The Journey is The Reward

The Journey is The Reward

A story of courage, hope, and inspiration

by Doug, Renee, and Kim LaViolette
with Karolyn A. Gazella

Doug, Renee
+
Kim LaViolette

Cover artwork by Archetype Group
Family photo pages designed by Mike Connell

Library of Congress Catalog Number: 2001-086574

ISBN 1-890694-35-5

Published by:
BDL Publishing
Green Bay, WI 54307

Printed by:
National Graphic Solutions
Appleton, WI 54911

www.briansjourney.com
e-mail: tjitr@aol.com

Dedication

To those who have experienced the loss of a loved one,

and to the children of today
who will become our future leaders—
enjoy the journey!

Acknowledgments

from Doug, Renee, and Kim

This book is, in part, about our life and how we coped with the death of our son and brother, Brian. It would be impossible to thank all of those caring people who prayed for us and helped us along our journey. There were hundreds of cards, letters, and e-mails from families who encouraged us. Our families and friends were incredibly supportive and are in our hearts forever.

We are thankful to Brian's friends who have not forgotten him, and the students his Foundation is now helping. We are confident they will have a positive impact on this world.

Thanks to Karolyn Gazella, our co-author, for her continued encouragement. She kept us moving ahead to complete this book even while we questioned whether anyone would really want to read about the life of the LaViolettes.

We are grateful to Heidi Mours, Natalie Beth and the other people who participated in this book. The people who were interviewed shared their pain in an effort to help others heal.

We are thankful for each other. Together we managed to get to the other side of grief and experience healing. Throughout the process, we have managed to strengthen our bond of love and respect.

Of course, we want to thank Brian—our first born, only son, big brother, and friend. He continues to guide us and give us strength years after he left us. It was said that if Brian had lived, he would have gone on to accomplish great things. We are sure he is accomplishing great things in heaven. We hope sharing Brian's story will help you accomplish great things in your life.

Acknowledgments

from Karolyn

I would like to thank Doug, Renee, and Kim. Telling their story with honesty and vulnerability took courage and great strength. I appreciate them and have learned so much as I worked with them to complete this book.

Also, a special thanks to the individuals who shared their stories in the healing chapter. Those people, along with the LaViolette family, are today's true heroes. They are the ones who have climbed out of the depths of despair to show the rest of us that it is possible. I also appreciate Austin Rios, Peter Mancuso, Lisa Petrikas, Sue LeTourneau, Kristin Kreuser, Darrel Burnett, Jack and Ginny Riopelle, Connie Payton, Ollie and Helen Bogsted, and the many others who took time to help make this book better.

Thanks to my good friends Kevin and Todd for sharing their Door County retreat with me, and to my talented editor, Frances E. FitzGerald, who is also a dear friend. Thanks to my dear friend, Maria Dalebroux, for her unconditional support, love, and patience as I obsessed for months over this book. I am also very grateful for my sister, Kathi, who is an inspiration to me and a source of strength. I also feel blessed to have my mom's loving spirit inside me—she was the one who taught me how to truly live life with passion and commitment.

Finally, my most humble gratitude is extended to God who continues to guide me on my journey.

Preface

by Karolyn A. Gazella

I first met Doug LaViolette the year after my mom died. I owned a publishing company and we were featuring a story about the Brian LaViolette Scholarship Foundation in one of our magazines. Selfishly, I wanted to talk about my mom and the possibility of getting Doug's help to start a cancer foundation in her name. I was immediately struck by his kindness and willingness to help.

Doug became more like an older brother to me than a business associate. We belonged to the same entrepreneurs' group, Silent Partners, and we had lunch periodically to catch up on things. One day, both Doug and I arrived early to our Silent Partners meeting. I had always thought about approaching Doug about working together on a book about healing, but the timing was never right—until that morning.

"Doug, have you ever thought about writing a book about Brian and healing from loss?" I asked.

"You're not the first person who has approached us about writing a book. We're just not sure," he said.

"What's holding you back?" I asked.

"The only way we would do a book is if we knew it could help people," he said. "Interestingly, just this week I received a call from a mother who lost a child. She actually asked if there was a book available that told our story."

"If you do decide to do a book, I would love to be your co-author," I said. As soon as Doug heard I was interested, I could tell he was considering the idea. I sensed he felt a certain comfort level with me and knew that this project would be close to my heart.

I submersed myself in Brian's story. I got to know a young boy whom I had never met. I also got to know Renee and Kim. Like mother, like daughter; they both are warm, honest, and authentic.

"Today, someone asked me what we hope to accomplish with this book," Doug said one day during one of our meetings. "Within an hour of that conversation, I heard the news about a 19-year-old boy who was missing in the icy waters of Lake Michigan. He was fishing with two of his friends and their boat capsized. My heart ached for that family. I was reminded again, just what our mission is."

This was an important project for me. When it came time to write, I knew I needed to get away. Fortunately, I have friends who own a beautiful home in picturesque Door County. That would be perfect, I thought. I could write this story of healing as I gazed out onto the Bay not far from where Brian drowned. I felt close to his spirit there.

For months before I started writing, I prayed to Brian and my mom for guidance. I wrote a special prayer that I said every day before I began writing. On the way up to Door County, I stopped by a beautiful chapel to pray. I bought a candle and lit it the moment I entered my friends' home and it stayed lit around the clock. The day I left Door County, the candle had burned down completely—perfect timing.

I sensed Brian every step of the way. I envisioned him and my mom encouraging me, Doug, Renee, and Kim. In my mind, they became the light we would follow until the project was complete. In the end, everyone involved helped create an honest view of how we can heal from incredible pain. I learned something about the transforming power of loss. For this, I am thankful.

Table of Contents

Dedication . . . .

Acknowledgments VI

Preface. VIII

Introduction: The Message 1

Chapter One: The Journey Begins 5

Chapter Two: The Accident 25

Chapter Three: The Faith 57

Chapter Four: The Next 12 Months. 71

Chapter Five: The Foundation 89

Chapter Six: The Healing 103

Chapter Seven: The Journey Continues 163

Appendix: Scholarship Foundation 170

The Message:

From Doug, Renee and Kim

"Don't be afraid to be different, your way may be the better one."

It has been said that angels walk among us. Their transparent forms are believed to follow us, watching our every move. Do they guide, prod, or cajole us into making positive life choices? Or, is their influence much more subtle and unobtrusive? Are they watching our lives unfold, like spectators in a theatre? Or, do they simply sense when they are needed?

Belief in angels is not a new phenomenon. Neither is the hope that the soul lives on long after it disappears from the world we are so familiar with. The idea that death is not an ending, but a new beginning has been debated and studied since the dawn of time. No doubt, this topic will continue to draw scrutiny for centuries to come.

Answers about angels, souls, and death will not be revealed in this book. While loss of life is a part of this story, it is not about dying; it is about living. This is not a story about an angel among us. Rather, it is about the angels within us—angel characteristics, that is. It is about the human spirit and its ability to survive devastating losses.

Yes, this is a story of pain and an agony so intense no description can depict it. And despair so immense that it's as if it will swallow you whole. This is a story of our journey through those depths of despair and how we re-emerged.

Peace, joy, and happiness are the bedrock of a fulfilling and vital life. Learning, loving, and respecting are the emotional tools we use to create our own life's map. As we navigate, we may encounter the barriers of depression and grief. It is during these times when our course is tested and our spirit may falter.

Whether your grief or depression is caused by the loss of a job, the break-up of a relationship, or the death of a loved one, meeting Brian may help. This 15-year-old boy has been described as an "old soul." We are sure his wisdom and philosophy about life will inspire you. His angel characteristics may help bring yours to the surface. If you allow him to influence you, you may begin to influence others more positively.

Brian's confirmation mentor said this about him: "I found out early on that Brian was no ordinary 15-year-old...he formed very clear and mature ideas about his life and the world around him. He took the risk of being open, honest, and candid...His spiritual faith had the confidence of a 50-year-old, not the average 15-year-old."

Brian said the most important day of his life was his confirmation, May 17, 1992. In his confirmation journal he wrote: "Death and resurrection is a sacred, but happy event. There is life after death."

While Brian was an ordinary teenager in most respects, he had special gifts to share. He loved to write and he posted inspirational sayings in his bedroom. His life's mantra was "The Journey is The Reward." Brian enjoyed every day, appreciated his family and friends, and tried his best to be a good person. As you can tell, we are very proud of him.

After his death, the same inspirational sayings Brian wrote on 3x5 cards that decorated his bedroom became spiritual messages that would guide us to resolution. These sayings are used in this book to start each chapter. They are the words that motivated and encouraged him on his journey. They are the words that live on even after he is gone.

In order to tell our story, we also wanted to provide the different perspectives of our family and friends. Throughout the book, we all share insights and reflect on Brian's life and his death. You will also read excerpts from Brian's own autobiography he wrote when he was 13 years old.

We use our own story to lead up to the most important chapter of all—the chapter on healing. It is here where we provide practical information about healing from loss. We appreciate the many people who participated in this chapter to tell their stories with the hope of helping you heal from whatever pain you are experiencing.

A passage from the Book of Proverbs states: "Length of days is not what makes age honorable nor number of years a measure of a life."

Although Brian left this world at the tender age of 15, his legacy of optimism and zest for life continues to inspire people. He truly believed that "The Journey is The Reward." His example was contagious to those of us who knew him. He was sensitive, bright, and motivated. At a time when we frequently hear about negative behavior in children, Brian's life gives us cause to celebrate the many children who exemplify the positive. Although he was just an ordinary child, Brian continues to influence others in extraordinary ways.

We invite you along on our journey…

—Doug, Renee, and Kim LaViolette

The Journey Begins:

The early years

"The more I want to get something done, the less I call it work."

Nestled to the north of Green Bay, Wisconsin, is the blue-collar town of Oconto. What it lacks in big-city appeal, it gains in lush scenery. To the east lies the Bay of Green Bay, while the west holds miles of thick forests. It's a small, cozy town where everyone knows everyone else. These rugged north woods provide a great place to grow up. And an even better place to fall in love.

Theirs wasn't the typical small-town romance. He was an office furniture salesman who also owned a local newspaper. She was working in a doctor's office. He was persistent. She played hard to get. It was love at first sight, at least on his part. Looking back, they were soulmates, destined to be together. Innocently, they pursued the American Dream—not knowing the tragedy they would be forced to overcome.

They met in 1973. From that fateful day in the doctor's office, hard-working, young Douglas LaViolette (pronounced La Va Let) was confident he had just met his future bride, Renee Bogsted. Now, he just had to convince her.

Doug

Let the courtship begin

It actually took me an entire year to convince her to marry me. I asked her three times. I was determined.

At the time, I was printing *The Reminder,* the local shopper newspaper. On Valentine's Day, I ran a full-page ad for Renee. It was one of those real mushy, I-know-of-love-because-of-you ads. Of course, I signed it, Love Always, Doug. We weren't even engaged at the time. It was actually pretty early in our relationship.

That night I called her up and asked if she had gotten the paper that day. She said yes, but she didn't say anything about the ad. I thought, "Oh no, I blew it...she's never going to marry me now." I was convinced that she thought I was crazy. I was also worried what her family and friends thought.

I am a persistent man, however. Even though it took three tries, she finally said yes.

Renee

His persistence paid off

Doug tells people that he came into the doctor's office for a physical and that I fell in love with his body. That's not what happened, of course. He was selling furniture and we were introduced. He asked me out on a date right away.

The first time he asked me to marry him, we had only been dating for three months. I told him "no" because I didn't really even know him yet. The second time was also too soon. I guess he knew what he wanted because he tried again.

We were married on September 7, 1974. I found out I was pregnant in 1976. We were both so excited. We definitely wanted to have children. Brian was born at about 9:30, the evening of January 23, 1977. It was the happiest day of our lives.

The pregnancy was very easy. I ate well. I felt good. But when it was time to deliver, there was some difficulty. The monitors were showing problems with the heart beat. As the heart beat dropped, the commotion started. I had to move on my side and they made Doug leave the room. It was tense for awhile. But then he was born—Brian Douglas LaViolette. He was a little blue, but he was still beautiful. He was 7 pounds, 13 ounces. We were so excited. We felt ready to be parents.

Doug

A first-born son

It was the happiest day of a father's life—to have a healthy first child, a son. We cried. It was incredible. But it wasn't without its complications. I could see the heart beat dropping. I got really upset. The doctor wasn't there. I insisted that the attending nurse call him right away. I guess I was getting pretty hyper. They asked me to leave the room and not come back. I didn't want to leave. Then, when they "asked" more forcefully, I waited in the hall.

But everything turned out just fine. You should see the baby pictures. What a sweet little boy. And he was a good baby, too.

We had heard horror stories from other parents whose babies wouldn't sleep or eat. Brian wasn't like that. He wasn't cranky at all. He was healthy and had big, expressive eyes. He was such a good-natured baby. When he woke up, he took his bottle and went back to sleep. Renee would put him down for a nap in the afternoon and he slept peacefully. He was great.

Now, Kim, our second child, was a different story. She wasn't sleeping through the night even at seven months old. Renee and I often joke that if Kim would have been the first, she may have been an only child.

After those first seven months, however, Kim was great. And Brian loved her. He was the perfect older brother. He was three when she was born. We encouraged him to be "our little helper" and he fit the role perfectly.

Renee

A daughter to be proud of

We waited three years before having our second child. Our daughter, Kimberly Renee, was born on November 18, 1979. She was 6 pounds, 12 ounces. I had the same problems delivering Kim as I did with Brian. Oh well, at least I'm consistent.

She was definitely a different type of baby than Brian. During the day she was just fine, but at night she had trouble sleeping. I really felt bad for her.

It was a difficult first seven months with Kim not sleeping through the night, but I really think it was a way for me to become a better mother. In one sense, maybe it prepared me somewhat for future difficulties. Little did I know that nothing could have prepared me for a mother's worst nightmare.

Our daughter was a beautiful, blonde-haired, blue-eyed wonder. And I think Brian was just as fascinated with her as Doug and I were. He was such a good little helper and very protective. It's funny, that's the same way he was with her as they grew up—protective.

Brian

From his autobiography at age 13

Being the oldest of the siblings in our family isn't too bad. My sister and I don't fight. She does what I tell her, but I don't boss her around a lot. Our parents treat us generally the same, too. I just hope the rest of my life will be this nice.

Kim

A great older brother

It may seem hard to believe, but Brian and I never fought. OK, there was one time but we made up right away. He was more of a friend to me than a typical older brother. I really looked up to him. We were close.

We played a lot together. We would build these huge forts in his bedroom. He had one of those tent beds. We would connect blankets and make a big maze. We both liked music so we would even make sound effects. I would play the "jaws" sound on the piano and Brian would say in his scary voice, "You have now entered the fort zone." Of course, I would then let out a big scream.

One time we were playing with Legos and had this great idea to drop our Lego man in the bean bag. What a great idea.

I don't know if you've ever stuck your hand in a bean bag, but it isn't the smartest thing in the world to do. We were vacuuming little static-cling balls for quite some time trying to find our little Lego man. But even that wasn't so bad because we were dealing with the mess together.

We would play for hours. We seemed a lot alike. We were both pretty creative. We would write notes to mom and dad. We would even put on little performances for them and the kids in the neighborhood.

Brian was very protective of me, always looking out for me. He was the wise older brother. Once when I was much younger, I confided to him that I was scared to go in the basement. Brian gave me some great advice. He told me to just sing or hum while I was down there and it wouldn't be so scary. From that day on, I hummed every time I went into the basement. Even as an adult, I catch myself humming when I am scared.

I was protective of Brian, too. We took a family vacation to Dyersville, Iowa. That's where the movie *Field of Dreams* was filmed. It was dad and Brian's favorite movie. Mom and I were watching as they tried to recreate parts of the movie. At one point, dad was pitching to Brian and the ball hit the ground, bounced up, and hit Brian in the forehead. Brian must have bit his lip when it happened because it was bleeding. Mom and I ran over to him. He said he was just fine, but it really upset me so I started crying. I didn't want him to be hurt. That's the way the two of us were—we looked out for each other.

Brian was very easy to talk to. Even as a kid I thought he was a cool older brother. He was active at school and had lots of friends. He didn't treat me like an irritating little sister. Oh sure, there were times I would get in the way. But, overall, we were very close.

You know how you hear stories about siblings that actually got along when they were kids but you don't believe it's true? Well, Brian and I were the exception.

Brian

From his autobiography at age 13

In the basement, my sister and I perform shows for the neighborhood. Our latest show was a haunted house. Out of all the rooms in our house though, my room is my favorite place. When you walk into my room you know I like things clean. Another thing you will notice is that I like sports.

Doug

Time to teach values

Looking back, I wonder if we were too hard on him. Both Renee and I grew up under modest circumstances. We valued hard work and knew we wanted our kids to know what it is like to earn their way.

We never gave the kids an allowance. If they wanted something special, they had to earn it. Brian really took that policy seriously. At a young age, he worked at our company, cleaning on Saturday mornings. We would get up early, go to a local restaurant for breakfast, and then head to the office. This was our Saturday morning routine for years.

After he died, I couldn't go to that restaurant. Years later, I finally made it to the restaurant and I thought I was going to have an anxiety attack. The first time I walked into work after he died, I noticed the garbage cans and started sobbing. These reminders of those Saturday mornings that I cherished were just too difficult.

Brian also mowed lawns and worked at a local golf course. He loved to play golf. I loved to go golfing with him. He was very good. Brian was a good athlete in general, except for basketball. He was a lousy basketball player. He laughed about it and confided to me that he would foul someone just so he could get his name in the record book.

In the beginning, he worked at the golf course just to golf for free. That was a big deal to a young kid who loved golfing. He did such a good job, they moved him to the kitchen and he started getting a paycheck.

The first time he wanted to buy something big, Renee and I loaned him the money. I drew up a handwritten "contract" describing how he would pay off the debt. I still have that contract. I wrote down how much money he would get if he mowed the lawn, pulled weeds, cleaned the office, washed the car. We both signed it. Soon after, I remember getting a note from him, thanking me for teaching him how to mow the lawn.

He was very responsible even at a young age. He took a lot of pride in his work. And that was something that came naturally. We didn't have to harp at him.

He may have reminded you of the character on *Family Ties* that Michael J. Fox played, Alex P. Keaton. Although Brian didn't carry a briefcase, he did like to wear ties and sweaters. He used to say, "style before comfort."

He wrote his first note to our employees when he was just 13. He told them to please pick up their paper clips because they were hard to pick up and could damage the vacuum cleaner. The employees really got a kick out of him. He got along well with everyone.

He typed another memo to the employees a year later. He found letterhead with the words THANK YOU! big and bold at the top and then typed:

April 23, 1991
TO: Entire Green Bay Staff
FROM: Brian
If you have any large garbage items that do not fit in your waste-basket, please stick a post-it-note marked GARBAGE on it. This will help me to know what to throw away.
Thanks a lot!

I often think that he would have made a great boss—definitely a good salesman. When he was about 10 years old, he would bring candy bars he was selling to the office. Rather than just set the box on the front counter, he would write a note. "Hi, my name is Brian LaViolette and I am going to sell you some terrific candy." He would describe the features of the candy and why people should buy it. He would sign it, "Thank You, Brian." He was always very polite and respectful of people.

When he mowed the lawn at the office, he actually sent invoices and a monthly statement to our landlord, Isadore Mednikow. "That boy is so organized," Izzy would say. Brian liked those checks the most because they were business checks written to him. Sometimes he wouldn't cash them for weeks. I think he liked to just look at them every now and then. He really appreciated having a job.

Brian

From his autobiography at age 13

My dad puts everything he's got into everything he does. He had a paper route that still puts a spark in his eye. Throughout his lifetime, he must have had twenty jobs. Not because he was fired. My dad just had to keep moving on. Currently, he is the president/owner of Executive Office Interiors. ...the main reason I wrote a tribute to my dad is because I love him.

...above anything else, I want to be happy—even if that means jumping out of a plane with a parachute when I'm eighty years old. That way I wouldn't have to sit around a hospital and be unhappy. Why live if you aren't happy.

I would like to go into either advertising or sales. I'm sure I would like both of them. To get that type of job, I would need at least a college degree, which I plan to get.

Renee

Proud of her young son

Doug and I felt the kids needed to know that money doesn't just get handed to them. Brian caught on very early. He even created a chart that he hung on the side of the refrigerator. He kept track of everything he bought, borrowed, and owed. He had a running total and he would subtract amounts for the extra work he did around the house or at the office.

It wasn't as if Doug and I ruled with an iron fist. It was just the way it was in our household. Brian was naturally just a hard worker. And as a typical 12 to 15-year-old, he wanted things. These were things that we weren't going to buy for him; he had to earn them.

Once, we loaned him money for an entertainment set for his bedroom and he also had to pay half the amount for his new trumpet for band. Right before he died, he paid off his debt completely. Even though it didn't make sense, at the time I thought "Maybe if he still owed us money, he would've been able to hang around a little longer."

After he died, all of that hard work stuff went right out the window. Doug and I would say "Kim, what do you want?" We definitely went in the opposite direction. You begin to think, "life is too short." Thankfully, Kim had already learned the values that Brian embraced. We are so proud of her. She is in college and has become a caring, intelligent, young woman.

Brian

From his autobiography at age 13

This person I owe my life to, and I'm not exaggerating one bit. She brought me into this world and has probably wanted to take me out of this world, too. My mom has guided me through the stressful, tear-rolling hours of my life. She has taught me right from wrong and always finds a way to make me grin. One thing that she has taught me that I will never forget is the value of trust. That five letter word has helped me throughout my life. Even more important than trust is a four letter word that will always be between us—love.

Renee

All work and no play...

The week before the accident, I remember actually saying to myself as I was driving to pick up one of the kids: "Life is good!" I was really living my dream. Granted, we didn't have a lot of money, but we did have each other. As a family, you couldn't ask for anything stronger. The kids were great, and Doug was, and still is, a wonderful husband and father.

Our life was pretty basic. The kids and the business kept us very busy. Both Kim and Brian were good students. Brian was getting straight A's in high school. He was involved in band and he was on the soccer and golf teams. He was a very good athlete and loved soccer. He started playing when he was in kindergarten. He could actually use both of his feet to kick and move the ball. I guess that's unique because most kids can only use one foot. As a freshman he made the varsity team. We went to nearly all of his games.

As with soccer, Brian also really excelled at golf. He and Doug golfed often. He said he liked golf because it was an individual sport and "if you miss a putt you can't blame anyone but yourself." The day before the accident he had to work at the golf course and mow a few lawns.

The week of the accident was a busy week for him. Doug told Brian he had to paint the deck before he could go to Door County with his friends. He had to scrape off the old paint and then re-paint it a dark grey. The scraping was the hardest part. As I glanced out the kitchen window, I noticed something odd. Brian was no longer on his hands and knees working on the deck. He had duct-taped a scraper on one of his feet to make the job a little more bearable. At the time, I laughed at his ingenuity. It may sound weird, but to this day, I actually get sad when I see duct tape.

He not only got the deck painted, he did a great job. All except for one spot. He got grey paint on one of the white benches. Doug teased him about it, "Brian, you left your mark." Brian just smiled and nodded.

A few years after his death, we donated a tree to the church garden in honor of Brian. At the dedication we asked some friends if they knew which tree was Brian's. They pointed to a tree not far away. Doug and I went to get a closer look. It may sound strange, but there, on the trunk of the tree, was the same grey paint—even the same width as the mark on the deck bench. We have no idea how it got there. Needless to say, we've never had any problems locating Brian's tree in the church garden—it's the one with "his mark."

Brian was a good son. He wasn't perfect by any means, but he had a good heart. When he was 8 years old, he typed a letter to me after I yelled at him for taking a toy truck from another child in the neighborhood. Here is what our insightful little boy typed:

"Mom. I feel really bad about what happened. I hope this will not affect our relationship. I LOVE YOU so much you could not say how much I LOVE YOU and DADDY. Your son, BRIAN."

As a family, we always took vacations together. We had some great vacations and we always had fun. It was actually relaxing to vacation with the kids because we all got along so well. There was no bickering between Kim and Brian. In fact, before each trip, Kim and Brian would get together and in spiral note books make up schedules of what they wanted to do. They called these hand-written itineraries, "Spiral of Fun."

It wasn't unusual for us to just hop in the car and go. In fact, a couple weeks before the accident, we drove to St. Louis. We stayed in a nice hotel that overlooked the Arch. Doug and I commented on how we thought some day soon the kids wouldn't want to vacation with us. We were determined to appreciate and enjoy the time we had right then.

Brian

From his autobiography at age 13

Not all of our vacations were peaches-n-cream. On a vacation to Washington, DC, our travel guide hooked us up with a hotel that literally had rats running through the wall. I was scared to sit down on the bed for fear a skeleton would pop out of the sheets. We took the hinges off the door running out of that place. Our family had a lot of memorable moments on those vacations...

One thing I also do for fun when I'm not going around town, is stay with my family. Some of the fun things we do are pretty cool. We go out for dinner about once a week. Sometimes we go out to a movie. But, like any family, we have the boring traditions. We have the famed LaViolette Meat Pies for Christmas. On New Year's Eve we eat by candlelight. Every year we have thumbprint cookies for Christmas. Notice I didn't say we eat the thumbprint cookies. I just hope my life goes on as long as these traditions do.

Remembering Brian

Reflections from his friend, Austin

The thing I most appreciated about Brian was his sense of humor, mostly because it was not all that different from my own. Some of my favorite moments with him were spent exchanging witty remarks during games of ping pong at his house, or pool at mine.

Beyond his humor, he was trustworthy and accepting. As an eighth-grader who had just moved to Wisconsin after living in Texas and Louisiana, I found Wisconsin to be a different planet. Brian and I became friends quickly. Brian helped me make the transition more easily.

Once we became better friends, we also showed our flaws. We argued at times, not always civilly. He could be stubborn—and so could I. Although he was trustworthy, especially when it came to things said in confidence, there was one time when he really let me down. We both worked at the golf course and Brian needed me to work for him one day. When the time came for him to work for me, he wouldn't because he didn't want to. That really hurt my feelings. It was really one of the only times I ever thought of him as selfish. This experience was obviously the exception rather than the rule.

Brian was a great friend. Just like all great friends, we spent enough time with each other to see the not-so-great sides of each other.

Aunt Sue

Respecting the strong family bond

My husband, Duane, and I also have two children. Kristin is our oldest and Paul is just one year older than Brian. We really enjoyed spending time with Doug, Renee, and the kids.

Doug and Renee are such good, caring parents. The four of them were a "true family" in the sense that they did everything together. Doug and I come from a large family of seven. Our father was always so busy working, trying to make ends meet, that he was not really around much when we were young. I am sure Doug wanted things to be different with his children. He and Renee were protective of Brian and Kim—protective in a good way, always watching out for their kids.

Brian was really a model child. He was so shy at times, and yet very sensitive and compassionate of others. He not only excelled in academics and sports, but also as a person. And Kim adored him. They were more than brother and sister; they were true friends. It was such a joy to have them around. What always impressed me was how well behaved they both were. Of course, that came from their home life with Doug and Renee.

Kim was a very reserved, sweet child. Although there is an eight year age difference between Kim and Kristin, they have become very close.

Kristin Kreuser

Thoughts from Kim and Brian's cousin

Uncle Doug, Aunt Renee, Kim, and Brian...they seemed like the perfect family. As a child, I remember thinking that Doug and Renee were overprotective. Now, as a mom myself, I only think of them as exceptionally loving and understandably cautious.

Brian and Kim were very close. They always stuck together at family functions. I remember driving by their house one fall afternoon during homecoming week watching Kim help Brian take toilet paper out of a big tree in their front yard. I remember thinking that I couldn't imagine my brother and I working together like that. But Kim and Brian were different. They really got along well and you could tell they liked each other's company.

Kim was quiet and seemed to follow Brian's lead. After Brian's death, Kim needed to grow up more independently. And she rose to that challenge. Today, Kim is a kind, respectful, friendly person. I no longer look at her as a little girl. The years between us seem to have been erased as we are now adults together going through life's many challenges.

Kim and I talk on a regular basis. I enjoy our friendship and admire how she has grown as a person despite the tragedy she experienced as a child.

Darrell Burnett

Admiring Doug and Brian's relationship

Doug and I have always had the kind of friendship that doesn't diminish with time or distance. We can go weeks and sometimes months without talking and it's like we've been in the next room all along.

My career had taken me far from the Green Bay area since I left in 1985. I hadn't seen the LaViolettes in nearly three years when Doug twisted my arm and made me commit to coming to visit the end of July 1992. In retrospect, I can't thank Doug enough—it was the last time I would see Brian, just a week before his death.

We decided to play a round of golf. Doug had some appointments, so Brian rode with me. We had a great conversation, talking about school, his future, a recent concert he attended with Kim, and various other subjects. I can remember thinking how I hoped my sons would turn out to be like Brian, a good person.

As my oldest son turns 15, I spend time just looking at him and thinking how he is changing so subtly, yet so distinctly. I know how quickly fate's path can change our lives and I never take anything for granted, thanks to Brian.

I used to have my life perfectly planned out in stages right down to the specifics. Now I make it a point to try and live more for the moment and maximize the potential of everything I do. I have Brian to thank for that. To say that he influenced my life in the past tense is inaccurate. He continues to influence my life even today. He continues to remind me that "The Journey is The Reward."

It was obvious that the LaViolettes were an ordinary family. They moved through life fairly easily. They worked hard and played hard. They were surrounded by family and friends who loved and admired them.

The family business was beginning to take off. They added a second location in Appleton, a city about 30 minutes from Green Bay. They were all healthy and happy. Brian and Kim were doing well in school and seemed to enjoy their friends and their extracurricular activities.

Brian was looking forward to the upcoming soccer season. He would soon complete Driver's Ed and in less than six months, he would turn sweet 16.

The LaViolettes appreciated life. They appreciated each other. As the summer of 1992 was coming to a close, they were hopeful for the future.

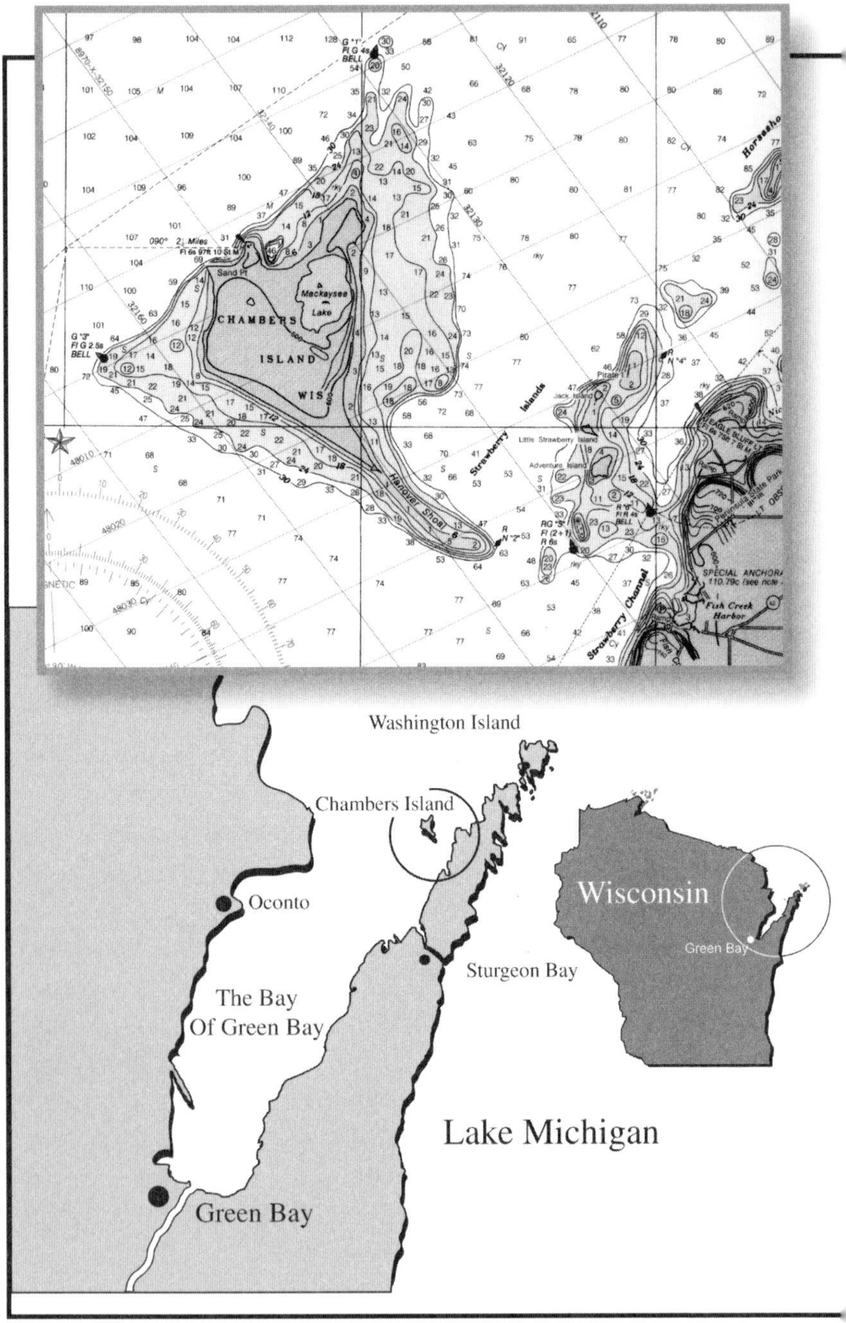
CHAMBERS ISLAND
Mackaysee Lake
Sand Pt
Hanover Shoal
Strawberry Islands
Little Strawberry Island
Adventure Island
Jack Island
Pirate Island
Strawberry Channel
Fish Creek Harbor
SPECIAL ANCHORAGE
Washington Island
Chambers Island
Oconto
Sturgeon Bay
The Bay
Of Green Bay
Lake Michigan
Green Bay
Wisconsin
Green Bay

The Accident:

When life stops

"You don't appreciate things
until they are taken away from you."

As you look at a map of the United States, Wisconsin is shaped like a left-handed mitten. With that image in mind, Door County is the "thumb." Because of its rugged beauty and picturesque water vistas, Door County has often been called the "Cape Cod of the Midwest."

This unique peninsula juts out like a knife, separating Lake Michigan to the east from the Bay of Green Bay to the west. If you drive the winding road through the small, inviting towns, it takes nearly two hours to reach the very tip of the peninsula from Green Bay.

Door County extends approximately 80 miles into Lake Michigan. Glacial activity chiselled and created this grand limestone peninsula. With nearly 250 miles, Door County leads all other North American counties in total shoreline footage. Yet, there is a mere eight miles of land between the Lake shore to the Bay side. It has been estimated that nearly 95 percent of the county remains undeveloped as a result of the county's effort to protect its rustic ambience and pristine environment.

Rocky shore lines, sandy beaches, parks and preserves, make this landscape a sought-after hot spot. People who own cottages or homes on this slice of heaven are the envy of many. Vacationers from all over the United States enjoy the inns and resorts. With more than 30 caves, 100 miles of trails, five state parks, 600+ state park campsites, and the most lighthouses in the nation, Door County has much to offer interested tourists and fortunate residents.

In addition to the many peninsula attractions, the islands that dot the Bay add to the peace and tranquility of this rugged yet gentle landscape. The breathtaking beauty of these Midwest natural treasures offer additional appeal. These remote hideaways are steeped in mystery, history, and unrelenting beauty.

The second largest island off the peninsula is known as Chambers Island. If you stand in Founder's Square in the community of Fish Creek and look out to the Bay of Green Bay, you will see Chambers Island about five miles to the northwest. It is a privately owned island, except for one section. The Town of Gibralter owns and maintains the 40-acre public park on the Island. The park's peaceful, sandy beach is the only public access to this summer haven. Few roads with even fewer vehicles meander through the one-half mile by four mile-wide Island. In addition to the historic lighthouse in the park, a small air landing strip lies a short distance from the public beach.

The tranquility of Chambers Island can be deceptive, however. Beyond the protection of the neighboring Strawberry Islands, bordering lake swells can become treacherous. The placid charm of this area can disguise the water's hidden undercurrents and dangerous drop offs. In a moment's notice, the sandy bottom can go from just a few feet deep to more than 70.

It is on this very Island where a devastating accident took place on a warm summer day in August 1992. One might ask, how can such a beautiful, peaceful setting be the scene of such a horrible tragedy?

That Saturday morning in August, sunshine combined with the overwhelming beauty of the natural landscape to create another picture-perfect day in Door County. Although it was already late morning, the Island was fairly quiet except for the muffled voices of four 15-year-old friends as they walked toward the beach, excited to go for a swim.

Matt and Mike walked ahead, eager to test the water. Brian and Austin were not far behind. They were two close friends sharing a serious conversation about their dreams.

"As we walked up the beach, we talked about our future," recalls Austin. "We both wanted to attend a good college, get married, and get a good job. These are typical goals of many young people. But as the water washed sand over our bare feet, and the sun bounced off the ripples in Brian's eyes, I saw something special on his face. He gave one of his patented smiles and said, 'I just want to be happy.' It wasn't what he said that struck me, but how he said it. He spoke sincerely, and I could tell he truly meant the words he spoke. I can remember admiring him for that sincerity."

The night before, they had played their trumpets around the campfire, stayed up late, and laughed a lot. Later that Saturday, the four boys were planning to run in a 5K race on the Island. Mike won the race the previous year. This was the first year Brian would participate.

When they got to the water, Austin and Mike wanted to "conserve their energy" for the race, so they remained near the shore. Matt and Brian ventured further out. Brian never returned from that swim.

What appeared to be an ordinary day in an extraordinary place changed in an instant. The warm sun would turn into an emotional darkness never to be forgotten by those present on the Island. For those still at home, their nightmare was just beginning.

Kim

One last time

I was only 12 at the time. I actually don't remember much about that day or the time leading up to it. But one thing sticks out in my head.

I was getting ready to ride my bike with my friend, Brianna, who was at our house. We were going to go back to her house. I recall seeing Brian's duffel bag sitting by the front door. I said to myself "I hope he doesn't leave before I get back. I'll want to say good-bye to him." When I got back from my friend's house, the duffel bag was gone.

That day, my friend and I wrote him a letter and put it on his pillow for him to read when he returned from Door County. I took the letter from his pillow after I heard the news.

Renee

A mother's worst nightmare

It was a hectic week. We were having a busy summer. Brian was in Driver's Ed. Because I was a stay-at-home mom, I would take Brian and his friends to Driver's Ed almost every day. They used to get a big kick out of teasing me about my driving. That Thursday, I took them to Driver's Ed, but I didn't have to on Friday. After the accident, I couldn't even drive by the intersection where I would turn to take them to Driver's Ed. Something so simple, yet so difficult.

Brian had been working very hard that summer. He was mowing lawns, working at the office and the golf course, and he even painted our deck. He really wanted to go to Door County with his friends. Doug and I knew the family he'd be staying with on Chambers Island and we didn't think there was anything wrong with him going.

Mike's mom drove Brian, Austin, and Mike up there on Friday. Matt and his family were already there. Austin's dad was going to go up to get them and bring them home on Sunday.

Brian got paid that day from his job at the golf course. He asked if I was going to go to the bank because he wanted me to get him a $100 bill. He had never had one and thought it would be neat. He endorsed the check and I was off to the bank. When I got home, he was waiting for his ride to Driver's Ed. I showed him the $100 bill and he smiled real cute and gave me a thumb's up.

Brian was very organized. He was all packed and had his bag by the door so he could leave when Mike's mom got to our house.

That day, we were invited to go on the Mancuso's sailboat in Door County. I actually am not that big of a fan of the water or sailing, but Doug really enjoyed it. I remember Doug and I pointing over at Chambers Island and saying "That's where Brian is." Brian was so excited to go to Chambers Island. He was also excited to spend time with Austin, Mike, and Matt.

On Saturday, it was business as usual. Kim had a hair appointment and then we had lunch together. Doug had to work. He had to make a delivery about 30 minutes from Green Bay. That night, we had plans to go to the Green Bay Packers pre-season football game. We were supposed to go with the kids but Brian really wanted to go to Door County and Kim wanted to go swimming at a friend's house. So, Doug and I decided to go to the game with another couple.

I was waiting for Doug to get home from his delivery. That's when it happened. The phone rang. Matt's dad was on the other line and said "You've got to get up here, something has happened to Brian." I panicked. "What do you mean, something happened to Brian?" He said that the boys were swimming and they couldn't find Brian and the Coast Guard was looking for him.

My panic heightened quickly to an indescribable chaos. "You've got to find him," I kept repeating. We needed to get up there. How could we get up there quickly? Even more panic. It was decided. A pilot from Chambers Island would come to the Green Bay airport to fly us up to the Island.

In the meantime, Kim called from her friend's house. She wanted to stay overnight. I kept my composure and said yes. What was I going to do? How were we going to tell Kim? More panic.

Through that black cloud, I thought of Doug. Thank God I couldn't get a hold of him. For some reason, he forgot his cell phone that day. It's a good thing, because he would have never been able to drive the 30 minutes to get home.

The wait for Doug seemed like an eternity. When he got out of the car, I met him in the driveway. All I remember is him dropping to his knees, crying.

Later, we threw out that phone and the clothes we were wearing that day.

Doug

A father's pain

The shock was so profound. It just didn't seem real. As we flew to Door County, I looked in the back seat of the small plane and saw Renee rocking back and forth. She hated flying. I knew her tears and peaked complexion that day were not because of her fear of flying.

It was a beautiful day in Door County. The sun was shining and the Island was just gorgeous. We had never been to Chambers Island before—and we haven't been back since.

It seemed ironic. Even though it *looked* like a peaceful place, the sounds of the helicopters, jet skis, and rescue boats reminded us that this nightmare was all too real. As we got off the plane, I saw all these people gathered. I later found out that those were the people signed up to run in the 5K race.

I glanced to my right and saw Austin, Mike, and Matt. I thought, "Wait, there should be four standing there… four best friends…a golf foursome…where is the fourth?"

We went to the beach, taking the same route the boys took earlier that day. All I could think of was, "Where's our son?"

As I looked out onto the water and yelled Brian's name, I thought of the Thursday night before he left—it was the last time I saw him alive. He came in our bedroom to say good night. We were watching the Olympics. Swimming was on. He came over to my side of the bed to say good night and "I love you," just like every other night. But that night, he sat on the side of the bed and watched swimming with me. We talked about how competitive swimming was. He was very competitive. After the accident, I wondered if he thought of those Olympic swimmers that day as he swam in the Bay.

That same week I remember driving home from work thinking, "I don't know what we'd ever do if we lost one of the kids."

As I called out Brian's name in vain, I thought, "This can't be happening." I just wanted this nightmare to end. I wanted him to come walking out of the water, following my helpless cries to safety.

I remember that day on the beach so vividly. There was unbelievable activity all around us with so many people wondering how they could help. And yet, as Renee and I sat on the sand, we were wrapped in an odd silence. We were in shock, stunned that this was all actually happening. But then I noticed a young family docking their boat on the beach—a mother and father with a son and daughter. I noticed, even from a distance, that they appeared to be a loving and close family. I couldn't help but think of how lucky they were.

As the minutes ticked in slow motion, the father quietly came up to us and handed us his binoculars so we could follow the search effort. He asked me if we knew the young man who was missing. I told him he was our son. For a long time, this stranger sat with us in silence, occasionally putting a comforting arm around us or holding us as we wept.

Then, it was time for us to fly back home to tell Kim what had happened. The young father walked with us back toward the truck. I told him how much we appreciated his kindness and then I asked him his name. He said Brian. I had not told him what our son's name was. When he said his name, it was as if our Brian was there and had sat on the beach with us, comforting us.

His full name was Brian Eller, a young cardiologist from Appleton, a city 30 minutes south of Green Bay. We stayed in touch with him. In fact, a month to the day after the accident (September 8, 1992) I had lunch with Brian Eller at the Butte Des Morts Country Club, where I had golfed many times before with my son. I couldn't eat, and I couldn't even look at the golf course. Brian Eller began to tell me about his residency in Detroit. He said he worked in the emergency room where he brought people back to life from gun shot wounds, stabbings, and beatings. So many times, he said, the person was upset with him because they said they were in such a peaceful place. Somehow that gave me some comfort then, and even more now.

I will never forget how that stranger was drawn to us and comforted us. Even to this day, for me it represents the good that exists in people. And it makes me thankful that we experienced such kindness during one of our darkest hours.

That day, we asked questions about what happened, but there were no answers. Only more questions that added to our emptiness. Brian was an athlete, he was a good swimmer. What happened?

There was talk of "horse-play." I was asked if my son was a "risk-taker." Yes, he was adventurous, I thought, but no he wasn't a risk-taker—he wasn't careless. All I could think of was the many times as a young child he would actually ask permission to unbuckle his seat belt if he had to get something off the floor or from the back of the car. It was only for a second, then he'd buckle up again safe and sound.

He wasn't afraid of taking the kind of chances you want your child to take. He made the golf and soccer teams, participated in band, applied for a job. There is always a chance you won't make the team or get the job. Those are the chances that Brian took.

For whatever reason, Brian may have been reckless with his life that Saturday morning. We will not know exactly what happened until we meet again.

That night we came back home. It was a difficult decision, but we wanted to be with Kim. We flew back to Green Bay—over the soccer field where we watched him play the week before, over Lambeau Field where we were supposed to be at the Packers game. As I paid the pilot, I looked closely at the date—8/8/92—because from that day forward I knew that nothing would ever be the same.

As we aimlessly walked around our house early the following Monday morning, Brian's alarm in his room went off. For months after, the echo of that alarm followed me every morning as I attempted to start my day.

Brian

From his autobiography at age 13

One thing I didn't like in the beginning was swimming lessons. I used to get really nervous driving to the YMCA where I took my swimming lessons. A nervous habit I had was bobbing up and down in the water. That was good, however, because my mom was able to pick me out from the other wet heads. I do enjoy swimming now, but I still get nervous on the drive to the YMCA.

Kim

From her journal at age 12

Julie's mom, I call her Juanita, walked out of her yellowish house onto the porch and told Julie and I to get out of the pool because my mom and dad were coming over.

Well, I thought this was very strange, like a chair with two legs, because my mom and dad were supposed to be at a Packers' game. I knew something was wrong then. My mom and dad came over and told me that my brother was swimming and they couldn't find him.

Everyone in Julie's house was crying then. It sounded like a house full of babies. The first week was the hardest of them all. First of all because they couldn't find Brian yet. Second because there were so many people at our home...which was very nice, but there were almost too many people.

My cousin, Jenny, stayed with me the second and third night after this happened, and that helped a lot. But we didn't go downstairs much because of all the sad people, and we were trying to be happy. We had someone at our house every single minute of the day. All of my friends were and still are really great.

The funeral was probably the hardest time for me because I knew I wouldn't see Brian for a long, long time. And I couldn't and still can't hear anything back when I talk to him, even though I know he's listening.

Peter Mancuso

A friend in need...

It was one of those weekends in Door County where the perfect weather nearly takes your breath away. In the summer, when the sun is shining and you can hear the waves crash along the shore line, Door County provides a peaceful place that you just can't find in the city. My wife, Deborah, and I are fortunate to own a home on the Bay side of the Door County peninsula. We were having one of our typical weekends, enjoying our surroundings.

We went sailing with friends, including Doug and Renee, on Friday. Saturday afternoon I remember reading the paper, relaxing, and looking out onto the Bay. About mid-afternoon, I saw a helicopter flying over Chambers Island. We have a great view of Chambers and Green Islands from our home. I've been sailing these waters for many years and I knew what that helicopter meant—something terrible had happened. Soon after, I got the phone call. It was Doug. He was so upset, I could barely understand him. However, he was able to tell me that Brian went swimming on Chambers Island and was missing. It didn't sound good. That explains the helicopter, I thought.

Deb and I immediately offered to drive to Green Bay to help in any way we could. Although Doug and Renee said no, our intuition told us differently. We knew they were so vulnerable and would need some help—someone to manage all of this. We packed our bags and got to Green Bay late Saturday night. We stayed for more than two weeks.

Doug and Renee were so upset. Their situation was even more complex because Brian was still missing.

Deb and I are very similar in that we are take charge people. I own a business and am used to being a leader. For years, I worked with Doug on a variety of issues regarding his business. It only seemed natural for us to help our friends during this desperate time of need. My wife and I decided to develop a game plan. Deb and I are very process oriented. Deb is also a professionally trained gourmet cook, so we knew that providing quality meals would not be a problem.

The amount of decisions that needed to be made was overwhelming, even for a command and control person like me. Because Doug and Renee know so many people, their front entrance became a revolving door with people constantly coming and going. I give Doug and Renee a lot of credit because they were not afraid to share their grief.

There was also the issue of working with the search team, dealing with the local media, and making other arrangements. Doug and Renee were not in the frame of mind to handle any of this. They were in shock. We felt very protective of them.

At one point, I had heard of special dogs trained to find drowning victims. I made a few calls. I arranged to have a specialist from Minneapolis come to Door County with the dogs, as well as experts from Dane County (Madison, WI). We had these professionals stay in our house in Door County. The search effort was incredible. So many people volunteered their time and worked tirelessly. Even the out-of-town experts and specialists with the dogs only required that we pay their expenses.

It was clear that Doug and Renee needed closure. It was especially painful to watch Renee. She would just sit in the chair, rocking back in forth in a fetal position. Our hearts were breaking for them.

I remember the day Brian was found as if it were yesterday. I went out on the waters with the search specialists early in the morning. We searched all morning and were ready to come in for a break. Then we heard someone on the boat radio say they spotted something in the water. The person said it looked like a body. I knew what Brian was wearing so I radioed back to the sailor to ask the color of the swimming trunks. When the man said "green," I knew it was Brian. The man in the sailboat circled the body until we arrived. We went to the area and watched as the Door County sheriff's deputies pulled Brian out of the water. As soon as we got to shore, I called Doug.

Deb and I had no time to grieve with Doug and Renee; we were too busy. We took turns sleeping so one of us would be awake around the clock. We were especially concerned about Renee. She would get up during the night and wander around the house. She was taking medication and we were afraid she may do something rash during this time of deep despair.

There was such an enormous amount of heartache.

Aunt Sue

Searching for Brian

It is often said that some people have strong intuition. I think I may be one of them. The day of the accident, before I knew what had happened, I had such a strong feeling that I "had" to call Renee. I wasn't sure why, I just needed to talk to Renee. I tried calling at 2:30 and then again at 3:00. First, there was a busy signal and then there was no answer. I later found out that at that moment, Renee was being told her son was missing.

My husband, Duane, and son, Paul, are both pilots. We were all feeling so lost and helpless. Duane wanted to do something to help. In the early evenings when the waters were calm, Duane, Kristin, and Paul went up in the plane searching for Brian. We just wanted to find him. We wanted closure.

Renee just kept saying she wanted her son home. As a mother, my heart ached for her. Those five days were the longest, darkest days any of us have ever experienced.

On August 12, I decided to go up in the plane with them, even though I knew it would be difficult. I thought I saw something. That night I had a dream that Brian was found. He was found the next day in that same spot that I noticed the night before. Maybe God didn't want us to be the ones to find him.

We had the horrible job of telling my mother, Brian's grandmother, the news. The ironic thing is that my father had gone to Chambers Island on a Catholic Retreat for years. He always called it his "heavenly retreat" because it was such a serene and peaceful place. In hindsight, it now seems appropriate that Brian would begin his journey to heaven at such a spiritual place.

At the time, it was one of the most publicized stories in the Green Bay area. The front-page headline of the local paper screamed: "Summer Fun Turns to Tragedy." The follow-up stories of the missing 15-year-old boy were equally troubling.

Just two weeks before school was scheduled to start, four young friends were swimming in the Bay on a beautiful, sunny Saturday afternoon. They were at the public beach on Chambers Island. Off the south end of the Island is a ridge that extends about 200 yards in thigh- and waist-deep water before it drops off to about 70 feet.

Two of the four boys stayed in the shallow water while the other two ventured farther out. Matt and Brian were in water that was about waist deep, nearing the area that dropped off. It was estimated that they were about 400 feet from shore when Brian became tired.

"They were out there for about 30 minutes," explained Austin. "They were about 50 yards from Mike and me. I didn't see anything out of the ordinary. I could see their silhouettes and there was no indication that there was a problem. I just remember the panicked look on Matt's face when he came into shore saying that something was wrong. Matt and Mike went for help. I just waited helplessly hoping Brian would reappear. He never did."

It was speculated that Brian became tired and was caught by an undercurrent in the deep water. While the specifics of the drowning are uncertain, it is clear that Matt worked hard to save his friend. He said he put Brian on his back and tried desperately to bring him to shore, but then he became fatigued and Brian slipped off. It was then that Matt went for help.

Austin Rios

Reliving the nightmare

Looking back, the day was definitely one of pairs. After leaving the jeep, Mike and Matt strode ahead and Brian and I followed behind. I was very lucky to have had a particularly deep conversation with Brian during what turned out to be our last encounter on this earth. Later, Mike and I talked together while Brian and Matt ran out into the water.

Even years later, these thoughts I remember strikingly:

- The look on Matt's face and the sound in his voice when he told us he couldn't find Brian.
- The frantic way Mike and Matt ran off to find help.
- Staring across the Bay, feeling utterly helpless.
- Matt's mom's knees buckling on the beach.
- The boats searching the waters.
- The plane flying over the Bay to land on the Island.
- Doug and Renee walking the same stretch of beach that Brian and I had walked earlier.
- Renee's knees buckling on the beach.
- Being interviewed by the policeman and the hint of blame in the officer's voice; I remember the overwhelming sense of blamelessness about the situation.
- Being numb.

Brian's death made me grow up quickly. Each time I talk about the circumstances of his death, I learn more about myself. His death has become a link between me and anyone who has lost someone dear to them.

For about 10 hours that first day of the search, the Coast Guard and other volunteers combed the area using a nautical grid system. Each day, their efforts were fruitless. Each day, the local newspaper reminded the family that their nightmare was not over yet: "Hunt for boy's body off island to continue." And then finally, the search was over.

For five days the body of young Brian LaViolette drifted. The search crews worked diligently, trying to bring this horrible tragedy to a close. However, it wasn't the Coast Guard that finally found Brian's body—it was one of his favorite teachers.

That summer, Brian's teacher was taking sailing lessons in the Bay just south of Chambers Island. During one class, the teacher reported that something told him to veer left as opposed to following his other sailing mates. He discovered the body of his student and radioed the Coast Guard for help. Brian's body was 10 miles south of Chambers Island, floating toward home. He was still wearing his confirmation cross. He was found at 2 p.m. After a positive identification by a friend of the family, Brian was brought home.

Peter Mancuso

One of the most difficult things he had ever done

I followed the coroner to the local funeral home in Sturgeon Bay. I made the positive identification at that time. I told the coroner I wanted to take the silver cross that Brian wore around his neck to the parents. I thought the cross would confirm to Doug and Renee that yes, it was their son. I didn't want to have them feel the need to view the body. At first the coroner said no, that everything had to stay with the body. Fortunately, I know the sheriff well, so I phoned him and he gave the coroner permission to give me the cross.

When I handed Doug the cross, I gave him something more than a piece of jewelry—I gave him closure. I also told him that he and Renee should not view the body at any time during the process. It was in their best interest. They agreed.

I think of myself as a pretty tough guy. I'm not overly emotional and I can usually maintain control. The sight of that boy's body after floating in the water for five days in the hot Door County sun is something that haunts me even today. I am glad my intuition told me to help Doug and Renee during this time. I am especially glad I was the one to identify Brian and not one of them.

It was a very emotional experience. It is surprising how vividly I still recall that time. The pain of those two weeks runs deep for me and my wife—I can't imagine how difficult it must have been for Doug and Renee.

Renee

Harsh reality

I was worried that the coroner wouldn't be able to identify Brian because of the number of days he spent in the water. We were advised not to view our son. I'm glad we didn't. I want to remember his smiling face and bright eyes. I don't want to live with the picture of his body after he had drowned. Fortunately, Peter confirmed it was Brian.

During the search, I always knew deep down that he was gone, even from the moment I received that call. Oh sure, there is always some hope.

Doug and I have since talked about how we wish we would have gotten more information about the Island before letting Brian go. We should have found out where they were going to go swimming and looked at a map with Brian. Maybe we could have warned him about the drop-offs and undercurrents. Since the accident, we've heard other stories of how people have drowned in that same area—people who were good swimmers, like Brian.

Just recently, we heard a story of a woman who drowned while trying to save her son. She was able to guide her son to safety, but was not able to save herself. Every time we hear such a story, we relive our own pain and can empathize with the family who is left behind. We always say a little prayer that Brian welcomes the person with his warm smile—we are convinced he's on Heaven's welcoming committee.

Doug

No more hope

We stayed in contact with the search crew each day Brian was missing and provided some of Brian's things so the dogs could identify his scent. I remember thinking that the Coast Guard was so compassionate, yet very professional. My dad was a former Coast Guard officer. I thought of how proud he would have been of them.

As they searched, we knew Brian was gone. Of course, we secretly hoped he would be found alive. However, parents have a certain intuition that just can't be denied. Both Renee and I had that same feeling—a dark, empty feeling.

Peter and I cried as he handed me the cross Brian was wearing when he died. The cross was a confirmation gift he received from his Grandmother LaViolette three months before the accident.

The Mancusos became a fixture in our home as they stayed with us for two weeks after the accident. Early on during the search, Peter was sitting in our living room with the lights out in the early morning hours as I entered. I told him, "It's even worse today than it was yesterday." Little did I know, it was the beginning of a painful trend—a downward spiral into a deep depression.

Austin's dad brought us Brian's duffel bag. I could see the pain in his eyes as he handed me the bag. Later, when I got the courage to look inside the duffel bag, I realized that Brian's clothing had been cleaned and folded neatly just as Brian had packed them. Brian would have appreciated that—I appreciated that.

The support we received was incredible. Not only were our friends and family supportive, but all of the cards and letters from strangers who heard our story were heart-warming.

It was the longest week of our lives. People were afraid that we were going to snap. I am not sure we could have gotten through it without the outpouring of support and kindness from the communities involved—Door County and Green Bay.

We wrote a hand-written, personal response to every card and letter we received. It was challenging to keep up because there were so many. We would count them and each day there were more than the day before. On Tuesday, August 18, there were 116 pieces of mail and the total was even higher on Wednesday. In the months and years to follow, we received more than 1,000 cards and letters.

The newspaper did a follow-up story about the overwhelming support and printed the following thank-you note from us, which appeared under Brian's picture on the front page:

"On August 8, 1992, the LaViolette family learned that tragedy does not make your family smaller. Rather, we've grown by the thousands. Your overwhelming love and support to us is deeply appreciated...The same love we have for Brian, we now share with you."

We also received gifts. Kim got a locket from Jolyce Rupp with Brian's name on it "to give her something to hold on to when she's lonely." The owners of our previous home offered to send over a tree that Brian helped plant on Arbor Day when he was four years old.

Renee and I talked about our concern that Brian struggled before he died. We couldn't get the vision out of our minds of him gasping and reaching as the current took him under. We couldn't let go of that nightmare, until we received a letter from Leon Bond.

At the time of the accident, Mr. Bond was 97 years old. He lived in Oconto, where Renee and I lived after we were married. We had never met Mr. Bond before, but something caused him to write to us: "Some few years ago, we lost our only child, a daughter, after she had a long, painful struggle with cancer...Doctors tell me that death by drowning is not all the struggle it is often believed to be. Instead it is a rather painless and peaceful departure. That thought might be a small comfort to you."

I started asking doctors and friends about Mr. Bond's theory. Our doctor said drowning only takes about four minutes. The first minute is the only struggle as you gulp for air and your lungs fill up with water. The doctor agreed that it would be a peaceful way to die.

The other day, nine years after the accident, I watched *Titanic* for the first time. I even kept my eyes open during the drowning scenes. As I watched Leonardo DiCaprio slip off the raft and sink into the water, I wondered if it was like that for Brian.

I know I'm making progress in my grief—a few years ago, I would never have been able to even think of watching that movie.

We also have a friend who nearly drowned when he was a child. He said he just remembers it being very peaceful before they revived him. He doesn't remember struggling at all. Other experts tell us that Brian did not suffer and that he did simply "slip away" into the waters. While this is a small comfort, it is an important one to parents who never want their children to suffer. Thank you, Mr. Bond, for providing us with that image. The other one was difficult to bare.

After we received that first letter from Mr. Bond, others from him followed. Our individual losses created a new friendship. Mr. Bond was one of the founders and former president of the Bond Pickle Company in Oconto. The company was established in 1921 and is still in existence today.

Mr. Bond donated more than $4 million to establish a community center in Oconto. He and the president of the Bond Community Center, Earl J. DeCloux, dedicated the outdoor soccer field in Brian's memory. Today, soccer enthusiasts enjoy playing at the Brian LaViolette Soccer Field in Oconto. It was a proud moment for us. Brian loved soccer and I am sure he is enjoying the fact that a field is named after him.

A Special Letter

From Peter and Deb Mancuso (8/24/92)

Doug, Renee, Kimberly:

We have seen firsthand the overwhelming support of those unknown to you, hundreds of caring friends, and your loving families. The sincere pain we have felt for each of you has gone beyond a threshold we thought possible.

Losing a child so warmly loved, so sensitive and full of promise, can only be imagined by those of us who have never faced that painful experience. Although there will forever be a void in your lives, Brian will always have been and continues to be your son—your brother. He and you three will continue to be an inspiration to all of us who have been touched by your pain and loss.

The journey is now beginning along roads that appear unknown—the reward will eventually come. Whatever we can do to help along the way is yours for the asking.

Love, Peter and Deb

Marilyn from New York

A 9/11 witness shares her thoughts and support

Your story is one of great compassion and love. I admire you for sharing your journey that holds so much hurt but also so much hope. On September 11, as I heard the plane hit the first World Trade building from across the street where I worked in Manhattan, I saw the fire spread across the top floors of the building and realized that so many people have just died in that split second. It is impossible to process that type of information as you are in the middle of trying to deal with such a devastating outcome. It was only in the days that followed, as families of victims came out looking for their loved ones, that I could actually cry. I think we have a built in survival mechanism that kicks in during times of danger and overwhelming grief. You experienced this first-hand as you dealt with the loss of your son. All we can hope for in life is that we find some meaning. Our value is measured by the way we touch other lives. Brian has done that in so many ways for so many people. His spirit is strong and his journey continues in the words, deeds, and hearts of his beloved family.

Kind Words

Incredible support from friends and strangers

"...I had the good fortune of knowing Brian. He taught us so many things, but one of his greatest lessons to me, is a simple one. I will never forget Brian's smile. The memory of Brian, I think, is a constant reminder for us all to take time to smile..."

"Your personal sacrifice has impacted and bonded so very many parents and children in ways you will never know. The memory of Brian will always remain in our hearts, thoughts, and prayers. We are so privileged to be a part of his continuous journey."

"During this incredible, almost indescribable affair, we have witnessed Brian's departure and the empty despair which is beyond human scale. Yet, curiously and ironically, his death has brought rebirth with: Christians renewing their faith; parents re-evaluating their roles and responsibilities; individuals rekindling their family relationships; business people reconsidering their priorities; youth reviewing Brian's foundation for living. Similar to your bright, young son who selected the best principles, philosophies, and guideposts as his foundation and pathway through life, we are reminded that the journey is the reward and the trip is best when taken together. We are deeply saddened by your loss. Yet, we are enlightened by the examples of wisdom of young Brian."

"You are fortunate to have experienced such a wonderful person and human being in your son. The time with him was short but what he gave of himself is something that will live forever. My sympathies are with you but I would like to also express thanks that you shared such a wonderful person with the community."

"You can be very proud of your son and hold in high regard the type of life he led and the many positive values he stood for. He truly was a great young man and all that you could ask for in a son! Your terrible tragedy helps reinforce my desire to spend even more time with my children."

"The paths that you went down with Brian for these past wonderful 15 years has diverged so tragically and unexpectedly. Within the span of those years I have had the privilege of watching your family mature in love and unity. Though Brian may no longer move among us physically, the sunshine legacy of his gentle, loving spirit will guide your thoughts through the cloudy days and nights that lie ahead."

"My husband and I golf out at Mystery Hills and one day were paired up with Brian and his friend. We want you to know it was a very refreshing day to golf with your son. He was a joy to golf with. We were certainly impressed with him and wish the circumstances were different now. You have a son whom you can always be very proud of."

"Brian was known by his efforts and his beliefs. Despite his young years, he did not live or die in obscurity, nor was his light extinguished with his passing. It takes such courage to make your spirit known to others."

Lisa Patrickus

Heart-felt thoughts from December 1, 1994

I will never forget when my friend, Brian, died. It feels like it happened yesterday. It was a warm summer's night and I was at our family cottage. I was watching the closing ceremonies of the summer Olympics in Barcelona. The news was about to start. I had heard that a boy drowned in Door County and I wanted to see if there was any more news. The boy was from my town. They hadn't released his name yet.

All of a sudden the phone rang. My dad answered it.

I got up to see who it was. From the look on my dad's face, I knew something was really wrong. I took the phone and on the other end was my best friend, Erin. She was crying. She couldn't say much but she said a couple of words that I'll never forget: "Lisa, Brian's dead. It was Brian that drowned." I couldn't believe what I was hearing.

I was still on the phone with Erin when I overheard it announced on the news. The newscaster even pronounced his name wrong. That made me even more mad. I went out to sit on the porch. I remembered the last night I saw him. He came over to my house just five days before. He left early that night and I didn't say good-bye. I wish I would have said good-bye. I never thought it may be the last time I would ever see him.

Erin and I went to the funeral home together. We were both so nervous. What would we say? How should we act toward his parents? Our turn slowly came up and we introduced ourselves to Brian's parents. Instantly, they gave us each a hug and we all started to cry. I had never met his parents before, but at that moment, I felt so close to them.

The next day we went to the funeral. The church was overcrowded with people who came to honor Brian. I will never forget when one woman sang, "Forever Young" by Rod Stewart as the casket went down that long aisle. We went to the grave site to see Brian buried. I had never seen a casket lowered into the ground like that. It is something I will not easily forget.

I often go to his grave site where I talk to Brian. He helps me with my problems now, just as he did when he was here. I visualize Brian smiling down on us.

Although Brian has been gone for more than two years, that experience will be with me forever. Not only do I try and say good-bye to everyone when I see them, but I also try to let my feelings show more. I never told Brian what an important friend he was to me. I don't take my friends for granted anymore, because someday they may not be with me.

I have only good memories of Brian. I try to be how he would want me to be. Brian's death also made me realize that no matter what, I should be happy. Even if today would be my last, at least I will have lived my life to the fullest, as Brian did. I will never forget Brian or how the end of his life has made such an impact on mine.

Renee

The dream

Within a few weeks of the accident, Brian came to me in a dream. Doug was watching TV in our bedroom and I was dosing off. That's when it happened. I saw Brian at the foot of the bed. My heart ached. I wanted to jump out of bed and hug him—never to let him go. He smiled, a quiet, peaceful smile and said: "Don't worry Mom, I'm happy and safe." With that he was gone. I sat up in bed and asked Doug if he saw him. He didn't. I felt so blessed that I did.

It was just an innocent swim with friends and in a moment's notice it turned into an ugly nightmare. It's always hard to believe that so much can happen in such a short period of time. In an instant in those waters off beautiful Chambers Island, many lives were changed forever.

That accident produced a gaping hole in the LaViolette family. With a blink of an eye they were now frozen in time.

Horrified to move forward and unable to look back, each member of the family was emotionally lost-exhausted, depressed, and filled with anxiety. How would they recover? How would they live without their golden boy—the protective big brother, their son who truly shined? This would be a test they were not sure they could pass.

As they collected their courage, they struggled to hang on. Could they some day make it to the other side of this intense grief?

"My family, including my parents, were coincidently up at Chambers Island the day Brian was missing," explained Brian's confirmation coach, Michael "Buz" Weas. "We were aware there was a young man missing and there was plenty of activity on the Island that indicated something was wrong. But we had no idea it was Brian who was missing."

"My mother wrote a poem that tells about that experience along with reflections of Brian." Buz read the following poem at Brian's funeral:

A helicopter filled the air.
The beautiful, fresh summer air.
I walked along a sandy lane without a single care.

My day was filled with sweetness,
Watching children play in the sand.
The stillness of the moment was broken,
By its invasion of the land.

For a moment, just a moment, I looked up
And caught a glimpse of a low flying plane,
And my own heart filled with the sadness
of someone else's pain.

BRIAN

He was here for awhile,
then suddenly on a warm summer day
The life that was Brian softly slipped away.
You search for an answer, you wanted him to stay.
He was handsome and tall, so young yet so wise.
He had it all together, you could see it in his eyes.
Brian was loving and kind, he had so much to give
He seemed to really understand how great it was to live.

The answer is out there in the endless waves at sea,
Where the patterns in the sand send a picture back to me
Of peace and calm and a quiet summer breeze,
That turned into a song, when it rustles through the trees.
I see gently shifting water that took that quiet lad
Away from his wonderful family and up to his Heavenly Dad.

On a still summer evening if you listen with your heart,
You can hear Brian gently telling you, "We will never be apart,
I am with you now in spirit for all your many days,
And I am etched deep in your memory in oh so many ways.
I love you all so much," he whispers very soft.
"And I am waiting for you patiently
in my beautiful heavenly loft."

—Tina Weas

Brian Douglas LaViolette
1977 - 1992

The Faith:

The soul lives on

"The man who goes alone can start today,
but he who travels with another
must wait til the other is ready."

Like a shadow on that sunny day in Door County, Brian has spiritually never left their side. The LaViolettes cling to their faith in God and their belief that the soul lives on. Immediately, their faith became their lifeline—their safety net against insanity. They knew in their hearts that if they did not believe they would be with Brian again some day, the pain could be maddening.

And it wasn't just their faith that protected them from emotional demise, it was Brian's faith, too. Less than three months before Brian's death, he was confirmed. He called it his "proudest achievement." He cherished his religion—he believed in God.

Spiritually, he was said to be wise beyond his years. In his confirmation handbook, Brian wrote this about daily prayer: "You should pray when you really want to. No fake stuff."

"Brian was not about fake stuff," explains Buz. "...he wanted to learn and grow. He could have just easily slid by or simply fed me with what he thought I might want to hear, but he understood our meetings were a great learning opportunity and he would not let them go to waste."

Brian's confirmation on May 17, 1992 charted the course for his final destination. He read the Bible and even marked passages he liked. After he died, his parents noticed that the bookmark in his bible on the nightstand next to his bed, was at this verse (Mark 16, 19-20):

Then he led them out of the city as far as Bethany, where he raised his hands and blessed them. As he was blessing them, he departed from them and was taken up to heaven. They worshiped him and went back to Jerusalem, filled with great joy, and spent all their time in the Temple giving thanks to God.

The words below this verse on the program handed out at the funeral appropriately concluded: "Brian now takes his rightful place at God's hand. Brian, may you walk hand in hand with angels, and smile down every day on those of us who love you so."

As the Coast Guard searched for Brian's body, the family took some time to think about his funeral. "It is to be a celebration of his life," someone declared. So, the planning began.

The family wanted a personal service that represented who Brian was.

Ironically, there was a question in Brian's confirmation workbook that read: What would you like your funeral service to be like? According to the Reverend David Blackmer, "Brian's answer was characteristically short and filled with a very simple wisdom. He wrote that he would like his funeral to be 'emotional, but keep on living'."

The first wish turned out to be an easy one to honor—it was an emotional funeral.

The visitation was on Sunday night. The funeral home nearly burst at the seams.

The journey is the reward.

BRIAN LAVIOLETTE

The funeral service took place at 10 a.m. on Monday, August 17, 1992. It was a warm, sunny morning. The "celebration" was held at the family's church, First United Methodist Church in Green Bay.

The pallbearers were six of Brian's friends and cousins, including the three boys he went swimming with on Chambers Island. Other students filled the church as they mourned the loss of their young friend.

The church was filled with people, songs, tears, and sadness. Family and friends fidgeted with their funeral program that featured Brian's smiling picture on the front and the words, *The journey is the reward* in his handwriting, with his signature. The program read: "The love of his family and his smile were Brian LaViolette's constant companions every day of his fifteen years."

It was "A Service of Death and Resurrection Celebrating the Life of Brian Douglas LaViolette." It was a service that those present would not soon forget.

One person wrote, "I am writing to tell you how tremendously impressed I was with the service for Brian. It was the most personal and beautiful service I have ever attended. Though I never met Brian, I left the church feeling I knew just what he was like if I would have met him."

Another family friend wrote, "As a parent myself, I cannot comprehend the pain of losing one of my children. My parents taught me that God has a plan for all of us and you can take comfort in knowing that Brian was a fine young Christian and has found a home in Heaven."

"I didn't know Brian personally but the irony is that since attending the funeral, I feel like I've been privileged to know him through those whose lives he touched and affected. I think of the famous poem, 'Tis better to have loved and lost, than never to have loved at all'."

Page three of the program read:

"...A young child of wonder grew into a star athlete and excellent student. He lettered in golf and soccer while just a freshman, and established even greater successes in the classroom as an honor student." (That day Kim pointed out an error in the program to her dad—Brian was a 'high' honor student, she said, not just an honor student.)

"In between, Brian filled his remaining free time with band, jazz band, and he still found the time to work at Mystery Hills Golf Course, mow lawns, and work for his parents. Not lost was Brian's entrepreneurial spirit, whether responding to the challenge before him, or working to improve existing methods. He embraced every challenge with his best. Through all of his achievements, the badge he wore so proudly was his faith, and it is his faith that carries him to his rightful place at the right hand of God, and that will carry us through."

Reverend Blackmer was first to speak. Buz and Darrel Burnett, a family friend, provided the eulogy. Both men tried desperately to contain their tears as they talked about a young man they admired—a young man they will miss.

Following are excerpts from Brian's funeral.

Reverend David Blackmer

A life well lived

Brian LaViolette was a delight to me and to the confirmation class here at First United Methodist Church.

The Apostle Paul said: "Whether I live or die, I am the Lord's." I believe Brian, like the Apostle Paul, had grown to understand that life is a gift. He believed that his life was a gift from God to be enjoyed and shared with others.

A life well lived is a full life. We can say with genuineness that Brian led a full life. Brian knew the everyday joy of a life well lived. I found Brian to be wonderfully honest. His confirmation folder is just loaded with straightforward language. He was easy to get to know and he was comfortable with himself and with other people. Many of us experienced Brian to be an exceptionally insightful person.

Brian was a good listener. People who are comfortable with themselves don't need to talk over another person. This characteristic of Brian's reminds me of a poem:

His thoughts were rich,
His words were few,
And seldom formed to glisten,
But he was a joy to all of his friends,
You should have heard him listen.

During the confirmation process, Brian indicated, in no uncertain terms, that his family—Doug, Renee, and Kim—were by far the most influential people in his life. He credits his practical spirituality to his father, his kindness to his mother.

I think Brian would be troubled to have us make him out to be bigger than life. Because, you see, he was a real person. He was very much plugged into life.

Michael "Buz" Weas

A tribute to a young man of faith

Brian knew he was loved and he did not take that love for granted. This love was not only evident in his writing about it or saying it, it showed in his values, in his strong self-esteem, in his optimistic attitude, in his very being. I believe this powerful love was at the very center of Brian's zeal for life.

Brian appeared to me to be extraordinarily prepared for the journey to manhood. There is no doubt in my mind that Brian would have seen success in his future. He already was an achiever. But bright future aside, I believe Brian would have grown up simply to be a good human being in a world that badly needs more good human beings.

Darrel Burnett

A family friend remembers

We are often reminded that children are our future. In truth, children are also our present. On that most basic of foundations, the strongest of all families was built—the LaViolettes.

Never, ever did Brian have to ask for love and respect. And he always returned it many times over.

We have all asked ourselves the question, Why? The answer is far too complex. Perhaps we will never know. I, personally, choose to believe that God is no different than us, that He likes to surround himself with friends. Today, God has a new best friend.

In a private moment the other night, Doug told me that I had in some small way greatly influenced Brian. As proud as that makes me, let the record show that Brian influenced me far more than I ever influenced him.

What Brian accomplished is not nearly as important as how he accomplished it—with diligence, dignity, and complete dedication. And most of all, with compassion and love.

Brian insisted that he earn his way in life. It is now our responsibility to follow the wonderful blueprint of life that he established.

Kimberly, Renee and Doug, we pray for you. Brian Douglas LaViolette, may God be with you. You would have gone on to accomplish great things. In your name and memory, we will accomplish great things.

Rest now my friend...your journey is complete.

Reverend David Blackmer

The committal at the cemetery

Doug mentioned to me just a few moments ago that one of his and Brian's favorite movies was, *Field of Dreams*. As we looked back at the line of cars cresting, streaming over the hilltop, all with their lights ablaze, he mentioned how much it reminded him of the final triumphant scene in that movie.

My friends, this is the promise in which we stand today. The significance of this moment is not merely in the number of people here, although there are many. And the significance is not only in who Brian was to each and every one of us, but who we were to him also.

Each one of us was an important person to Brian. We helped, by God's grace, to shape his life. And now, today, even in our grief, this is the promise we share. As we hold hands here, we know that God is with us. God comforts and cares for us through one another. That legacy, of which Brian was so aware, continues today and will go on as our source of comfort.

Cousin Kristin

An amazing tribute

The funeral was an amazing tribute to Brian. As I scanned the faces at the funeral home, the church, and the cemetery, there was grief, shock, and bewilderment. What was most difficult was seeing so many "kids" upset.

As I sat in church the morning of his funeral listening to people speak so thoughtfully about Brian, I couldn't get over the fact that I never really got to know him the way others were so fortunate to know him. In many ways, Brian was more of an adult at age 15 than I was at the age of 20.

For me, because I didn't see Brian on a daily basis, it wasn't losing him that changed who I am, but watching those I love experience such a profound loss and sense of grief. That was difficult. For a long time after he died, I often thought I saw him when I went places. It would happen at the mall or maybe a restaurant. I would catch a glimpse of someone that I thought looked like Brian. I think it was wishful thinking because I knew I would never get the opportunity to really know this special person.

Renee

Everything was a blur

I don't really remember much about the funeral, or the days leading up to it. I think I was still in shock for a long time after I received that horrible phone call.

A lot of people were around. I know many of them were helping Doug plan the funeral.

After the funeral, people told me the service was beautiful—a real celebration of Brian's life and his faith. It's hard to believe the funeral of a 15-year-old boy who died so tragically can be considered a beautiful celebration. But it was. Someone audio taped it for us. We have not been able to listen to it. I'm not sure we ever will.

We felt blessed that we had Reverend Blackmer, Buz, and Darrel. We were fortunate to have adults that could speak about Brian. It would have been so difficult for a friend his own age to speak at the funeral. Buz and Darrel really loved Brian, and he respected both of them.

After Brian died, it seemed like I stayed in my room a lot. It really took every ounce of strength I had to get out of bed and even attend the funeral. The depression had already begun its attack and it was unrelenting in its pursuit of me. Even though I knew the funeral was to celebrate Brian's life, secretly I was not sure that I would even make it through the day. But, somehow you do, I guess. Our friends and families were wonderful. Although Doug was better at reaching out to people than I was, I really appreciated all the kindness and compassion I felt from them during this horrible time.

And then there is the finality of walking out of church behind a casket that contains your son's body. It is a feeling I will not forget in this lifetime.

Doug

I wish he were here

Both Renee and I agreed that we wanted to remember our handsome son as he was before the accident. Like the day of his confirmation, just three months to the day of the funeral—smiling, filled with pride, and yet humbled by that important religious experience.

The funeral was very emotional. It may sound weird, but I kept wishing he were there. Oh, I know he was "there." But I wanted him there, sitting next to us—just as he did every time we went to church.

Those five days, while he was missing, gave us a chance to plan the funeral. We had so much help, it was amazing.

We wanted him to wear the suit he was confirmed in. Renee and I commented the day of Brian's confirmation what a handsome young man he was. We were so proud of him.

A couple days before the funeral, I put the suit on a hanger with such care, it was as if it were made of glass. Because Brian would never get a class ring, I gave him mine. I slipped the ring on a string and looped it on the hanger beside his belt and his tie. Tears rolled down my face as I realized that his lifeless body would soon replace that hanger.

I imagined him there with me that day, with his hand on my shoulder saying: "Everything will be all right, dad." It was an image I clung to, because I knew if it left me, I would be lost.

Peter Mancuso

Happy with their progress

After the funeral, Deb and I decided to go back to Door County to resume our lives. The funeral was a very emotional and special service. I remember thinking how proud I was that Doug and Renee had made such progress in their grieving before that important event. Making it through that day without breaking down was a major step out of their deep despair. I think all of the support they received really helped. I was glad for both of them.

While it may be difficult to admit, when we go through something like this with friends or family members, we can't help but think, "Thank God it isn't happening to me...thank God it wasn't my child." This type of tragedy gives you pause to think of the true wealth in your life. It helps you appreciate each day a little more and enjoy your loved ones fully.

Since the accident, I have looked out our living room window and been able to see the area where we found Brian. It is a haunting memory that continually reminds me that life is not always fair.

Although Brian has become somewhat larger than life, he can best be described as a good son and a good kid. He had strong values that Doug and Renee worked hard to instill. Today, if he were alive, I am sure Doug and Renee would be enjoying his many accomplishments with him just as other parents do with their good children. But instead, Doug and Renee must keep his spirit and memory close to their hearts.

Brian's faith began very early in his life. Often Doug and Renee would tuck him in bed and read him the following prayer. It is a prayer that Brian could eventually recite by heart.

A BOY'S PRAYER

I pray, whatever wrong I do,
I'll never say what is not true;
Be willing at my task each day
And always honest in my play.
Make me unselfish with my toys,
And generous to the other boys;
And kind and helpful to the old,
And prompt to do what I am told.

Bless everyone I love, and teach
Me how to help and comfort each;
Give me the strength right living brings,
And make me good in little things.

After the burial, there was a lunch at the church. The family decided to donate some of the food from the occasion to the Family Violence Center. A warm letter of thanks followed:

"We thank you for the generous donation of food. We appreciate that you remembered the needs of others especially at this most sorrowful time. Family Violence Center could close its doors if the community abusers had the characteristics of Brian. How very fortunate you are to have experienced his special giftedness."

This would be a legacy of giving back that they would hope to continue in Brian's honor.

Attending the funeral of a loved one can be a very complex event. Although grief is the overriding feeling, an emotional tug of war can also take place. While you dread the event, there is a part of you that doesn't want it to end. After all, the funeral provides the last physical connection you will have with your loved one. It is a small comfort but the fact remains that the casket holds the body of your loved one. It's their last physical presence with you here on this earth. When that casket is taken away, the reality of the loss unfolds quickly.

The 12 months that follow a loss can feel like an eternity. It is a time filled with haunting memories, incredible loneliness, and a despair that manifests itself not only emotionally but physically, too. The physical pain is not unlike a heart attack or a broken limb. It is a deep pain that can surface in all kinds of ways. The sadness is so heavy it can make it difficult to walk, while the anxiety actually steals your breath. There is no magic pill or potion for that frustrating, physical pain. There is no cure—other than time.

The LaViolettes were not immune to this pain. They were now experiencing the agony and hopelessness that cloak those who have lost someone they love.

How would they get through it? How would they overcome the desperate pain that accompanied every moment of their days?

Their answer was with Brian. They would lean on this "old soul" as they tried to find ways to make it through each day. They would look to him—and each other—to help them continue on their journey.

The Next 12 Months:

Going through the motions

"We will either find a way, or make one."

It may happen while you are listening to the radio, driving in your car, or innocently walking from one room to the next. Those feelings and memories of your loved one are as steady as your own breathing. They are like a ball and chain hooked to your heart. With them comes the pain. It is a pain that can strike like lightning or creep into your day like the morning fog. You are the hostage as it takes over.

When you lose a loved one, your world as you knew it is gone—forever changed, only to hopefully be reborn with time. Your life comes to a sudden stop. You are a wounded bystander as those around you continue to actively move through their days. Participation in life is not only difficult, it can sometimes be impossible.

It's as if you are driving at night without the headlights on. Or in the midst of a white out blizzard. It's nearly impossible to see forward. And yet, your intuition tells you to keep moving. As you go through the motions, you feel more like a puppet on a string, rather than a human being. You are not really sure how you are getting through each day. But you are—one at a time.

Nearly every minute of the day holds the reality that you no longer have your loved one. The 12 months that follow the funeral are filled with "firsts." Birthdays, holidays, anniversaries, soccer tournaments, and golf outings serve as reality set-backs that magnify the tragedy and keep the pain alive. Then there is the emptiness—the empty bedroom, the empty chair at the dinner table, the empty feeling in your heart.

The LaViolettes struggled to find a way to divert their pain. They needed to outsmart this monumental adversary. While they knew they would not defeat the pain, they searched for a way to channel it. Their answer *was* their son. Their love for Brian and his positive attitude would be their saving grace. That would be the foundation they would use to rebuild their lives.

Kim

From her journal at age 12

Right now, almost two months after it happened, we are still getting cards. People still call and come over, too. Even though we're seeing a counselor named Lucy, who is very nice, what I think is helping the most right now is the people. I'm growing away from the problem of Brian's death, but I'm not growing away from Brian.

Renee

Getting through each day

After the funeral, I stayed in bed a lot—maybe too much. Kim came into the bedroom right after Brian died and said "Mom, now you don't have to worry about Brian." I'm a worrier. I always was and probably always will be.

After something like this happens, you know your life will never be the same, but nothing can prepare you for the pain of that first year. It's as if nothing else matters. It is really difficult to keep on living.

We had so much support. We had one couple, Jack and Ginny Riopelle, who came over to our house literally every single night for months. They would just visit with us or have dinner with us. Even if they went out to dinner, they would come over afterwards. When the doorbell rang, we knew it was Jack and Ginny. Many times I didn't want to see anyone. But I would come out of my room and force myself to smile a few times. That was a good thing. Because for a moment—no matter how brief—I actually felt like I was living again, instead of dying inside.

We had another friend, Ron, who sent us a weekly postcard with an inspirational saying. The number of cards and letters we received from family, friends, and even strangers was unbelievable. Because of the publicity of the story, we had people reaching out to us from all over the area.

We were interviewed for a front-page story a few weeks after Brian died. The picture showed me, Doug, and Kim with all the cards taped up on our family room wall. The headline read: "Love carried De Pere family through the loss of their son." That was so true. There were hundreds of cards and letters from people who had lost a child. There was a large poster signed by the children at the Boys and Girls Club.

Doug was on the local Boys & Girls Club board of directors for eight years. The people we met through that volunteer effort were very supportive.

There was also a prayer letter with 200 signatures from people attending an East Coast prayer workshop with the mother of one of Brian's friends. The support we received was remarkable. Our families were also very understanding.

The Thanksgiving after Brian died, my sister invited us over, like she had always done for years. Instead of eating at the dining room table like we always did, she set up tables and chairs in the kitchen. Everyone worked with us to try and help get us through as best we could.

Ginny suggested that we hire someone to put up the Christmas tree and decorations that first year because then it would be different than in years past. We thought it was a pretty good idea. It did help.

Although we are still sad at times, at Christmas, we've managed to make the holiday season special. After all, Kim deserves to have a special Christmas.

I received two special gifts from Doug the Christmas before Brian died. He had a local artist, Martha Carpenter, do a charcoal drawing of each of the kids. The sketch of Brian is on page 56 of this book. On the back of his sketch, Brian wrote:

"Mom, as we pass through our lives, nothing will stay as still as this portrait…except for your constant kindness and love. Merry Christmas! Dec. 1991 Love, Brian."

The picture on the cover of this book is the one that the artist used to sketch Brian. Those sketches of Kim and Brian are the most precious Christmas gifts I've ever received.

Doug

The first Christmas

Yes, Christmas can be difficult. Of course, our first Christmas without Brian was the most painful. But something inspiring actually happened that first Christmas. I was glancing through the local newspaper when a letter in the "In Memorial" section caught my eye. Here is that letter, as it actually appeared in the paper:

Dear Brian L.—
Although we never met, it's as if I have known you a long time. I had just arrived in Door County when I heard the news of the accident. Much like many mysteries of this world, I will never understand why things like this happen to wonderful people. And the first chance I get to ask Him, I will.

I want you to know that out of everything comes some good if you look for it. Life in our home has changed since that August day. My children know a more understanding mother. Sometimes being a parent can be very difficult and also a lot of fun.

It's the little things I see more clearly now and how precious they really are. On those days when I come home from work, I'm tired, the house is a mess, and I'm out of patience. Because of your passing, I reach down just a little deeper.

Christmas in our house will be different this year, not because there will be more presents under the tree, but because I will watch their smiles, I will listen to them and hear them, I will catch them doing things right, not wrong. I will say "I love you" more often, hug and kiss them more, and not get caught up in the day-to-day stuff, like making a living.

Until we meet, A FRIEND

We were so impressed that someone would take the time to write this message and pay for it to run in the paper. We also were touched by the message. What is even more special about this letter is what happened months after it ran.

Of course, we didn't know who put the letter in the paper. Months later, I was at a tradeshow and a woman came up to me and asked "Are you Doug LaViolette?" There was something about her. I said "Yes" and then it hit me...she was the person who put the letter in the paper the Christmas before. I started crying and she confirmed that yes, it was her. To this day, I'm not sure how I knew it was her. Maybe Brian told me.

Renee

Painful reminders

Brian's bedroom was the most difficult. No matter what we did—door open, door closed—it didn't help. He always had his door open during the day and closed at night. We tried it both ways. Some people told us to convert it into a den. That didn't seem like an option to us.

His room was always so neat. After the funeral, however, we started putting some things in there from the funeral and gifts from people.

When Doug would go to work and Kim would be at school, I would go into his room by myself. I would hold his pillow and cry. I would get up, look around, and leave his room, only to do it again the next day. The pain felt like a slow torture.

When his 16th birthday arrived, Doug and I thought that maybe going on vacation would help us get through it. Boy, that was a bad idea. You know what they say, "You can run but you can't hide." We could've gone to the ends of the earth and the pain would have followed us.

As I look back, I feel bad for Kim. She lost her brother and for a time, she lost her parents—at least, emotionally. Her father and I cried a lot. Kim didn't show a great deal of emotion at the time. I think she was afraid that if she cried it would make us feel worse. I worried about her, but I knew she had supportive friends and was getting help at school. It must have been difficult for her, though. Doug and I were so totally consumed with the loss of our son.

And there were so many reminders that Brian was no longer with us. The newspaper and television covered the story when they discovered that his high school soccer team dedicated their season to Brian's memory. That year, the year he died, the team played in the state championship game. One news report really stands out in my mind. We kept a copy:

The De Pere Redbirds are a talented team worthy of their unblemished record. But a lot of talented teams don't make it this far. De Pere wasn't going to be denied after tragically losing a teammate.

"Brian LaViolette drowned a week before soccer season started," according to coach Dale Rhodes. "He started for me as a freshman last year at left wing. Just a really super kid. And, the players dedicated the season to him."

"We decided we'd dedicate the season. Some people just dedicate games. He would have been on this team and he would have been a major contributor," said teammate Robin Rameker.

Brian's memory has been a major contributor. The Redbirds play an all-out, hustling, total team game. And when they get a little tired, they think of Brian.

"Our motto this year is The Journey is The Reward. Brian had that statement over his bed. It was something that Brian took into his heart," said Coach Rhodes. "...there isn't a game that goes by that we don't talk about Brian."

"It feels good to know that he has a major role in this yet. We all loved him dearly and this is the least we can do for him," concluded Rameker.

If De Pere beats West De Pere tonight, they will be just one step from their ultimate goal: State.

Well, they did make it to state that year. Those games were exciting to watch and yet very difficult for Doug and me.

After he died, Brian's school had an athletic awards banquet. Doug and I were invited because they honored a soccer player and a golfer in Brian's memory. Even though everyone was saying such nice things about Brian, that banquet was very hard for us to attend.

I have had dreams with Brian in them—mostly good ones. I often sense that he is in the room. Or, I will go into a specific room and I will smell him. Even in our new house, I still get those feelings. They don't frighten me—they actually comfort me. Sometimes I even wish that they happened more frequently.

Doug

Physical agony

I was physically sick for so long after the accident. My heart hurt so much that at times I thought I was going to die. And at that point in the grief, I secretly wished I would just die. The only thing that kept me going was my love for Renee and Kim.

I cried so much. I cried in the shower when I would get up in the morning, and I would cry before I slept at night. Sometimes, I even cried at work.

Both Renee and I lost our appetites. It's as if your throat is closing. It's not only difficult to eat, it's difficult to talk. We both lost weight.

A few days after the funeral, I had to make a delivery to our other store location. As I drove down the freeway, I passed a flatbed truck carrying casket vaults. I noticed it was the same company that made Brian's casket vault. Those types of reminders were almost suffocating.

For me, the worst part was the realization that he's never going to come back. That I'm never going to walk through the front door and hear him say, "Hectic day, Dad?" He could look at me and tell the kind of day I had. He would come over to me and tell me that everything was going to be OK.

We would never have another "snow day" when the four of us could throw a log on the fire and watch movies and laugh. Our family was no longer whole.

I remember the day I worked on a Saturday a few months after he died when I replaced Kim's school picture on my desk but was not able to replace Brian's picture.

It was difficult to go into his bedroom. When he was alive, I went into his room nearly every night. I would like to think that I am a pretty observant guy. After he died, I went into his room and noticed—for the first time—all these inspirational sayings in his handwriting on 3x5 cards. Somewhere along the way, he saw those sayings or tweaked them into his own style and decided to stick them up in his room. These were sayings that represented his young life and his values. He used them to stay positive and motivated. I wish I would have noticed those sayings before he died. I would have loved having a conversation with him about why he picked the ones he did and where he found them.

We think he liked "The Journey is The Reward" the best because it most clearly represented how he lived his life.

Some of the sayings even represented his wonderful sense of humor, like "Men play football, real men play soccer." He had a great sense of humor—kind of "tongue in cheek."

Just before the accident, I got upset with him because he didn't cut the lawn like he was supposed to. After he died, I actually felt bad about that argument. That day, however, he let me blow off steam and then he said with a smile, "Dad, I'm strengthening the root system."

A few days before he died, he walked into the kitchen and I noticed he had a diamond studded earring. Before I even had a chance to get upset, he pulled it off and showed it to me—it wasn't real, it was magnetic!

After he died, it helped to talk about things like that—like his sense of humor and his faith. I was actually kind of jealous of his faith. He was only 15 years old and yet he was so confident about God, Jesus Christ as our savior, and that there was a heaven. Even though he had a lot of questions, he used to say, "I guess that's why they call it *faith*."

My own faith was very fragile after he died. I asked the same questions every parent asks when they lose a child—why our child, why Brian? I still struggle. But it helps know-

Brian's first pose 1977

Even at 5 months it was certain Brian would always carry a smile

Storing up firewood for a Wisconsin winter.

Grandpa Bogsted's gift of golf clubs set the stage for Brian's love of golf.

A close shave...caught in the act.

And baby Kim makes two!

Leaving home on the first day of school
Brian's educational journey begins.

Brian always enjoyed looking out for,
and protecting his little sister.

Brian and Kim on their cousin's 1988 wedding day.

A future soccer star in the making at 6.

There isn't anything like seeing a friend on that first trip to Disney World!

When mowing the grass even a light rain could not hold him back.

Brian demonstrating that sweet swing on our Florida vacation

Brian the soccer player having a little fun.

Confirmation at the United Methodist Church May 17, 1992 was Brian's proudest day. Here he poses with his sponsor and good friend Buz Weas.

In between sports and school Brian found time to play the trumpet in the DePere marching band. He was so proud of this picture Kim took of him before his last Memorial Day parade in 1992.

From an early age Brian had a great respect for history and loved our country. He and Kim stand in Abraham Lincoln's office in Springfield, IL on our family vacation - July

Early morning fishing - the LaViolette family poses for our last father's day as a complete family.

Brian's sense of humor and competitive spirit came to light with a bumper sticker he had hung in his room that said "Men Play Football, Real Men Play Soccer"

Hopes, Dreams, Destiny

This shot was one Kim's favorites and shows Brian and Kim overlooking the Bay of Green Bay in 1984. Ironically, 8 years later Brian's body was found in that same area.

ing that he was such a spiritual young man. It seems odd, but he is the example I follow. I know he wouldn't want me to stop believing—he wouldn't want this to shake my faith.

A few weeks after he died, I was getting ready for church. It was actually one of the few times I've gone to church since his death. Something inside me was telling me to "look over here." I turned my head and on the dresser was a funny looking note with a big black spring-like paper clip on it. I opened it and there was his handwriting:

"Unfold slowly, love Brian" it said.

I opened the first fold and he wrote, "I LOVE YOU";
second fold, "I ALWAYS HAVE";
third fold, "I JUST WISH...";
fourth fold, "EVERY KID COULD HAVE IT AS GOOD AS I DO."

It was like he was speaking to me from heaven. As hard as it was to discover that note and read his handwriting so soon after we had lost him, it was as if he was saying, "I like it here!" Along with the sadness, came some comfort.

He still gives me little signs. When we moved into our new house, I received a sign. We now live on a golf course—Brian would have loved that. I was in the back yard on a sunny fall day. It was a typical beautiful Wisconsin afternoon. I noticed a golf ball lying on the grass. I know this is not surprising, considering we live on a golf course. However, it was the first golf ball I found and it was a Slazenger 4, the exact style of ball that Brian always used. I picked it up, smiled, wrote the date on the ball, and put it in a safe place. I've only golfed a few times since Brian died. Maybe I will enjoy the game again someday, but right now, I just don't.

There were so many reminders of him at work. Not only did I have to force myself to go to work, but I had to run a business. I think I was just going through the motions. Some people throw themselves into their work, others do as I did and retreat. I think my reaction had something to do with the fact that Brian was so involved with the business. Just showing up at work was difficult, let alone actually working.

As a business owner, in hindsight, I made a huge mistake. We had a very "flat" organizational chart. I was the key salesperson and I was also running the business. As I retreated into my own depression after the accident, sales dropped like a rock.

A close business associate has said I was like Ripp VanWinkle—I was asleep. And I took years to wake up. By the time I woke up, we nearly lost the business to bankruptcy.

If you own or manage a business, you must realize that your company will be affected by your personal loss and that you will never be the same. For a time—measured in years not months—you will not be able to effectively run your business. It took more than four years for me to be able to feel good again. In today's competitive marketplace, you're lucky if you have four months let alone four years. You must ask for help from your staff. If you don't have the people who can run the company from within, look to outside professionals. There is a tremendous pool of talented people who will be willing to help. Don't overlook those who are retired or semi-retired.

We worked hard to rebuild the business and in 1999, we sold our company. Today, our new company is called TenFold. I work as a marketing consultant with many of the companies that supported us over the years. I also devote a lot of my time to the Brian LaViolette Scholarship Foundation.

The Foundation began the week Brian was missing. We wanted to find a way to honor his memory and help others. Jack Riopelle mentioned setting up a scholarship fund and it seemed like a great idea.

Renee

The Foundation

I just wanted to donate the lights for the high school sign. Oh, and I also wanted a bench at the cemetery. No lights and no bench yet, but we are working on it.

For me, the idea of starting a Foundation was kind of overwhelming. We were also worried about Kim. Doug and I didn't want the Foundation to take our attention away from Kim. We didn't want her to think we were focusing on the child who died versus the child who was still living.

We knew our family was no longer the same. The Foundation helped us create a new routine that would allow Brian's memory to not only live on, but also help and inspire others.

Kim

It helped with the grieving

I think starting the Foundation was a good thing. It especially seemed to help with the grieving process for my parents. It also helped because we were able to talk about the tragedy and about Brian. For the most part, talking helps a lot.

Starting the Foundation was our way of keeping Brian's memory and his positive qualities alive to inspire others. It is a very good feeling knowing that you are turning a tragedy into something that is helping others.

I'm glad we started the Foundation. Today, it's going strong and still helps with the grieving process.

Doug

Letting go of Kim

It became unbearable to live in our home. We sold it and moved into a duplex. We were all excited about planning and building our new home and building new memories together.

Not surprisingly, we built a new home right across the street from where Kim went to high school. We became very protective of her. From the house we could see her as she walked home from school. It can be difficult seeing your youngest child grow up, but it's even worse when she is your only living child. Renee and I worried about everything. But as time went by, we were able to let go. In fact, as the last chapters of this book were written, Kim studied abroad in Soenderborg, Denmark, just north of the German border. We are so proud of her.

Renee

The death of dreams

When you lose someone you love, your world stops. And yet, everyone else's life continues to move forward. You are forced to participate even though you want to succumb to the desire to remain motionless. It is during those times—when you realize that "life goes on"—that you may experience the most painful grief of all.

As a parent, you look forward to watching your children grow. You have hopes and dreams that you await with eager anticipation:

- When they learn to drive a car.
- Their first date.

- Their first love.
- When they graduate from high school, then college.
- The start of a promising career.
- When they get married.
- Their first child, your first grandchild.

The day Brian drowned, those dreams died with him.

I remember the night Austin and Mike came over to our house before their Junior Prom. They looked so handsome in their tuxes. I would have liked to have seen Brian in his Prom tux heading out the door with his friends.

As the months turn into years, we find ourselves being invited to Brian's friends' college graduations and weddings. While we are thankful to have remained close to these ties to our son, we watch with sadness and sometimes even jealousy. I know that's only natural.

We feel blessed to have a daughter that we can dream with. Kim has become an intelligent, responsible adult and has helped us through this tragedy. There is no question that without Kim, we may have never survived the loss of Brian.

We are on this earth for a short time and we need to make the best of it. It has been said that God will only give you what you can handle. There have been many times (too numerous to count) when I was convinced that God made a mistake and gave me more than I could handle.

But now, I live my life with the goal of seeing Brian again. He believed in heaven, and so do I. Until we meet again, I will not complain or question what God has given us. I will treat others with respect and I will give back to this world as much as I am able. If I have that attitude, I have a chance at achieving my most valued goal of all—to be reunited with our son.

I AM ALWAYS WITH YOU
Author Unknown

To those I love and those who love me
When I am gone, release me, let me go.
I have so many things to see and do
You mustn't tie yourself to me with tears.
Be happy that we had so many years.
I gave you my love, you can only guess
How much you gave me in happiness.
I thank you for the love you each have shown
But now it's time I travel on alone.
So grieve awhile for me if grieve you must
Then let your grief be comforted by trust.
It's only for awhile that we must part
So bless the memories within your heart.
I won't be far away, for life goes on
So if you need me, call and I will come.
Though you can't see or touch me, I'll be near
And if you listen with your heart, you'll hear
All of my love, around you soft and clear
And then, when you must come this way alone
I'll greet you with a smile and a "Welcome home."

The only way to make it through each year after you've lost a loved one is to string the days together one at a time. After experiencing a loss, this methodical process can appear unsurmountable.

However, if you have ever competed in a race, hiked a mountain, or overcome an illness, you realize that small steps lead to big gains. The year after a death is similar. Each day brings you closer to the next month, until finally that first year is complete.

Don't look for the clouds to lift or the pain to end. It is just a milestone—one small step that confirms you can and will survive. Yes, there will be set-backs. Don't be afraid. They are a part of the process.

As the first year blurs into the second, the reminders will still be there and the suffering may continue. But take a moment, however brief, to relish your victory. Because with each passing moment, you are building a lifeline. As each year ends, in your mind's eye, tie a knot. The more knots you have to hang on to, the better chance you will have at achieving your ultimate goal—to heal.

The Foundation:

Helping others

"Genius is the gold in the mine, talent is the miner who brings it out."

The human spirit is resilient. Even though at times it appears to be so fragile that a single breath could cause it to shatter into a million pieces. The human spirit can rebound even during the most challenging of times. Through unfathomable loss can come inspiration. Triumph can somehow rear up like a knight in shining armor even when the spirit has been beaten down by tragedy.

One family's loss has been converted into an opportunity for others to pursue their dreams and aspirations. A horrible accident claimed a promising future. However, children now benefit from this loss, and others are inspired by the story. This is the human spirit at work.

The Brian LaViolette Scholarship Foundation was formed to help children obtain the education they desire. Just days after his tragic death, the family made a commitment to Brian's memory. They hoped this commitment would help children accomplish one of life's key goals—a college education. This was a goal Brian had. Now, they would help others achieve it.

With the support of the many contributors, the Foundation can assist and influence young lives, while keeping Brian's incredible spirit alive. In addition to touching the lives of college-bound high school seniors, the family hopes the Foundation will make an impact on parents as well. After hearing Brian's story, it is the hope that parents will be inspired to spend more quality time with their children. The dream is to help people appreciate and savor their lives a little more than before.

Those who knew Brian say that if he had lived, he would have accomplished great things. Thanks to the Foundation, others can now accomplish great things.

The five simple words that hung above Brian's bed have become the Foundation motto: The Journey is The Reward. For the family, this simple phrase became more than merely words of inspiration; it became an extension of their son. This simple phrase would become the cornerstone of the new life the LaViolettes would create.

The LaViolettes' old life was gone. Their "normal" was no longer normal. They would need to reinvent themselves, their family, and their daily routines. They would need to create a new life that would allow them to traverse their way through the depths of despair that come with losing a loved one. They would attempt to carve a tolerable existence out of what seemed to be an intolerable landscape.

The unconscious decision was made to redefine their family and their future. They would become a new family with a mother, father, daughter, and a son's spirit. Intuitively, they must have known that reshaping their lives would not mean they had to give up their son. Deep down, they believed his soul could live inside them, remaining an integral part of their new family unit.

BRIAN LAVIOLETTE
SCHOLARSHIP FOUNDATION

THE JOURNEY IS THE REWARD™

The Foundation logo symbolizes adults helping and guiding youth. The three figures holding hands also represent Doug, Renee, and Kim. The waves below symbolize the Bay of Green Bay where Brian drowned.

Their lives would be dramatically different. They were unsure if it was even possible to rebuild. In order to accomplish this daunting task, they needed to somehow fill their lives with Brian's positive spirit. They needed to make his journey their own. They needed the Foundation.

In hindsight, the Brian LaViolette Scholarship Foundation served many more purposes than originally planned. It also created many challenges not anticipated. But the LaViolette family has no regrets. There is just the future. A future they know will continually change based on the Divine plan. This future includes a loving marriage, a daughter's dreams, a son's inspiration, and a Foundation that will help and inspire others.

NOTE: The following was excerpted from a feature in the *Phillippine Daily Inquirer* taken from the Compassionate Friends web site, www.compassionatefriends.org. For more information on this organization, call 1-877-969-0010.

Moving on after losing a child

by Cathy Babao Guballa

There are many ways to keep our children in our hearts and in the hearts of other people as well. There are rituals we can perform or little things we can do to keep the relationship with the one who has gone ahead of us.

Migi (her son) had always been fascinated with dinosaurs, and in that first year after his death, I found myself buying every little dinosaur book that I could find in the bookstore. Perhaps it was my way of coping and remembering him.

This experience reminds me of a sad story I heard about a lady whose only daughter died at birth. For many years until she had a child again, she would buy a doll on her daughter's birthday and bring it to her grave. Her family and neighbors could not understand the gesture, and thought she was going out of her mind.

It was only many years later, when she told the story to her counselor, and the counselor said, "What a lovely gesture" that she broke down and cried. All those years she had been hurting from the comments of neighbors and friends, and it was only when this one person appreciated and understood what she had been doing, was she able to work through her grief.

I have found that it is in reaching out to others, in stepping out of the shadow of one's sadness that one is also able to heal. Investing oneself in activities that give meaning to the loss helps alleviate the pain and aids in building a new life that will keep the memory alive and well in our hearts and, I am certain, make our children proud.

Kim

Brian would be proud

I have always been proud of my mom and dad for starting the Foundation. I think Brian is, too. Now that I am going to college, I am not as involved with the Foundation. When it first started and I was living at home, I was able to help a lot more.

When I was still in high school, I had the opportunity to talk to some of the recipients. They all said receiving the scholarship was more about the honor than the money. It made me feel good to know that my brother was liked and respected by so many people.

I think Brian would be very thankful that we started the Foundation. He would love the fact that so many people are benefitting from something he is connected with—something that he inspired.

Even though the Foundation continues to help a lot of people, it still is helping our family in the grieving process. I am thankful for that and I am very proud to be a part of the Brian LaViolette Scholarship Foundation.

Doug

Not without a struggle

Believe it or not, the creation of the Brian LaViolette Scholarship Foundation was somewhat controversial. Living in a small community, we did consider the impact the Foundation would have on the three boys who were with Brian that day. Would reliving the memories be too difficult? We still decided to go ahead with the Foundation. Of course, we hoped people would understand that this was something we felt we had to do.

So far, Renee and I have invested thousands of hours and some of our own personal finances in establishing this Foundation. We know that if we work hard, we will be able to give out more scholarships and honor Brian's memory. That's our payment—it makes all of the hard work worthwhile.

Fortunately, nearly everyone has been supportive. The Foundation receives a lot of media attention. We also had billboards put up and have held a variety of fund-raising events. We are happy that most of these events received good coverage in the local newspapers and on television.

Over the years, some people question why we would want to relive the accident every time there is a story about Brian, hold a fund-raising event, or drive past a billboard.

Yes, it has been painful for us to relive the accident. But talking about it and talking about Brian was the only way we felt we would be able to turn this tragedy into something good. The only way we knew how to do that was through the establishment of a Foundation that would help other kids—kids like Brian.

We weren't trying to relive the accident, we were trying to keep Brian's memory alive so he could inspire others. We knew we wouldn't be able to see our son go to college, but maybe we could help other kids get there. That's really what the Foundation is all about—helping kids achieve their academic goals.

Brian was a great student and a hard worker. We wanted to find a way to honor those characteristics. The Foundation is helping us accomplish that goal.

I am a typical father and like most fathers, I was looking forward to living vicariously through my son. I wanted to savor his successes and help him through his challenges. My ability to do that remains in the waters of the Bay.

I guess the Foundation is something that I can do "with" Brian—something he would be proud of, something we can share together.

Renee

It has been difficult at times

I love my husband. One of the characteristics I've always loved most is his determination. I typically don't think on as grand a scale as Doug. He is the dreamer in the family—the planner, the goal-setter, and really, our leader. Doug gets excited about new ideas pretty easily. I've learned over the years to just let him go. Things happen almost always as he plans. Even though I was concerned about the amount of work involved in starting the Foundation, I was sure it would turn out as Doug's projects usually do—a big success.

When you start a non-profit organization, there is a lot of paperwork and some up-front costs. We knew we needed the advice of an attorney and an accountant. Who was going to do all the work involved? How were we going to raise money for the Foundation? The practical side of me began asking all sorts of questions. We methodically addressed all of these questions one at a time.

We thought of turning the inspirational sayings in Brian's bedroom into full-color posters that we would sell for a profit. All the profits would go to the Foundation. Even though it is very labor-intensive, we still have this program today.

There are eight framed or unframed prints available. People really like them. They have been distributed in 29 states and Canada and Mexico. A family in Oklahoma City ordered a complete set of the prints after the bombing. Many of Doug's business clients have ordered them for their offices to inspire employees or to give away as gifts. One of the posters is a photo of Brian's high school soccer team the year they became state champs, with the saying "The Journey is The Reward."

Sure, we occasionally questioned whether starting the Foundation was a good idea. But when we think of all of the people our son's story has touched, we realize it is the right thing to do. We have been complimented for turning our tragedy into something positive. We are actually just average parents who wanted to keep our son's memory alive while giving back to society. There is really a dual advantage because while we're helping others, we're helping ourselves heal from the pain.

People have asked if it is difficult to be surrounded by his picture and his story everyday. The fact is, whether we have the Foundation or not, we are surrounded by him everyday. The reminders of him in our minds are far more powerful than those reminders on the Foundation literature. He is alive in our hearts and souls forever.

The Foundation has blessed us in so many ways. Because of the Foundation, even though a great part of us is lost, new friends were found, and old friends mean even more.

The Foundation has been successful because of those old and new friends. We give credit to Brian's spirit and the many people who supported us very early on. The Foundation really began the day of the funeral. We set up a memorial fund for the Brian LaViolette Scholarship Foundation. All of the donations meant so much to us and have helped deserving high school seniors.

To us, the Foundation is more than simply a way to memorialize our son. It is a way for us to introduce Brian and his values to others who weren't lucky enough to have met him. Most importantly, it is a way for us to help other kids.

Of course, the Foundation will not bring Brian back. Our hope is that when we see him again some day, he will say "Great job!" Until then, we will continue to do the best we can.

Doug

A very rewarding experience

I feel so thankful to have a wife and life partner who is trusting and caring. Without Renee's support, the idea of the Foundation would have been lost. Kim was equally supportive. She could have been a spoiled little sister wanting attention, but she wasn't. She was involved with the Foundation right from the start and has encouraged Renee and me every step of the way.

I'm not going to say it was easy. In fact, there was a lot of learning that took place those first few years. We did some things amazingly right, even though we had no experience with this sort of thing. And we did some things horribly wrong, because we had no experience with this sort of thing.

I was able to use my experience as a business owner and

also my years as a volunteer with the local chapter of the Boys & Girls Club. Being involved with the Boys & Girls Club was a very rewarding experience for me. In fact, the year before the accident, I was named board member of the year. As a part of that honor, a family picture is put in the newsletter. For whatever reason, that never happened for our family. The following year, Brian was gone. I really regret not having that newsletter with a recent family picture in it.

One of my favorite memories of the Boys & Girls Club is the year I was in charge of ticket sales for the NFL Banquet, the largest fundraiser of the year. That year, Brian and I decided to take two kids from the Club golfing. Even though we had never met the two young guys that we were going to golf with, we had a great time. For the record, I can't remember who won. I think it's because that day wasn't about competition, it was about sharing the day. I'm glad we did that—not only for the kids but for Brian and me as well.

Even though starting the Foundation was difficult at first, the bottom line is that we did it. And it is still going strong today. We are proud of the fact that we do not take a salary from the Foundation. We donate our time and efforts fully. That means that other than direct costs such as postage for mailings or printing, all proceeds donated to the Brian LaViolette Scholarship Foundation go directly toward helping the kids. That's important to us. We also get a great deal of "in kind" support from printers, designers, and others who are willing to donate their time or expertise to the Foundation at no charge. For example, the cover of this book was designed free of charge by the talented people at Archetype Group. We are also proud that all the profits from this book are going directly to the Foundation.

On January 23, 2000, Brian would have celebrated his golden birthday; he would have turned 23 on the 23rd.

Although we still miss him every day, the Foundation allows us to continue to celebrate these special occasions with our extended family. That same year, the Foundation awarded a record 26 total scholarships in Brian's memory.

If you have not yet volunteered for a non-profit organization, I highly recommend it. While it won't feed your pocketbook, it will nourish your soul in unexpected ways. We have found our work with the Foundation most rewarding. Not just because it's a way for us to honor our son's memory, but it is a very personal way we can give back to the world in which we live.

NOTE: For more information about the Brian LaViolette Scholarship Foundation, refer to Appendix A in the back of the book.

Darrel Burnett

A noble cause

When Doug first shared with me their idea for starting a scholarship foundation, it was the day after Brian's funeral. I remember thinking to myself that I shouldn't question the timing or suggest a healing period. If Doug wanted to start a scholarship foundation in Brian's name, I knew we would pour our hearts and souls into it to make sure it was a great tribute to Brian.

As the years have passed and the list of scholarship recipients grows, I revisit emotions I have for Brian. As I look at Renee and Doug, I know that they see Brian in each recipient's face. I know it is difficult for them wondering what Brian would look like or what he would be doing with his life. I have immense respect and admiration for their ability to be gracious in the face of having lost such a wonderful human being.

As the years come and go, I am certain there are times, as there would be with any parent, when both Doug and Renee wonder if all of the hard work is worth it. Then there always seems to be a reason to continue. Perhaps it is someone else's tragedy on the front page of the local paper, or a letter they received, or another student in need. Whatever the reason, Brian's Foundation just continues to gain strength and reach out to more and more deserving young people.

I can't think of a more noble cause or a more fitting tribute to their son. I think Brian would be proud of Doug, Renee, and Kim.

Aunt Sue

The Foundation's enthusiastic "ambassador"

Being a part of Brian's Foundation has been very rewarding for me. When we first started carrying "The Journey is The Reward" banner to the Green Bay Packers football games and handing out literature, it was difficult to tell the story. My friend, Jeannie Martin, who has been an "ambassador" along with me, would have to finish the story.

I am now able to convey Brian's story without getting choked up. I am so proud to help continue Brian's wonderful legacy, knowing that the scholarships are going to deserving young people. It really makes it worth all of the effort.

In one of his many inspiring speeches, the immortal Dr. Martin Luther King, Jr., said: "Not everyone can be famous, but everyone can be great because greatness is determined by service."

Service and giving back to the community can be an accurate measurement of a life well lived. Peace and fulfillment can often be found through service.

The LaViolettes discovered a different kind of peace through their service. Their peace is not euphoric contentment. Rather, theirs is the peace that comes from acceptance.

They are well aware that the happiness they once dreamed of as a physical family of four is gone. As their course has been changed, they have adapted accordingly. Today, the Brian LaViolette Scholarship Foundation takes a firm place in their new family unit. The Foundation has developed a life of its own. In addition to helping others, it stimulates future dreams and aspirations for the family. The same passion the LaViolettes used to raise their young son is now channeled into their new family unit and their service to others. It's what Brian would want—it's what they want.

The Healing:

Overcoming loss

"Nothing is often a good thing to say."

A person can often learn profoundly important lessons of life while experiencing the death of a loved one. When death enters your life, it generates a whirlwind of emotions. Some of those emotions may have been under lock and key, while others are entirely new.

Feelings of fear, anxiety, deep sorrow, despair, loneliness, and anger can spin uncontrollably in your head and heart. But with those feelings can also come positive emotions, such as appreciation of life, enhanced communication, and spiritual awakening. Death is an inevitable part of life and our best coping option is to be open to all the emotions that come with it. Suppressing the feelings that accompany death may eventually breed bitterness, resentment, and self-pity. Like a cancer, these outcomes can eat away at your soul and hasten your own demise—emotionally and physically.

Dealing with all the emotions of death is the best way to travel down that winding, healing path. Taking that path requires hard work. There will be setbacks. However, there will also be progress. As with any journey, you make progress as you move forward.

It has often been said that time heals. However, as the famous columnist, Andy Rooney, said: "Love, not time, heals all wounds."

Without love, time just passes. With love, time brings growth, change, and healing.

When an individual loses his or her sight or cannot hear, the other senses compensate for this loss. Something similar happens when we heal from the loss of a loved one. The parts of ourselves that have not died can grow stronger to help make up for our loss. This doesn't mean we forget the loss. After all, the blind person is always aware he or she cannot see, but that person can still move forward to live a fulfilling life.

Nature is filled with examples of remarkable adaptations to loss. If you cut the top off of an evergreen tree, it will create a new point the following year. If you barricade a stream, it will work diligently to find a new path to continue its forward movement. Depending on how big the barricade, the stream is definitely challenged. Challenges also occur during the healing process. These are the times when it feels as if you are slipping backward. Don't panic. Setbacks are inevitable.

Tapping into our natural desire to survive and thrive will enhance our healing ability. Understanding that this power comes from a higher source can also expedite the process. Spirituality—no matter what the religion or method of practice—is believed to be a critical healing link. Depending upon or connecting with a spiritual power strongly affects how an individual reacts to death and heals from loss.

The healing process is acutely individual. Even if two sets of parents lose a child the same age and in an identical manner, chances are, they will grieve differently. There are no easy answers and no special blueprints to follow. However, there are general concepts we can use to help rebuild our lives after loss. We can also learn great lessons from others who have experienced loss.

Decades ago, Swiss-born psychiatrist, Dr. Elisabeth Kübler-Ross, developed an easy-to-understand description of the five stages individuals go through when dealing with death—denial, anger, bargaining, depression, and acceptance.

Dr. Kübler-Ross' work has been helpful for those suffering from terminal illness, however, there are many other theories and professional opinions. "It isn't like a disease, with stages," explains Kenneth J. Doka, Ph.D., professor of gerontology at the College of New Rochelle in New York. "It's more like a roller coaster. You have ups, you have downs. And sometimes it takes you by surprise."

Grief is a very complicated, individual life process. While Dr. Kübler-Ross' five stages involve feelings that can and often do occur during grieving, these feelings are much more complex than they appear. As you move through your own stages of grief, each emotion will have a unique expression. It is important to experience each of these emotions fully, without "stuffing" or discounting them. People who do not allow themselves to grieve fully, often report that a more intense grief resurfaces years later. Sometimes it is difficult to grieve immediately following a death because there is so much to do. If you are the person in control of making arrangements, or if you are faced with your own personal challenges during that time, you may not be able to grieve at that moment. Make the conscious decision to take time to process your emotions after things settle down.

Acceptance will not come with a quick sigh of relief, bright light, or ringing bell. Rather, acceptance happens over time. It is often said that we should "adopt the pace of nature; her secret is patience." This certainly applies to grieving. Be patient with yourself and those around you.

Letting go of the pain associated with loss does not mean you are letting go of your loved one. When you settle into the acceptance stage, you are able to incorporate your loved one's soul into your everyday life without the strong feelings that surfaced during the previous stages. During the acceptance phase, you quietly and peacefully embrace your loved one's positive characteristics. You make them your own so they can continue to positively influence other people through you.

Grieving is an emotional and physical process. It only makes sense to consider the connection between the mind and the body. Science has made the link between our emotions, our health, and our quality of life. Researchers have also discovered ways to enhance life by controlling or enhancing specific positive emotions. Understanding this mind/body connection can assist with the grieving process.

It is believed that you can dictate specific emotional outcomes by the messages you send yourself. For example, if you tell yourself continually that you are depressed "all the time," chances are, you will become depressed more often. In reality, you are not depressed all of the time. By focusing on the moments, or even seconds, that you are not depressed, you can give yourself a different message.

A word of caution: pretending that you feel great when you are actually consumed by grief and feeling lousy can be destructive. There is a fine balance between focusing on the positive, while allowing yourself to honestly deal with your emotions.

Focusing on the thoughts you give yourself may help put you back in the driver's seat. Key components of grieving are the feelings of helplessness that come with loss. Gaining control of your emotions, even for short periods of time, may help speed up the process.

Feelings such as grief, depression, fear, and panic can negatively affect your health, while laughter, love, faith, and self-acceptance can positively affect you. To help tip the scales to the positive side, surround yourself with loving, accepting people. Try to avoid negative or draining individuals. Loving support is one of the most powerful medicines you can "take" for grief.

Laughter can also help you on your way down that healing path. While the death of a loved one is no laughing matter, remembering the fun and funny times may help ease the pain. Don't be afraid to giggle about the silly things your loved one did or have a belly laugh on his/her behalf. You may even want to rent funny movies, watch cartoons, or buy a joke book.

"It's no joke that laughter is healing," explained health expert, Andrew Weil, M.D. "Preliminary research suggests it may boost immunity, relieve pain, lower stress levels, and even protect against heart disease."

According to *Dr. Andrew Weil's Self Healing*, UCLA is presently involved in a major study evaluating the effects of laughter on immune function, pain management, and quality of life in kids with cancer, AIDS, diabetes, and other major illnesses. "Regardless of the science," said Dr. Weil, "it's clear that a good guffaw brings people closer together, offers physical and emotional release, and helps us cope with unpleasant situations."

Other mind/body techniques include:

- Meditation—the ability to quiet your mind and clear your thoughts can generate tranquility even during times of chaos.
- Self-talk—giving yourself positive messages (either out loud or to yourself) can reinforce healthy healing.
- Visualization/guided imagery—lying quietly and visualizing positive images may also help guide your recovery from grief.

- Prayer—no matter what your religious inclination is, strengthening your spiritual foundation through prayer may also help.

Perhaps the most dramatic way to make the connection between the mind and the body is through physical activity. Exercise is a powerful tool we can use to enhance our mental health. It's been called the most powerful antidepressant of all. Physical activity increases the release of endorphins in the brain. These are natural "feel-good" substances that actually lift your mood. According to health writer, Frances E. FitzGerald, "Depression may result, in part, from a person's loss of control. Exercise can become a form of mastery, a way to regain control…People who exercise regularly are generally happier, feel more alive, and enjoy higher self-esteem than their sedentary counterparts."

How do you know if your depression is out of control? The American Psychiatric Association's *Diagnostic and Statistical Manual of Mental Disorders* indicates that you are clinically depressed and in need of psychological treatment if you exhibit at least four of the following symptoms nearly every day for at least two weeks:

- Poor appetite and significant weight loss, or increased appetite and significant weight gain;
- Insomnia, or increased sleep;
- Agitation, or sluggishness in movement and thought;
- Loss of interest or pleasure in usual activities, or decrease in sexual drive;
- Fatigue and loss of energy;
- Feelings of worthlessness, self-reproach, or excessive or inappropriate guilt;
- Diminished ability to think or concentrate, or indecisiveness;
- Recurrent thoughts of death or suicide, or suicide attempts.

If you feel you are clinically depressed, you need to seek help from a qualified professional. Do not self-diagnose or self-treat your depression. Mind/body techniques may not carry you through this dark period. Medication may be helpful. Be open to the various treatment options available to you.

Chances are, the mind/body techniques outlined in this chapter will have little effect on the early stages of the grieving process. Keeping these ideas in mind as you move forward may help you come to terms with your loss. The goal with mind/body methods is to help you to become proactive rather than reactive or submissive to the despair.

Know that you will one day enjoy living again. It has been said that if you desire true happiness you need to "work like you don't need the money; dance like nobody is watching; and love like you've never been hurt." This is sound advice.

True healing requires emotional balance. As you attempt to come to terms with your grief, remember that the mind and body are one. Take care of both—physically and mentally.

It was William Shakespeare who wrote: "Our remedies oft in ourselves do lie." As you search for ways to overcome your despair, look in the mirror. Your solution may be right in front of you.

Judy Hodel

A professional perspective

I have been a family counselor for more than 32 years. I have worked with families who have lost loved ones and I personally have experienced the grief that comes from losing a loved one.

I have heard the LaViolettes' story and seen what their Foundation has done in the community. I often use them as an example of how a family can proactively move forward. Rather than becoming stuck in their grieving by simply hanging on, the LaViolettes have chosen an action-oriented course. This is healthy because it involves growth. It appears they have come to a resolution in the truest sense.

Remember resolution does not mean the thoughts and feelings about the person who has died disappear. Resolution is actually just the opposite. It allows you to keep the person's soul alive. It is an acceptance of that person in a different form and a subconscious awareness of the ongoing presence of that person in your life, even after he or she is gone.

Grieving is certainly not a black-and-white issue. It is a complex time that can trigger many unfamiliar feelings. I try to describe and acknowledge the five stages of grief to my clients. I then focus on the following:

- Pay attention. This is a vulnerable time for all those involved. Be sensitive to the other family members and especially to your partner. Unresolved issues within the family may surface and become exaggerated.
- Get support. Identify what's best for you during this time. Allow people to be supportive. It is important to grieve with others. Develop a support system that includes friends, family, priest/pastor, counselor, etc. Surround yourself with loving people.

- Children grieve differently. There is a different dynamic when children are involved. Children may not talk to parents. Sometimes, children feel as though they need to take care of the parents.
- Find a spiritual source of strength. I find that people who believe in a higher power are more likely to come to a positive, healthy resolution.
- Be open and honest with yourself and others. Ask yourself what is getting in the way of your progress toward acceptance/resolution. Be aware that feelings about your own immortality may surface. Be open to the various issues that come up and deal with them.

According to The Compassionate Friends, Inc., government statistics estimate that each year 228,000 children and young adults in the United States die. These statistics do not include miscarriages, stillbirths, or the deaths of older adults who are survived by a parent.

Losing a child can complicate the grieving process immensely. There is the issue of guilt, because as parents we believe that no matter what, we are supposed to protect our children from harm and death. There is the issue of nurturing any other living children. And there are the issues unique to the other partner and the dynamics within that relationship. Unlike the LaViolettes, many relationships cannot withstand the pressure that comes with grief. They separate because of the unresolved anger or to escape the pain.

Losing a child is the most painful event parents can experience. Healing from that loss can be overwhelming. It is during this time when the simple saying "one day at a time" holds much meaning. There is no denying that the grief associated with the death of a child is all encompassing. Only when you recognize the pain that comes with the loss, will you begin to heal from it.

There are many organizations that can help during times of loss. Most experts offer the following advice:

- Don't grieve alone. Isolation will only add to the depression that can come with grief.
- Talk about it. Do not try to protect other family members. Share your feelings—if not with family, then with a friend. Talk often. If someone tells you to "snap out of it," find another person to confide in.
- Keep busy. While you should avoid frantic activity, staying busy with purposeful work will help occupy your mind.
- Eat well. Your body needs proper nourishment more than ever. If you have a poor appetite, you may want to supplement the diet with vitamins.
- Exercise regularly. The biochemical changes that come from consistent exercise can help relieve symptoms of depression. Exercise may also help you sleep better.
- Postpone major decisions. This is an emotional time. Wait before selling your house, for example, or changing jobs.
- Turn your grief into creative energy. Find a creative outlet or a way to help others. Keep a journal about your feelings or write about the loved one you lost.
- Become spiritually connected. If you have religious affiliations, you may want to enhance that activity during your grieving time. Daily meditation or prayer may also be helpful.

What about those of you who find yourselves in a supportive role? What can you do? A lot! Your actions can either help or hinder the healing process.

Some people react to a death by distancing themselves from the person who has experienced the loss. While death may make you feel extremely uncomfortable or awkward, you must fight those feelings in order to be a supportive friend or family member. Your efforts will be greatly appreciated. It has been said that to express sympathy you say "I'm sorry." To express compassion, you say "I'll help." Only when we learn the difference between the two can we really make a difference.

Don't be afraid to bring up the loss and talk about it. And when they do, just listen. Don't try and talk the person out of his/her feelings or try to "fix" the pain. Volunteer to help in practical ways, like running errands or helping around the house. Here are some general guidelines to consider if you find yourself in a supportive role to a loved one who has experienced loss:

- Don't talk just to break the silence. As one of the quotes in Brian's room so appropriately stated: "Nothing is often a good thing to say." Don't force conversation if the person doesn't want to talk. Compassionate listening, a brief embrace, or a quick note to let the person know you care may be all that is necessary.

- Be yourself. Show your concern in your own way, with your own words. Avoid using cliches like "He's in a better place," "She's no longer in pain," or "Everything happens for a reason." Avoid pity.

- Be available. Keep in touch. Even if some time has passed, it's never too late to express your concern or willingness to help.
- Attend to practical matters. Volunteer to prepare meals, clean the house, care for children. This type of help may be needed beyond the initial grieving period.
- Do not judge. Do not try to tell the person how he or she should feel. Phrases like "You must feel relieved" or "I know how you feel" are presumptuous. Let the individual lead the conversation. Don't criticize grieving methods. Everyone grieves differently.
- Avoid small talk. Even if you are trying to distract the person, do not chatter aimlessly about the weather, sports, or other trivial things.

Remember, grieving is not just an emotional experience. The person who is grieving may experience physical, social, intellectual, and spiritual reactions.

Grieving not only affects how a person feels, it can also affect behavior. Physically, the individual may have trouble sleeping, become weak, or experience a rapid heart beat. The person may also become detached and withdrawn or have difficulty concentrating. These physical manifestations and behavior changes are due to the grief. Make sure the individual is receiving proper professional care during this time of grieving. An experienced grief counselor can provide assistance. Some people may also choose to involve a priest, rabbi, or other religious leader. Grieving should be a group effort. No one should grieve alone.

Being supportive means being honest, open, and considerate of the person's feelings. Oftentimes, people who are dealing with loss say it helps to talk about the person who has died. Honor that wish, because remembering a loved one can provide comfort during the grieving process.

THE ELEPHANT IN THE ROOM
by Terry Kettering

There is an elephant in the room.
It is large and squatting, so it is hard to get around it.
Yet we squeeze by with, "How are you?" and "I'm fine"...
And a thousand other forms of trivial chatter.
We talk about the weather.
We talk about work.
We talk about everything else—
except the elephant in the room.
There's an elephant in the room.
We all know it is there.
We are thinking about the elephant as we talk.
It is constantly on our minds,
For you see, it is a very big elephant.
But we do not talk about the elephant in the room.
Oh, please, say her name.
Oh, please, say "Barbara" again.
Oh, please, let's talk about the elephant in the room.
For if we talk about her death,
Perhaps we can talk about her life.
Can I say "Barbara" and not have you look away?
For if I cannot, you are leaving me
Alone...In a room...With an elephant.

The following poem was written by Kim after she turned 15—the same age Brian was when he died.

UNTIL WE MEET AGAIN...
by Kim LaViolette

As I looked at the water
with a tear in my eye
I realized my brother was gone
and I didn't get to say good bye.
I wanted to tell him I love him
and ask God why he had to die;
I wanted to tell him I miss him
and give him a hug while I cry.
I know he watches over me
and he's another angel in the sky.
I know one day we will meet again
and we will stand eye-to-eye.
But to wait for that day
I will have to be strong
and remember the memories we had
will never be gone.

Grandparents Grief

Ollie and Helen Bogsted share their thoughts

We are Renee's parents and Kim and Brian's grandparents. Renee is the youngest of our four children. We have four grandchildren. We are proud that our family is so close. We have always supported and loved each other during the good times and bad.

Nothing can prepare grandparents for the pain that comes from losing a cherished grandchild. But the love and support that makes up our family's foundation, certainly helped us get through the tragedy of losing Brian. As grandparents do, we love our grandchildren and Brian was no exception. Brian was a very special young man. We cherish the memories we have of him and the cards and letters he had written to us during his short lifetime.

It's easy being loving and supportive during the good times, but the true test of a family's love comes when tragedy strikes. You will find out just how strong the extended family is during these times. We were so fortunate to discover that our family became an even stronger unit during this horrible nightmare. We were there for Doug, Renee, and Kim and we were there for each other.

We experienced great loss and grief during that painful time. And we each handled the grieving differently. But the thing that kept us moving through the grief was that we helped each other. It helped to talk about Brian and our deep love for him. But sometimes, we didn't talk at all—we were just together, showing our support and love.

Our advice to grandparents and other members of the extended family of those who have experienced the loss of a child is to be available. Also to be honest and open. Don't be afraid to talk about how you feel with other family members.

Don't be afraid to express your sorrow. Show your love and support and allow your tragedy to make your family even stronger. That's what your loved one would want. We are sure that's what Brian would want.

Peter Mancuso

Advice from the LaViolettes' supportive friend

On my 22nd birthday, my father died of cancer. I was the oldest child and I was expected to take care of the details. Just the week before, my wife gave birth to our first child. I learned early on what it meant to be responsible.

When Doug and Renee needed support, those same instincts kicked in. While every situation is different, my wife and I give this advice to people who find themselves in a supportive role:

- Understand the personalities and needs of the people you are trying to help.
- Develop a plan and follow your instincts. You may have to be the one to initiate and anticipate.
- Help them feel hope. You need to believe in their ability to recover.
- Be a resource and tool they can use in whatever capacity that's necessary.
- Remember, everyone heals at their own pace.

When my father died, I really didn't have time to grieve. I was the one in charge. I was happy to be able to be the one in charge for a time for Doug and Renee. Hopefully, it gave them some very valuable time early on in their grieving process to concentrate on the goal—to heal from this terrible tragedy.

Renee

No rules for grieving

I must admit, since the accident, I interact with others who are experiencing grief differently than I did before the accident.

A number of years after the accident, Doug and I were at a social event and a couple whom we had just met asked if we had any children. I said "Yes, two. Brian died nine years ago when he was 15 and Kim is in college." What amazed me is that they did not acknowledge what I had just said—that we had lost a child. Nothing. They just kept going, telling us how many children they had. I expected them to say "Oh, that's too bad. How did he die?"

I think people are still so fearful of the topic of death, they just don't know how to react, especially when it is a child. Sometimes people don't send a card because too much time has passed since the death. Don't let that bother you. Grieving parents grieve for a lifetime—a card is nice anytime.

After you lose a child, all you can think of is that you just want your life back the way it was—you just want your child back. It's difficult. You've got to really look for a reason to get out of bed every morning. You need to push yourself. You need to push each other.

Unexpected things may bother you. For example, it was difficult for us to sit at a table with four chairs. Sitting with that empty chair was so difficult. In fact, when we built our new home, we decided not to use a "conventional table." Our dinner table has no corners—it's called an amoeba. Sometimes you have to be creative to overcome certain issues.

Early on in the grieving process we were told that some marriages do not survive the death of a child. The relationship ends in divorce. Doug and I have often been asked how we have been able to make it through the tragedy of losing our son while keeping our relationship intact and stronger than ever. We have been blessed to have each other. Doug and I make a good team.

Marriage can be challenging and so can having children. I think that's why they say, "In good times and in bad." Doug and I have been there for each other during those good times and bad.

Kim has also helped both Doug and me get through those difficult times. She quickly became wise beyond her years. We had to remind ourselves that while Doug and I lost a son, Kim lost a big brother. Even today, we lean on each other for support.

The grief of losing a child travels so deep. But time does help. Today, ten years later, I can go a couple of hours or more without thinking of Brian. Not too long ago, it seemed like I thought of him nearly every minute. You become so totally consumed with the loss.

Our grieving process is made more bearable because Brian was such a spiritual young boy. That helps.

Doug

Two important pieces of advice

Actually, I'm not sure how we got through it. It seemed like every day was an effort.

I've always admired Bart Starr, the great NFL quarterback. When Bart and Cherry lost their son, Brett, I saw a family that reacted to that tragedy with such grace and dignity.

Bart and Cherry lived in our neighborhood. I remember the day they moved. I asked Brian if he wanted to go over to the Starrs' house and say goodbye to Bart. When Bart came to the door, the phones were ringing, there was a moving van outside, and there were boxes everywhere. Yet, Bart took the time to really talk to us. It meant so much to Brian. Me, too.

Eighteen months after losing Brian, I was beside myself with the pain of his death. I decided to call Bart and ask him how long it would take for me to feel good again. I wanted something to hang onto, some type of goal to shoot toward. Bart paused for what seemed like a lifetime and then finally said, "I'm almost afraid to tell you." He said it took him four years. I was devastated. How could I last another 2 1/2 years?! Of course, he said that everyone was different. Surprisingly, as every August 8 anniversary came and went, I felt a little better until four years later, 8/8/96. It seemed like a huge cloud lifted and I knew I should reach out to others the way Bart helped me. He helped lead me out of my darkness through his example.

The day we began this book project was a big step toward our healing. We had to dig deep inside and relive all of the horrible memories and feelings that had been buried for so long. But it also meant we could relive all of the good times. For so long, we could never even look at the thousands of photographs we had taken prior to the accident.

There is obviously no right way or wrong way to grieve. There are no magic formulas that ensure you will heal from your loss. The most important advice I can give people is to:

1. Surround yourself with supportive people;
2. When you feel you can, help others get through a difficult time.
3. Don't be afraid to cry.

A grief counselor told us that crying can be helpful and can positively impact your health. She said medical studies have even confirmed this to be true. These studies have demonstrated that tears of joy are made up of saline, a harmless substance. Tears of sadness and grief, however, contain a poisonous substance so toxic that, when injected into a mouse, will actually kill it. Amazing, isn't it? Just think, crying could save your life. It will certainly save your soul.

It is definitely worth repeating that we had very supportive people in our corner. If you are going through something difficult, identify and search out those types of people. Surround yourself with friends and family who are positive, and avoid people who bring you down.

During my grieving, I was also inspired by then President George Bush. He and his wife, Barbara, lost their daughter, Robin. President Bush moved on to raise a wonderful family, become President of the United States, raise his son to become President, and accomplish important things for this country. I thought, if President George Bush can move on to become one of our great leaders, I surely could find the courage and the will power necessary to carry on without Brian. I have discovered that there are many inspiring people in this world.

Kim

Growing up fast

Losing my brother made me grow up pretty fast. I actually blocked out many of the details about the accident and that time in our lives. I still think about Brian often. I even talk to him sometimes. I think he's watching out for me.

I notice that I am able to help my friends who are going through a difficult time. I can be there for them. I can help calm them down and be supportive. It's during those times that I really think Brian works through me.

During the first few years of the grieving process, I was pretty distant. I was afraid to talk to my parents about how sad I was because I thought it would make them even more sad. I was lucky, though; I had support from my friends at school.

My advice to young people who have lost a loved one is to take time for yourself and try to help your parents as much as you can. You need to allow yourself to grieve. If you need to talk, find someone you can trust to talk to. If you need to be alone, don't be afraid to communicate that as well. But don't distance yourself from the ones who love you. Stick together. As hard as it is, you need to stick together as a family and help each other as best you can.

Today, I am able to miss Brian and feel sad that I don't have him here to talk with and just hang out with. But I also don't dwell on that sadness. I recognize it and move on. I like the way it feels to be positive. In life, bad things will happen and everyone has to suffer at one point. You need to move on and try to focus on being happy with yourself and your life.

Cousin Kristin

Admiration for Doug and Renee

Throughout my life, I have always told Uncle Doug and Aunt Renee that I wanted to have a marriage just like theirs. Their marriage is so loving and affectionate, and they always seem so happy.

When Brian died, I watched as the two of them grieved in very different ways, yet they still managed to keep their marriage strong and together. I'm sure they have had their challenges, but I admire their ability to survive such a tragedy together. So many times I hear of families that fall apart after the loss of a child.

Doug and Renee have definitely overcome many obstacles. I hope my marriage has as strong of a foundation as theirs does.

For many years after Brian's death, I never talked about him with Renee and Doug. I was too worried about making them sad. However, as time has passed, I have grown more comfortable talking with them. I have been able to draw on their amazing strength. Their willingness to share their tragedy with me has made me feel like a special part of their lives and has helped me come to terms with the overwhelming sadness one can feel after losing someone. I see how much it took for them to deal with Brian's death every day for the past ten years. I have seen them deal with it and survive. It shows me that if I had to survive such a tragedy I could too. It is a true gift they have given me.

Jack Riopelle

A business associate becomes a close friend

I've known Doug for more than 20 years. We began as acquaintances. We would see each other at business functions. Then we became business associates sharing our thoughts and strategies on how to run a better business. It wasn't until Brian died that we became close friends.

When my wife, Ginny, and I first learned about the accident, it was the Sunday after it happened. I had never met Brian, but I was overwhelmed with grief for Doug. I just felt I needed to go see Doug.

I will forever remember that day as I rang the doorbell, not knowing what to expect. Doug answered the door and we hugged and cried. Doug's body just shook in my arms. I had never felt grief like that. It seemed so deep and painful.

Then I hugged Renee and we cried together. After they

filled me in as to what happened, I felt I needed to get Doug out of the house. So, we went for a long walk. It was a beautiful summer day. I can still remember many of the things we talked about. Doug went through the long list of things Brian would never experience. He described his pain and how it shook him to the core. I couldn't help but think about my own two kids.

There were so many people coming and going that day. It made me think of how special Doug and Renee are to have such an incredible support system.

I had the idea that Ginny and I should go visit Doug and Renee each night to spend time with them as they grieved. While we knew we couldn't take away their pain, we knew we could give them a valuable gift—our time.

For months, Ginny and I went to the LaViolettes every night. We always let Doug and Renee tell us when they were tired or if they didn't want visitors. It's funny, these nightly visits became a part of their routine. It was a regular part of their schedule and it became a priority for us.

When we arrived at their house, one of the first things we did was go through the sympathy cards. There were so many cards, many from people they didn't even know. I think sharing the cards with us was very therapeutic for Doug and Renee. As a result of that time we spent with them, we have a deep appreciation of what they went through and how they were thinking and feeling.

I was the one to suggest having a scholarship fund in Brian's memory. It created a little spark in Doug and Renee and I think it helped with their healing. I have been proud to be on the scholarship committee every year since it began.

It was obvious that some people were uncomfortable with the intense grief that surrounded Doug and Renee for a time. But I am so glad that Ginny and I were there for them.

Looking back on our lives, I think the time we spent with the LaViolettes ranks up at the top in our efforts to help others. It was one of the most important things we've done for other people in our lives. It also taught us a lot. Recently, Ginny lost a close friend. For months, she spent nearly every day with her friend before her friend's death. I think our experience with Doug and Renee helped prepare Ginny for this role with her dear friend.

As human beings, we have a moral and spiritual obligation to support our loved ones. Don't be afraid of the grief or of showing your own emotions. Open your heart, give your time, and be committed to the cause of helping your loved one. Also remember that when people are grieving, they are not thinking clearly. They may need friends and family to help with some of the tough decisions.

Ginny Riopelle

Supporting her husband's instinct

I had only met Doug and Renee once prior to the accident. At the time, neither Jack nor I had experienced the death of someone close to us. How did we know Doug and Renee needed us? I guess it was instinct. Jack suggested we visit them consistently during this crisis period. I thought that was a good idea.

Every time we came for our nightly visit, we could tell it was appreciated. That helped reinforce the need and kept us coming back. It became a comfort, something Doug and Renee could rely on at a time when their world seemed out of control. We were consistent and we knew that was important to them. Each visit gave them the opportunity to talk about the little things that happened in the last 24 hours.

Renee and I seemed to click right away. I remember one of the first conversations we had was about the "How are you doing" question. She didn't know how to respond. We wondered why some people were so afraid of grief. They just wanted to keep things surface. Well, that's not what Doug and Renee wanted.

I think it helped that Jack and I had never met Brian. It gave Doug and Renee the opportunity to tell us all about him. It was perfect timing, because that's really what they wanted to do—talk about Brian.

There is a misconception that people think those who are grieving don't want their loved one mentioned—that bringing up the name will make them suffer more. Nothing could be further from the truth. I think the opposite is true. The fear is that no one will remember the one who died. In the case of Doug and Renee, it was their precious child.

By talking about the person who has died, you are helping to keep the memory alive. And more importantly, you are helping get the grief out. I think it is true that it's more healthy to grieve outwardly than to hold it in.

We really didn't have a plan to help Doug and Renee. It just happened. It was something we could do that seemed to help them.

It's important to be open and honest about your emotions during grieving. It is also important to be consistent. If you find yourself in a supportive role, follow your instincts, follow your heart. Just go with it. Don't push things. Follow the lead of your loved ones. And don't be afraid to show them you care by listening and grieving with them.

Scott Roberts

Friendship from afar

As a United States Secret Service Agent, I was assigned to protect former President George H. Bush when I first met Doug. He was persistent in getting the President's signature on a miniature Air Force One replica for the Brian LaViolette Scholarship Foundation annual auction.

Since our first encounter, Doug's family and my family have become friends. Doug, Renee, and Kim have not only opened up their home and their hearts to us, but have provided us with a sense of renewal in the human spirit. When my family goes through difficult times, we reflect on the triumphs and tragedy the LaViolettes have endured and that provides the strength we need to continue.

When we first met the LaViolettes, my wife and I did not have any children. We are now the proud parents of a 2 1/2- year-old son and a six-month-old son. I can only hope that we are able to instill in our sons the same commitment, values, and guidance that Doug and Renee have provided for their children.

Words to Live By

by Brian D. LaViolette (8/21/90)

NOTE: Brian wrote the following "Sports Hints." Today, we realize that these athletic tips from a young 13-year-old boy are not just about sports. They not only apply to living, but healing.

1. Never, ever say you're sorry when you miss a ball, shank it, etc. I know you didn't do it on purpose so don't ever say your are sorry. Got it?!?

2. Don't be a ball hog. It annoys your teammates and cuts down your overall performance.

3. Don't be cocky. I could type pages upon pages on this rule, but you know what it means.

4. Be nice. You can gain a lot more respect this way. By being nice I don't mean not hitting somebody in football. Just be a good sport when you lose, win, or tie.

5. Trust people when you have doubts. Who knows? Maybe they'll surprise you!

6. Above all, maintain a good attitude. Whatever you do, wherever you go, try your hardest at everything you do. It can take you places you never even dreamed of.

7. Enough talk…Go out and have some fun!!!

NOTE: This certainly illustrates that we can learn a lot from our children.

Following are inspiring stories of others who have overcome the tragedy of losing a loved one. We are each other's best teachers. These stories are unique, but they share a common thread of strength. They demonstrate our ability to survive and thrive, even during tragic circumstances. Each story shows us what death can teach us about life.

Judith Rybicki

Three deaths in six months

My mother's first child was a boy. He died of pneumonia when he was nearly two. One month later, I was conceived. During that same year, my father lost four of his family members. My parents were a couple who knew sorrow too well. After I was born, my parents went on to have three more daughters. In all, there were five girls.

In April 1997, I received a call from my closest sister, Jackie. She had shocking news. After months of abdominal discomfort and a series of misdiagnoses, she was finally diagnosed with fourth stage ovarian cancer. She was to have a complete hysterectomy the following day.

Jackie was only 42 at the time, one year older than me. We were so close. I was grief stricken, knowing what she would go through and that I may even lose her. Over the next year and a half, I would drive up to Boulder, CO, from Albuquerque, NM, every six weeks to be with her and support her in any way I could.

Jackie blazed ahead, her bright spirit and luminous smile shining a positive light on everyone she met. Through the course of her illness, she was determined to heal her cancer, trying every treatment that offered the tiniest bit of hope. She had always been successful in her life as an interior designer and single mother. She wanted to be successful in healing from her cancer. Flanked by the support of many friends and family members, Jackie traveled around the country for close to three years searching for a cure.

Then, in May 1998, my mother suffered what the doctors thought was a stroke. She was a very sensitive person and the stress of possibly losing another child was too much for her. That summer, her symptoms worsened. I'll never forget when both Jackie and my mother came to my graduation from Acupuncture College in August. Jackie laid on the hotel floor barely able to breathe as the cancer had spread to her lungs. My mother was having difficulty speaking and remembering the simplest of words.

I knew something was deeply wrong with my mother. I was right. Just two weeks later, while on a meditation retreat in Virginia, I received an emergency call the morning I was to leave. My mother was having surgery that afternoon to remove the most insidious brain tumor known. I was on the plane that afternoon and spent my 41st birthday with my dear mother during her recovery from surgery. The bond I had with my mother was very deep.

That next Christmas was the last one we would spend together as a family. In January, Jackie became extremely ill with a collapsed lung. We almost lost her then. My mother was holding her own after radiation and interferon, doing surprisingly well. During the next few months, Jackie rose again from the ashes as she had done on several occasions. It would be short-lived, however, as the summer of 1999 bloomed they both weakened dramatically.

While Jackie had multiple courses of chemotherapy and

several lung surgeries, her treatments were barely keeping her cancer at bay. She became quiet and accepting but still did not give up hope. Meanwhile, my mother was losing more of her memory and speech but gaining an undeniably beautiful part of herself. I always felt my mother was losing her mind to gain her heart. Her love was flowing along with the feelings she had kept locked inside her whole life. Everyone wanted to be with her to help, but we were the ones being helped by her openness and humility.

That fall I moved from New Mexico to Green Bay to help my parents. There I spent three amazing months in the house I grew up in, helping my sister, Joann, take care of my parents. On Thanksgiving, we received a call from Jackie. She had a multiple intestinal block and she was opting not to have surgery. That meant she was going to Hospice. I told her I was going to come out to be with her no matter what.

My other sisters who lived in the Midwest would help my parents and I would be with Jackie. I never wanted her to be alone, especially just before she died. So on Thanksgiving Day, I flew out to Boulder to be with her, even though I knew I would never see my mother awake or talking again.

Our family had been through so much in the last several years. All of my sisters tried to be with Jackie or with my mother whenever they could and whenever either needed them in spite of their own families' needs. The deep faith and support we carried was absolutely astonishing. We knew that this was one of the most, if not the most, important times of our lives—a time to give back what they had given us.

Jackie still had so much strength but my mother rapidly lost all her capabilities. On January 18, 2000 with Joann's family and me at her side, my mother passed away. The day after her funeral, we received a call from Jackie's nurse saying that she was unresponsive. Was she going to leave us immediately now that our mother was gone? I wasn't going to wait to find out. In an hour I was on a plane off to Colorado again.

Jackie was so happy to see me. Of course, she revived herself one more time so that we could properly grieve the loss of our mother and Jackie's life, too. She could finally die, knowing our mother was resting now. Six weeks later, on March 4, she passed on with all four of her sisters at her side. Her boyfriend and close friends were there as well. Later, her teenage son, Ben, came. Ben had such a hard time leaving his mother, yet he said something so wise. He said he was happy for her because she was finally free.

Four weeks later, my father had a heart attack. I believe that the sorrow caused his heart to break because he did not know how else to express his sadness. I was still in Colorado, and Joann was taking care of him. Shortly after, I went back to Wisconsin. After all that happened, I needed to be with him, too. The stress had really taken a toll on him. He was very thin and weak. It was in this vulnerable state that we were able to heal old issues and develop once again a loving trust between us. Then on July 10, 2000, with his daughters by his side, he passed on to join his beloved wife and daughter.

Losing three family members in six months was very difficult. But we made it through. The support of my sisters, Jackie's boyfriend, and other family and friends made our big family one of strength and love. We discovered that the deeper the pain you experience, the greater opportunity to love. Learning to love yourself and those close to you is what life is all about.

I feel my life is a work in progress. The grieving process is giving me the strength to really know who I am and what I am destined to do to make this world a better place. Life is truly a precious gift that God has given us. Although my heart aches for those I've lost, it is also expanding.

To those who find themselves in the midst of despair, I can offer these suggestions:

- Listen very closely to the person who is dying and support them in whatever way you can so they can leave this life more peacefully.
- If possible, help them to finish unfinished business before the final hour.
- Find refuge in God or something bigger than you. Use this time to see the larger picture.
- Open your heart and allow yourself to feel love—love for yourself and love for your loved one. If you feel like a victim, your heart will close and you will blame and become bitter.
- Value your feelings when they surface. Losing someone close to you can bring up every feeling imaginable. Find someone who can listen to you honestly and openly.
- Pay attention to your physical health. Rejuvenate yourself on a daily basis. Physical activity will help replenish you emotionally as well as physically.
- Try to avoid addictive patterns such as excessive drinking, smoking, gambling, etc., to help ease the pain. This behavior is just a quick fix and is not a healthy outlet.
- Keep the spirit of your loved ones alive.

My sister's death has left a hole in my heart that will only be eased through time, but will never be filled. I feel her spirit now guiding me on my journey in this crazy life. In a sense, I think we'll grow old together after all.

As for my mother, her brilliant spirit blessed me at the moment of her death. She was like a fountain of light that went right through my entire being. At that moment I saw who she was. I feel so grateful to have known her.

The Ambrosius Family

Losing a child to cancer

Rob and Melissa Ambrosius have been married for 10 years. They are the proud parents of three beautiful children, with another one on the way. Lauren is six and Brooke is two. And then there was Ross, their only son. He was a typical little boy who loved the outdoors and enjoyed helping his dad cut the lawn with the riding lawn mower. He was always smiling and, like most boys his age, he was very active. But suddenly things changed. Just before Ross turned three, he was diagnosed with cancer.

Hearing the word "cancer" is traumatic. But for parents, hearing that word describe their child can be even more devastating. Ross had an inoperable muscle tumor near his brain. Once the Ambrosius family recovered from the initial shock, they moved into action. They were determined to help their child beat this deadly disease. Soon, however, the cancer took charge. Ross was unable to talk and eat. His parents became desperate participants in a brutal battle to save their son.

Prior to his diagnosis, Ross was having trouble sleeping and had pain in his ears. He was diagnosed on a sunny Friday afternoon in July 1999. He was given a 50 percent chance of survival. That weekend Rob and Melissa packed up the kids and went to the family cottage. It was a place Ross loved. That Monday, Ross underwent five surgeries. The following week he began radiation and aggressive chemotherapy. Melissa and Rob would later discover that the treatment was just as bad as the illness. In fact, the side effects were not only painful for Ross, they became life-threatening. Not surprisingly, Melissa and Rob still have difficulty recalling those months.

Rob

It was painful to watch him suffer

The chemotherapy really knocked him down. But he was a little toughy. I was proud of the way he made it through his treatments. Soon after he was diagnosed, he was in and out of the hospital a lot. We got to know many of the nurses pretty well. They really liked Ross.

About three years prior to Ross' diagnosis, we started our own business, a photography studio. As a small business owner, I was still working a lot of hours when Ross got sick. Fortunately, we had incredible employees. We couldn't have gotten through it without them. I do regret, however, that I did have to work so much during Ross' illness. There is not a day that goes by that I don't think about the time I was away from him while he was sick. I guess I was so convinced that we would be able to beat this thing. We were so sure Ross would be healthy again.

Our daughter, Lauren, was very close to Ross. She was the perfect little helper. The illness changed Ross' appearance and really took its toll. Lauren wasn't afraid. She just wanted to be with him. Even when he was in the hospital, Lauren would visit Ross often.

Melissa took care of Ross when he was home. When he was in the hospital, I would work during the day and then spend the night with Ross. Melissa would go up to the hospital during the day. We spent a lot of time at the hospital. There are so many bad memories from the hospital that, to this day, I have trouble driving down that street.

On December 9, 1999, less than six months after we first heard the diagnosis, our son died at the hospital. That day, we came home to a house filled with medical supplies, one daughter with lots of questions, a younger daughter with lots of needs, and so many reminders of Ross. It was the worst day of our lives.

Melissa and I dealt with our loss differently. I am more private and tend to hold things in. I talk to Ross often. I go to the cemetery often. And I have a gold ribbon with an angel on it pinned to nearly every jacket I own. I also make it a point to give these little reminders out as often as possible. The gold ribbon signifies the fight against children's cancer, and the angel represents our son who lost his battle.

Today, I pay more attention to the other kids. And we really do "stop and smell the roses." Life is too short and I refuse to sweat the small stuff. I've allowed Ross' death to change my life. Now I try to live life to the fullest.

Obviously, it was unbelievably painful to lose our son and see him suffer with that horrible illness. He is in our thoughts and hearts forever.

As a result of our son's illness, however, we received incredible support. It showed us the good that exists in this world at a time when it was difficult seeing past the bad. We met a lot of new people. The positive support from our parents, families, friends, neighbors, and even strangers was almost overwhelming.

This summer we are going to organize a golf outing in our son's honor and memory. It will also be dedicated to Cory, our friend's child, a three-year-old who lost his battle with brain cancer. The proceeds will go to the National Children's Cancer Foundation and local families who have children with cancer. It's our way of giving back to others who are in need.

Melissa

The mother becomes the nurse

At the time of the diagnosis, I was working part-time for an insurance company. My employer and my co-workers were incredibly supportive. From the day of the diagnosis to well after Ross' death, I did not work and still collected a paycheck. My co-workers actually donated vacation time so I could keep getting paid time off. People I didn't even know gave up their vacation time so I could stay home to care for our son. It was such a generous gift.

There were also various fund-raisers. The money helped us with some of the bills. I remember hearing a story about one young girl who donated all of her first communion gift money to a fund-raising event for Ross. In addition to these touching stories, people also delivered meals to our home, cleaned the house, mowed the lawn, and really gave us unconditional support during that time.

Out of the nearly six months Ross fought his battle, he had maybe a handful of good days. The illness was awful. He was at the hospital nearly as much as he was at home. When he was at home, I became his 24-hour nurse. I was taught how to feed him and care for his special needs. During that time, Rob and I didn't get much sleep. I think God kept us going. There's really no other way to describe how we got through it.

In September, Ross' condition became dramatically worse. The cancer treatment weakened his immune system, which made him susceptible to infection. He constantly battled one infection after another. But we still remained positive. I guess that's why at the time, I didn't mind being the nurse rather than the mother. We were so convinced we were going to have our healthy son back. I always thought there will be plenty of time for mothering after he got better. I just wanted to nurse him back to health. Each time Ross would bounce back from an infection, it reinforced our hope that he would be able to overcome this illness.

The day Ross died was actually quite a shock. We knew he was still very sick; however, just the day before, the doctor told us the cancer was gone. We were so happy. Now, we thought, it would be just a matter of helping our son get stronger. We worried that the treatment was too harsh, but we really didn't have a choice. The day before he died, he was operated on for another infection. As we waited for him to recover from the surgery, we were told that he developed a deadly strep pneumonia infection. The doctor told us it would be touch-and-go for the next 24 hours.

Even then, we were still hopeful. However, this time it was different. We watched helplessly as each of our son's organs started to fail. Ross never woke up from that surgery. He died at 10:30 the following morning.

I was never angry with God, but I did question why he took our beautiful little boy. I now take comfort in our faith. Our belief in heaven assures us that we will be with Ross again some day.

It is very important for us to keep Ross' spirit alive in our family. Each night, when we get the girls ready for bed, we pray as a family. We take turns talking to Ross and telling him about our day. We pray for him and we pray for each other.

For me, getting past that one year milestone was important. It also helps having our girls and looking forward to a new baby. I am glad we reached out to people during Ross' illness. They have touched my life in a profound way. Their love will never be forgotten. Today, I treat every day as if it were my last. And I continue to search for the good that has come from us losing our little angel.

Maria Dalebroux

A close friend commits suicide

Wendy and I were friends for about eight years. We met at a marketing research company where we both worked. We quickly became best friends, spending time together outside of work. Wendy and I just seemed to click. We had a lot in common. We graduated from the same high school and we both enjoyed biking and other outdoor activities.

I jumped into the role of the motivator and Wendy was the comedian. It was a perfect partnership. I always wanted to go a little faster, a little farther. I was a true competitor. Wendy, on the other hand, never wanted to take things too seriously. She had such a great sense of humor.

Wendy was one of those "once-in-a-lifetime" friends that you can tell anything to. She was a great listener and she was always there for me.

Soon after we first met, Wendy shared stories of a painful loss in her life—her mother. Her mom committed suicide when Wendy was just a small child. As Wendy would share details of the story, it seemed to put her in a place so unreachable. The pain of abandonment and her grief over her mom's death was still very apparent. It was as if it happened yesterday. She missed her so deeply. She always carried a picture of her mom in her wallet.

Occasionally, Wendy would spend time with me and my family. She especially liked to be with us at Christmas and Thanksgiving. My mom and Wendy bonded. They had an unspoken connection. My mom understood Wendy's loss and Wendy appreciated my mom's motherly influence. Every summer my mom would make Wendy's favorite—canned pickled beets. I think it was comfort food for Wendy.

I knew Wendy suffered from depression, but I had no

idea how serious it was until a few years into our friendship, Wendy tried to take her life. Fortunately, she was able to stop herself and she called me. I could tell something was very wrong. I immediately went to her house where I found her unresponsive. I called 911. I couldn't believe this was happening. Because her suicide attempt was so serious, she was placed in the hospital. She didn't want anyone to know. I kept her secret as I supported her during this traumatic time.

We were soon able to put that nightmare behind us and Wendy seemed to be getting the help she needed. Life went on and we remained very close.

I moved to Arizona, but Wendy and I still stayed in touch. One Christmas I wasn't able to come home so I talked Wendy into visiting Arizona for the holidays. With a group of friends, we headed up to the Grand Canyon. The spectacular views, laughter, and good times from that Christmas are memories I will cherish forever.

When I moved back to Wisconsin, Wendy and I found ourselves working for the same employer once again. Like close friends do, we picked up right where we left off. Everything seemed to be going great.

A year later, however, I could tell that Wendy was suffering from depression and anxiety. She was receiving professional help and even checked herself into the hospital. I was convinced she was getting the help she needed. Even though she had many supportive friends who were reaching out to her, she continued to sink into those depths of despair that she had felt before. But I still thought she could climb out, like she did in the past. Deep down, however, I was frightened for her.

In the spring of 1997, Wendy took her own life. She was just 35 years old.

I remember our last conversation together. I called to

check on her. She sounded so down. By this time, she had taken a leave from work. I encouraged her to try and go into work for even a few hours. I thought it might help. I asked her directly if she was feeling as if she wanted to take her own life. She said no. I asked her again before hanging up. She said no again and told me that if she started to feel that way, she would call me. That's the last time I heard her voice.

The next day a friend was at my front door to deliver the news. I was shocked and angry. She promised me she wouldn't do that! Why didn't she reach out to me? And then I felt guilt. Did I do enough? Why didn't I go over to her apartment to check on her that day? Of course, I could think of a million things I should have done. Now, I know that this was something that Wendy must have planned. I think the lie was all a part of it.

Soon after the suicide, I became very frightened for Wendy's soul. I was always taught that God does not look favorably on those who take their own life. I was unsure of where she was. I wanted her to be safe and finally happy. Then I realized that the God whom I believe in is a forgiving God. I couldn't imagine that He would turn his back on Wendy. I then started to visualize her safe and happy. This helped with my grieving.

After the shock wore off, I actually felt some relief for her. Wendy was obviously in so much pain. She seemed like such a tortured soul during the last few months of her life. I wish she would have found her answers without taking her life. I wish she could have gotten the help she needed and deserved.

I had not experienced the death of a loved one prior to Wendy's suicide. It was a painful, difficult time. The experience was worse because she took her own life. When a loved one commits suicide, there are so many unanswered questions and so many emotions that are not present with a natural or accidental death. But in the end, I learned that the grieving process is still fundamentally the same. With a suicide, you need to come to terms with lingering anger, guilt, and resentment. The quicker you can move toward peace, the better chance you can move on.

Since this has happened, I've had a chance to research the topic of suicide. If you have a friend or family member who is experiencing depression, consider these facts I discovered about suicide from the American Institute of Preventive Medicine:

1. Suicide is a by-product of severe depression and suicidal threats must always be taken seriously.
2. Most people who threaten and/or attempt suicide more than once, usually succeed if someone doesn't stop them.
3. Suicide is the third leading cause of death among 15 to 24-year-olds, after accidents and homicide.
4. More than 70 percent of people who commit suicide suffered from depression right before their deaths.

For Wendy, it's too late. But maybe for someone reading this book, or someone's family member, it's not.

I remember on one of our outdoor hikes, Wendy and I made a pact that we would be lifelong friends "no matter what!" After her suicide I was angry that she didn't hold up her end of the bargain. Today, every time I have a good belly laugh or think of her innocent blue eyes sparkling, I think of Wendy and realize that she kept her promise after all.

NOTE: To find a national directory of support groups for survivors of suicide, as well as helpful information on coping with this type of loss, visit www.suicidology.org.

Jill Miller

A tragic accident takes her young son's life

We lost our son, Mitchell, when he was 8 1/2 years old to an accident that took place in our garage. Our other son, Matthew, who was three at the time, was with him but was not physically injured in the accident. We had a step ladder hanging on a hook, with a large roll of plastic standing below it. The roll was secured with bungee cords.

On that summer day, Mitchell chose to take the ladder without asking. Typically, he would have asked permission. We are not sure exactly what happened. I heard the crash and ran to the garage, only to see my son's lifeless body laying on the floor. He apparently chose to climb the plastic to unhook the ladder. The roll unhooked and tipped. The sudden impact of Mitchell's head hitting the concrete caused serious injuries that resulted in death.

My husband and I could have blamed each other, but we didn't. We knew we were careful parents. My husband and I grieved differently. He needed to stay busy. I needed time alone. I went through pictures, thought of Mitchell's routine, remembered his favorite foods, and grieved about the future I would not share with him.

As a mother, I searched for reassurance that my son was safe and happy. I wanted to learn as much as I could about heaven and life after death. I read many books. Some of them I agreed with and others I did not. I found that studying this topic actually helped me with the grieving process. I also went to a support group, which had many helpful aspects; however, I found that I preferred the individual path.

It was important that Matthew wasn't lost in our grieving. Children are very resilient, but it can be difficult to know the impact an accident like this can have on a young child.

It was interesting the way people reacted to our loss. It seemed many had different opinions, suggestions, and judgments. My husband felt his friends didn't know what to say, and therefore they avoided the topic.

It seemed like people were uncomfortable even hearing Mitchell's name mentioned. He was still my son and always will be. If a conversation relates to something in his life, I will still mention his name. Just because he is gone now, does not mean he never existed.

At the time, I didn't even like hearing "Time heals." Today, of course, I realize that there is a lot of truth to that. You never forget. However, if you are willing to accept the loss and try to heal from it, time does give you the opportunity to learn from the experience and move on.

It takes work to grieve the loss of a child. In the beginning, I wondered how God could take Mitchell from me. Today, I believe that life is meant to be enjoyed. We are on this earth to learn our chosen lessons. It isn't always easy. However, our perception and attitude help determine how we handle the struggles. Many people have recovered from tragic losses to move on and live a joyful and fulfilling life.

After the loss of Mitchell, and even today, when I am feeling down, I just think of all the blessings in my life.

Donna Pagel

Watched her two sons suffer and die of cancer

When the twins were born, I was just as surprised as the doctors. First there was Justin James, 3 lbs. 14 oz. Then, seven minutes later Jason John, 2 lbs. 11 oz., Justin's identical twin brother, was born. It was touch-and-go with Jason. He was so tiny. Justin stayed in the hospital for two months and Jason was there for three months because he was so small. They were such a blessing in my life. I was so happy and relieved when I was able to finally have them both home with me.

When the twins were born, I was personally going through a difficult time. My marriage was in trouble and we were on welfare. When the twins were two, I finally got the courage to divorce my husband. It was just me and the boys.

In an effort to get off welfare, I was going to school to be an EMT and volunteering as a 911 dispatcher to gain valuable experience. I was getting my life back. The boys were thriving. They both had large blue eyes, blonde hair, and bright smiles. They meant everything to me. They had so much fun playing together. They were inseparable.

I landed a job in a community about 40 minutes from where I lived, but I was ready to make the move. And then, my world crumbled right before my eyes.

Justin got sick when he was five years old. Odd as it may seem, it was his school picture that told me something was wrong. In the picture, one side of his face seemed paralyzed. It was subtle. Everyday that I looked at him I didn't notice it. But in the picture it was obvious.

Justin was in so much pain. But nothing seemed to help. He cried because of the pain in his ears. The doctors just blamed his pain on ear infections. I knew it was more than that. He wasn't sleeping or eating. He was vomiting. I took him to several doctors, searching for answers, searching for relief for my child. It took two months to get the final diagnosis—Rhabdo-myosarcoma, terminal brain cancer. By the time the doctors operated on my beautiful little boy, the tumor had already eaten through his skull and damaged his right eye. The cancer had spread throughout his body.

Desperate times require desperate measures. They bombarded his body with very high doses of chemotherapy. Soon, he couldn't hear, he couldn't walk, and he wore an ominous black patch to cover up the gap where the cancer stole his eye. The suffering that my poor little baby went through was incredible. He was only five years old and he wanted to come home. So, in the fall of 1988 I took my child home to die. I was his only caretaker at the time because I didn't have any support.

Jason was devastated as he watched his best friend suffer.

A couple of days before he died, I glanced into his room one night and saw a bright figure standing over him, comforting him. Maybe it was my imagination, maybe I was just so exhausted. But even today, I believe in my heart it was real. I didn't feel afraid when I saw that image. I knew we weren't alone and I took comfort in that.

It's been more than a dozen years, but I remember the day Justin died as if it were yesterday. It was a gorgeous fall day. He didn't want morphine. It was amazing how aware he was that day. He sat in the living room with a contented stare, just taking everything in.

The boys always shared a room. That night Jason came into the living room and said Justin was breathing heavy and he wanted to sleep in my room. I said sure and continued my work; I was writing my son's eulogy. Then, just as I was about to get up and check on him, I heard him say "mamma."

I was shocked. He had not spoken for weeks.

I held my son and told him everything was going to be all right. He reached up and brushed the tears from my cheek. I talked softly as I described what it would be like for him in heaven with God. He would be able to walk again, and play, and God would take good care of him. My little Justin took a couple of difficult breaths and then died in my arms.

I felt so alone and so angry. At the time, I hated everyone, including God. Now I realize that my belief in God is what gave me whatever little peace I had.

My story would be tragic if it ended there. But it doesn't.

Jason was really lost after Justin died. He not only lost his twin brother, he lost his buddy, his confidant. But he seemed to be able to move on from his loss. I was so paranoid about him getting sick that I wanted him thoroughly checked over. The doctors told me not to worry, that it would be unusual for Jason to get the same type of cancer as his brother. They told me to try the best I could to get on with my life. So I did.

Jason was very active. He was always the fighter. Justin, on the other hand, was more quiet and preferred to write and draw.

Jason seemed to be doing well in school and adapting just fine. At age nine, he was quite a ladies' man already. He had such a great, fun-loving personality. Everyone seemed to like Jason. And again, just when I thought our lives were back on track, the walls came crashing in around me.

Jason was eating supper and said "Mom, I can't feel the right side of my face." He said he had also been having headaches and didn't really have an appetite. You can only imagine the thoughts and fears screaming in my head. I immediately made an appointment with the doctor.

The tests confirmed that it was the same brain cancer as Justin. When Jason got home from school, I gave him the news through my tears. "No!" he cried "No, please no!"

Even though he was only five years old, Jason remembered everything about his brother's illness and death. He was so afraid to go through the same pain and agony.

When we received Jason's diagnosis, I was planning my second marriage to my present husband. Jason was going to give us the rings. Because he was so sick that day, he had a difficult time just sitting through the ceremony. The next day I took him to the hospital.

I was soon faced with the same decision. The chemotherapy was taking its toll, just like it had with Justin. I decided to stop the treatments and took my nine-year-old son home. Jason's cancer spread so fast. It travelled across his throat to the other side of his face. We tried desperately to keep him comfortable. He fought hard.

The last nights of Justin's life, my husband's family stayed by my side to keep him comfortable so I could rest. Within those horrible days and nights of thrashing and fighting, we tried to keep him as comfortable as possible. The final morning, as he slipped into a coma, I laid next to him as he succumbed to the cancer. I thanked him for giving me enough love to last a lifetime. He loved the song *Silent Night*, so I sang it to him. I told him everything was going to be all right and that his brother was waiting for him and they would be happy together forever.

Justin died peacefully, but Jason left this world hard. Jason died at 10:30 in the morning on November 6, 1992, four years after he watched his brother die.

I had so much support during Jason's illness. It was completely the opposite when Justin died. My new husband's family helped out so much with Jason. When Justin died, I felt alone and bitter; but when Jason died I had a group of people I could share my pain with, because they were in pain, too. They had lived through the tragedy with me. Together we were able to share our stories and our pain.

Losing two sons to such a horrible illness tested my strength in more ways than I ever could have imagined. There were so many times I thought I was going to break from the pressure of the pain. The years of healing have not been without their struggles.

Today, my husband and I have a beautiful four-year-old boy named Jacob. He is outgoing and active, like Jason, but also loves to color and draw like Justin. One day he said to me, "Mama, there are boy angels in heaven. I came from heaven just for you." Jacob is our little gift from heaven.

I don't take anything for granted and I have gotten much better at learning when I need to grieve and keep my boys' spirits alive. I was raised a strict Catholic and taught to fear God. Now, I believe He is a kind and loving God. I have entrusted Him with my two babies. He is a compassionate God who will take good care of my children. I no longer fear God; I rely on Him.

It is so important to reach out to others during your times of need. If you don't talk about your pain, it will be an emotional type of cancer. Find some way to express your pain before it grows beyond your control. Find somebody who can help you through the difficult times 24/7. After Jason's death, I took steps to get help during the grieving process.

One thing that has really helped me heal is yoga. It may sound odd, but taking yoga classes helped me find a balance and spirituality that I was searching for. For me, yoga is a form of meditation, a time when I connect with my sons in heaven. I visualize my kids being happy and safe. I am in touch with them and that calms me.

Don't rush your grief. People told me that it was time to move on, that I should be done with the pain. Well, you are never "over it." You just learn to cope with it.

Be patient and flexible with yourself. Grieving is a roller-coaster ride. There are down times that take you by surprise. Allow those times to come.

It is important to find some type of activity that you can connect with. In addition to yoga, I found that journaling has been very helpful to me. I started journaling when Justin was first diagnosed. Don't be afraid to go back and read your journal entries. When you're ready, look at old pictures and take the time to remember.

Following is an entry from my journal less than a year after Jason died:

I don't want to be anywhere. I don't want to do anything. I don't want to feel anymore. I don't care about anything.

I am so tired of everything, I can't fight for anything. I want to sleep all the time. I want to cry all the time. I want to be angry. I want to be sad. I want to miss my children. I want to remember how much they went through. I want to scream sometimes.

I want my children here with me.

I want to be left alone in my pain. I want to feel the pain I want to have hope again. I want something good to happen. I want to be normal.

I am normal!

If you are dealing with despair and pain, realize that you can get through it. You must believe that. It is that hope that will help you make it out of the darkness to the other side where the sun is shining.

And always remember that those who remain in our hearts will live forever.

Remembering Walter Payton

Impressive both on and off the field

If you are a football fan, you know that the name Walter Payton is synonymous with athletic greatness and superior achievement. For more than a decade, fans, sports writers, and other athletes marveled at his performance on the football field. Walter Payton's list of NFL accomplishments is impressive. During his 13-year career, he:

- earned more rushing yards and combined net yards than any other player in NFL history;
- held an NFL record 3,838 carries with 16,726 rushing yards;
- was selected to the Pro Bowl nine times;
- missed only one game in his rookie year and went on to play 186 consecutive games;
- was twice named NFL Player of The Year and Most Valuable Player of The Year;
- was recognized by ESPN as one of the 50 greatest North American athletes of the past 100 years;
- was enshrined to the Pro Football Hall of Fame the first year he was eligible.

He is believed to be one of football's greatest all-around players. What many people don't know, however, is that Walter Payton was more than a sports legend. His most important accomplishments occurred off the field.

Walter was a devoted philanthropist, championing the cause of needy children. He worked tirelessly to provide motivation and support to youth throughout Illinois. In 1989 he started the Walter Payton Foundation, dedicated to helping disadvantaged youth. In 1998, the Foundation distributed more than $3 million in toys and clothes to more than 35,000 Illinois children.

In 1999, while Walter was bed-ridden due to terminal illness, he demonstrated once again that he was more than a great athlete—he was a great person. Because of his illness, Walter was unable to make personal appearances to secure funds for his Foundation. Instead, while he fought his personal health battle, he spent two months signing limited edition lithographs titled "Whatever It Takes." Amazingly, Walter signed 2,534 prints to be sold after his death to help keep his legacy of giving alive.

Today, it is his wife, Connie, who is the champion. She keeps her husband's spirit alive by carrying on his tradition of giving. In addition to the Walter Payton Foundation, she helps run the Walter Payton Alliance for Children and the recently formed Walter Payton Cancer Foundation.

For Connie Payton, the memories she holds close to her heart do not involve football or amazing athletic accomplishments. She remembers her husband as a truly caring individual and a great role-model for their two children.

Walter Payton started writing his biography entitled *Never Die Easy* before he died. The book was completed the year after his death and is presently available in book stores.

NOTE: The Walter and Connie Payton Foundation provides financial and motivational support for youth. In 2000, Walter Payton and his non-salaried staff distributed more than $3 million in toys and clothes to more than 35,000 wards of the State of Illinois. The lithographs he signed sell for $499 and can be purchased at www.paytonart.com or by calling 1-888-284-8330. Donations can be sent to Walter and Connie Payton Foundation, P.O. Box 5128, Elgin, IL 60121, (847) 645-1202.

Connie Payton

Lost her husband to cancer

My husband was a complex person. He had many sides. Walter liked to sit back and observe. Even if you thought he wasn't paying attention, he was keenly aware of what was going on. He was also a practical joker. He loved having fun, especially with our two children—Brittney, who is now 16 and Jarrett, who is 20. Walter would hide behind the door and jump out at them when they least expected it. He was such a kid at heart. As a family, we had so much fun together.

Walter was also a very giving person. It gave him such joy to know that he was making a difference. He was very generous and never wanted anything in return. More than a decade before he died, he started the Walter Payton Foundation. He especially liked to help children in need. He was a spiritual man who was thankful for the many blessings in his life.

He was definitely not a complainer. Even if he was sick, you never really knew it because he kept it to himself. He didn't want to be a burden. That's why when he did get sick, it was such a shock—especially for the children. After all, to them, their father was bigger than life. Jarrett was particularly in shock. How could his dad, a great athlete, get this serious illness? It was an incredible shock to all of us, including Walter.

In hindsight, there may have been more symptoms. But it was easy for Walter to shrug off health issues and blame them on old sports injuries. Before his diagnosis, he began to lose a significant amount of weight. Then we knew something was wrong.

It was the fall of 1998 when Walter's local doctor referred him to the Mayo Clinic for more tests. They discovered that

Walter had a rare liver disorder called primary sclerosing chonlangitis (PSC). The only cure was a liver transplant. I was in shock as the doctor explained the need for the transplant that would hopefully save my husband's life.

In typical Walter Payton-style, he remained positive and upbeat about the possibility of receiving a liver transplant and beating the disease. We found out later that a small percentage of PSC patients can develop cancer. Walter became a part of that group.

In May 1999, doctors discovered multiple tumors. The news was devastating. He was no longer a candidate for a liver transplant. Even worse, the doctors told us that the cancer had spread to his lymph nodes and was inoperable. There was nothing they could do for him.

The last six months of my husband's life were a struggle. The cancer tore through his body, causing pain that was difficult to control. He was like a zombie when he took the medication, but without it, the pain became intolerable. I searched desperately for ways to make his last months comfortable. And then I heard about a special cancer hospital in Zion, IL. The Cancer Treatment Centers of America helped give Walter some important quality time prior to his death by focusing on his nutritional needs, as well as his emotional needs. Hospice also helped us immensely. Everyone at Hospice was wonderful.

As a family we had accepted what was happening to Walter. We knew we fought a good fight, but we also knew Walter was ready. He held his head high and died with dignity on November 1, 1999.

Walter's spiritual energy was contagious. In fact, throughout his life, many people, including his own grandfather, said Walter would have been a great preacher. He relied on God and scripture throughout his life, but especially while he was dying. His spiritual strength helped all of us cope with his passing.

Our family's spirituality was always important. Both Walter and I grew up in the South, where your religion is your foundation. There is no question that this spiritual foundation helped get all of us through this most difficult time. Because Walter was able to touch so many lives with his giving attitude and spirituality, I think he fulfilled his calling after all.

The first year after his death is really a blur. His loss was felt throughout the world. I attended many tributes and events that first year. A lot of people, not just his family, needed to heal from his loss. At times, I found myself comforting those whom I met along the way. I think people appreciated the fact that our family included them in the grieving process. They were happy we chose to share Walter with them.

Although it was tiring, that flurry of activity was actually a part of my own healing. It made me realize the impact that my husband had on so many people. I felt proud of Walter and shared many of the stories with Brittney and Jarrett. They, too, felt proud.

Staying involved with my husband's Foundation, a cause he loved so dearly, is one way that I am able to keep his spirit alive. Just as he did, I want to make a difference in people's lives. His spirit is also very much alive in our children. From time to time, one of them will do something that reminds me of their dad and I will comment on it. Even they notice certain things they do that are like him. It makes all of us smile because we were so proud of Walter. For me, I take special comfort in seeing his spirit in their eyes. It is still another way that he lives on.

Doug
You are not alone

The people who shared their stories in this book represent just the tip of the iceberg. They are courageous individuals who have been able to heal from their profound loss. But there are so many others like them.

A year after Brian died, Renee and I were invited to a dinner at St. Norbert College in DePere, a city adjacent to Green Bay. It was an annual event for us. Our good friend from St. Norbert College always made sure we had assigned seats with a group of new people he thought we would enjoy meeting. That night we all started talking about our families. As we all shared stories, it turned out that we had all lost a child. This was the table nobody would want to sit at—a club that you never want to be a part of.

At first, I questioned why our friend didn't warn us or give us a choice about that table. However, as the evening went on, I found out that all of us had started scholarships to help other kids in a lasting tribute to our children. These common bonds we shared let us know that we were not alone in our tragedy and that we could make it through.

During our family's healing, so many people who had lost a child reached out to us to tell us their stories of how they healed. It showed us that we were not alone. It also showed us that if they could do it, so could we. With each story, we gained more strength and momentum toward our healing goal. Today, we hope that sharing our story and the stories in this book can give people the same strength others gave us as we continue on our healing journey.

Renee

Gaining courage from each other

On Brian's 18th birthday, three years after he died, we received a mailing from a razor blade company addressed to him: "Dear Brian, Happy Birthday…" It was not the first time we received mail addressed to him. I remember feeling very angry at the mailing services and marketing companies who were so insensitive. To them, our son was a mailing label. It's amazing how much pain a small, typed label can cause.

When we first discussed doing this book, I admit I was concerned. I knew the process would stir up all kinds of feelings. I knew I would be thinking about the mail that came addressed to Brian, the day I got that phone call, the funeral, and all of the other painful experiences that have come and gone over the years. But what I didn't realize is how good it would feel to remember Brian's sense of humor, re-read the letters from the many people who thought he was such a good person, and be able to reach out to others who may be struggling just as we were years ago. Because we feel so blessed by those who have helped us, we feel it is our turn to give back.

Although it is difficult, it is important to reach out to others during your time of need. Even though I have always been a private person, it has helped talking about Brian and the emotions associated with his loss. Our hope is that no matter where you are on your journey, you will find hope and inspiration from the many stories we have shared. We can all gain courage from each other.

Today's society is obsessed with creating superheros and clinging to celebrities. Rather than gaining strength from the real-life successes of each other, we live vicariously through the actions of these famous people, idolizing their make-believe power.

But today's true heroes are not found on television, at the movies, in a sports arena, or on stage. Life's real winners are often sitting right next to us. They live in the house next door, work in the cubicle adjacent to ours, or serve us dinner at our favorite restaurant. They are our neighbors, our friends, our co-workers, and our family members. They are real people who have overcome real tragedies. They are the ones who have conquered despair only to stand at the foot of the mountain, poised and ready to start climbing again. These are the people who make a difference. They influence us by their actions and they encourage us with their strength and quiet confidence.

The people who have shared their stories in this book are our everyday heroes. And there are so many others. We can gain inspiration, courage, and hope from those who have made it through the difficult times. These people have their own badge of courage, a shield that helps protect them from future despair.

Our loved ones, who have gone on before us, serve as reminders of all that we often take for granted—kindness, spirituality, and love. Their deaths and our losses demonstrate that sometimes growth is preceded by pain. Through the pain, we can hopefully become better people.

When we experience the growth that comes with change—even forced, traumatic change—we are somehow able to stand a little taller, be a little stronger.

Life can be challenging and unfair. Most of us have gone through some type of difficulty. How we choose to respond to that time can either be a life-changing turning point, or a soul-damaging event.

The dictionary defines grief as "deep mental anguish." It is an agonizing physical and emotional pain. The pain of losing a loved one—especially a child—can torment us for years, sometimes for a lifetime. Healing comes at a time when we realize we have choices in the process. Will you be an unwitting victim that cowers in a dark corner? Will you be an angry dragon, spitting fire at those in view? Or, will you be the defiant warrior who fights the anguish with every ounce of your being? These are the choices you face.

As you face life's battles, remember the profound words of Eleanor Roosevelt, who said, "Anger is only one letter short of danger." Staying in the anger mode too long can cause serious emotional and physical health problems. Anger also does not allow you to honor the spirit of your loved one, or the needs of your own soul. It can cloud your view, making it impossible to see past the red haze, through to the light at the end of the tunnel.

According to Joan Borysenko, M.D., a popular motivational speaker and author of *Minding the Body, Mending the Mind* and *A Woman's Journey to God*, "The most remarkable thing about death is its insistence on harvesting life's meaning even in those not prone to introspection."

We can learn many lessons from those who have experienced grief and have broken free from its grasp. Their wisdom can help us on many different levels, not just when dealing with loss. If we allow them, they can teach us from their example that life is to be enjoyed, and loved ones are to be appreciated. They have confirmed for us that the journey truly is the reward.

The Journey Continues:

Moving on after loss

"Well begun, is half done."

Why do things happen when they happen? What is Heaven like? What is the true meaning of life? We can toil and contemplate such complex questions for a lifetime, but we will still be left with no answers, only more questions. As with many things in life, sometimes we discover that knowing all the answers is not what's really important.

Finding the meaning of life, for example, is not nearly as important as finding meaning in each day. Obsessing about Heaven may cause you to miss parts of it here on Earth. And we all know that second-guessing fate can be a waste of valuable mental energy.

Life provides us with many opportunities and challenges. The loss of a loved one is just one part of the complicated mix of events, personalities, personal awakenings, parties, trials, and tribulations that we face during our lives, however long or short that life may be. Life is certainly a package deal with few ala carte options available. While it would be nice to pick and choose your life events, that's just not possible. After all, that would result in far too many lottery winners.

If you believe "The Journey is The Reward", you will want

to celebrate all aspects of the journey. If you are riding a bike, for example, the flat roads may be easier, but they won't make your leg muscles any stronger. In fact, if your muscles are not used, they will atrophy, or waste away and deteriorate.

Just as exercise strengthens muscles, researchers have found that mental challenges strengthen the brain. Scientists have documented that elderly patients who read more frequently have a better chance of keeping their communication skills strong, continue to learn as they age, and have a far less chance of developing senile dementia, or brain atrophy.

Perhaps researchers will someday find that appreciation of life is the mechanism that keeps the soul alive. It may be discovered that tapping into our spirit helps reduce soul atrophy. That would be the most important discovery of all.

As the LaViolettes continue on their journey, they have incorporated the spirit of their lost loved one into their daily lives and their future dreams. They nourish their souls with Brian's spirit as they continue to support each other along the way.

Kim

A future filled with hope

Looking to the future can be difficult, because we never know exactly what will happen. When I look forward, I hope to have a good job, children, and a loving family. It may sound corny, but that's really what I hope for the most. I also hope I can have the opportunity to travel and meet a lot of different people. If none of that happens, however, I hope I find something else that makes me happy.

Brian wrote in his journal that "First, above anything else, I want to be happy..." That is my sentiment exactly. Life is too short not to take full advantage of each day. I have learned early on that things can change in an instant. That's why I am focused on living life to the fullest.

"The Journey is The Reward" is such a fitting saying. Not only does it make me think of my brother, it reminds me that life is full of so many ups and downs. No matter what part of the journey you're on—good or bad—you can always get something from it. To me, "The Journey is The Reward" inspires me to do something good with each day and my life.

Renee

New dreams

After the accident, I honestly didn't think I would make it through. Deep down, I thought if I ever do make it through, I certainly would never be happy again. But today, I feel differently.

When we were writing this book, I told Karolyn how happy I was before the accident. I shared with her the time I was driving in the car and actually said, "Life is good." She asked if I have felt that way since the accident. No, I have not. But that's not to say I have not experienced happiness. It's just that that exact same feeling will never be here because Brian isn't here.

When Brian died, our dreams, hopes, and aspirations for him also died. But over the years, we have replaced those dreams, with new ones. The Foundation has now taken its rightful place in our hearts, never to replace, it is there to honor his memory in a positive way. But most of all, I look forward to helping our daughter accomplish her dreams and aspirations. I am eager to see her find happiness in her relationship, as well as her career. And I am hopeful for the day we are blessed with healthy grandchildren.

Today, Doug and I enjoy an active life with family and friends. While the Foundation keeps us busy, we are able to sit back and appreciate the little things life has to give us. We take each day as a gift and try to enjoy it fully. And we have gained strength in knowing that we made it through the horror of losing a child. Even on the worst of days, you realize deep down that you can make it through because of that strength.

Doug

Looking forward to a bright future

Today, our future revolves around our daughter and the Foundation. We are really looking forward to helping Kim along her journey. As parents, we want her to experience all life has to offer. We also want to ensure Brian's spirit touches the scholarship recipients and that the Foundation continues to help young people.

As the three of us move forward, we know that Brian's soul will continue to guide us as we reach new heights in his name and spirit.

After the death of their son and brother, Doug, Renee, and Kim found it difficult to look forward, to look beyond the pain. It was as if they were trapped with nothing to propel them. For years, they drifted. But today, things are different. Their son's spirit inspires and strengthens them as they set a new course.

Egyptian mythology features a popular story about a beautiful bird called a Phoenix. It is said that the Phoenix lived in the desert for 500 years and then was consumed by fire, only to later rise from the ashes.

Your personal power to create a fulfilling, peaceful, happy life is like that Phoenix rising from the ashes. There is a beautiful bird in each one of us just waiting to soar.

Realizing that we have choices, even when things seem out of control, is the first step toward finding fulfillment. According to best-selling author, Gary Zukav, "Even if you are feeling empty or lost, you are meant to live a joyful, fulfilling life...Open your heart to what you are feeling and you can heal yourself."

Living life to its fullest is a conscious choice we all can make. We have the ability to turn tragedy into triumph or despair into a deeper appreciation of life. The power lies within each one of us. Finding meaning and purpose in our lives is determined by our ability to tap into that personal power.

Ralph Waldo Emerson said it best when he wrote: "What lies behind us and what lies before us are tiny matters compared to what lies within us."

Epilogue

September 11, 2001

As this book was nearing completion, the world was struck by a profound tragedy. On Sept. 11, 2001, terrorist attacks on the United States killed thousands of innocent people. This most horrific event has affected the lives of all people living freely in our modern world and has struck terror and grief in the hearts of Americans everywhere.

Through this profoundly devastating tragedy, we have witnessed the heroic actions of our fire and rescue personnel, our police force, our friends and our neighbors. And we have seen firsthand the true power of the human spirit.

One of those who witnessed the terrorism inflicted on New York City was a friend and former soccer teammate of Brian's, Joel Blecha. Joel was in his first week of teaching third grade at a public school in Brooklyn when the hijacked airliners struck the World Trade Center's twin towers. His school was just across the East River from Lower Manhattan.

He watched with horror through his classroom window as the smoke and flames shot into the sky and the towers collapsed onto themselves. He worked to calm the fears of his students, some who had relatives working in Manhattan.

We thought of Joel then and of the heartfelt letter he sent to us a few years earlier, in the spring of 1998, during his sophomore year at the University of Wisconsin-Madison.

Here was Joel's message to us:

Dear LaViolettes,

Greetings to you from the dressing room of a political play I'm acting in here in Madison.

I began my busy week of classes, exams and rehearsals with the making of a panic attack. On a whim, I left a lecture to attend a noon campus church service. Sitting there in Mass, I just opened myself up to God, hoping to find some direction…some clarity.

God sent a messenger. That messenger was Brian. "The Journey is the Reward," he told me. When I remembered that lesson –those eternally wonderful words of wisdom – I found clarity, and my heart was at ease. I wasn't going to be defeated by stress.

Instead, I looked at this week as an adventure, a challenge, something to revel in and enjoy, not to conquer me…no. It's that struggle and adventure filled with both smiles and tears that I will always remember. It makes the end result that much more gratifying when you can look back on that tumultuous road and feel proud.

On opening night of the performance, I made a card for each cast member with the words, "The Journey is The Reward…tonight the journey continues."

I am convinced that Brian was put on earth for a definite reason. I am so blessed to have known him, and to have considered him a friend. Each night before I go on stage, I think of Brian and whisper, "This one's for you, buddy!"

Love and peace, Joel Blecha

What a touching reminder of how Brian has influenced many lives.

Finally, we offer our thoughts and prayers to those who have lost family and friends to the intense acts of violence on Sept. 11, 2001. We share our admiration and praise for those heroes among us who have risked their own lives to save the lives of others. It is in their honor that we reaffirm our belief that "The Journey is The Reward."

Appendix A

Brian LaViolette Scholarship Foundation

Brian LaViolette
Scholarship Foundation

1135 Pleasant Valley Dr.
Oneida, WI 54115
(920) 405-9929
fax (920) 405-9928
e-mail tjitr@aol.com
www.briansjourney.com

THE JOURNEY IS THE REWARD

Proceeds from the sale of this book go directly to the Brian LaViolette Scholarship Foundation, a 501 3(C) non-profit organization. If you would like to make an additional donation, send a check or money order to the above address.

Manufactured by Amazon.ca
Bolton, ON

23445841R00081

A dark fantasy novella

the summoner's cry

ANA C. REIS

Print ISBN: 978-2-9579401-1-0
Legal Deposit: DLE-20211122-78375

Kindle ISBN: 978-2-9579401-0-3
Epub ISBN: 978-2-9579401-2-7

Cover designer: Saint Jupiter
Chapter headings and title page designer: Saint Jupiter
Editor: Jess Lawrence
Beta-readers: Day Leitao, Catarina Pinto, Carolina Gonçalves

Connect with the author

Instagram
@anareis.poweredbybooks

Twitter
@poweredbybooks_

Facebook
@poweredbybooks

For my grandparents, who taught me
how to be strong and gentle

"We honor our parents by carrying their
best forward and laying the rest down.
By fighting and taming the demons that
laid them low and now reside in us."

— *Bruce Springsteen, Born to Run*

TRIGGER WARNINGS

THE SUMMONER'S CRY contains instances of graphic violence, adult language, blood, death, and discrimination. If these topics are sensitive for you, please read with care.

Author's Note

Dear reader,

Thank you for reading The Summoner's Cry. This is a self-published book. Even though great care has been given to revising and editing this novella, some mistakes may have slipped through. If you spot any grammatical errors and typos, please contact me via email.

This book also contains some elements of the Portuguese culture and tradition namely the consumption of *aguardente* which literally translates as burning water - a popular alcoholic beverage obtained by fermentation and distillation of sugared or sweet musts, vegetable macerations, or mixtures of the two.

A Portuguese saying and a glimpse into the everyday life of traditional fishing communities are also included in this book with additional explanations when needed.

The use of *Kunai* throughout this story, short Japanese blades typically associated with ninja, is meant to honor the anime series - Naruto - that has played a huge influence in my life.

Happy reading,

Ana C. Reis

anareis@poweredbybooks.com

Prologue

Lilith peered at the crystalline waters and was not displeased by her reflection.

Irises stained a deep crimson that matched her plump lips. A soft glow irradiated from her pale skin. Feral black hair intertwined with fragments of bone from her enemies.

Not all of it was nice, though. There were hungry bags under her eyes, too. A consequence of the months spent underground healing, waiting, trembling with rage. Soon, she would have to go to the surface to replenish, and then the hunt could begin.

For the time being, she marveled a little longer at her reflection. Clawing her way back from the edge had left its marks on her body, and she was enraptured by them.

She was not quite who she used to be. But it was hard to say if she was a witch, a demon, or a goddess. She thought about it while licking her dry lips. And then the answer hit her. Godhood fit like a black velvet dress, and she would wear it like an armor.

Walking away from the natural pool and her newly discovered nature, a pang of pain made her shudder. She leaned against the cold rock to steady herself.

First the shock, then the humiliation. She cursed into the empty cave, and her rough voice reverberated through the slimy walls. She had underestimated the damage inflicted upon her, and her patience was running dry.

Months had passed since she had been forced to hide like vermin in a cold underwater cavern. Cut off from the kingdom and throne she had sat upon for centuries. All because of a sad creature she had raised as her own.

If she thought carefully, the signs had been there from the very beginning. A propensity for rebellion. A heart too human to kill without mercy. But pride and love had blinded Lilith, and because of that, she had let the weeds grow and fester.

None of that mattered now.

A crooked smile surfaced on the face of the newborn goddess. She would use that anguish to recreate herself, and the effort would only make her revenge all the sweeter.

CHAPTER ONE

The Woman Who Was Born Twice

I picked up the delivery box, locked the door behind me, and wrapped my thin scarf over my nose.

Cold no longer bothered me, but pretending it still did gave me a fleeting sense of belonging and, most of all, it muffled the shouts of fishers and dockworkers echoing through the thick fog.

They were only trying to get their boats safely back to the harbor. But their shouts reminded me of other nights filled with terrors and made my medallion feel heavier than it should. I touched it warily, hidden beneath my wool sweater, and hurried through the docks, trying to leave my grim thoughts behind.

Surely this fog was playing tricks with my mind, or maybe it just reminded me too much of home. The place where I had been born twice, amid pools of blood and piercing cries. I could never return there because everything that happens twice is bound to happen again, and I wasn't ready to face it. Not until I fulfilled my promise to Adam. Not until I broke his curse.

Less than a year had passed since Adam and I arrived at Latis Island, a beacon for tourists whose definition of the supernatural had been ripped out of a children's book. I couldn't care less about their bizarre superstitions, but after months of chasing shadows, I was beginning to wonder if there wasn't a ring of truth to their tales. At this point, hope was my only sustenance.

Locals believed we were a family of misfits and runaways and we saw no reason to deny it. It wasn't such a wild stretch. Adam appeared to be on the verge of puberty, and I could pretend to be his young guardian. Albeit a very careless one.

A tattoo of a dragon spread from the tip of his fingers to his left cheek, imbued Adam's pale skin with a mixture of black, orange, and crimson. My brown skin wasn't any less odd, but instead of tattoos, I had a collection of scars. Not deep enough to be visible from a distance, but sufficient to keep people from asking awkward questions.

But then again, I doubted we needed any kind of pretense to fit into this place. It was Latis' thick veil of weirdness that allowed us to hide in plain sight. Truth be told, I had never felt so plain and normal in my life.

The locals were simple, feral, and practical. Nothing like the horde of tourists that visited the island each summer, eager to quench their thirst for a watered-down version of the supernatural. Living among Latis' strange inhabitants, sharing their bread and butter, caring about their insignificant little troubles, made it easy to believe we could make a home of this place. But it was when I shook with terror and lay awake in the dead of the night that I remembered why we could never again settle on this earth.

I was trapped in limbo. Too strange to be human. Too frail to be whatever I had been in the past. Never in my long life had I met someone like me; I only knew what I really was from old stories.

I was not a witch. Although I had earned my place among them and managed to learn a little trick or two. But what I did wasn't magic. It was a way of willing Spirits into existence, of summoning beasts lurking beneath the fabric of reality.

It was useless to think about that now because most of it was gone, shattered by a cascade of shitty decisions. The only Spirit I could still summon was trapped in someone else's body, and extracting it would get its host killed.

I eyed my surroundings cautiously. The fog brought another layer of blindness to my already scrambled perception. Halfway across the harbor, I almost crashed into a shape and the heavy delivery box nearly slipped from my grip. Before I could stop myself, a loud "Who goes there?" escaped my tight lips. I almost drew my blades alongside it.

"Lau, dear!" a familiar voice said.

My muscles relaxed in a heartbeat. "Saul!" I said, feeling embarrassed by my reaction. "How are you? It's a bit dangerous to be so close to the water in this weather."

The old man raised his hands in defeat, as if I'd just caught him doing mischief. "Alright, alright, ya worry too much, Lau. I'm an old man, ya know." He winked. "I've lived a long and fulfilling life. No point in being too careful just to stretch my life by a couple of years. Might as well not live at all." His smile was broad and filled with sunshine.

I hated when he said those things, but I didn't press him further. The townsfolk already called me Old Sister when they thought I wasn't listening, and they didn't mean it in a good way. It took me a heartbeat to notice the pouch of Latis' smelling salts on Saul's hands. He had drawn a near-perfect line at the entrance of his boat, almost as a warning for unwanted visitors. "What could you possibly need so badly that couldn't wait 'til morning?"

He laughed heartily and the tension that had been building around my shoulders lifted. When his chuckles dissolved, a worried expression took hold of his features. "I was looking for ya, gal! Help this old man one more time, will you?"

I smiled, knowing well what he was talking about. "Alright, but only if you tell me what the hell is going on here." I pointed to the salt at his feet.

He looked puzzled at first, but quickly turned his attention to the fog that thickened around us. "One can never be too careful with this weather," he said, then snickered.

It sounded so unlike him. It made me shiver. I waited for him to elaborate, but he stepped onto the deck as if he had just stated the obvious and left me chewing on my thoughts. I rolled my eyes and sighed, glanced one last time at the dark line of salt at my feet, and stepped inside his floating home.

He had fashioned it after one of the many local stories. Sirens' tails decorated the hull, and the prow had been shaped in the form of a female fisher carrying a lamp while pointing towards the horizon. *Carlota*, the Brave. One of the rumored founders of the town.

Saul gestured at the table when we entered the cabin. Coffee was brewing on the stove and the unmistakable smell of cinnamon buns filled the air. It felt like home here, as much as I hated admitting it. Better than home, actually.

The letter was on the table alongside pictures of smiling young children. Once I sat, I couldn't help staring at them and a strange longing swelled in my chest. When Saul put the mugs of coffee down and sat in front of me, I was lost in thought.

Like his grandchildren, I had lost my mother too soon. The most vivid memory I had of her was as still as a picture. She sat on a bench, unsmiling. Her skin had been a shade darker than mine, but we shared the same golden eyes and a nose too big for our faces. In my mother's case, that nose had failed to spoil her beauty; I wasn't so sure about mine.

"They've grown," I said, trying to shake the longing.

"Yes," he said in a quiet tone.

"Will they come this summer? You think I could meet them then?" The words flew from my mouth before I could quench them.

"I'm counting on it, gal. I even talked to Sally about renting a little room at her inn. *Carlota* isn't big enough for all of us," he said, referring to his boat.

"Are you sure you want your grandchildren near the town's most boisterous fishers?"

He chuckled. "Those idiots helped me raise their mother," he said. "Besides, ya know how much Sally is dying to meet the kids…"

He gripped his mug and stared into the distance. Sadness drew deep lines in his face. If he knew how

much I wanted to stand up and hug him right now, he would laugh at me. Instead, I picked up the letter and read it aloud, translating its contents in the process.

Two cinnamon buns had found their way into my stomach by the time I finished penning Saul's reply. In all these years, he never learned how to speak or write in French. But he also never doubted he would one day convince his grandchildren and son-in-law to visit him.

It looked like Saul's persistence was about to pay off, and that made me feel like a coward. Deep down, I knew I wasn't going to be around to witness it.

CHAPTER TWO

The Heart of a Pirate

The high season was almost upon us, and the weather would soon be bearable enough for the mainlanders. A few of them already ventured to the island, hoping to quell their silly thirst for adventure. In a few more weeks, many more would follow and would soon pester the narrow streets of the town I'd come to love.

How I hated them for it.

I liked the quiet, the cold, and the harshness of these people. Their feral nature was refreshing compared to the countless feigned friendships that had almost got Adam and I killed.

When I left Saul's *Carlota*, the fog had thickened, casting imaginary dangers in the back of my mind. For some reason, I found myself squeezing the small pouch of salt Saul had slipped into my jacket. The old man had tried to be discrete about the deed because he knew I would mock his gift, but he had been so obvious I had to pinch myself to avoid laughing in his face.

Thoughts of Saul's warm kindness filled my head as I

made my way towards the Fishers' Guild. The sound of metal sliding and crashing echoed around me as others closed their workshops for the day. Their eyes shone with something akin to terror; I wondered if it had anything to do with the fog and whatever terrors they believed it held.

Their superstition was probably rubbing off on me because the more I looked at my surroundings, the more terrifying they seemed. Adam would taunt me for sympathizing with the locals and their superstitions, but there was something unnatural about this fog. It was thicker than it had any right to be. It crept into our bones and wrecked us from within. No amount of wool sweaters could prevent that. Only a bottle of the island's strongest *aguardente* would. Luckily for me, Jeff had a surplus of those in his storage room. And he was always too drunk to keep track of his inventory.

A smug smile forced its way to my lips, and then Sally's voice reached me.

Even though I still hadn't mastered the dialect, her songs were like a balm to my soul. The melody pierced the thick fog like a hot blade.

"Oi Oi, Sally," I howled.

"Oi, Lau! It's a bit late to be wandering around, don't ya think?" She had been cleaning her fishing tools and gutting knife at the entrance of her guild. As I approached, the colors grew more vivid around her, heightened by her furious red hair. "Did that hoarder make ya close the workshop again?"

"You know Jeff," I said. "I swear the bastard can smell easy money in the air. He took off as soon as the fishers brought the mainlanders to shore. 'Money to be made,' he said."

"I think he meant money to be lost." We both laughed at that. Her voluptuous giggles enveloped me and almost made me forget about the vicious fog.

When we both caught our breath, I passed her the box filled with bottles of *aguardente* and noticed the thick line of salt encircling the entrance to the guild.

"Have any more rounds today?" she asked, picking up the box with an unusual agility for a woman her age.

I shook my head. "Na, today's just you. Er… what's with the salt?" I asked.

She stared at me as if I'd just asked her why the sky was blue. "For protection. What else?"

I fought the urge to roll my eyes. "Protection from what?"

"Are ya sure ya wanna go down that path again?" Sally whistled without bothering to look me in the eye. *She's still mad*, I realized. My skepticism was common knowledge among the townsfolk, but maybe I'd been a bit too enthusiastic about it the other night. In my defense, Sally had started the whole thing when she picked up that ancient bottle of whisky and decided telling ghost stories around candlelight was a great way to spend a stormy night.

I lifted my hands in defeat. "I won't laugh," I said, and when she turned to look at me, I added, "I swear."

She gave me one of those looks that made my stomach twist. "Fog always draws the worst creatures." Her features twisted with disgust. "They crawl like cowards, trying to find their way inside. The salt will burn them if they try to cross these lines. And don't look at me like that, there's nothing wrong with being prepared."

There was no fear in her eyes, only wariness. I'd seen her use that look on obnoxious tourists, and I didn't

want to be the one receiving it. I cleared my throat and changed the subject. "Where's Adam, by the way?"

"I sent him home earlier. The kid deserves a break." Sally's gaze softened, as it always did whenever we talked about her protégé.

"Why is that?" I asked, unable to conceal my surprise.

"He's been busting his ass off, that's why." She placed the box into a small cart. Nobody owned a car on the island. Nobody needed one. It would be a nightmare to fit them into the town's narrow streets and a terror to trade with the mainland for gas and car parts. "He's been mending and patching fishing nets since the sun came up this morning. He's good, you know. Julien has been talking about promoting him." A hint of pride touched her voice.

"Is that so?" For some reason, it was hard picturing Adam enjoying manual labor. "And Adam's happy about it?" I asked, trying to hide my feelings of betrayal. Our relationship had been strained lately. Fatigue and despair had been driving us apart, like two planets cast in opposite directions by a supernova's blast. But I hadn't expected him to find some comfort here and, worst of all, not tell me about it.

"Happy? I'd say he's content. But the kid's a fucking genius, I'm telling you. He might even become a Guild Master sooner than anyone that has ever joined our ranks." She proudly displayed the Crest sewn on her right sleeve. I raised my eyebrows. "What, ya don't believe me?"

"Oh, c'mon, I didn't say anything! It's just…"

"Ya worried we start taking the kid on our fishing trips?" She picked up a hose and started rinsing her tools,

turning her back to me.

"Maybe…"

"He'll be alright," Sally said. "Besides, I don't think that'll happen soon."

"Why is that?"

"Old age has turned Julien into a prick."

"Wait, what?" I chuckled. "What does that got to do with anything?"

"Julien is always complaining that the damn kid is too good-looking. If you ask me, he's jealous of the mob of silly girls that come to watch yar kid work every day. You should hear their giggles when he takes off his shirt!"

Nothing I hadn't witnessed before Lilith had shattered our lives into a million pieces. But I blushed regardless and hoped the fog concealed the crimson in my cheeks from Sally's eyes.

To my relief, she changed the subject. "Have you eaten, girl? I swear you keep getting thinner."

"I'm eating all right." I chuckled. Sally's motherly instincts emerged in the strangest moments.

She hummed and gave me one of those 'I don't believe a word you just said' looks and vanished through the entrance of the Fishers' Guild. With surprising stealth for a woman her size, Sally returned holding a cream package. She dropped it in my arms with a wink.

"Sally, I can't," I started.

She shushed me and grabbed me by the arm, pulling me away from the fence. "Ya idiot, stop behaving like an outsider. Ya're one of us now. Embrace it. Can't keep living yar life like every place you set foot on is temporary. Someday, ya gotta start taking roots. Might

as well do it here." She winked. "Maybe ya'll even start believing our tales!"

Inside, my heart wrecked. Putting down roots would get me killed. My past had claws and cunning, and it would not rest until I'd been torn to shreds. For Sally's sake, I forced a smile.

"Tell Jeff I'm gonna need you for a fishing trip next week," Sally continued, deaf to my inner struggle.

"In this weather?"

"You think *Alice* can't handle a bit of fog?" she said, referring to her illustrious little boat.

I shook my head and raised my arms in defeat. "I believe *Alice* and her owner could sail to Hell and back without batting an eyelid."

"Really?" The old woman placed her hands on her hips. Her pose and unruly red hair made her look more like a pirate than the fisher she was.

I chuckled. "Really!"

A smug smile appeared on her face and before I knew it, she was pulling me into a bear hug. "There, there." She patted my back, and I dared to dwell on the warmth of her embrace as I hadn't in decades. Something about Sally always nudged the part of me that was still inexplicably human. No matter how many years passed, I couldn't truly bury the scared little girl I'd once been. She pulled me away gently. "Off ya go."

I winked and walked away with a soft smile on my face. Being around her made me feel safe, and I'd forgotten how right it was.

The red-haired fisher had been there the day Adam and I first laid eyes upon this strange land. Perhaps it had been our strangeness to bring us together. We bonded

in an instant over a bottle of *aguardente* and a plate of grilled fish with lemon.

Maybe I was finally getting soft. But I should know better. Softness was the last thing we needed if we wanted to survive.

CHAPTER THREE

The Boy Who Lost the World

Oblivious to the bizarre fog, Adam was sitting on a bench across from the town hall. Old dark buildings higher than any tree cut off the sunlight that touched the island after midday. This had been Adam's favorite spot since we'd arrived. I never understood why, because all I ever felt here was an impending sense of doom.

But Adam fit into the scenery perfectly. He had tied his dark hair in a samurai bun, drawing attention to the dragon tattoo on his neck. As I crossed the gardens to meet him, two giggling girls passed by. Arm-in-arm, they whispered in each other's ears while stealing glances at Adam.

When they saw me, their cheeks turned a deep crimson, and they dashed across the gardens, laughing even harder than before. A rowdy chuckle escaped my lips. How good it was to be young, foolish, and unscarred. Unfortunately for them, Adam was neither.

As I drew closer, the dragon trapped in his skin gleamed angrily. His black claws stretched towards

Adam's mouth, and a smirk danced around his white fangs. That was never a good sign. I groaned. Enduring Adam's foul mood on top of the crazy weather was not the soiree I had in mind.

His brows furrowed as he scanned the contents of an old book. He looked like a kid enjoying a good story, but I knew differently. He was connected to life and death around him as I had never been. He sensed me a mile ago, but whatever that book contained, it was good enough to hold his interest. I just hoped it was more substantial than the shadows we'd been chasing these past few months.

The book looked odd, unlike any book I'd seen him reading since we'd arrived. Dirt soiled its cover to the point where it was impossible to guess its original color. As if Adam had dug the darn thing out of a graveyard. Whatever happened, I preferred to be spared the details.

By the time I sat beside him in silence, the fog had mutated into something much more vicious. Everything was a blur except for the bench we were sitting on, Adam, and his vibrant tattoo.

I searched my backpack for the bottle of *aguardente*, two paper cups, bread, and Sally's grilled fish. Adam continued glaring at the book, perhaps expecting to eke out its secrets.

"The weather looks exquisite today." I beamed, taking a piece of bread and stashing the warm fish within.

He barely registered the irony. "You're late," he said, without meeting my eyes.

I ignored his bitter tone and threw him a piece of bread. The bastard caught it between his long fingers without looking up. He placed the soiled book on his

lap and reached for the remaining fish.

"And you sound like an arrogant brat. You should thank me for bringing you dinner. Most of us don't have the luxury of sitting around reading old books," I spat.

He ignored my remark and dug his teeth into the sandwich. For a long moment, he savored the food with closed eyes.

I wanted to tell him I knew our lack of progress frustrated him. I wanted to scream that perhaps it was time for us to move on, but I nibbled my dinner instead. My stupidity had dumped us here. If only I'd been able to undo his curse back then, none of this would have happened. If I had been skilled enough, Adam would still have his body and his world.

We could be recruiting witches to our cause or seizing Lilith's throne for ourselves. Instead, we were running like rats from a storm. Latching our hope to the one thing that could save us from this mess – Adam's grimoire, which refused to be found.

After an uncomfortable minute of silence, I changed topics. "Found anything useful today?" I pointed to the book on his lap.

"You mean… have I found a way to free both of us without killing either of us in the process? No, I haven't." The dragon trapped in his skin glimmered in reply. We hadn't spoken his name out loud in ages. "I'm tired, Lau. I think wicked ghosts are playing tricks with our minds," he added in a hushed tone.

This was my chance. I cleared my throat, filled the paper cups with Jeff's yellowish *aguardente*, and handed one of them to Adam. Jeff could be the town's drunk, but he was also its finest liquor producer. When he was sober, at least.

Surprisingly, Adam took the cup, our fingers brushing lightly, and he looked me in the eye for the first time since I'd arrived. I raised the cup in reply and said, "To us, the finest witches the world has never seen!"

He chuckled. "To us!"

We drank the cold liquor in a single gulp. Adam's eyes sparkled and his cheeks turned pink.

"That was interesting," he said. "That's not Jeff's usual."

"No." I smiled. "I added something special."

"Oh, you're using me as your guinea pig?"

"Wouldn't be the first time," I said. We both laughed.

He had the same rough laugh I remembered. It made me feel vulnerable in a way I did not hate. I could swear it had been ages since I last heard him giggle.

"You like it here, don't you?" I asked, my brain still struggling to wrap itself around the idea of Adam enjoying a peaceful and near-normal life.

He sat very still and straight, gripping the paper cup with both hands. I could almost picture the man he'd been before the curse turned him into a child. "Well, we can't really leave with this weather." He chuckled nervously and then I knew I'd hit a nerve. Adam was never nervous.

"Sally is planning a fishing trip soon and she might give us a ride back to the continent then," I said, preparing myself to express the idea that had been wrecking my mind for the past few weeks. "Maybe we need to face the facts." My voice trembled. "Maybe your grimoire isn't here. Could it have been moved?"

Adam was quiet for a while, and I refilled our cups, trying to ease my nerves. Tension was palpable in the air, so solid I could almost touch it. "Aren't you tired,

Lau?" he said. Vicious fear stirred in my soul. "Don't you ever think of just… stopping?"

Anger and surprise mingled in my chest. I took a deep breath. "What do you mean?" I say, trying to hide the bitterness that wrecked me from within.

"I mean, just stopping…" I glanced at him. He was still holding the cup and staring at its contents as one stares at the skies on clear summer nights.

"There's no stopping for people like us." My jaw tightened. I sounded every bit like the Lau I used to be and I hated myself for it. "We don't have the luxury of craving a normal life." *No matter how much we want it*, I thought, but did not say. "You won't grow up, Adam. Even if we stay, people will notice and they will fear you… and you know what fear does to humans." *Look what it did to us.* I swallowed.

"I'm not a fool. I know we can't stay here forever. But…" He blushed slightly, and it took me a while to recognize the excitement in his voice. "Even if my grimoire isn't here, there's something odd about this island. Can't you feel it?" His eyes sparkled.

I shook my head. "It's just a sad little rock in the middle of an ocean."

"I thought the same at first, but then I started noticing the small things. They were so insignificant I almost dismissed them. Until I couldn't ignore them anymore…" His voice trailed off.

"Adam, what are you talking about?" Was he going insane? Was the dragon I'd trapped in his body to save his life driving him mad?

A smile settled on his face. He stood and fixed his gaze on me. I moved uncomfortably as unease lodged

itself in the pit of my stomach. "I can do magic again," he said in hushed tones. "Nothing complicated nor useful for now. But it's still magic and I'm getting better at it." I must have stared at him as if he'd transfigured into a bird because he didn't let me speak. "It's true, Lau. In a few months, I may be able to practice more complex spells, and then we can…"

"Wait!" Exasperation tainted my voice. "How long have you known this?"

He lowered his eyes. "A few weeks after our arrival…" His voice was barely a whisper.

My breath quickened. "We've been here for months!"

"I wanted to be sure."

I covered my face with my hands and swallowed the resentment I wanted to throw at him. Had I been naïve to trust him?

"Do you not… trust me? After all we've been through?" I asked through my clenched jaw.

"With my life," he said. Those words nudged at the knot of frustration in my chest.

"Then why? Why didn't you tell me before? Are you… What do you…?" I inhaled deeply and then the words were out of my mouth before I could stop them. "Do you hate me for what I did to you?"

He exhaled, and suddenly I could almost see the bundle of pain he had been carrying since that night. "I don't hate you. I just… can't stand the way you look at me." He averted his eyes and a violent crimson claimed his cheeks. "Like I'm made of glass. Ready to break at the smallest provocation. I don't want you to babysit me anymore."

"You want me to leave?" I blurted. He refused to

look at me. Hot, painful tears stung my eyes. I stood in haste. I would not let him see me cry. "You always got what you wanted," I said, feeling discarded and lonelier than ever. Bitterness clawed its way up my chest and I swallowed it as hard as I could.

"Not always," he said, looking torn. He opened his mouth to speak and then closed it again.

I glared at him and picked up my backpack. "As you wish, my Lord," I spat, bowing and turning to leave. Before I could take two steps, Adam grabbed my wrist.

"Stay," he said, so softly I would later think I'd imagined it. I turned to face him and I thought I'd seen yearning in his eyes.

But before any of us could speak, a harrowing scream pierced the night.

CHAPTER FOUR

An Unwanted Visitor

I'd learned from ancient texts that every summoner has a token that links her to the Spirit world.

The medallion was mine. Winding silver ropes binding a large garnet. Crimson like my mother's blood when I'd taken the medallion from her corpse.

That day, I summoned a Spirit for the first time. Vanara, a one-thousand-pound gorilla with green feral eyes. Confused, I watched in terror as he crushed the robber that had taken my mother's life. I was twelve years old.

Spirits still allowed me a glimpse into their world, but it never lasted more than a heartbeat. Fear always made me more aware of their presence. But they wouldn't let me bring them into the flesh world until I fixed my mistake.

When the scream pierced the atmosphere, the Spirits were the first thing I saw. So close, I could almost touch them, and, at the same time, so far away. They vanished in the blink of an eye and, for a moment, I was blind. All

I could hear was my pounding heart.

I turned to Adam for guidance, but he was staring at something I could not see. Eyes wide open and livid, he seemed to have given in to despair. Only the dragon appeared to be enjoying the moment by the look in his bloodthirsty eyes.

I drew my *Kunai* and its familiar weight brought me back to reality. Eons might have elapsed since I last used them in a proper fight. My mind could struggle, but my muscles remembered.

I shielded Adam with my body, inhaled the stale evening air, and fell into my favorite stance. Blade held behind my back, my other hand pointing at the ground in front of me. Humans called it the ambush stance, and I excelled at it. After all, I had been trained by a trickster.

A heartbeat later, the fog shifted as something heavy and unnatural cut through it. Then the smell reached us. Spices and filth mixed in a nauseating perfume. My skin crawled as realization hit me.

It couldn't be. A demon.

What was it doing here? How had it eluded my protection spells? Was I that weak?

I craned my neck in Adam's direction and whispered a silent question. Did he let it through?

He shook his head, some color finally returning to his cheeks.

I tightened my grip on the *Kunai* and turned to face the demon. No matter how many times I'd seen one, I never got used to the creatures. They corrupted the definition of the supernatural.

Part of me believed they would respect the Treaty my kin had used to bind them with blood, bone, and

magic. Another part of me didn't want to bet our lives on it.

What if they knew about the price on our heads? Would the Treaty protect us or hasten their attack? Demons liked to bend the rules, and one should never forget how much they craved witch blood. Even tainted blood like ours would be hard for them to resist. Especially if we were right there for the taking.

In vain, I tried recalling the ancient spells we used to repel them. We'd spent so many decades fighting and killing other witches, I'd forgotten they were not our only enemies. The faint memories kept slipping from my mind until it was too late. While my brain frantically searched for an answer, the demon reached the gardens. My ears popped as he broke free from the fog.

I muffled a scream.

His appearance was as repulsive as his smell. It was taller than any demon I had ever seen and a dark cloak covered in white runes concealed its massive body. Only a crooked nose and nine-fingered hands remained in plain sight.

"Oi," I howled. My throat burned at the contact with his powerful smell.

His head snapped in my direction, and I took the chance to move away from Adam. Killing a demon would be messy, especially one this big. There was no need for Adam to get involved in the fight.

I had enough *Kunai* in my pocket to keep the creature distracted, but I was going to have to touch his skin for the finishing blow. When he shrieked again, I threw the first *Kunai* directly into his eyes.

He dodged it easily, but I was already throwing my

second. This time, I didn't miss. The blade buried deep into what I hoped was his right eye socket.

My jaw tightened as I waited for the beast to scream in pain. But he never did.

Instead, he grabbed the *Kunai* with his dirty hand and threw it at the ground.

Sweat burst from my skin and a gasp escaped my pursed lips. It shouldn't be possible. Those blades had been infused with magic. He shouldn't be able to touch it without burning. The demon lingered at the edge of the fog, glaring at me. And then he turned into a blur. My reaction came a second too late.

I tried to jump away, but the demon's fist buried into my jaw the minute my feet left the ground. My skull shook with the impact and I felt my body being tossed against a tree. I coughed blood and stood as fast as I could. The demon's next blow shattered the tree trunk behind me.

My vision was blurred from the blow. Adrenaline was the only thing keeping my senses sharp. The demon pursued me, unyielding, and I knew if the fight didn't end quickly, I would soon become dead meat.

Blinded, I climbed the town hall, a stupid and dangerous idea forming in the back of my mind. Through the blurriness, I spied the massive form of the demon climbing behind me at a slower pace and smiled. Demons had always been terrible climbers.

When I reached one of the towers of the town hall, I ran towards the light switch. I would return the courtesy to the beast and blind him momentarily with the electrical light. A moment of distraction was all I needed.

I heard his shallow breathing right before he reached

the top of the tower. In that second, I turned on the lights.

His scream was deafening and nauseating. I threw myself at him and pushed him out of the tower. I buried my fingers in his eye sockets and started chanting a simple spell. I would boil the beast from within.

As we fell, his dark nails pierced my skin. In the cacophony of noise, I didn't feel the ground approaching and jumped away a second before he crashed against the floor with a thud. I heard bones cracking and stone shattering as I landed a few feet away from him. I went to my knees, breathing hard, my skin burning with the fresh wounds.

Everything was silent for a while and I allowed myself a smile. But my enthusiasm was short-lived. Barely had the dust settled, the demon was already dragging himself to his feet.

His hood fell, revealing silvery skin pierced by a thousand scars, and a lipless mouth twisted into a grin. The beast screeched again in anticipation, and the shock wave pierced through my skull and raged against my body. I couldn't help but close my eyes.

When I opened them, his arms were stretched in my direction. I felt the bloodlust in his eyes. He would shred me to pieces. I grabbed a handful of *Kunai* and threw them at him.

He evaded every single one.

I cursed under my breath and reached for the medallion. I begged for the Spirits to come, but they remained deaf to my pleas. My throat tightened as a scream clawed its way from the depths of my being. Before I tried to force a tear in the veil of reality, Adam stepped in.

His tattoo shone in the darkness and his voice carried the weight of a thousand suns.

I ran to his side in time to see the demon crouching in pain. Before I could move to strike again, the massive creature turned and dissolved into the fog.

CHAPTER FIVE

A Restless Dragon

Adam collapsed the minute the demon disappeared. I caught him just in time.

He was thinner than the last time I'd held him. His breath came out in rags and sweat colonized his skin. My heart wracked at the sight of him.

The dragon glared at me from his nesting place on Adam's neck.

"I know," I whispered. After grabbing my backpack, I carried Adam across the gardens. The town's small church seemed as good a place as any to lay low for a while.

The fog had started dissipating by the time we reached the entrance, yet no sunlight touched its inner walls. Its stained glass windows had been placed too high. The tall basaltic walls culminated in an arch adorned with shards of blue glass. The place was supposed to be beautiful, but it had always made me uncomfortable.

Musty incense and cheap candle wax made the atmosphere hard to breathe. We had no choice but to

endure it; I could not carry Adam in my present state, nor could I risk another encounter with the demon prince without a plan.

I lowered Adam into the cushioned red steps of one of the side altars and placed his head on my lap. My hand trembled as I cleaned the beads of sweat on his forehead with my sleeve and my mind kept gravitating towards the same thought – *we have to get out of this place.*

Saint Andrew frowned upon us from the top of his wooden shrine. Fishing nets adorned his frail figure and a school of tuna swam at his feet. I snickered at him, stole the bread fishers had left as offering, and soaked a small piece in water.

Adam was feverish and murmured nonsense in his restless sleep. His dark hair was still dripping with sweat. I held the bread to his mouth, but he refused it. I had to swallow back my agony.

"Come on, Adam. You gotta fight this…" I begged. "Eat. It will make you feel better. Stay with me…"

If he's going to die, you should at least release me. An indolent voice spoke directly to my mind, rasping it in its wake.

Give me a chance, I begged in reply.

A chance to do what? The voice asked. I could feel his anger burning. *To run away? Do you mock me, summoner?* He uttered that last word with disdain.

My stomach twitched with shame and longing. "I do not," I spoke out loud, looking directly at the dragon ingrained in Adam's flesh.

You lured me. Lied to me. Trapped me in this body so you could save your little friend, he hissed. *You promised me this would be temporary.*

"We have a contract," I hissed in reply. "Don't you dragons have honor?"

We honor power, not weakness. Release me and I'll happily dig my claws into your enemy.

Fatigue overwhelmed me. The dragon ignored my heavy sigh and continued. *We used to be powerful, you and I.* His hoarse voice felt as soft as velvet in my mind. *You were the greatest summoner the world had seen in generations, and I was proud to be your Spirit. Now you're just this sad little human that jumps every time there's a rustle of leaves. All you ever think about is running with your tail between your legs. What happened to your courage?*

"I was not brave, you fool." I sighed and massaged my temples. It had been years since I had let him slip into my mind. "I was greedy and reckless, and it was killing everyone we crossed paths with. Until he came along…"

He burst out laughing, and it felt like being drawn into a thunderstorm.

In this world, we either kill or get killed. You're too old to believe otherwise. He snickered. *And how do you plan on taking us out of this mess, oh mighty summoner? Without my help, without your powers…?*

The medallion burned against my skin. Just a moment ago, the Spirit world had almost been within my reach. Now, I was blind and lonelier than ever. "It will be alright…" Courage failed me, and I could not meet his eyes.

If you release me, we can beat the demon. Together. Just like old times. Remember?

"And then what?" I burned with despair. "Have you forgotten who's hunting us? This demon is the least of our worries."

I have not. I was there the night you tried to rip off the Queen's head. I carried you and the Witch Lord out of that place. And made a pact with you on a hilltop. A pact I'll break if your life is endangered. Even though I no longer believe your life is worth saving.

I stared at him, and he glimmered in reply.

I wish there was an easy way out of this war. His voice sounded tired and sad. *But there isn't. You're not powerful enough to save everyone. Sooner or later, you'll have to stop running and start fighting back.* He cut out our connection and my chest filled with dread. I swallowed the lump in my throat. It had been a mistake to hope he would offer anything but despair. I stood, shaking the insecurity that clung to my limbs. The dragon's words echoed in my mind.

What was happening to me? I had never been this vulnerable before.

Adam was still feverish, but I could not sit around waiting for disaster to strike. I pulled the bottle of *aguardente* from my backpack and used its contents to disinfect my wounds. It stung like a swarm of wasps.

Cursing, I dragged one of the massive wooden benches to the entrance of the church and spilled the rest of the liquor on it. When confronting demons in the absence of sunlight, flames were the next best thing. And I knew how brightly this shit could burn.

It would do little to stop a demon prince, but it would buy us time. Seconds were all I needed to disappear with Adam through the back door, too tiny for the demon to slip through.

I left the front door ajar and placed as many candles as I could on the top rail. If the demon came through it, the candles would fall directly onto the bench and set it ablaze.

After setting the trap, I returned to Adam's side. His breathing had stabilized, and he had stopped talking gibberish. I sat one step below him, grabbed a *Kunai*, and held the medallion between my fingers. Its fiery rage burned through my skin and its gem shone a sickening red.

I pressed it against my palm, desperately seeking the once familiar coolness among its grooves and plains. But even that was gone now, devoured by my very own stupidity.

CHAPTER SIX

A Foul Taste of Blood

The sound of a door closing jolted me awake. I squeezed my *Kunai* and jumped to my feet.

The front door had not been opened, but the church was too dark to catch any movement past the candles' frail halo of light. I turned to the back door, fearing that by blocking the entrance, I had trapped us inside. I had been so sure that door was too small for the demon to slip through. But could I have underestimated his cunning?

Thankfully, the atmosphere still only reeked of incense and wax. So, whatever it was, it had been no demon.

The *Kunai* rested in my hand while I scanned the room. Only a second later did I realize Adam was missing. I cursed under my breath and hurried for the back door. Before I could reach it, Adam emerged from the shadows with a grin plastered across his face.

"Hey there!" He raised one hand above his head and walked down the aisle. I released the breath I'd been holding, but prepared to scold him for his recklessness.

"Where have you been?" My tone came out harsher than I intended.

"Someone has to do the grown-up's work while you get your beauty sleep." He smirked, but his expression softened when he came closer. "Did he hurt you badly?" Concern shadowed his face.

"I'm fine, I can handle it."

He nodded, but did not take his eyes off me. I averted my own, feeling vulnerable under his gaze.

"You haven't answered my question," I quickly added.

"Look, you built that little trap for our friend, but we can't hide here forever. I went back to the gardens to recover your *Kunai.*"

"Are you insane?" I asked, drawing closer to him. Anger smoldered any fear I might have felt just seconds ago.

"Don't worry, the fog has lifted, and we still have a couple of hours left of daylight." Before I could reprimand him further, he lifted a *Kunai* to my eye level. "Plus, this one will be useful to track him down. Or do you plan on sharing this island with a blood-thirsty demon?" He was holding the only one that had hit its target. Smears of dark blood spread unevenly across the blade. Just the sight of it made my stomach churn.

No, I was planning on running away as fast as I could. At least that's what I wanted to share, but I sighed instead and went back to the altar. He had a point, but I wished he discussed his plans with me before gambling with his life. I could swear he had a secret death wish, but I couldn't blame him for his recklessness. Our lifetime of planning had imploded in a single evening, and I still bore my scars as a testament.

Adam handed me the other *Kunai* and kept the

bloodied one to himself. I picked them up without looking him in the eye, sat on the steps with my legs crossed, and pretended to clean my weapons.

"I'm not sure I can beat it," I mumbled.

"You can't. Not alone." I lifted my head and looked straight at him. He was still grinning again for no reason, and it pissed me off.

"Care to explain that smug look on your face?"

"Don't you see it, Lau? It's a demon prince!" His eyes shone with excitement under the light of a dozen candles.

"I've seen enough and I'm not looking forward to another encounter, thank you." If the damn creature was a prince, we had better chances of survival if we swam to the continent with nothing but the clothes on our bodies.

He crouched until he met me at eye level. "Look, demon blood can be useful."

"Blood magic… useful?" I spat. "Are you willing to bow so low?"

Adam averted his gaze, but not before I caught a glimpse of shame in his eyes. "Are you gonna sit there and judge me? What choice do I have?" he said.

I stood, hot anger stirring in my stomach, and my tongue suddenly tasted of ash. I didn't fail to notice he had used *I* instead of *we,* as if what I did or wanted didn't matter. "There are choices you can't unmake. This is one of them. What will set you apart from Lilith if you do this?"

Adam sighed so loudly his voice rasped the surface of my skin. He sat on the red steps and held the bloodied *Kunai* in his hands, looking like a lost little boy. Saint Andrew's frown appeared to deepen from the top of his wooden shrine.

“We’re so close,” he whispered. His soul lay bare in front of me. I could feel the vortex of despair pulling him away. Lilith had a terrible talent for tainting everything she touched. She would be so proud to see her tentacles still stretched across the ages, dragging another soul to darkness with her. After all this time, she was still fighting us, every step of the way.

“You once told me your grimoire was part of your soul. So why can’t you summon it like I summon my Spirits?” I bit my tongue. “Like I used to summon…”

He stared at me, and his eyes stung like needles. “It’s not that simple.”

“Why?”

“Have you ever tried to will your heart to stop beating? Grimoires are a piece of a witch’s soul. I can’t command it, not more than I can command my own heart. I can only wield it.”

“But shouldn’t you be able to sense it?”

“Not if it doesn’t want me to.” He dropped his shoulders as if the knowledge weighed him down.

I walked towards the altar and sat by his side. It suddenly dawned on me that there was an entire universe behind Adam’s eyes I could not fathom. Neither Lilith nor any of her minions had ever carried a grimoire. It was ancient magic. *Weak magic*, she had said. It shamed me to admit that, until now, I had never questioned that belief. After all, Adam had become powerless without his artifact.

“Are you telling me your grimoire is hiding… on purpose?” I asked.

“There’s no other explanation.”

“Why would it do that?”

Adam's hands trembled slightly, and the *Kunai* slipped from his grip. The blade fell with a muffled thud. He picked it up, and I realized he was sweating. "Who cares! Besides, we don't have the time to sit around and talk about it. The demon prince is here. My grimoire isn't. The choice is obvious."

I could tell there was more to it than what he was telling me. Grimoires were a mystery to me. Blood magic wasn't. Lilith had used blood to bind me. I still craved it after a lifetime of abstinence. The thought of Adam consuming it made me sick. "It will change you forever," I said, shuddering. "You don't know what it'll cost you."

"Then enlighten me!" he screamed and stood, and it suddenly became harder to breathe. I stared at him; arteries throbbed furiously in his neck. All traces of kindness and uncertainty gone from his eyes. I shrank, unwittingly, under his sharp gaze.

And then it hit me.

I jumped to my feet, seized the bloodied blade from his grip, and tossed it into the nearest basin filled with holy water.

Adam's posture suddenly softened. His knees trembled, and he sat on the very spot where he had been standing just a heartbeat ago. I walked towards him and crouched.

Sweat covered his forehead.

"How did you survive this?" Adam asked, his voice little more than a whisper.

"I think part of me didn't," I admitted. "I still owe you your freedom, Adam. But don't you ever ask me to sacrifice what makes you good for its sake. I won't do it.

Even if I have to drag you out of this island against your will. This is but a taste of what blood magic will do to you. You don't want to lose your heart just to get your power back." *Like I lost mine*, I almost added.

Months had passed since Lilith had cursed Adam. I still felt it, the panic rising in my throat as the time-reversal spell almost devoured him alive. I had anchored his soul to my Spirit dragon just in time.

He swallowed. "Still, we can't flee…"

"Why not?"

"We can't leave the humans to fend for themselves. Not against an enemy they don't understand. We owe them that much. Wouldn't you say?"

I sighed and stared at him. His puppy eyes made me avert my own. Fighting the damned creature was better than letting Adam consume his blood, wasn't it? I guess I had to stick around to find out. "At least tell me you have a plan."

The town had disentangled itself from the vicious fog and red sun rays bathed its narrow streets. The old Witch Lord stood a few steps ahead of me on a hilltop. From this spot, the town could fit into the cup of my hands.

Eyes closed and arms stretched, he seemed like a blind lighthouse in a violent twilight. His hands curled into a loose fist and small arteries pulsated on his neck. It would be hard to track the demon prince without his blood, but I had faith Adam could do it anyway. His mind must have been boiling with anxiety. But there was something else too, hiding just beneath the surface of his skin.

The feeling was oddly familiar, but I couldn't articulate it. It was right there in his countenance, posture, and in the glimmer behind his eyes. Almost as if he was looking forward to whatever was about to happen. Before I could read too much into it, he inhaled sharply and opened his eyes.

"Did you locate him? Tell me you have good news," I begged.

"I located him, but I don't have good news. He's not alone anymore," he muttered.

"Shit… How many?"

"Twenty… maybe more. It's hard to say."

I sighed. "A swarm of demons."

"We're lucky the fog lifted and forced them to retreat, but we don't have much time."

I stared at the dying sun, wondering if I would have another chance to bask in its light. "Okay, Adam. What do you wanna do?"

"We need to get help."

CHAPTER SEVEN

A Crack in Reality

The sun had already dipped its toes in the ocean by the time we reached Sally's Little Hell. Yellow light leaked from the small windows of the pub. In concert, sad guitar tones woven with enthusiastic voices spilled to the quiet streets. The prospect of wasting the last sun rays talking with rowdy fishers was not what I had in mind when I woke up this morning.

I was so absorbed in my thoughts, I almost crashed into Adam. He stood as rigid as stone. His breath had quickened, and he stared at the pub as if the idea of stepping inside horrified him.

I placed my hand on his shoulder. It still shocked me how thin he'd become. "I can try to talk to them. Or maybe we could just ask Sally for help…?"

He shook his head. "I have a plan."

Before I could reply, he walked right through the front door, leaving me behind to ruminate.

I cursed softly and took my favorite detour. I had a feeling Adam wanted to do this by himself and, for

once, I would try not to interfere. He had been right. I'd been treating him like a child lately.

As usual, Sally had left the back door ajar. I slipped through, careful not to disturb the line of salt drawn around the entrance, and closed it behind me. The kitchen reeked of grilled fish, and a swarm of pans lay unwashed in every corner. On any other night, I would roll up my sleeves and start washing. But tonight was different. Adam needed me in the other room. If only as a spectator.

The music was still playing when I reached the bar. Sally and her nest of violent red hair walked from one point to the other, cracking dirty jokes while serving warm beer to a mob of patrons.

A small group of mainlanders clustered in a corner, eyeing the chaos with wonder. For them, these boisterous fishers were part of the attraction. For me, it was a regular Friday evening.

Sally glanced at me with confusion and worry from across the room. I hadn't seen myself in a mirror, but I imagined my fresh wounds were painfully obvious even under the faint light. I articulated a quick apology and promised I would explain my tardiness and state later. The mainlanders were the ones who raised their hands next.

"Miss," one of them said. He was in his mid-fifties, bald, and with thick golden rings around his fingers. I'd seen his kind around here before, wealthy and extremely bored. Eager to infuse their meager lives with adventure, but too cowardly to venture beyond the traditional tour packages crafted by unimaginative travel agents.

"How are you doing, sir?"

His brows furrowed, and his eyes scoured every

inch of my dark skin. "What happened to your face?" he asked.

"Fishing accident."

He hummed and continued scanning my body. My skin crawled under his gaze. "You're not from around here, are you?" he asked in a high-pitched voice, apparently losing interest in my wounds.

Weariness overwhelmed me and I latched my best fake smile onto my face. "No, sir," I forced myself to say, hoping that whatever Adam was planning to do would steal this man's attention from me.

"How did you end up here? Surely you miss the sun and warmer weather! It must be hard for you living here." My weariness turned into annoyance. I had heard this speech before and wasn't in the mood to hear it again. I had spent my childhood knee-deep in gray snow. Sunny days had been rare, and my mother and I had shared a bed to avoid freezing to death overnight.

"What's it gonna be, sir?" I asked, evading the question, the smile erased from my face.

He opened his mouth to speak, but before he could say anything, Caleb, who had been looming nearby, stepped in.

"Ya have a problem, sir?" he said, sitting at the mainlander's table. His cheeks, red from the drinking, failed to soften the angry look in his eyes. I'd never felt so grateful to have him around.

The mainlander raised his hands. "No problem at all, I was just curious." He chuckled nervously, eyeing Caleb's ripped muscles with dread.

"We have a saying around here: '*A curiosidade matou o gato.*'" Laughs erupted all around us and I muffled a

chuckle too. I hadn't mastered the language, but it was hard not to remember what the saying meant.

Confusion and annoyance surfaced on the mainlander's face. "What does it mean?" he asked, sensing he was being mocked.

"It means it's time for ya to go to bed!" Caleb replied. The laughter of the fishers intensified, deepening the mainlander's exasperation. 'Curiosity killed the cat' was the saying's official translation, a delicate way these fishers used to tell someone to fuck off.

"We are paying you a lot of money to give us a tour of the island." The bald man's voice deepened, and his companions nodded. The laughter died on the fishers' lips and a sharp static filled the air.

"So?" Caleb asked, taking a sip of his warm beer and winking at me in a way that made me roll my eyes.

"Listen," the man said, his cheeks quickly turning pink, "this is not how you treat your clients." His words made the fishers laugh again, so hard it threw him off balance.

Before he could say anything else, Sally stepped in, as I knew she would. "Something bothering ya, sir?" Sourness tainted her voice.

"Your patrons are being extremely unpleasant for no reason," he said. Sally's eyes turned into slits. Tension was palpable.

"Oh, I see…" she said. "Well, there's a simple solution to yar problem."

The bald man sneered. "Thank you, I appreciate your sensibility."

"Of course, sir. Anything for our best paying customers." She smiled and bowed slightly. "Caleb,

would ya be so kind as to accompany these gentlemen to their quarters?"

The mainlander opened his mouth to protest, but before he could say anything, Caleb rose from his seat. He towered over everyone else at the pub. He'd inherited Julien's height and posture. Some said he would soon succeed his father as Head of the Fisher's Guild too. The bald man swallowed his protest readily as the statuesque figure stood before him.

"If ya're unhappy with the service, feel free to look for another place to spend yar money on, sir," Sally said, adding the last word with a sneer.

"But we're paying you a lot of money, woman. It's low season, we're your only chance of surviving this winter. You need us, you need the money. If I were you, I would be grateful," another man from the group spoke with a trembling voice.

Sally sighed, put her hands on top of the table, and stared at the man who'd spoken. His resolve cracked under her gaze.

"Would ya now? Be careful, sir," she said. "This is my property and I don't have to put up with yar shit. If I say it's time to go, then I suggest ya listen. Or we can talk to the authorities and tell them ya're unwell… I'm sure they would love to take ya back to the continent right now with this lovely weather."

The man swallowed, and a single drop of sweat ran down his face. "This isn't over," he muttered and then turned to leave the building with his companions. Applause rained on them from every direction and I laughed so hard I had to hold on to the bar behind me to steady myself.

When I caught my breath, Sally drew closer. "So…" she said casually, "what took ya so long?"

"Sorry, something came up."

She hummed and grabbed me by the chin. "Lau… what's happening? Who did this to ya?"

"You will see," I replied.

Before I had the chance to elaborate, the patrons roared. I turned my head in time to see Adam on top of a table in the middle of the pub. He looked so small and frail, I almost pitied him.

"What's that silly kid doing?" Sally asked. I grabbed her arm before she had the chance to interfere.

She stared at me long and hard until her eyes caught my cheeks on fire. After a heartbeat, the patron's roars started forming a single word. "Dance!" was the word they kept screaming in unison like the senseless mob of drunkards they were.

For all I knew, dancing could be part of Adam's plan to get their attention.

"Lau… I swear…"

Before Sally could finish, a blinding brightness subdued the crowd. Like a supernova, it irradiated from the place where Adam had been. The room fell silent as everyone crouched and shielded their eyes from the glow.

When it dwindled, gasps erupted all around me.

My heart pounded when I lifted my head and stood. *What was Adam thinking, exposing us like that?* My angry thoughts died once I set my eyes on him. The breath caught in my throat, too.

"Demon!" someone cried.

Unwittingly, I jumped and landed on top of the bar.

All eyes turned to me. "Let him speak," I screamed at the top of my lungs.

The boy had bewitched us with a single breath and transformed into the man he used to be. But the pain in his eyes was palpable as he struggled to maintain the illusion.

I basked at the sight of his strong and lean body, and something within me quivered. He stood a head taller than Caleb. Runes covered his exposed chest, and an old scar blemished his perfect torso.

Those were wounds not even an illusion could hide.

His firm jaw moved as he whispered a silent 'thank you'. I nodded, not quite believing my eyes, and he returned his attention to the crowd. With his back turned to me and the humans cowering at his feet, I wanted to believe these harsh years had been nothing but a nightmare. But the man in front of me, the man who had once led a legion into battle, had been broken beyond recognition.

His voice trembled as he said, "I am not your enemy!" The same words he said to me the night we first met. I shivered as the memories raced through my mind. "And I am not a demon."

"Why should we believe you?" someone urged. Other voices rose in agreement, and some cursed loudly, disappearing through the front door without a second glance at Adam.

"Have we not shared meals with you?" he said. "Battled the sea by your side? Buried your dead and celebrated their lives with a bottle of *aguardente*? Have we not spent days helping you untangle your fishing nets? Repairing your boats? Watering your fields?"

Amid Adam's words, fishers hissed, booed, and some even murmured into their prayer beads with their eyes fixed on the Witch Lord. Adam's voice was barely audible amid the sea of discontent. Dread burned my throat as the conversation derailed into a million different squabbles. But as chaos brewed, a crazy idea started forming in the back of my mind.

"We're not evil," I screamed, unable to hold it back any longer. Silence fell, and suddenly all I could hear was the loud beating of my heart. All eyes turned to me, including Adam's. I cursed because I obviously hadn't thought this through. With trembling hands, I reached for the pouch of salt Saul had slipped into my pocket, and when my fingers finally brushed the rough cloth, a relieved smile reached my lips. Luckily, I hadn't lost it in the fight. "I can show you," I said, holding the small bag in my hands for everyone to see.

Most still regarded me with skeptical eyes, but a few expressions softened under my gaze. One of those belonged to Caleb. He opened his mouth and closed it again, probably struggling with the words. But these fishers had only one real leader, and I knew it wasn't Caleb. Not yet. So I met his gaze and shook my head. He swallowed the words that barely had the time to form on his lips and a hint of shame touched his eyes.

When I turned to Sally, all eyes moved in the same direction. She had gone still as a rock and pale as chalk. For a heartbeat, I thought she would throw us out of her pub as she'd done with the tourists. I prayed to no one, bracing for the worst. "For heaven's sake, girl," she said, gravely. "What the hell are ya waiting for?"

The lump in my throat faded. I nodded, almost

laughing with relief, and then jumped to the floor. The fishers stepped aside as if stung by a blowfish. It saddened me to realize they did it out of fear, not respect. There was no hint of kindness in their eyes, as if all their good memories of us had been devoured by the wicked monster of distrust. As I walked through the crowd and saw myself reflected in their eyes, I wondered what they would do to me if they caught a glimpse of my past life. Despite the closeness of their warm bodies, I shivered.

When I reached the table at the center of the pub, Adam's hand was waiting for me. On any other day, I would have rejected his help because gestures like that made me look weak. But today weak was certainly better than dead. So I grabbed his hand without a second thought and allowed him to pull me onto the table.

Once we stood face to face, I got lost in his dark eyes. For a moment, I wanted nothing but to dive into them and disappear. But someone cleared his throat loudly, breaking the spell.

I swallowed and lifted Adam's hand, exposing his palm. Without a word, he helped me untie the knot around the small bag. The pungent smell of ammonia stung my nostrils and shivers ran down my spine. With trepidation, I glanced at Adam, but there wasn't a trace of fear behind his eyes. He winked and took the pouch from my trembling fingers and, without a second to waste, spilled its contents into the cup of our hands.

The room gasped in unison.

My chest tightened, and momentarily, I forgot how to breathe. If these salts held the power to repel evil Spirits, I doubted I would pass their test. Because evil dwelled in me.

Eyes fixed on the large amorphous crystals; I counted the seconds with the rhythm of my heart. *One, two, three, four, five…* Sweat ran down my neck in fat beads. My coat turned into a straitjacket. A dry sourness filled my mouth.

Clenching my muscles, I stood there waiting for the salt to burn us alive. But nothing happened. It took me a minute to lift my gaze and, when I did, I found Adam was staring at me, amused.

I gaped at him, confused, and was suddenly possessed by the need to kick him. And I almost did. But before any of us could say or do anything, the sound of the front door being slammed shook us.

We craned our necks and, standing at the entrance, we found an all too familiar face peering back at us.

CHAPTER EIGHT

Pride Wins no Wars

Disheveled hair and bloodshot eyes, Jeff stood at the entrance of the pub. Panic and confusion mingled in his features. Wrinkles carved deep grooves under his eyes. *Gods, something terrible must have happened*, I thought. I'd never seen the old man so agitated. He had always been a happy drunkard, and a rather cheerful fellow, even when he was sober.

Now, he appeared to have shrunken, consumed by an invisible evil.

Adam and Sally were the first to react. Before anyone could speak, they arrived at Jeff's side and helped him to the nearest seat. I kept waiting to see a hint of distrust in Sally's countenance, but there wasn't any. She and Adam worked in perfect synchrony, as any normal master and apprentice would. Was she doing it out of habit or simply because our performance had convinced her we sought no harm? I couldn't tell.

When I descended from the table, Sally had a glass of water in one hand and a first aid kit in the other.

Without a word passing between them, Adam grabbed the kit and started taking the old man's temperature and pulse. Of course, he didn't need the instruments, but I suspected he used them to avoid stressing the humans. We were already walking on a frail thread.

Jeff babbled something, but it wasn't until our eyes met that his words started making sense.

"Ya," he screamed.

All heads turned in my direction. I froze in my tracks and instinctively reached for the blades in my back pocket. I muttered a silent prayer to the Spirits. Warm bodies clustered too near, making it hard for me to breathe.

"Ya," Jeff repeated, and I swallowed the fat lump in my throat. He rose from his seat, against Sally's protests, and took a step in my direction.

Adrenaline pumped through my veins, and, in a blink of an eye, my brain cooked up an escape route. I would have put it into motion if I hadn't glanced at Adam. He was calmer than I expected, and his eyes begged me to wait. I cursed silently and sighed louder than I'd intended.

The silence became so heavy, I could hear the floor creaking under Jeff's feet. We stood eye to eye for a moment and then, to my surprise, the old man broke down in tears. Before I knew it, he locked me in a tight hug and whispered in my ear, "Ya're alive. I thought I'd lost ya, girl."

It turned out Jeff had witnessed the fight with the demon prince. As soon as the creature dealt the first blow, the liquor master had run to the village looking for help,

but no one had believed him. Dejected, he had returned to the town hall to find us gone and then he'd come straight to Sally's pub.

"I saw it with me own eyes," he said. "*Demónio*. I'd bet me life on it."

To everyone's surprise, Adam used a bit of magic to return some color to Jeff's drained cheeks. The old man had looked so relieved even I ended up laughing. Telling our story after that had been a breeze. Convincing the fishers we needed to fight the creatures, a little less so.

Only a handful stayed. To my surprise, Sally was among them.

At some point, Adam's illusion shattered, and he returned to his cursed body. His cheeks were flushed, sweat dripped from his hair, and exhaustion weighed on his shoulders. But this was the most excited I'd seen him in years. Somehow, it felt right.

We all agreed Adam would prepare the trap near the town hall, Jeff would use the lighthouse as a distraction, and I would lead the group responsible for luring the demons 'like fish to the hook.' Sally's words, not mine.

While I gathered Caleb and some of the strongest fishers, Sally volunteered to join my party. When I begged her to reconsider, she just stared at me with a hand on her hip and howled, "I'm not an invalid, ya know! Someone has to watch out for these blockheads." She pointed at the young fishers. "And that ain't gonna be ya! Ya can roll your eyes all you want, kid. I'm going with ya."

I opened my mouth to protest, but ended up sighing instead. Sally had held her ground against an entire school of tuna, survived an encounter with a hungry

great white shark, and regularly pulled fishing nets all by herself. I knew how strong and stubborn she could be. But human strength was useless against demons. I just hoped it provided the distraction we needed to lure them into our trap.

The streets were quiet as most families retreated indoors to enjoy their meals or gathered around in pubs. I had to control myself not to go knocking on every door and beg them to leave.

"Trust me, kid, in this case, ignorance is bliss," Sally said, sensing my frustration. She was right. These people were more likely to throw a pan at our heads than to believe us. But it pained me to walk past their homes in silence.

Sally approached me when we crossed the edge of town. "Where do ya really come from?"

I glanced at her sideways and laughed nervously. "Does it matter?"

"It matters to me."

I stopped and pinned my gaze to the ground. Guilt cast an ugly aura around me. The group paused a few steps ahead, probably confused.

"Why don't ya go ahead, boys? Pick the lighter harpoons from the shed and wait for us there." They promptly obeyed Sally's command.

When they were out of earshot, I spoke without daring to meet her eyes. "Do you believe anything good can crawl out of the shadows?"

What a stupid question to ask. Crushed by my choice of words, I crouched and hugged my knees. Cold sweat formed on my palms.

Sally sighed, and my stomach twisted. Was she

frustrated or disappointed? I couldn't tell. Before I had time to think, she sat on the dirt in front of me. With her calloused hands, she lifted my chin. A gesture she often used with foolish young children. It crossed my mind I was probably old enough to be her grandmother. I wondered if she would still grab my chin if she knew.

"Would I live on a cursed island if I didn't?" she said. A hint of a smile touched her lips.

The crushing weight on my back lifted just enough for me to breathe. Would it be so bad to tell her the truth?

"I wanna help ya, kid. I do," she said, and her eyes glimmered with sadness. "But I can't if ya keep tossing dirt to my eyes."

She dropped my chin. The wind howled around us, enveloping me in a chilling embrace. Who was I fooling? I didn't have the guts to tell her about my past. But what choice did I have? I had to give her something or risk losing her friendship forever.

"Fine," I said, swallowing my fears and pushing the words out of my mouth. "You want to know who I am? Where do I come from? If I'm worth helping? I'll tell you… I'm the monster in every child's nightmare. The mad huntress born from the death of the night. You're wasting your kindness on me. I'm full--"

"--of shit?" Sally cut me off. I stared at her, dumbfounded. There wasn't a hint of amusement in her eyes. "I can see that just fine. Ya think ya're the only one with a past around here? Ya think ya're surrounded by saints? I don't care about yar sob stories," she said, waving her hand dismissively.

"Then, what do you care about?"

"I care about yar heart," she said, leaning so close our noses almost brushed.

I laughed, not without feeling bitter. "My heart?" The word tasted odd in my mouth, as if I was savoring it for the first time. "Now, who's the one tossing dirt to my eyes?"

A motherly smile seized Sally's features. Her hair seemed to flare up under the sun's dying light. "Ya're incredibly thick sometimes, aren't ya? Ya're probably ancient, I can tell by the look in yar eyes, but ya've never aged, have ya? And believe me, old age changes everything, kid. So, I'll ask ya again, where do ya come from?"

Thoughts stumbled on each other in my mind. Sally had the tongue of a trickster and the heart of a devil. I suddenly realized honesty was the only way out of her scrutiny. I scratched my temple and smiled. Beaten by her words and cleverness, I lifted the veil of my past life. "Adam and I come from a faraway land. A land that remains hidden from human eyes by a web of complex spells. We used to be enemies," I finally said. A strange light flickered behind Sally's pupils. "It was never personal. Wars rarely are..." I left my voice trail off, and for a moment, I was back at that small hunt in the middle of the woods, pressing a dagger against Adam's throat and staring at the dark ocean behind his eyes.

"Then what?"

"Then... I tried to kill him."

The sun had almost drowned in the ocean by the time we reached the nest of demons. Despite our depressing

circumstances, Sally's laughter still echoed in my ears. Apparently, the story of how Adam and I met and came to work together had been enough to convince her my heart could still be saved.

A nudge on my shoulder brought me back to the present, where life hung by a thread. The horde of demons clustered at the old cannery. A once imposing building that was nothing more than ruins. According to Sally, it had once belonged to a 'sorry-ass rich man, who thought he could make money off the backs of hardworking people.'

I had asked her why they didn't destroy the place and build something new on top of it. She told me the ruins served as a reminder that this little town was immune to rich-ass pretensions.

It was ironic we ended up here, in the place where pretensions came to die.

We were close enough to the cannery to smell the demons, but not close enough to see them. I crouched behind the old guardhouse and picked up my radio.

"Jeff, we are in position. Over."

"Roger that, Lau. Can ya see the bastards? Over."

"Not yet. But we can smell them alright. Get ready to grill them at our signal. Over."

"Roger that! Hum… Lau?"

"What's the problem, Jeff?"

"Please be careful. Over."

The old man was getting sentimental on me. If he only knew how vulnerable that made me feel. It was a promise I could not make, but my human side compelled me to lie. "I will. Over."

I turned the radio to Sally and swallowed the lump in

my throat. The group stared at me, their eyes brimming with questions. I tightened my grip around the harpoon as if that would ever suffice to stop a demon. For all our sakes, I better start believing it would.

“Demons are immune to most weapons,” I said. “Don’t try to fight them. That’s not our job. Tonight, we’re nothing but bait. Always move in pairs and never run in a straight line. These creatures are faster than sailfish and meaner than piranhas. You can’t beat them, so don’t even try. Jeff is watching over us from the lighthouse. He’ll grill the creatures with the light beam if they get too close, but that won’t kill them. It will piss them off, blind them momentarily, tease them, but it won’t make them stop. So, don’t let your guard down. I can’t guarantee your safety until we reach the town hall. Do you understand?”

They nodded. Sally had a strange smirk on her face while she nodded in approval. Without even realizing it, I had sounded just like her.

“I’ll go ahead and lure them. When you hear the screams, cut your flesh and light your harpoons on fire. Demons are drawn by the smell of blood and the fire will help you in case they get too close. Once you do this, don’t wait for me, just run as fast as you can, and don’t dare to look back.” I placed my hand on Sally’s shoulder. “Give the signal to Jeff when the time comes. Good luck.”

I stood, feeling terrified and exhilarated. The old part of me who had thrived in battle stirred and howled in anticipation. The other part of me feared the wild bloodlust that thickened my veins.

Before I could take a step in the nest’s direction, Sally

dragged me into a hug.

"Ya got this, kid. I have yar back."

I wrapped my arms around her and inhaled the comforting smell of saltwater and wet wood. Part of me knew that whatever happened tonight, we were saying our goodbyes.

CHAPTER NINE

Hell Unleashed

Heart pounding, I dashed across the gap that separated me from the cannery.

The stench grew stronger with each step, and soon the demons' twisted voices reached me. They spoke in Hellspeech so loudly I could hear their muffled cries through the thick wall. Just recalling their language made my skin crawl.

A lifetime ago, I had spoken it almost as well as any native. But I was sure to gag if I tried to speak it now. Like all other memories of my old life, this one was damaged beyond salvage.

I climbed the outer wall and reached the first floor. When I peered through the small windows, my heart sank. Wrapped in filthy robes embroidered with runes, the creatures filled the entire ground floor of the cannery. Like cockroaches on a hot summer night.

At first, I couldn't spot the prince, but when a brawl erupted at the edge of the ruins, his thunderous voice drowned every other. Sickened, I strained to make sense

of his words. The sun lingered by a frail thread on the horizon. Whatever he was about to say, it had to be important.

I watched the other demons gathering around the prince. My senses sharpened at the familiarity of the scene. The last time I'd seen demons bowing to another creature, I had been standing right beside her.

The memories of my foolish younger self disgusted me. A powerful summoner enraptured by the lies of a wicked witch. If I was going to be honest with myself, I hadn't followed her because I didn't know any better; I'd followed her because I loathed my own weakness and Lilith had a special talent for making me feel strong.

I almost expected to see her here among these rotten souls. But all I saw was a swarm of demons and my terrified expression reflected on the window. I buried my nails in the soft moss and growled in frustration.

Hell's foot soldiers couldn't be much taller than me but compared to the prince, they looked stunted, and their voices almost sounded mellow. Next to them, the prince shone like a lighthouse wielding darkness instead of light. His voice was sharp, like the tip of my blades. It crawled under my skin making me shiver. Yet, because the demons were so numerous, it was hard to hear him above the frenzy. Demons were volatile creatures; the only language they understood was pain. But when I was about to give up, Lilith's name emerged above the noise.

I almost lost my grip then.

Panic pulsed in my veins. My breath quickened. Nausea rose from my entrails. My mind imploded in pain.

If Lilith was here, it changed everything.

There was no trap big enough to contain her, no

plan solid enough to evade her, and no spell strong enough to elude her. She'd found us a century too early. Our wounds had barely healed, and my Spirits would rather see me burn than come to my aid.

Trembling, I slipped down from the building. Sweat formed fat beads on my neck. I sat on the dirt as furious tears burned my cheeks and dread claimed my every limb.

If I stayed here, the demons would sense me. If I left without warning, I would leave Sally and the others exposed and at the demons' mercy. My soul twisted and my mind screamed in terror as I glimpsed the frail human figures clustered behind the guardhouse. Even if I was no longer Lilith's favorite executioner, I had willingly brought them to her doorstep. Again.

Sally's lone and curvy shape, with her nest of unruly hair, stood out from the rest of the group. I bit my lip, urging my mind to solve this mess. It was too late to bring them to safety. Whatever was about to happen, they would be part of it, whether or not I liked it.

I touched my medallion, searching for answers. My fear thinned the veil of reality, and the Spirits I'd once commanded gawked at me. Their heavy gaze told me all I needed to know. I was on my own. Blood and betrayal defiled my soul. If I was going to die in this place, I'd better make my peace with the ones that had been there for me in my darkest hours.

I closed my eyes in prayer, and resolve burned within. My legs shook as adrenaline pumped through my veins. I stood and leaned against the ruins, snatching one last glance at Sally's immobile figure. Covered in sweat, I reached for one of my blades and pierced the palm of my hand.

Dark crimson blood emerged from the shallow wound.

The response was immediate. The horde of demons screamed in unison and the ground rumbled in their wake. I looked at my former companions one last time and sensed Sally's growing confusion as the demons blasted the doors of the cannery.

I could pinpoint the exact moment when her bewilderment turned into realization. I pointed in the direction we'd just come from and screamed into the night. "RUN!"

Instead of waiting for their reaction, I turned my back to them, feeling torn, and ran into the woods behind the cannery. What would they think of me? Would they believe I'd abandoned them? Betrayed them? Would their faces come back to haunt me if they lost their lives tonight?

Knowing Sally, she would be cursing right now. I wish I could have told them they would be safer without me, especially if Lilith was coming for my head. But life never waited, not even for supernatural creatures like me. It just dragged us through the mud in an eternal circus of pain. Whatever happened tonight, I could only hope Jeff, the lighthouse, and the harpoons wrapped in old cloth and drenched in liquor would keep the fishers out of harm's way.

My mind scrambled as I raced through the woods. Around me, tall and slim trees encircled a massive blood moon. *Such a fitting night to die*, I thought.

Only when I slipped did I realize it had started to rain. I roared and punched a trunk with my bare hands. Rain was the last thing we needed. The water would mingle with my blood and mask my smell. It would make it impossible for the cloth to burn and give the

demons all the coverage they needed to move and kill undetected. The reality was almost too cruel to be true.

But my protests amounted to nothing because, a few seconds later, several hooded figures emerged from the shadows. Rain blew on their capes and their long noses sniffed the air. If I'd counted the demons at the cannery correctly, barely a third had followed me into the night.

Not nearly enough to ensure Sally's safety. But more than enough to make me sweat.

Pain stirred in the pit of my stomach, and I threw my bloodied blade at the demonic beasts. "Eat shit, you creeps," I screamed as the blade buried deep into an eye socket.

The demon I'd hit fell shrieking, and his companions stared at me with blood thirst in their eyes. It had been so long since my blades and I had danced with demons in the night. I licked my lips, suddenly energized, and I vowed to drag as many of these foul beasts to Hell with me.

CHAPTER TEN

Behind the Veil

My muscles burned. Wild screams clawed their way up my throat. Red and black blood mingled as I jumped from the shadows and butchered one demon at a time. The rain poured from the skies like an angry beast who wanted nothing but to drown me in sorrows.

I steered clear of the houses and ran in circles through the woods, dragging a dwindling swarm of demons behind me like a vengeful storm. I didn't see it coming when a pair of muscular arms seized me and dragged me into a small shed. "What the fuck?" I screamed.

A calloused hand covered my mouth. I bit it and the bastard who'd grabbed me howled. "Caleb?" I asked. "What the fuck is happening? Let go of me."

Surprisingly, he did. "Hell of an exit, Lau," he said, rubbing the hand I'd just bitten.

"You need to go…"

"Not without ya, those are my orders."

"Who the fuck gave you those orders?"

"Ya really need to ask?"

I sighed. Of course I didn't. "I don't have time to explain. I'm taking care of everything."

"Of course ya are. Ya're doing a great job burying yar ass in the sand out there."

"What…? Why are you even here, Caleb?"

"Sally figured ya'd do something stupid at some point, so we agreed I'd come to fetch ya once ya did. Don't get me wrong, we know ya can take care of yarself. But that's just not the way we do things around here. And ya know disobeying Sally's direct orders is almost as fun as stirring a demon's nest." A smirk danced around his lips.

I stared at him, anger and humiliation boiling in my stomach. "Asshole," I finally said.

His sneer deepened. "We know ya love us. No need to hide it." He winked, and I slapped him on the arm.

"Ouch!"

I rolled my eyes and sighed. He was right though, I was damn happy to see him, but I'd rather lose an arm than admit it. The only thing I was willing to admit was that I needed all the help I could get. "Okay…"

"Okay, what?"

He was going to make me say it. "Okay, I could use your help."

He raised an eyebrow in reply. "Surrendering without a fight? Ya're getting soft, Lau."

"Spare me, Caleb."

He raised his hands in defeat. "Bad timing? Fine! We should lure them into Adam's trap. Now."

"No," I shook my head. "Adam and the others will have their hands full with the rest of the demons. We should kill as many as we can here and now."

"Ya know Sally wouldn't approve this, don't ya?"

"I've fought these creatures before, Caleb. We can take them on."

"How?"

"I have an idea," I said, and a wicked smile danced on my lips.

The rain poured madly from the heavens as if someone was Hellbound on seeing us perish at the demons' hands. Not that it mattered now, because the place we were heading to was dry as dust and brimming with liquor.

Caleb went ahead to prepare for our arrival while I forced the demons to chase me in a maddening spiral. Despite my caution, my head had already started to spin from the blood loss. My movements were becoming sluggish and my aim less accurate. Exhaustion grinded my muscles and bones, and still, my Spirits refused to listen.

I'd always been alone, but never had I felt so lonely.

When the pier entered my line of vision, my legs were aching and my throat was burning with thirst. I forced myself to keep running, but my speed was no longer enough to give me an edge over the reeking beasts. Seconds away from stepping into the harbor, a demon grabbed me by the arm.

My reaction was slow and awkward, and the creature took advantage of it by throwing me against a wall. I screamed as one of my ribs broke on impact. Before I could move, several of the hooded beasts had me surrounded.

I pushed the wall behind me, but my legs wouldn't move. The demon's thirst for my blood filled the air like

bad static. Exhaustion overwhelmed me. I was famished, outnumbered, surrounded, and I'd run out of cheap tricks.

For once in my life, there was nothing I could do to flip the odds. Strangely, I felt at peace with myself. Then the medallion burned bright against my flesh. I gasped, my mind reeling, my chest aching with longing. Fingers flexed, I raised my hand, trying to grab the thin veil of reality.

It was there, like it always had been, and grabbing it felt like touching velvet. A pool of cold air formed around me, and the demons stopped in their tracks. I smiled and cried as the gap between the two worlds closed before me. Buzzing gravity pulled me into a strong embrace and the demons cowered in fear.

Brown fur and eyes soft and green like moss materialized in front of me. "Vanara," I said in a whisper. I extended my hands, dying to feel his lustrous simian fur between my fingers. Sadly, I caught nothing but empty air.

"I don't understand," I said.

Vanara shook his massive head, and sorrow filled his eyes like a storm. He pointed at my chest, where my medallion still burned like fire, then a deafening buzz washed over me. Convulsions took over my body. I covered my ears and screamed as Vanara's pain rattled my soul.

"Help me, please..." I begged through clenched teeth.

My vision blurred, and agony infected every atom of my being. When I was certain my soul would crack, the buzz stopped. I opened my eyes, hoping to see the giant gorilla one more time, but Vanara was gone, and

the coolness of his presence washed away too quickly, replaced by the copperish smell of blood. Wretched, I swiped angry tears from my eyes, and forced myself to stand. Every muscle burned in protest.

Despite Vanara's power surge, the demons were back to their feet in a heartbeat. The hooded beasts licked their thin black lips and their stares bore holes into my soul. They approached like a black wave, intent on crushing me.

My legs refused to move and, this time, I closed my eyes and braced for the impact of their putrid flesh against my bones. During that last second, I wondered if there were better ways to die.

Silence, the smell of liquor, and then a flash of light.

An explosion breached my shadows and cracked open the tight demonic rows around me. Caleb thrust through, hands clasped around a bottle of liquor with a burning cloth hanging from its mouth. With an elegant swig of his arm, another explosion followed. He shielded me with his body at the last possible minute. The world shattered around us, and thick smoke forced its way down my throat.

Caleb had gone still after the blast, and his massive weight pressed against my body. "You fool," I screamed, coughing, and punched him hard on the chest. To my relief, he woke up coughing too.

"Ya okay?" he asked.

"I'm fine. We need to move. Now." I pushed him.

He stumbled to his feet, and I followed him, only to stop and crouch when a sharp spasm pierced my back. I gasped and held Caleb's arm to steady myself.

"Lau…?"

"I'm fine," I repeated and forced my back to straighten. The injury was more serious than I'd thought, and I smiled to disguise my discomfort. Not even Caleb believed my act. Against my will, he took me in his arms and broke into a run.

"Sorry, Lau."

"You idiot." I punched his chest. "We'll never make it if you take me with you. It's me they want. Put me down. Now."

Instead of obeying, he smiled. "Ya think ya're the only one with a plan?" I stared at him, wide-eyed. "Can ya trust me for a minute?" His voice was barely a whisper. I nodded in reply. "Good…" He seemed relieved. "Because I'm gonna need yar sweater."

CHAPTER ELEVEN

Bad

Caleb used all the shortcuts only a local would know to outrun the demons.

His plan was simple, but effective. Demons didn't need to catch me, they only needed to think they did.

He lured them to the empty brewery, using my bloodied sweater as bait. At the same time, I dove into the freezing waters to disguise my smell. A spark in a workshop filled with liquor did the rest.

When I resurfaced, the hungry fire roared, glass shattered, and black smoke mingled with the cries of the demonic beasts. While Jeff's old brewery burned, Caleb's long shadow rushed in my direction.

He pulled me from the water, and I shuddered. The effort had inflamed my broken rib with fresh pain. Caleb probably mistook it for hypothermia because the next thing I knew, he was taking his shirt off with a single elegant motion and pulling me into his arms. When he started rubbing his body against mine, hot blood claimed my cheeks, and all protests died on my lips.

"Ya're warm," he said after an awkward minute of silence.

I cleared my throat, tightened with embarrassment. "I'm fine…" It dawned on me then I'd been saying the same worn-down words for the past hour. Cold wouldn't touch me, but Caleb couldn't know that. Would he still hug me like this if he knew the truth?

"Why didn't ya say so earlier?" With a gentle motion, he pushed me away, and I lowered my gaze. Suddenly, I was too aware we were both shirtless. I couldn't stop myself from gawking at his chest and defined abs. Even though I didn't think it was possible, I blushed a bit more.

His fingers brushed my cheeks and grabbed my chin. "Lau," he said. My eyes refused to stop staring at his thin, dark lips. Before I could speak, he withdrew his hand from my face and put his shirt around me. "It looks like ya're stung by blowfish. Are ya sure ya okay?" He smirked.

I swallowed and cursed internally, fighting to keep all emotion from my face. Had I just imagined this moment? "Yeah, thanks," I mustered, panting for no good reason. As soon as Caleb backed away, a chill went through my body. It was hard admitting I'd missed it. The touch of someone else's warm body against mine. How long had it been since I'd allowed myself that freedom?

Ignoring my inner struggles, Caleb started buttoning the shirt. I averted my eyes, fearing he would see too much into them.

"Ya're always wearing that necklace," he said after a while. "What is it?"

The words were out of my mouth before I could stop them. "It was my mother's."

He whistled, impressed. "Was yar mother a duchess or something?"

I laughed, and the pain flared in my torso. "What? No! She was a maid."

"A maid? Why would a maid have something so fancy?"

I opened my mouth to reply and closed it again because I had no answer. All I remembered was her stern and melancholic gaze, and the winter nights we'd spent huddling together on a tiny bed. I'd told no one about her. Not even Adam.

When Caleb finished buttoning the shirt, his hand slipped to the garnet around my neck. Then dizziness and fatigue overwhelmed me, and the strength drained from my legs.

"Lau," he said, concern drawing troubled lines on his sweet face. "Lau, what's happening? Talk to me."

Dark spots filled my vision. I fell and Caleb held me in his arms. He was still uttering my name when his face dissolved and another took its place.

"Lau," a feminine voice said. "Lau, listen to me. Run as fast as you can."

My vision focused, and Caleb's face resurfaced for a second before being swallowed again by darkness.

"Mama, I don't want to!" I heard myself saying. "I wanna stay with you."

Delicate fingers held my chin. "Stardust, do you trust me?" My vision focused again and instead of Caleb, I saw someone else. Shivers ran down my spine. For a moment, I saw a ghost or, perhaps, my own reflection. Then it hit me.

Wrinkles carved deep lines on her forehead. Black hair disheveled. Heavy bags under her golden eyes. Mother. She smelled of flowers, mornings, and freshly cut grass. Exhaustion perspired through every pore of

her body, but her beauty didn't falter. Part of me wanted nothing but to reach across time and hug her.

"Mama, please…" I said instead in a childish voice. My younger self stretched her tiny hands and mother grabbed them, her expression softening. She engulfed my hands and kissed my fingertips. Warm nostalgia filled my chest.

"I love you, stardust," she said. As she uttered those words, a shape moved in the corner of my eye. She craned her neck in its direction. "I'm trusting her to you," she whispered to the shadows. "Please take her as far as you can from here."

The darkness stirred around us, and the shape that had been concealing behind trees and rocks stepped into the clearing. The child I'd been and the woman I'd become gasped in unison. Eyes like embers. The same rough red and orange scales I'd come to love. The one whose name I couldn't think or say aloud. The dragon hesitated, his piercing eyes lingering on my frail body. I thought I saw sadness in them. And then he bowed.

In a blink, the world exploded, and a myriad of images flashed before my eyes. A dark forest. A dragon's lonely figure in the skies. Blood-red eyes. A wicked smile. A hand pressed against my chest. Pain tearing me from inside. Blood. An inhumane cry ripping the night.

Before I could react, someone tossed fresh water on my face. My mother and my precious dragon faded, their image eaten away by reality.

"Lau?" Caleb asked. I opened my eyes and looked around. I was inside someone's boat. Saul's *Carlota*, I realized. "Hey, ya okay? Ya're gone there for a minute."

"Sorry, Caleb." I licked my lips, and the taste of salt

and copper filled my mouth. "I think I lost too much blood." Another lie. But the alternative was telling Caleb I had either hallucinated or glimpsed a few scattered memories of my old life. I had no words to describe what had just happened. Maybe all the terrible things I'd done were finally catching up with me, pushing me beyond the edge of insanity.

Caleb nodded, deaf to the chaotic ramblings of my brain. Then he walked towards the small kitchen, apparently appeased by my excuse.

"I think Saul left some cinnamon buns in the oven," I said, slowly dragging myself to a sitting position. Caleb had put me on the table where Saul and I had sat earlier today. The wound grinded in response to my sudden movement and I did my best to ignore it.

Caleb returned with the entire rack and a glass of water. I was about to make fun of him when my stomach growled. He laughed. "I always knew ya had an appetite," he said, placing the rack and the glass on the table. I swallowed my pride and dove for the buns with a hunger I didn't know I had.

"Now can ya tell me the truth?"

I choked and forced a chuckle to disguise my discomfort. "What do you mean?"

Caleb sat on the table next to me, his naked chest moving to a steady beat. The shirt he had given me smelled of salt and algae, just like his skin had smelled when he'd hugged me earlier on the pier. For some reason, I felt safe.

"How long have we known each other?" he said, nibbling one of Saul's famous buns.

"Eight months…" My voice cracked.

"Ya'd think that after eight months of going out fishing together, ya'd learn to trust us. I know we're a weird folk. But we've got yar back. Can't ya tell that by now?"

His words stung like wasps. I guessed I deserved to hear them. I sipped the cold water. Sweat formed on my forehead. *You wouldn't understand*, I almost said. Thankfully, I bit my lips before the words came out. I owed him an explanation. "I'm not human," I said, half-expecting Caleb to get up and leave, but he didn't. He just sat there, staring at me with his soft golden eyes, urging me to continue.

"Adam isn't human either..."

He snorted. "That much is obvious."

"I know, but it felt good to say it out loud." I looked into his eyes, and he surprised me with a smile. There was no fear there, just genuine curiosity. A weight lifted from my chest.

"There's more, isn't there?"

I sighed and nodded. "Yes... Someone powerful is coming for our heads." I took another sip. "When she gets here, no one will be able to stop her, not even us..."

"She a demon?"

I shook my head. "Something worse."

"What did ya do to piss her off?"

"I tried to kill her."

He raised his eyebrows. "Why?"

Because she's a bad person, I almost said. But that sounded immature and fake, even in my own head. Part of me knew that wasn't the truth. Not the whole truth, at least. And to be honest, if we started measuring our deeds, I would be forced to admit I was a bad person too.

I stared at the half-eaten bun in my hands. How could

I justify what I did all those years ago? "She was someone I loved…" I finally said, and my voice failed me. "A long time ago." I glanced at Caleb. Surprise flashed across his face. "But her love was suffocating… And no matter what I did to please her, it was never enough. Trying to contain her love was like fishing with a torn net."

"What does Adam have to do with that?" he asked.

"She and Adam were enemies long before I even existed. I guess Adam and I formed an alliance against her out of necessity."

"I see," he replied, but his eyes were filled with turmoil. "What are ya gonna do now?"

"Run," I said. From the corner of my eye, I saw Caleb swallowing and staring at the ceiling. Nothing would have prepared me for what he said next.

"That's yar big plan? I thought ya're the one with the brains." He pointed at my forehead with a serious look on his face.

"We can't win, Caleb…" *Not while I'm this powerless*, I almost added.

"Then why go stirring the demon's nest in the first place? Why give us hope?" He opened up his arms.

"I didn't know she was coming. I heard it from the demons when I climbed the walls of the cannery."

"Ya speak their language?"

Revulsion filled my stomach. Caleb stirred in his seat, and I realized he didn't know what else to say. "It was a lifetime ago…" It sounded as lame as I thought it would.

"Fine," he said. "I think I saw enough craziness for a lifetime. We need to get going. They need us at the town hall." His voice was strained.

I cleared my throat. "You're right," I said in a

tight voice. First my hallucinations, now the pain and disappointment in Caleb's eyes. My chest burned with a feeling I couldn't define. It felt raw and heavy, like a thunderstorm on a summer night.

Whatever it was, I didn't want it. Silently, I asked my Spirits to take it away. It was as if I had never left that clearing. The fear of abandonment resurfaced, and the inhumane scream of my memories echoed in my mind.

As much as I wanted to deny it, deep down, I knew that piercing cry was mine.

CHAPTER TWELVE

Bait for Demons

Caleb wrapped fresh linen around most of my wounds. He also forced me to shower and put on one of Saul's slacks. I looked ridiculous, but the alternative was wearing my previous attire, and nothing would please the demons more. For the sake of safety, I agreed to discard my clothes. We needed to move fast without those beasts clinging to our tails.

Surprisingly, Caleb let me keep his shirt because, as he put it, I was about 'five sizes too small for any of Saul's sweaters.' He blushed as he said those words, or perhaps I'd just imagined it. Either way, I kept it because the smell of the ocean embedded in the fabric made me feel safe.

When we were ready to leave *Carlota*, the clock was about to strike midnight. Caleb led us into the night at a relentless pace. I struggled to keep up. Occasional flares of pain tormented me, and I pushed them to the back of my mind.

The rain had stopped a while ago and the clouds dissipated, exposing a hungry blood moon. The sight

of it chilled me to my bones, but my mind burned with questions. Had my mother been a summoner? It sounded impossible. She looked terrified and exhausted and I had a nagging feeling whoever was chasing her couldn't be a simple thief.

Were all my memories scrambled? Was everything I remembered about my mother a lie? And if it was, how would any of it help us defeat Lilith? Drained and confused, I threw that knowledge into the pile of things I could neither solve nor explain.

I couldn't afford to lose focus now. Everyone's life was at stake. I thought I'd be protecting them by running away, but I only managed to make things worse. I'd been naïve to think only Lilith would be wicked enough to do something so heartless. Yet, here we were, and as much as I hated myself right now, I had to believe there was still a way to fix this mess.

Consumed by thoughts, I failed to notice we had reached the town hall.

Caleb stopped first, and I almost crashed into him. His back straightened and worry was written all over his face. A chilling silence reigned over the gardens. Vicious darkness enveloped buildings and trees in a powerful embrace. As we approached, a sense of gloom lodged itself in the pit of my stomach.

We paced towards the edge of the gardens and in the blood-red moonlight, I saw Adam's handiwork. Thin fishing nets intertwined with each other to create an impossible maze. The perfect trap for demons once we blinded them with light.

I stretched my hand and touched the nets, admiring Adam's cleverness. When he'd told me about his plan,

I'd laughed. Who would think of catching demons with fishing nets? But the result was marvelous, and I couldn't help feeling a pang of jealousy. Adam had relied on the fishers for help. In turn, my arrogance had almost destroyed his plan.

Caleb chirped like a bird, awakening me from my stupor. Leaves rustled in reply. We lifted our gaze, and the silent trees awoke. Shapes stirred in the shadows concealed by branches. Shivers of excitement ran down my spine.

Their figures came into the faint light. Their pale skin transformed by the crimson moonlight, whispers of war, and wails of terror brewed among them. Bewildered, I recognized every face. Their gaze shattered the heavy mask I'd been wearing for a lifetime, and I allowed myself a smile.

"Ya're late, assholes," someone said. Caleb and I stared at each other, confused.

The person who'd spoken descended from the tree, and we walked towards them. It turned out to be Julien, the head of the Fishers' Guild. He had a round nose and a tattoo of an anchor on his inner forearm. As usual, he wore a black t-shirt stamped with the drawing of a green siren with sharp teeth. Nothing seemed more fitting for the occasion.

"Pissed yar pants already, old man?" Caleb asked, and I stared at him wide-eyed.

"Ya wished. Oh, isn't it past yar bedtime, sweetheart? And don't tell me ya already let yar ass get kicked before the real fight even started?" Julien said, pointing at Caleb's clothes. The two men glared at each other and tension built around us. I almost put myself between them, but before I had the time to react, they cracked up laughing.

Their hearty laughs echoed through the gardens, and soon the entire town was laughing with them.

"Did a blowfish bite ya?" Julien asked me after a while. I swallowed, stared at him, and then I couldn't take it anymore. Muscles creaking, I laughed too. The broken rib grinded my flesh with each breath, but somehow the pain became a bit more bearable.

And then a shriek and the bright beam of the lighthouse burst through the night.

"Okay, ya cowards," Julien howled. "Ya know what to do. We're not gonna let a dumb pretty kid save our town by himself. Let's go."

The fishers reacted as one body and concealed themselves in the trees. The smell of liquor reached my nostrils and never had something so pungent, felt so sweet.

"Julien, where's Adam?" I asked.

"He went back for Sally and the others," he said, and guilt swelled in my chest. I couldn't help but lower my gaze. "He left ya a message. Does this nonsense mean anything to ya?" He took a creased piece of paper from his back pocket and handed it to me.

I recognized Adam's elegant scribbles and my breath quickened. *Lau*, he wrote, *I'll need you to trust me again. I've found the grimoire. To be more precise, as soon as I decided to go back and help Sally, it stopped shielding its presence from me. It was right under our noses. Can you go back to the place where it all started and bring it to me?*

Laughing, I hugged Julien. "Yes!" I screamed. "It means everything!" I kissed his cheek and let go of him.

Julien stared at Caleb and asked, "Are ya sure she is okay?"

"Hey, I'm right here." I punched him on the arm, and we both chuckled. "Can you hold the fort for me?" I asked.

"Lau, don't even think about it, I'm going with ya," Caleb said in a tone he meant to be menacing, but turned out to be concerned instead.

"Can you trust me for a minute, Caleb? They need you here, and I won't be much help in my current state," I said.

He shook his head and then turned his back to me. "Just don't let them corner ya again…" he whispered, and a soft smile emerged on my face.

"Kid," Julien said, putting his hand on my shoulder, "do what ya have to do. We'll serve ya demon's grilled flesh on a platter. Ya'll see." He winked.

I hugged him again, this time tighter than before. "Just stay safe, Julien. I'll come back for you."

For all our sakes, I hoped I did.

CHAPTER THIRTEEN

Wicked Things

Grimoires were wicked things, unpredictable and treacherous like souls often were. It was funny Adam's grimoire had chosen this exact moment to reveal itself. Perhaps, deep down, the Witch Lord cared more about helping others than saving himself. I couldn't help but smile to myself. Adam's heart turned out to be as soft as butter; but despite its good intentions, it surely had one of the worst timings in the history of witch magic.

I dug the ground outside the old cannery with my bare hands. "You little bastard," I cursed, and it chided in reply. I'd stood in this exact spot a few hours ago and the nasty artifact hadn't thought of revealing its presence to me. It took stubbornness to a whole new level.

My nails hit its hardcover, and I cussed. I withdrew my hand from the hole and found them chipped and bloodied. The little beast had a temper, and I had no time for its games. Eyes closed, I channeled a part of my body heat to the tips of my fingers. It was a cheap trick, but desperate times required madness. I just hoped

my ploy disguised as menace would suffice to calm its temper.

I stretched my hands and reached for its spine. "I will burn you if you don't come with me right now," I said, caressing it with my burning-hot fingers.

It chided again, but this time a bit fainter than before. Believing we'd reached an understanding, I let the warmth concentrated on my fingertips recede, and grabbed the grimoire with both hands.

I pulled it out of the hole and stared at it. Under the crimson moonlight, it looked like something a demon would have on his nightstand. Dark leather and golden runes wrapped around old sheets of paper. Tiny spikes decorated its edges. It was obvious this book didn't like to be touched.

"I'll bring you to him. Promise," I whispered and got back to my feet. My muscles creaked in protest, and then I forced myself to run.

As I approached the town hall, the air grew hotter and the night brighter with flames and the lighthouse's radiant beam.

Human cries and demonic shrieks mingled in the distance. My heart tightened with the same intensity as I urged my legs to run faster. *Please let me arrive in time*, I chanted in my head over and over again.

Adam's grimoire had made itself smaller and retracted its spikes so I could grab it with one hand. For some reason, that only made my anxiety spurn. If the wicked thing was willing to help me, it could mean we were in

deeper shit than I'd anticipated.

When I reached the garden, the first thing I saw was ashes. They covered trees and buildings in a grey blanket and turned all my anxiety into sadness. I gasped as my eyes wandered. Bodies with limbs bent at strange angles lay unclaimed at every corner. The living rocked back and forth, murmuring incomprehensible prayers.

My worst fear had come to pass. I'd arrived too late.

I dragged my feet through the soft ground and held the grimoire to my heavy heart. I wished I could reach it as easily as I once had reached Spirits, but the thing remained silent in my arms. Nausea overwhelmed me as if someone had put a noose around my neck.

It took me a while to realize I'd picked up my medallion and held it to my lips. The garnet felt unnaturally cold against my skin.

I trembled and scoured the gardens for Adam.

But I found her instead. A nest of disheveled red hair. Ashes clinging to deep and ugly wounds. I knelt next to her in horror. This was the consequence of my selfishness, but nothing could have prepared me for the sight of Sally's body pierced almost beyond recognition.

Sobs shook me, and I hugged myself.

"Why?" I cried. My powers, once beautiful, now served only to summon death and destruction. I grabbed her bloodied hands and kissed her strong fingers. "I'm sorry," I whispered, but there was no comfort in my lies. "I'm so sorry, Sally… I don't know how to fix it. Come back to me so we can fix it together… Please…"

As I finished uttering those words, someone cried. My neck snapped, and I found myself staring at Caleb. He was dragging Julien's inert body. An ugly wound pierced his

right leg. I put down Sally's hand gently and ran to them.

"Caleb, what's happening?" I grabbed Julien's free arm and put it around my shoulders.

"The big one saw through it..." I knew immediately he was talking about the mad prince of demons.

I clenched my jaw. "Where's Adam?" I asked, as we placed Julien's heavy body against a tree trunk.

"I lost them, Lau..." His eyes shone with pure fear and madness. I saw myself reflected in them, and that spurned me awake.

Holding his chin, I forced him to meet my eyes. "Caleb, listen to me," I said. "I need you. Please. I can't do this without you." His eyes focused. There was still fear in them, but another emotion had brewed underneath. "I have no right to ask you this, but please help me find Adam. He can end this."

Caleb nodded slowly. "Okay, what do you need?"

We left Sally and Julien behind and headed into chaos. Flames, ashes, and putrid meat had claimed every spot and we had to hop to make our way through the gardens. Our search started in the place where Caleb had last seen Adam. The rest was guesswork, luck, and an increasingly tormented grimoire that chided every time we took a wrong turn.

"Do I want to know what that thing is?" Caleb asked.

"No," I answered plainly.

Caleb spotted Adam first. He stood on top of a fallen tree, howling orders to the survivors and tossing bottles of *aguardente* – turned into Molotov cocktails – into the

night. The weight that had been crushing my chest lifted, and I dared to believe we could still turn the tables around.

But then my hopes shattered when the sound of claps echoed in the night.

"Bravo!" a woman's voice said. The blood froze in my veins. "Bravo, bravo, bravo!" Her voice swelled in a horrific crescendo.

I clenched my muscles, holding Adam's grimoire to my heart. Everyone that was still fighting stopped moving. I turned in the voice's direction, but the pain of reality was worse than any blow I'd received.

Her red eyes scrutinized the scene as she sat on a branch, legs dangling in the night. Her terrible beauty was unmistakable, even from afar. Once our eyes met, she laughed, and the sound was as chilling as I remembered. My stomach twisted in anger.

I placed the grimoire in Caleb's hands. "Remember when I said someone was coming for our heads?" He nodded; all blood had drained from his face. "Whatever happens, make sure this reaches Adam. Do not look her in the eyes. Do not stop running. Do not ask questions. Go. Now."

Caleb swallowed and turned to leave, gripping the grimoire so strongly his knuckles had turned to chalk. I rolled up my sleeves and reached for my *Kunai*, feeling deep in my guts this would be the last time I'd use them. I kissed the blades and prayed to my Spirits. As soon as Lilith's shape dissolved into thin air, I let my blades fly to meet her.

They didn't miss, but instead of gasps of pain, Lilith's mad laughs resumed, filling my ears like cotton. I knew

the blades wouldn't stop her, but I only needed to distract her. And as my ruse took effect, I crashed into Lilith's delicate figure and blocked her from reaching Caleb.

Her long fingers wrapped around my throat in a heartbeat. I choked, and from the corner of my eyes, I noticed Caleb had stopped running. "Asshole," I cursed. I kicked the air like an octopus trying to escape a trap. I stopped only when my leather boots met Lilith's ribs.

She gasped, released me, and I fell with a thud. My broken rib pushed the air out of my lungs, but I forced myself to breathe and scream as loudly as I could. "Caleb, go!"

My scream shook him from his daze. He looked at me one last time, nodded, and ran in Adam's direction. Lilith was too quick for me to react. Before I had the chance to stand up, she put her legs around my torso, immobilizing me. I tried to reach for my blades, but she buried her left elbow on my bicep and wrapped her long fingers around my wrist.

She stood on top of me and all I could see was the blood-thirst in her eyes.

"Dear Lauryn, let us not overreact, shall we?" she whispered in my ear. "Plus, do you really think your little friend is safe just because I'm sitting right here with you?" Malice dripped from her lips like poison.

Caleb, I thought. Heart pounding, I arched my neck. The strong, sandy-haired fisher was nothing but a dark shape within the limits of my vision. Until a massive shadow rushed to meet him. Too late, I saw it for what it was.

The beast caught up with Caleb in a heartbeat. I watched the fisher stop, hesitate, and turn around. *Run, fool*, I screamed in my mind. As if he'd heard me, Caleb halted again. My heart sunk like a rock. Before he moved

another muscle, I knew what he was going to do.

He swung his arm and tossed the grimoire as far away from him as possible. Then he hurled himself against the prince of demons. In one moment, Caleb was moving, his body brimming with life. In the next, the prince beheaded him in a single clean motion.

His body went limp. "No!" I cried, so hard my broken rib chewed my soft flesh. Sobs shook my body. Mind reeling, chest aching, I screamed. "You monster," I spat in Lilith's face.

She arched her eyebrows, feigning surprise. "Am I?" she asked. "This happens when you're soft. Don't tell me you actually cared for the weakling, sweet daughter?"

"I am not your daughter," I barked through clenched teeth.

"Oh, but you are, sweet thing. I claimed you. You're mine." She kissed my forehead, and her breath reached my nostrils. It reeked of death. My medallion reacted to the touch of her putrid lips and burned against my neck.

And then reality faded, and a different version of Lilith materialized before my eyes. She had the same red irises, but her cheeks were softer, and her hair shorter. Gasping, I realized this was either another hallucination or a glimpse into my past.

In my vision, Lilith grabbed me by the shoulders and whispered in my ear, "I claim you. You're mine." The child I had been sobbed.

The ancient pain reached me across the ages, slashing open long-forgotten wounds. Lilith laughed, and my skin crawled with revulsion. Then she took a medallion from her pocket. Almost identical to the one I wore around my neck. But instead of containing a garnet, it

was made of glass.

"Come find me when you wake up," she said, pressing the glass medallion against my chest. At first, silence swelled around us, until all I could hear were my ragged breaths and the frantic beating of my heart.

Then the world exploded, and a loud cry burned me from within.

Panting and confused, I opened my eyes to find present-day Lilith staring at me. My chest still hurt, and my mind struggled to understand. Lilith was mid-sentence when I regained my focus.

"... you can't possibly believe you can save everyone," she was saying. "It's either Adam or these weaklings. Choose."

Tears rolled from my cheeks, and Lilith drank from them, sending shivers down my spine. Through sobs, I said, "I'd rather die."

I closed my eyes, and my body braced for pain. Would she kill me quickly or bathe in my blood? Before I learned the answer, a burst of light washed over us. Warm and glorious, like an orange sunset.

Lilith recoiled and released my hand to shield her eyes. That moment was all I needed. I reached for my faithful blades and pierced one of them through her heart. Transfigured by disbelief, Lilith howled.

I punched her in the face with all the strength I could muster and freed myself from her suffocating embrace. When I stood, panting, Adam was there beside me and a black bird cawed above our heads. I opened my mouth in awe, but before I could speak, Adam grabbed my

hand and pulled me away.

He lifted his hand and ash, flesh, and debris flew out of our path. I smiled as his magic vibrated in the air, diffracting the atmosphere into a kaleidoscope of colors. We were running in the middle of a rainbow, and a faint smile dangled from my lips.

Then Lilith snapped her fingers, and the world wrecked beneath our feet.

CHAPTER FOURTEEN

What Once Was Lost

One moment, I was holding Adam's hand. The next, Lilith was standing between us with death on her tail. She tossed me and held Adam by his neck. The grimoire that he had transmuted into a crow dove from the skies and went straight for Lilith's eyes.

I heard screams and then my surroundings morphed into darkness as I crashed against a tree. Another rib cracked, and the pain blinded me. I tried to get on my feet, but the world whirled, my stomach twisted, and I retched instead. Curling, I fought to breathe. Each inhalation was an ode to agony, and my mind battled against insanity.

I felt him before I saw him with my own eyes. The demon prince arrived. And there was no way Adam could beat them both without my help.

It's time, the Spirit dragon whispered in my mind, and I screamed in despair. *I'm sorry, I can't let you die,* he murmured. There was a touch of finality in his voice. In that split second, the veil of reality lifted against my will,

and I cried my guts out.

Eyes closed, I saw Adam. He wore his favorite tunic, orange and red, like my dragon's scales. He smiled in that boyish and warm way of his. Nothing terrible had happened yet. And then his image broke into a thousand pieces. I opened my eyes, gasping, and watched the world explode before me as dragon and Witch Lord became two beings once again.

"Nagendra!" I screamed and sobbed. Anger and fear mingled on the surface of my skin.

The ashes stirred in reply, and Nagendra, my beautiful Spirit dragon, emerged from the chaos like a phoenix reborn. His roar reverberated through my soul, and a howl of joy and pain rose from my chest. I felt his talons burying in the soil, his wings stretching, and fire bursting like lava from his open jaws.

Lilith froze, her gaze fixed on the red dragon. With a swing of his tail, he forced her to release Adam and cast her away. The prince followed her into the night.

"Kill them," I begged.

With pleasure, Nagendra said. He shook the ashes, still clinging to his massive scales, and flapped his wings. The air shifted and heated under him and in a blink of an eye, he was airborne.

I felt his exhilaration as the wind caressed him, and the skies welcomed his return. And then I remembered Adam, and my joy died quickly. I stood painfully and dragged my torn body towards a bundle of clothes. I found him panting and curling on the floor. His body had shrunk faster than I expected. I wrapped my arms around him and buried my face in the crook of his neck. "I'm sorry," I said, sobbing and clinging to him.

"Lau," he replied in a weak, childish voice, and brought his hand to my cheek. "We're both fools, aren't we?" He grinned and the sight of his smile warmed my heart.

"Proud fools…" I said, tears mingling with my smile. "Can't you reverse the curse?" I asked, trying to keep the panic out of my voice.

He shook his head and my heart sunk. "There's no time." He winced as Lilith's curse consumed him, dragging him back in time. Hot tears streamed from my eyes, washing over me like a storm.

"No, no… Maybe I can still do something. There's still hope… isn't there? There has to be." My voice broke. Eyes closed, I reached for my medallion. A silent prayer in my mind. But only silence leaked through. "I don't understand," I said, opening my eyes and staring at the garnet. It seemed different. There were cracks and scratches on its surface I didn't recall seeing before.

Then Adam placed a tiny hand on top of mine. "You've done too much for me already." A weak smile formed on his lips. He was barely three years old now. His shirt hanged loosely on his torso. Small curls erupted from the top of his head. "Maybe I deserve this. This war… my selfishness brought us nothing but pain. I'm not that different from her. Just a different brand of the same nightmare."

I hugged him fiercely. "You're nothing like her!" Fear and longing danced in my chest. The curse kept pulling him relentlessly. His small body dwindling at a terrifying pace.

When his sobs turned into cries, I lifted my gaze. Adam was nothing but a baby in my arms. We'd spent decades preparing for this possibility, but my mind

refused to accept our reality.

I brought the medallion to my lips and sobbed. “Please…” I begged to no one.

Adam’s cries intensified, and then time froze.

Eyes like moss stared at me. The temperature dropped, enveloping me in an icy embrace.

“Did you come to watch us die?” I sneered. Vanara’s sorrow cut through my soul like a hot knife. “Enough,” I screamed, and the pain receded. “What more do you want from me? There’s nothing left for me to give.”

“You’re wrong,” he spoke, for the first time. His mellow voice hurt more than all my wounds combined. Then he pointed at my medallion, and my chest tightened with despair.

“I see.” I failed to hide my bitterness. “You were the first Spirit I ever summoned. Are you telling me you want to be my last?” Vanara didn’t reply, and anguish spread like fire on the surface of my skin. “At least tell me you’ll save him,” I begged, lowering my eyes to the newborn in my arms.

“We can’t.”

I closed my eyes and exhaled sharply. I’d forgotten you can’t bargain with Spirits. “What about Lilith?”

“We will seal her in our world. You have our word.”

A bitter laugh escaped my lips. Until this moment, I had built my life on broken promises. How many people had I damaged in the wake of my selfishness? I was rotten. Judge and executioner. The pale faces of Sally, Caleb, Julien, Jeff, and Saul danced in front of my

eyes. I should have shared their fate. Instead, I was still breathing, still clinging to life like a parasite. If there was a way to end this war, why couldn't I bring myself to pay the price?

Nagendra roared in the distance, shaking me from my daze. I felt the sharp pain in his torso as Lilith pierced one of his thick scales. I gasped and trembled. There was no winning with Lilith, was there? She always had the upper hand, no matter how hard we fought.

And then Adam's tiny and plump fingers wrapped around mine. I stared at the baby in my arms, mesmerized. He had finally surrendered himself to a heavy sleep. He smelled of hot chocolate and fireplaces, and although it tore me, I untangled our fingers and forced myself to wrap him in clothes that no longer fitted. Then I placed him on a heap of frozen ashes at my feet. With a last kiss on his forehead, I melted the ice surrounding Adam and whispered, "I love you." The truest thing I had ever said.

When I stood, I found Vanara's warm eyes settled on me. An emotion I couldn't name danced around his features. Somehow, it made me feel safe. But there was no certainty in what I was about to do.

Cold sweat formed on my palms. Breathing heavily, I took the medallion dangling around my neck. I stared at it one last time and stretched my arm in Vanara's direction. Emptiness and uncertainty mingled dangerously in my chest. There was no other choice, was there?

At the last possible minute, I withdrew. But by then, it was too late. Vanara saw through my cowardice and clutched my hand before I could blink. Wrapping his strong hand around mine, he said, "I'm sorry, stardust."

"What did you say?" I screamed, holding the cool garnet tighter. The giant gorilla smiled a sad and heavy smile.

"There's no other way," he said, crushing my hand and the garnet with it.

My breath quickened, and my heart raced in my chest. I tried pulling my hand away, but Vanara's grip was too strong. "What are you doing?" I screamed, punching his arm. "Let go of me."

In the cacophony of my struggle, I heard the garnet break. Pain claimed every atom of my being. I cried, panic burning through me. Then, cursing, I bit Vanara's hand until blood filled my mouth. My blood, not his.

Strength drained from my muscles. Life bled from my entrails as I knelt in front of my Spirit, sobbing like a child. "Make it stop," I begged.

"I can't, stardust."

"Why?"

"Because this is the only way to set you free."

I lifted my gaze and stared into his eyes. He crushed my hand so hard; I felt my bones breaking and sharp pieces of garnet burying deep into my skin. Bone and crystal touched, surrounded by my minced flesh. And then everything went dark.

I saw myself through Vanara's eyes. The same way I watched his unwaning figure through mine. I was him, and he was me. We were two beings and one soul. Two bodies and one mind.

We saw Nagendra fighting Lilith in the distance. Glorious and covered in dark blood, the Witch Queen

danced with screams and nightmares. Nagendra replied with fire and snarls. I bit my lips apprehensively, and saw myself doing it through Vanara's eyes.

The world faded before us in a heartbeat. It was only Vanara and me, in a world devoid of light.

"Listen to me," Vanara said. "When Lilith killed your mother and claimed you, she did something not even the strongest Spirit could undo." He lowered his gaze towards the spot where our hands met.

"The garnet was never my token, was it?" I asked.

"No, it was a curse, a powerful one used to bound you to Lilith's will. She stole your heart, stardust. And then she turned it into glass."

I nodded, strangely at peace with his words. Deep down, I knew he was right. "There was never a thief, was there?" I asked, crying.

"There was a thief, but he didn't kill your mother. He just saw the two of you laying on the snow. Cold. Dead. And then he tried to seize the moment. By then, you were no longer ours. You belonged to Lilith. So, when he started unfastening your boots, you snapped. And in your anger, you pulled me into the flesh world… I'm sure you remember the rest."

I nodded and closed my eyes, as if not seeing Vanara's face would make his words less real. "Why do you keep calling me stardust?" I urged, desperate.

"That's the last piece, stardust, something you have to figure out by yourself. Closing your eyes won't make it any less painful. Believe me." He was not wrong. "Spirits don't have a physical body. As much as Lilith tried to erase our existence, I'm sure you know this by now. We can change our appearances whenever we

want. But most of us choose to keep a certain shape. You see, it helps us deal with our own losses. With our own deaths." His voice cracked.

I lifted my gaze, suddenly electrified, and stared deep into Vanara's eyes. And then I saw it. The stern, melancholic gaze, staring back at me. How did I miss this?

Trembling, I forced myself to stand and dragged myself towards Vanara. I placed a bloodied hand on his cheek. Her cheek.

"Do you see it now, stardust?"

I cried and buried my face in her fur. And there it was. The smell of mornings and freshly cut grass. "Mama," I said. She released my broken hand and wrapped her arm around me. "Why did you wait so long?" I lifted my gaze.

"I'm sorry, stardust. Your heart had to be broken before I could show myself to you. And that wicked creature who calls herself the Witch Queen did it all by herself." Her peaceful features twisted in revulsion. "It was the only way to break her curse. Now, stardust, there's one last thing you need to do."

I inhaled the morning air and opened my arms. The vegetation stirred around me as if tormented by ghosts and Spirits. My medallion, once adorned with a precious gem, lay shattered at my feet. Its true and twisted form revealed by the faint sunlight.

Mother had brought me to the battlefront, where Lilith and Nagendra danced with blood, fire, and ashes. The demon prince lay on the ground right beside me. His carbonized body steamed and reeked with the smell

of death. *That one's for Caleb*, I thought, spitting on him.

Before Lilith could sense my presence, I gathered the last drops of strength left in my broken body and ran towards her. I smelled the death that enveloped her like a storm and gnarled, pushing through her defenses. I watched the smirk vanish from her face as she realized I no longer had my medallion.

Crying, I crashed against her delicate figure and hugged her as tightly as I could. In a heartbeat, Nagendra was right beside me, the coolness gathered around us like lightning, and then I closed my eyes and pierced the veil of reality, pushing my soul and Lilith's to the Spirit world, her terrified screams echoing in my mind.

As I descended into darkness, a smile formed on my lips. I was dying not in a forsaken corner of the world, but at home, surrounded by the people I'd come to love.

CHAPTER FIFTEEN

Stardust

In my dream, I was boundless. My fragmented soul floated in a sea of stars.

Memories came and went, but none stayed.

Ages or eons elapsed. I became stardust, and it became me. I could be in a million places at once. Witness death, rebirths, and the clash of titans in the skies. Sadness, happiness, and anger mingled with painful ferocity within the tiny fragments of my being. But nothing eternal can forever remain the same.

One day, the pull started. An invisible force wrapped itself around the microscopic pieces of my soul and stitched them back together. I struggled, cursed, and agonized, but the pull was stronger than my will. Once its work was done, I was trapped in the ugly confinements of a tiny new soul.

At first, I fled like a ghost ship in turbulent waters. My mind rebelled against the new boundaries of my being. I would have driven myself mad if voices hadn't pierced my shadows.

They called me Lau. A name I recognized but could not claim as my own. It had belonged to a different person when the world was still made of light. Relentlessly, the voices told me the most wondrous stories about dragons, demons, and pirates in the skies. I basked in their warmth and light.

Eventually, even they were absorbed by the vastness of the universe, and I was all alone.

Or so I thought.

Nothing extraordinary happened in the time it took me to traverse a galaxy. When my being was about to leave the safe boundaries of that cluster of stars, an explosion shook me.

Instinct drove me to cover my eyes, but my insubstantial being failed to shield me from the burst of light. I choked and screamed in pain. When my soul was about to crack, something immense grabbed me and devoured me.

Anguish took over, and instantly, the atmosphere became humid, toxic, and too heavy to breathe. Like being tossed inside the belly of a beast. I stretched my insubstantial hands and touched the slippery surface of dark, icy walls.

I shuddered and punched it with all my strength. To my surprise, the wall rebounded as if made of flesh.

Confused, I backed away. "Who's there?" I screamed, but the echo of my voice was my only answer.

As soon as I stood, slender arms wrapped themselves around me. Shivers went down every atom of my soul. "Stardust," a female voice said.

I gasped as realization hit me. "Mom?"

Turning around, I found her. We stood heart to

heart, two immaterial beings with kindred Spirits. I hugged her, crying with joy, as much as one could hug and cry when made of stardust.

"Mom," I said through sobs. She tightened our embrace and for the first time in a long time, I felt human again.

"Got you." She grabbed my hand and kissed the tip of my fingers. Warmth spread across my chest. "Let me look at you," she said, and I took a step back. "Strong and beautiful, as I raised you to be." Her voice cracked and I could tell she was on the verge of tears. I reached out to her and touched the edge of her being. Sadness spilled through.

"Mom, what's happening?" I asked, unable to keep the anxiety from my voice.

"Maybe I raised you too well. I thought we'd lost you there for a minute." She laughed and her soul turned into a kaleidoscope of colors.

"But you didn't," I said.

"I didn't. But we have little time left, stardust."

"I don't understand."

"You need to get back," she said, her voice failing again.

"No, I want to stay here with you. There are so many things I still want to ask you."

"You will, dear, just not today."

"Why not? I want to know all there is to know about you. Why there are no more summoners left? Why…" I sobbed and snatched the fringe of her soul.

"Look at me," she demanded, and I lifted my gaze. "We will have an eternity together. We'll travel to other galaxies and other universes. I promise you. Just not today. You need to go back to your people, to your

home, to your happiness…"

"I died… How could I ever go back?"

"Haven't you noticed, stardust? A summoner never dies. Lilith was foolish to think she could erase us from the face of the earth. The more violent our deaths, the stronger our Spirits become."

"Then… will you come back with me?"

"I can't… My body is gone, stardust…" Her voice cracked. "Spirits can't heal flesh wounds, but they can heal the rest." Her soul brushed mine and sent ripples down my spine. She grabbed my hands again and kissed them, leaning so close to me I could feel her warmth and light. "You'll have a lifetime to search for answers. The only ones you need now are these: I love you and I'm proud of you." Tears ran down my face as I clung to her embrace. "Goodbye, stardust. Be free."

"Mom, don't do it. Mom!" I screamed, and the world around me collapsed.

My mother vanished. Silence replaced her voice. Cold replaced her warmth. And then gravity pulled me so intensely I thought my soul would break in half. A cry pierced the darkness. Mine or my mother's, I could not tell.

It all ended with a burst of color and a flash of light. My flesh body convulsed, and I woke up coughing and gasping for air. Breathing painfully, I laid on a soft mattress in a dimly lit room. Sweat covered the back of my neck and my voice came out hoarse and dry.

My freshly forged Spirit uprooted the numbness that had taken over my body. The pain of the process was excruciating, like waking up from a nightmare, only to find your blood had stopped flowing. As the sensation

returned to my limbs, I screamed and tossed. It was like being pierced by a thousand tiny needles.

After a while, though, I realized it was better to stay still. In my flesh, death gave way to life, and numbness gave way to pain. I clenched my teeth and waited because there was nothing else I could do.

For all I knew, an eternity could have elapsed before the stinging finally stopped. I risked moving a finger and all the muscles of my hand trembled in protest. It took me a dozen more tries until the throbbing stopped and then I moved to the next finger.

My eyes wandered around the room. It dawned on me that every single piece of furniture and every layer of paint were unknown to me. I didn't know where I was, nor if I was safe here. All I knew was that it was best to leave before nightfall.

It took me hours, but I regained control of my body. And as soon as I did, I slipped out of the massive bed. When my feet touched the cold floor, ripples danced in my skin. I risked standing up, and for a moment, the world wouldn't stop spinning. I sat on the bed and noticed, for the first time, my hair had grown too long. Beautiful bushy locks had replaced my typically straight hair. I touched it, mesmerized, suddenly certain this was the way my hair was supposed to be.

I dragged my half-numb body out of the bed-chamber, and then through the front door. The light blinded me for a minute, and I shielded my eyes. I'd been among the stars for so long, it was hard to believe my eyes couldn't handle a little light. But then again, as my Spirit roamed the universe, this body had probably never left that bed.

Childish laughs, grilled fish, and exciting conversations reached me. I lowered my hand, bitten by curiosity, and my tired eyes finally focused.

White and blue reigned the skies above. Green grass stretched as far as the eye could see. And then I saw them, and my knees gave way. Townsfolk danced around fires or sat on benches around large wooden tables. I recognized Sally's nest of red hair, and Saul's laugh among them. My eyes filled with tears.

I grabbed the soft grass between my fingers and sobbed with pure joy.

After a while, someone blocked out the sun. "You're back," the person said in a husky voice.

I lifted my chin and saw Adam's dark eyes staring back at me. He was wearing a fresh linen shirt, with the top unbuttoned, and rolled-up sleeves. His long dark hair danced with the wind and a bright smile adorned his features.

He crouched and met me at eye level. No longer confined to a child's body, he looked comfortable in his own skin again. I lifted my hand and brushed his cheek; he closed his eyes, savoring the moment.

"I thought I'd lost you." He placed his hand on top of mine and opened his eyes. His irises were a mixture of sadness and longing. I could dive into them and lose myself forever.

He put his knees on the dirt and wrapped his hands around my frail body.

"I'm not leaving your side ever again," he said, his voice cracking.

A smile formed on my lips. "Good, because I'm not leaving either."

He pushed me gently and stared deep into my soul. I grabbed his hands and kissed his fingertips. They tasted of salt and lemon. His eyes lit up, and he cupped my face with his firm hands.

Leaning closer, our lips brushed, and the air filled with static. And this time, I dove and dared to get lost in the sweetness of his embrace.

THE END

Acknowledgments

First, I want to thank my husband for not letting me give up on my dream of writing this book, for helping me stay focused and motivated when life became overwhelming, and encouraging me to be brave and believe in this story. To my family and friends, for understanding when I needed to disappear, often for days at a time, to finish writing this book.

A heartfelt thank you to my marvelous trio of beta-readers. Day Leitao, for her eye-opening and constructive criticism on the first five chapters of this book and for being an amazing source of inspiration. Catarina Pinto for her incredibly honest remarks and countless conversations about what it means to be an author in this day and age. Carolina Gonçalves for her unique insights, for enduring my rambles, and for pushing me to finish this book on time.

To my fantastic editor, Jess Lawrence, without whom this book would never have found its own voice. I'm forever grateful for her valuable and thought-provoking remarks. Thank you for helping me see what was missing, what needed to be salvaged, and what needed to be rewritten. Because of you, many of the scenes I was ready to delete ended up becoming my absolute favorites of this book!

To Saint Jupiter, my amazing cover designer, for lending me her incredible talent and transforming the theme and key elements of this story into the most gorgeous cover art I could ever asked for. Thank you for helping me draw the right readers to this adventure with your beautiful skill.

To Susana Imaginário for being such a genuine, approachable, and incredibly talented role model. Thank you for allowing me to pick your brain and for your dark and beautiful stories that often accompanied me whenever I needed a break from life. To the amazing members of my ARC team and newsletter subscribers, thank you for the kind words, excitement, encouragement, and precious feedback. I heard you, and your words mattered in more ways than you could possibly imagine. Thanks for being amazing Andreia Delgado, Ana Jesus, Maria João Soares, Leonor Ferrão, Ricardo Balsinhas, Catarina Prata, Jéssica Reis, Cláudia Amaral, Joana Nunes, Ana Silva, Carla Correia, Tânia Pataia, Laura Silva, you are too many to name or count!

I want to thank my grandparents for being the most unconventional, inspiring, happy, and headstrong elders I have ever met. I miss you every day and wrote this book for you. I wish you were here to celebrate this achievement with me. Last, I want to thank God for nudging me in the right direction and fostering my resilience and creativity. This book would never have existed if God hadn't taught me, through great pains, that real power needs not come from strength.

Thank you, dear reader, for taking the time to read this book and for allowing me to take you on this journey! I hope you enjoyed this story. If you did, please consider writing a review. Without reviews, indie books like the one you just read are destined to remain invisible on retail sites. Leave your review on:

Amazon

Goodreads

About the author

Ana C. Reis is an author of weird and fast-paced stories. She lives with her husband in Strasbourg, France, a city made of fairy tales and warm wine. She has a PhD degree in biotechnology, a love for traveling, and an obsession with Costa Rican coffee.

Join her mailing list to receive FREE updates about her upcoming releases.

Subscribe for
Monthly updates

Back then, most parents knew very little about child psychology. At this young age, a child's name is closely related to their identity. These children require a loving hand and emotional support to adapt to this life altering change. I'm sure it's also difficult for new parents to adjust to an 'instant' child. The whole 'family' can benefit from a psychologist or counselor.

However, it was a common theme among my parent's generation to *never* attend counseling, let alone utter the word 'psychologist.' Anyone, who was 'weak' enough to need it, was labeled 'mentally unstable.' Insane asylums existed and the immense fear of even looking in that direction was enough to kill any thought of mental or emotional support.

This left a huge gaping hole in 'parenting' around the sixties. Imagine calling out to your eighteen month old, using a brand new name? My son, Brydon, knew his name when he was only twelve months old! He knew it well! When I think of the thousands of children who went through this split in identity without proper support, my heart aches for them and I hope they are able to heal.

"I'm sorry! I love you! Can I give you a hug?" A mother whispers, as she reaches for her child.

This kind of hope that is never lost in a child. A child will always yearn and rarely ever give up.

I can say with absolute certainty, that I never received a gesture of love and kindness in this home. Tough love was the medicine of my future.

I can only hope that I was held at least once by the Caregiver at the orphanage. I was told that one of them knitted me a beautiful pink outfit to go to my new home in. Perhaps, in a quiet moment, this kind woman was able to hold and comfort me in preparation for the hard, barren years to come. Perhaps she whispered a silent blessing.

My adoptive parents were tough and bled grit and sweat. My dad was wiry and had dark brown hair with unusual sea blue eyes that pierced through my being like a razor-tipped sword, swung to do maximum damage. I could never meet his eyes. The hatred in them was too painful to even fathom.

My mom stood only 5'4" but she was a giant to me, a Goliath. There was never a moment when I was NOT terrified of her. Her eyes were brown, as well, and just as scary.

They worked hard and were tough as nails. They held very strong opinions, quite like a boxer holds his gloves, tight to his chest. They hated anyone who was on 'welfare,' it didn't matter what the reason was. They believed in 'capital punishment,' a death for a death. Mom made so many inappropriate comments at my wedding reception just to get people to sign a petition for Capital Punishment.

They were staunch advocates in corporal punishment. They wielded weapons of mass pain with great fury and delusional justification. Whatever they did, they did well.

My mom actually announced at my wedding, "You will now become a respectable wife!" They didn't really care what society thought, but used this as their scapegoat. At my wedding they were released of the stigma that their daughter was, God forbid, a 'single parent.'

They adopted my brother, Robin, a few months

before me. He was a year older than me. He had tight, blond, natural curls—it was considered a true 'afro' at the time—and he had a wonderful mischievous nature.

As I browse through his school pictures, the wonderful sparkle in his eyes gradually disappears. I see hate burn through so intensely, that I must look away before I start to cry.

His eyes tell a harrowing story. Around 13 years old, they are weary and shrouded in anger and defiance. Every picture and every year, following, carries more and more sadness and devastation. These people were experts at breaking us down.

In our earlier years, mom wielded the wooden spoon like she was giving medicine on a regular basis. Pulling our pants down and bending over set us up for our daily dose. However, I could never grow a tough skin like my brother. I hated these moments, because every single hit with the spoon erased a teaspoon of trust and innocence from my soul. Soon, I would be left with an empty shell.

When I was about 5 years old, my mom was sitting in her favorite chair, knitting. My brother and I started arguing over some board game. I can't remember the name of it, but I remember pushing the clear, plastic dome in the middle and making the dice jump. It made a cool popping sound! I think I was popping it over and over just to irritate him.

Mom didn't like any interruption into her world. She didn't care that we were just kids. Children needed to 'be seen and not heard.'

She peered over her magnifying glasses, "Enough! Grab the spoon and come here! Both of you!"

No warning, no build up, no attempting to re-direct

us.

I dragged my feet as the familiar swell of fear rose in my chest, threatening to cut off my oxygen. My brother, however, bounded over with the spoon. "You can't hurt me!" He taunted her.

The look of surprise in her eyes morphed immediately to rage. I wanted to puke! Needless to say, she made sure the spoon broke and there was no doubt, the color purple stained my brother's backside for many days after. Due to my brother's defiance, I managed to get away with only a mild beating.

I don't remember my very first beating. There were too many of them. I don't remember going three or four days WITHOUT getting a beating. All I remember is a dark hole of intense fear and helplessness.

Over the years, my soul got lost in the pain, agony, and self-hatred, and my brother's got lost in anger and absolute revenge.

Many years later when I finally became a mother, I taught my son, Brydon, about 'corporal punishment' and 'capital punishment.' I taught him why I didn't agree with either. With corporal punishment, we are teaching people that if they are in power, then they are allowed to wield the stick, sort to speak.

Whoever is in charge at that moment gets to have ultimate power over another human being. It's like a bully who gets beat at home, then goes to school and beats his classmates. Each time, it's the person in power doing the beating. The same for the death penalty, the only message we are teaching others is: "It's okay to kill, if you are the one in power, right now."

As I reflect and begin to heal, I wish to tell this

beautiful little girl: “I know this is very scary for you! I know how lonely you feel! You are very brave and strong! I promise from now on, if you need a hug, I will be there for you. Anytime you want to come out and play, I will protect you and I will play with you! It’s finally safe to explore this wonderful, amazing world! I love you so much!”

Chapter 2

For the first 6 years of my life, we lived in the small town of Elk Point. I don't remember the town itself, except that my dad owned a blue garage with a blue house right next door. He worked as a very successful mechanic. My mom stayed at home and—well, I'm not sure what she did.

We were often sent out of the house to be babysat by my cousin, Wendy, who was six years older than me. She lived with us on and off. Her mother, my mom's sister, would get lost on long drinking binges and leave Wendy alone for days on end.

She was my mom's favorite—without a doubt. My brother and I came from "bad stock" as my mom was fond of saying. It wasn't my cousin's fault that she had an aunt who was biased and mean, but I resented her for years. My mom's voice would raise an octave and give off this sickening-sweet, child-like sound whenever she spoke to Wendy. "Oh sweetie, what did you do today with the kids? "Are you okay, do you need anything?"

She, actually, spoke the same way to her little Chihuahua. She called her 'Pup.' This dog honed in on the unseen realm, in other words, she knew my mom's innermost attitude and had no problem lapping up the attention. She would always growl and snap at us kids whenever we approached; then, immediately, she would lick mom's hand for more gum (had to be 'juicy fruit'); her tail and butt in a constant jig.

Many times, I wanted to put the damn dog in her place—or knock her off it! However, this thought had to be deeply hidden or I'd pay the price. Even the dog knew I was licked! The little bitch!

It was in this small town of Elk Point, where my arm was broken. It was a cold, wet, September day. Most people would be curled up by the fireplace or reading a book. The weather never bothered my parents. In fact, they seemed to take pleasure in the worst of it. They would ball up their fists and head straight into the storm.

I guess that's what they call two storms colliding—the perfect storm.

My parents were a storm to be reckoned with. They were scary. They made all the decisions. We obeyed. Everyone obeyed. End of story. It didn't matter who you were, if you ended up in their space, you were under their rule. It was like black magic, they could command strangers or people of authority, alike. It didn't matter who or where you came from. My parents were gods.

It's too bad they didn't get the handbook on 'Godly manners.'

On this day, they decided to go horseback riding. After a half hour of riding, my dad spotted a steep descent next to a fast moving river and directed us to follow him down. He made it safely, followed by my mom, and then my brother. Their horses were inhaling the cool, clean water as I started down.

I peer sideways over the horse and notice it's straight down. I shake my head. I'm not going down this cliff!

I'm not going to make it! I don't want to go! I don't like this feeling! It makes me sick to my stomach. My tummy really hurts! It's raining and wet.

I allow the reins to go loose through my tightly clenched fingers. I don't have a choice. As each leg of the horse finds purchase on the uneven terrain, my upper half starts bobbing in time to its abrupt movements. Our heads are going to hit! Another jolt and I will be knocked out cold. The horse probably won't notice. Their heads are so hard. What if I fall into the raging river at the bottom?

I shake my head. I can't get my mind to focus. I feel like I'm swimming already and there's a rock pushing me down! It's the fear crowding in and it won't let me think! Please stop! Each jolt creates an explosion in my brain!

My thighs are trembling and I can't squeeze them like I'm supposed to. I hope they don't notice! Why won't they give us saddles? My butt starts sliding forward. I try to scramble backwards and grab chunks of the horse's mane to hang on. It's more slippery than the leather! The horse is heading straight down! Oh no, I'm falling right off the front. This is going to hurt! I call out, "Help, I can't stop! Ahhhh..."

"Don't be so lazy! Tighten your legs around the

horse!" Mom screams. I can't do it. I've lost control. I'm riding a moving mountain on top of a mountain! I'm flying off the edge!

I fall hard on a root sticking out of the ground and almost miss being stepped on by the back end of the horse, as it rears to sidestep me. It's only focus is for its own safety. Mine is to blink away the fuzziness that's threatening to engulf me and to find my breath. It's been knocked out of me. I see stars and I can't get any air in! Something is squeezing my chest! The pressure around each eye, feels like a cork about to pop. Help me...

My lungs force air in with a painful gasp, and the world around me starts to clear. I hurt everywhere! I'm shaking like a leaf, probably from the cold and shock.

I see my dad run for my horse and grab it. A few moments pass before I'm able to sit up. The movement causes a jolt of pain up my right arm. Something is off. It won't move properly and the pins and needles are a strange sensation. There is sharp pain in one spot and the rest of the arm is numb. Something's not right.

I wipe away the tears and snot with my left sleeve. I'm scared, and in a lot of pain, and I want to go home. I'm wet and muddy from head to toe. I start trembling from the pain, the cold, and the fear. I want to be alone in my bedroom with my toys. Please! I hold my right arm and squeeze myself into a ball.

Wait a minute! Why aren't they helping me?" These last thoughts get thrown to the wind. My dad comes out of nowhere and grabs me by the back of my pants. He throws me up on the horse and makes me go up the incline first.

"Hang on and for Christ's sakes, don't let go if you

know what's good for you!" He looks like a distorted comic-book character, with a cigarette dangling from the side of his mouth. He is so angry at me! He swats the back end of the horse to send it on its way.

Irony is a strange bedfellow, as the same thing happened in reverse.

I can only use my left hand on the reins, as the horse lunges upward to get a foothold on the loose soil. This time, I bob back once and instantly slide off its rear end. I can't even remember hitting the ground this time. Everything shuts down.

I, actually, don't remember the rest of the day, that night, or the weekend. It's just a blur of pain and agony.

This happened on a Saturday. I spent the rest of the weekend holding my right arm. It wasn't until my parents were called in by the teacher at the school, that they finally took me to the hospital.

I received a cast and the pain settled down. The teachers signed it and drew happy faces all over it. I felt so special with a beautiful, colored arm canvas.

My parents convinced the doctor that they had never seen a broken bone and didn't know the signs. It was a small town and everyone covered for each other. I would hope that this feeble explanation wouldn't fly anywhere else, especially since my Mom had taken training as a nurse's aide.

They say that the brain creates neuro-pathways from our experiences as children. As adults, we revert to these same pathways when something similar happens. As I see my journey unfold, I can see where pain will be a huge mountain and obstacle to overcome. My relationship to pain and the agony it represents becomes, for many years, a blinding path of addiction and all-consuming obsession.

For many years, pain, itself, was the demon that held its grip on me and would knock me down into a tail-spin so fast that my head couldn't catch up. I would be lost in a blinding storm, not knowing how to climb out. My body and mind would respond to pain as if I was being held in a death grip. I couldn't even process what was happening. All I could do was endure it.

Pain was the ultimate enemy and I was going to vanquish it by any means necessary. Even if this meant multiple trips to the Emergency, only to discover, most of the time, that it wasn't life threatening. I was absolutely positive each time they were wrong. How could pain be this intense and not life threatening? The few times that it was life threatening, brought absolute redemption and satisfaction.

For a few years, as an adult, dealing with a lifetime of torture and abuse, I was caught in an extremely dysfunctional relationship with pain. It took a lot of work for my soul to remove the 'emergency' blinking lights each time a pain receptor lit up. 'Fight or flight' no longer had to be the only option.

Now, I'm able to tell this amazing little girl, "You were so strong and brave that day! These adults should never have taken you down that steep incline with a horse; and, definitely, should never have forced you back up the hill. It was their responsibility to cuddle you after the first fall, and ride back up with you on their lap, or carry you up the hill. They should have protected you with their lives! Anyone else would have immediately taken you to the hospital. You don't need to panic anymore when you have pain. We can deal with each incident together, as it happens. You are special and beautiful and loved! From now on, I will be there for you!"

Chapter 3

When I turned seven, we moved about 70 kilometers northwest of Whitecourt up the 'Windfall' road.

The Woodland Cree Nation was the first settler in the area around Whitecourt. They called it, 'Sagitawah' – "the place where the rivers meet."

The town of Whitecourt is located in a valley, on the eastern border of the foothills of the Rocky Mountains. There are four waterways winding through the area: the mighty Athabasca River, the majestic McLeod River, Eagle River, and Beaver Creek,

For years, the pulp mill was a major source of jobs. The softwood, used for lumber, grows large and hearty in the rich soil of this beautiful land; all maintained by these waterways. There is no shortage of fauna in and around Whitecourt. Moose, dear, bear, rabbit, squirrel, weasel, pheasant, and the occasional cougar roam the bush.

It doesn't matter what type of weather or season, the scenery is always breathtaking! This is true bush land, thicker than the eye can penetrate and teaming with life everywhere you look.

My parents brought in heavy equipment. They carved a long driveway, straight into the bush and then they cut down a wide swath of trees for the buildings. We all picked roots, out of the ground, for the next three years or more.

We had neighbors, but we were all spaced out by several miles. If we needed help, we were on our own.

My parents filled the farm with horses, cows, goats, chickens, geese, turkeys, and for a few years we even had pigs. We had three large gardens located at different sections of the farm. One was a large potato garden, another grew only raspberries and strawberries, and the one closest to the house, grew the rest of the vegetables.

There is ALWAYS work to do on a farm. It doesn't matter what the season is. In the middle of winter, we were expected to put our snowsuits on, and chop and haul wood for the furnace. This job never actually ended, time would just run out.

Whenever I come home from school, I would immediately be put to work or I'd be given a beating for some infraction that made no sense to me. I hated the walk up the driveway. I never knew what was coming, only that it would come and it wouldn't be good.

The following incident is similar in nature to so many others I endured. The only reason I remember this one, so vividly, is because it was the first time I thought about running away. However, it took a couple more years to get the actual courage, to finally follow through.

As I looked up that day, the trees had blotted out the sun. The wind blew in gust after gust, like an usher moving his guests back and forth. The trees weaved and danced in an ancient rhythm, building to a frenzy as their excitement grew. They were waving me in, but I don't want to come.

I was trembling with what they, now, call anticipatory grief, though I had no idea what that meant at eight years old. Knowing something horrific is coming and being absolutely powerless to stop it—that definition sounds about right.

I stepped down from the school bus, and began the long walk up the driveway with a deep heaviness and a portent that even the weather acknowledged.

The anticipation of violence and pain corrodes the soul like termites burrowing in day after day. Yet there is no release, nor does it get easier over time. The opposite happens. One loses hope and the exuberance of youth dies a slow and agonizing death.

I knew this was going to be bad. I was conditioned well at this age.

As my brother and I turn the corner of the house, I see my mom bent over the picnic table at the edge of the porch. They have spent the day killing the geese and rendering them in scolding hot water, so the feathers would come off easier. They were almost done and she was cleaning the table with a dishrag. "Good! I'm glad your home!" Her eyes zone in on me like a hawk. "Do something useful and clean up all the feathers!" Her hand sweeps the driveway, like a queen to her court. She walks into the house with the last of the pots. I glance around the porch and driveway. It seems like nature has branded the earth with cotton balls. The white down is stuck to the gravel, like it's glued to it. What isn't glued down is bouncing and weaving in the wind. It's a haze of white. It's going to be a long few hours. My brother, as usual, didn't have to help. He walked inside the house grinning. I was the stooge. He was the prince. I heard him talking to my dad through the open window.

I sigh and put my book bag down by the door.

I start picking up each piece of heavy, wet, down and each white feather and placing them in the bag. My mind starts wandering as it usually does when I'm doing something repetitive. "I wonder if that new girl will like me." I muse. It seemed like only a moment, but was probably closer to 30 or 40 minutes, when the door flew open, as if the wind snapped it to attention.

My dad is charging me! Oh, no!

"You lazy son of a bitch! We give you a job to do and you can't even do it right! It takes you all day to do a simple chore?"

The coiled rage was about to be unleashed:

He grabs the closest thing to him, the outdoor broomstick. It is an inch and a half round and solid. "No! Please no! I'm so sorry!!" I squeeze my eyes shut as the first crack feels like liquid fire, slicing through my thigh. I fall to the porch. Please, let me slip through these cracks! He beats and beats the stick along my backside. I'm wrapped in pure agony. Only the pain exists. It becomes its own entity; pulling me down to the fiery depths of hell. Every nerve ending is on fire, and what isn't, will be soon. I can't make it stop. There is no hiding. No mercy. He's like a man possessed. He's never going to stop! Each heart wrenching scream and every frantic movement seems to incite his demons further. They are egging him on.

I, as a human, no longer exist in this body.

I look down from a great distance. He is beating this jellied object, in front of him, with a stick; molding and shaping it to the force of his will.

The screams feel like they are coming from someone else. That object is shrieking and pulsating! Please, make it stop! I can't look at it anymore!

I'm falling, and suddenly I feel the weight of my body. The pain is excruciating! If only I can block it out again! At some point, I hear a loud crack. He swings the broom with such ferocity that it breaks in two. Stars explode into white hot pain splinters. For a brief second, it feels like lightening has struck. Molten pain burns clean through to my bone. Please let me die!

I didn't realize until years later that the bone in my right leg was cracked. I walked with a forked stick, like a cane, for weeks. About a month later, we were at an auction and my mom took the stick away, and forced me to put pressure on the leg. She didn't want anyone asking questions. Later that night, while I was silently crying into my pillow, my bother popped his head through my bedroom door.

He whispers, "They will kill you if you don't do something! If you want to run, I'll help you."

Wow! I'm so grateful, but I start to tremble with a different kind of fear. "Where will I go? What if they catch me?"

As my thoughts try to wrap around this puzzle, the pain recedes to the background. For the moment, I breathe evenly and deeply as my brain formulates a plan.

To this beautiful little girl, who is a survivor, "Please, know that you are loved! You have not been abandoned, nor forgotten. You were able to walk through the darkest dark so you could experience the lightest light. You are a beautiful spiritual being! You shine with the Light of God. You are able to really understand the Yin and Yang of the universe. Both are etched, deeply, and forever, into your spiritual, astral, and physical cells—and, most importantly, your soul! You will grow up and be a great teacher!

As an adult, I have beaten this little girl many times. I have pushed her off the ledge of existence time and again. Every time she tries to come back, I tie her up in the dark recesses of my mind, and leave her to fend for herself. For years, I raged at her as she cowered and hid. For years, I was my own worst enemy.

It was only when I started a spiritual journey, at the age of 20, that I was able to build a relationship with this beautiful little girl. One that is healthy and healing. The Universal Principle of Dawning indicates that it is step-by-step, and this is how this healing continues to unfold—slowly and with gentle care.

When I was 20 years old, my world turned on its axis. My neighbor gave me a session of divine light. It blew apart everything I knew about the universe! It opened my spiritual eyes in the most unexpected way. Prior to this, I was imprisoned in a world of hate. I hated the world. I hated myself. I especially, hated men. I had no comprehension on how to communicate effectively. I was so dysfunctional that I couldn't even leave the house. I was absolutely broken. My world had twisted down on itself to a very fine point. I wasn't the Center of the Universe—I was the universe. Nothing else mattered or existed. The term 'self-centered' probably doesn't describe it. Wrap that term around me 10 thousand times and throw me in a dark hole—that would cover it.

However, I don't want to get too far ahead here. I just want to give you a heads up, that with each painful, childhood event, I have so many spiritual questions as to why the universe allows these painful experiences to exist. If humanity is going through this pain, there HAS to be a reason that we aren't fully aware of yet. It's time to find out. I won't accept, "just have faith" in something vague, that's way out there.

As I reflect on these childhood memories, and share

them with you, they are too painful to bring up one after the other. So, please, indulge me as I go back and forth in time.

As I pull the painful memories to the surface, I will give my inner child a chance to share her story. I will connect with her brave spirit. Then, going forward, in time, to age twenty, I will allow my young adult to speak to Gabrielle, my spiritual advisor. With her help, I will have an opportunity to reflect on the connection with the unseen realm, and how these amazing spiritual forces gave me a road map to heal my soul.

Towards the end of my story, as a mature adult, I shall share with you how I followed that roadmap and consistently practiced the tools, and I will share some amazing, miraculous stories!

If God can create the Universe and can tease us with Quantum Physics, then He can give us absolute, concrete and specific answers. We just need to locate them. What are the rules in this unseen realm? What is the Astral World? What is the Divine World? How do these unseen realms function within the Universe?

How do they affect our daily lives? Where does this spiritual power come from? How are we all connected? Why are some people born into great, happy families and others born into horrific abuse? Why are some children born geniuses and others with handicaps? Why do some horrible, mean people get great physical wealth and some amazing, beautiful souls live in abject poverty?

There is an intersecting point in my story, where everything prior is dark and everything after is light. Of course life is never black and white, so I hope my story blends and the lines soften, much like life.

Gabrielle, or Gabby for short, ran the Spiritual Centre. (more about that later in the book) When I was 20, my life revolved around this Centre, as I learned how to give and receive this powerful spiritual energy. She was the one that taught me about the Universal Principles and how to put them into actual daily practice.

Gabby is from Quebec. She is a true Frenchwoman, who loves big floppy hats and a vibrant clothing style that advertises her amazing, rich, heritage. She grew up with nuns as teachers, and she adopted their strict and straightforward manner as her own.

Many people thought she was too strict. But, I understood her. I saw her love and passion for humanity and her desire to be straightforward to God. She was NOT one to take the easy road or sluff anything off, just because it was too hard.

She was a teacher by trade and I would, often, come to her for spiritual guidance.

As usual, I had questions about this horrific memory—this beating where my bone cracked.

I headed to the Centre. Gabby was in the middle of cleaning, so I grabbed a rag out of the drawer, filled a pail of water and joined her. I relayed my family's experience and asked for guidance.

She isn't one for public displays, so I was shocked when she grabbed me, hard, and gave me a fierce hug! "You are so brave and must have a great mission on this earth!"

"What?" I didn't expect that to come out of her mouth.

"Your soul agreed to come back during this lifetime and experience this intense 'soul scrubbing,' to erase your own negative karma, and so that you could guide others."

"Look, what we know of the universe is actually paper thin. What exists, however, is higher than the Empire State Building. What we do know, though, is that there are principles that function the same throughout the entire universe. They are immutable. One of them, is the Universal Principle of Balance. If there is an imbalance anywhere in the universe, energy will be moved to right it, as soon as possible. This happens on so many different levels, simultaneously. This is why we can never judge energy as good or bad. Everything that happens, to us, is the beginning of something positive, we just may not understand it yet. You accumulated this precise energy in a previous life by being the parent to your parents and committing the same abuses." Gabby grabbed her bucket and dumped it down the sink.

As clean water was running into the bucket, she continued, "All of us have lived many lifetimes prior to this one. This is why when we speak of the cycle of abuse stopping, it must be stopped within the entire reincarnation wheel. If you are reborn, as your parents were, with a grudge, you will continue the cycle of abuse. If, however, like you, you choose to sincerely apologize and stop repeating this vicious cycle, then true healing can take place. None of us are innocent and some of us are very old souls. We, are, however, all divine souls and God has torn off a piece of His spiritual essence to create us. It is, precisely, because we are spiritual in nature, that we are able to discern the deeper nuances of life's mysteries. Animals are not capable of this.

She started washing the floor again, but stopped after a moment, "Also, within the universe, there exist the Principle of hardening and its counterpart, the Principle of lightening or opening up." She said.

"The best way to describe this is to tighten a lid on a jar. It turns to the right and tightens down on itself. Then, turn the lid counter-clockwise, to the left and it opens up."

"Hitler actually researched this principle and used only one of the swastikas. Guess which one he used? The hardening one. The one that rotates to the right.

He did NOT use the spiritual one—the one that opens up and rotates to the left. He took away one from its pair and exploited it, by itself. He caused a massive imbalance."

She continued as I washed the kitchen countertops, "These symbols have been around since ancient times, and predate Hitler by thousands of years.

Both are required in balance throughout the universe, always going back and forth between Yin and Yang, the negative and positive, like a perpetual see-saw. This follows the Principle of the Wave. All energy and vibrations move in this wave pattern. This is why we have periods of 'soul scrubbing' and upheaval; then we have periods of rest and relaxation, where we say that 'everything is going smoothly.' It's like the nodes of a tree. Our soul will never grow strong and become fortified without adversity. Our soul is not actually growing when things are going well. This period is just a temporary break or recess until our next training arrives."

She turned the hot water on and filled the pail a third time. She bent down on her knees to finish scrubbing the floor, "A baby grows and ages and hardens. The physical body hardens, but the soul is supposed to lighten, to become pure, to become *enlightened* as it ages. This is the universal balance of the Yin and Yang occurring within us. But, that's just a minute example of how the two opposites work in conjunction. They exist everywhere and in all things, in a million different ways." She stood up and stretched her legs.

"I know you would stay here all day and listen to me, but these are all 'living' teachings, meant to be put into actual practice in our daily lives. You can start by offering gratitude for your suffering."

I looked at her like she was insane. "What? Gratitude? But I want sympathy!"

Gabby gently laughed, "Well, I could give you sympathy, no problem, if you need a break from your spiritual growth. However, what you really need is to learn how to move through life with grace and an inner strength; and how to become a great soul. The best way to accomplish this is to materialize gratitude as soon as you can. If you were to go to your friends place four to five times a week and eat and shower there, then leave each time with just a 'thank you' to them, how long before your friend gets frustrated with you?"

"Well, probably, pretty quickly!" I acknowledged.

Gabby nodded, "You need to find ways to put gratitude into actual practice. Like for example if you showed up with a bottle of wine that they really liked, or paid for their water bill, then they would feel your sincerity and want to continue helping you. It works the same in life. We need to find a way to help others, to be of service to others and the earth, without expecting anything in return. This is called Spirit-First. It is the best way to materialize our gratitude to God and the universe for all the blessings we receive every day. This way we are not taking them for granted or think we deserve them. Arrogance can grow very quickly and easily. Humility must be worked at, with consistency and persistency. It is one aspect of creating a great soul.

I pondered all she shared, as I watched her put away all the cleaning supplies.

I got excited as I verbalized my thoughts, "When I think about my life, my cells tighten just thinking about all the pain. I squeeze and tighten when something painful happens. My world becomes small. I squeeze myself into a tiny little ball."

"Over a lifetime, I have seen this hardening and tightening draw addictions, obsessions, clutter, etc. My world becomes smaller and smaller."

"The more dense something is, the more it draws similar density to itself. I have even heard that the human pineal gland, where our soul resides, is becoming hard and crystallized over time."

I continued to share my thoughts, "Yet the opposite is even more powerful. When I'm relaxed and filled with gratitude, and when I'm acting in a Spirit-First manner, my cells at the DNA level naturally open up. My entire world opens up. My intuition deepens. I become purer, lighter, etc. I am spiritually evolving. I'm in tune with the universe!"

My eyes were twinkling as I attempted to breathe in loving vibrations, and send them across the room to Gabby.

"So when you are always guiding me to offer 'true

and sincere gratitude', **even for suffering**, I'm starting to understand that there are precise laws and great power in the unseen realm. I can shift my whole existence simply by following them. Wow! I want to learn more. I don't want to stop learning. It's like a puzzle and the parts are precision cut. What's next?" I had the full exuberance of youth!

Gabby chuckled, as she walked me to the door. Time seemed to have flown by. She knew I would be back. This was just the tip of the iceberg. I couldn't wait to learn more.

We hugged as always, but this one felt deeper and warmer. I sensed energy flowing both ways. I felt a shift in my own energy. As I walked home, I felt happy, genuinely happy with every pore of my body! It felt like I was bathing from head to toe in a warm luxurious flow of joyful dancing ions.

I thought about our hug. I had decided to put the 'gratitude' teaching into actual practice and I purposely sent her loving and grateful waves of energy right at the moment I hugged her. By golly, I believe she did the same! It magnified the energy and created a powerful event!

I love it that I don't have to believe in something way out there, where I'm supposed to just 'have faith.' I love it when I can hear about something and immediately put it into actual practice, and then see for myself what the outcome is. I can repeat it over and over again if I want to.

I've had bad experiences with religions so I was a great skeptic going into this path. When I found out that this path is NOT a religion and that is open to all people, all races, all status, and you can keep your own religion, or have no religion at all, then I was hooked. This path practices all the Principles that every single material object, plant, animal, and person are subject to, that exist in the Universe.

They said, "We don't want fanatics. If you don't believe, that's okay. Just put it into practice and see what happens. Be a scientist, set up an experiment and observe."

So, for the last 27 years, I have been absorbing, practicing, and testing this spiritual path. (I started on this path when I was 20, so you must have figured out my age by now…) It is the most precious journey I have undertaken.

Let's check back in with the small child…

Chapter 4

My mom had a favorite horse as a child, called 'Lady.' My parents decided to move her off my Grandparents farm, in Tofield, and bring her out to our farm in Whitecourt. She was fully black with a white star on her forehead. She was average in height and would only connect with my mom, who had ridden her for many years.

My brother, Robin, got to ride a young gelding, with a lot of spunk. I, on the other hand, wasn't permitted near his horse. Any chance he got, he made sure we both knew who the best rider was. Shortly after receiving his new horse, he managed to fall off and break his leg. He was in a full length, leg-cast for several weeks. Looking back now, I think his ego needed to be broken a little to bring him back to reality. He was so full of himself! It did seem to tone his sarcasm down after the incident.

I don't blame him for teasing me—or breaking his leg. I was his punching bag for coping with his own world of pain and suffering. Our parents went at him too, just in a different way. He loved sports, especially basketball, and he was very good at it, and may have gotten a scholarship in a different lifetime. He was the Captain of the team for a reason.

Our parents refused to support him in his passion and constantly stepped on his dreams and prevented him from following them. They would tear him down and tell him he was not good enough and, therefore, why waste his time in sports? He needed to spend time studying for his "matriculation" if he wanted to get anywhere in life.

They would find any excuse to prevent him from going to the games or the after-parties. They tore into him every chance they got.

The only highlight of his sports career, at school, was that one time he and his team got to play basketball with the Harlem Globetrotters! These players were giants on the court and knew how to play up an audience, while teaching the kids outstanding sportsmanship! The audience roared with laughter! My brother even got his picture in the local Gazette, trying to dodge one of them with the ball. In the black and white picture, his large, round, blond 'afro' blended well with theirs.

He had a routine after school. He would come home and grab his snares, his BB-gun, and his dog and take off in the bush to trap and kill weasels and squirrels. He would sell the hides for money. As long as we were being 'productive' and not playing, our parents would let us go outside.

I had just gotten home from school and was trying to think of a way to get out of the house. If I stayed too long, I knew I would feel my mom's hard, long nails digging into my forearm, dragging me to where ever she thought needed an inspection. I had been beat many times for having left some baked food on a frying pan, or for having left some dirt hidden in the corner of a room. She would find something; it would just take a matter of minutes. The clock was ticking.

On this day, however, she had company and wanted privacy. Her one and only friend had arrived and I was not needed. "Go take care of Lady. Give her some exercise and make sure you give her a good brushing!"

I didn't need to be told twice. I headed to the barn.

We had a great log house on one section of the property, and a narrow path to the north of it that led to the barn and some outhouses. One of the outhouses stored the tack and all the tools needed for a working farm. I unhooked the squeaky door and grabbed the halter and a pail of oats. I knew Lady would be in the closest corral to the barn, as she never wandered far.

I was nine years old on this stifling, hot June day, having just turned in March. I had been riding horses for the past three years. I had learned many tough lessons on horses. I had broken one bone and had fallen off many times. I knew what was needed to stay on.

I found Lady to the rear of the barn and held out the bucket of oats so the wind would catch it and invite her with its lovely aroma. She may have been old, but her nostrils flared and took the bait. She would never turn down a heavenly meal. She trotted over, her tail twitching and swishing her backside to keep the flies at bay.

I placed the halter on her and tied it to a gatepost. I began to rake her with the horse brush. Again, with anything repetitive, my mind began to wonder and I was Nancy Drew's partner, circling the globe, solving crimes together. The heat from the late afternoon sun made it easy to zone out and daydream in vibrant colors. It was baking hot! Out of nowhere, Lady turned her head and bit me! She tried to take a chunk out of me!

"What the hell! Why'd you do that?" I was abruptly yanked back to reality. I grabbed my arm and saw multiple sets of red indents that were swelling fast. Some of the marks had thin trickles of blood appearing, like a ring of vampires materializing mouth-first on my arm. I shivered. Had I been rubbing her too hard? Usually horses like that. I was dumbfounded by her actions.

I was ready to unhook her halter and put her back out to pasture—but, NO of course not. Guess who was walking towards the barn with her friend and her favorite dog in tow? My mom decided to come out, at that moment, to watch me ride.

"Why are you brushing her NOW? That needs to be done AFTER you've ridden her!" she turned her nose up at me in utter disdain. "Don't you know better?" I swear her face smirked as she quickly looked away from my arm. If her friend hadn't been there, I know the next question would have been, "What did you do to Lady to deserve that?"

"Get on her and give her some good exercise!" she started walking towards me, leaving her friend looking on.

I went from freedom to imprisonment in a second. I was terrified she would smack me. I didn't like her close to me. It was never a good thing.

I scramble up the middle board of the fence and throw my leg over the horse. I pull the reins back to keep her still. She's taking off! Why isn't this working? She's never done this before. It doesn't matter how hard I pull on the reins! My heart's racing so fast! Oh no!

She doesn't care and she isn't stopping! She heads for the nearest and largest spruce tree in the field.

I vaguely hear a warbled tinny voice, far away, calling out to me, "Duck! Tighten your legs! For God's sake, show her whose boss and hang on!" My mom has stepped off the trail, and is yelling and flapping her arms like a goose about to take off.

Like that's going to help! Thank God she's nowhere near me!

All I can see is a massive tree looming directly ahead and this horse isn't turning! Of course I duck! There is nothing else I can do! Lady has picked the lowest and fattest branch there is. By the time we get to it, she's at a full gallop. It hits me in the midsection, scrapping past my lowered face and sweeps me right off the horse, like a battering ram. I fly off! I land hard on my back-side, as the wind is knocked out of me.

As I'm fighting to pull some oxygen into my bruised chest, my mom grabs her horse and spends a few minutes talking to her. "Whoah girl! It's okay! You're okay! No one's going to hurt you!"

Hello! What about me? I shake my head. Haven't we been here before? Yes, when I broke my arm. This time, thankfully, I think nothing's broken.

By now, I had enough schooling in hard-knocks to know this was far from over.

"Well she's fine and I don't think she's scared anymore. You need to get back on her or she'll be ruined for life!" My mom directs me back on, like I've caused this catastrophe! She hands me the reins. Her eyes indicate this is not a choice.

I want to run, but not on this horse! I'm shaking and my palms are sweaty. As I take the reins from her, I'm sure the horse is absorbing my fear. I attempt to climb back on. My gut is rock hard. Oh my God, I know what's coming!

Immediately, she takes off again. Only this time, she starts to gallop and then does an immediate stop. As my head almost whips into hers, I feel a memory forming of falling off the front end of a horse. Oh no, not again!

However, Lady has something else in mind, because that trick didn't work. I managed to hold on for dear life, so she bends her front knees to the ground. Again, I vaguely hear my mom yelling something, but I can't make out the exact words. It doesn't matter, I'm on my own. She's irrelevant at the moment.

It takes a few seconds, before the extent of Lady's plan is clear. She begins to lie down on the ground and roll to the left. I jump off just as she starts to roll on my left leg. As I scramble off to the right and away from her, I hear the loudest and happiest whinny ever. She starts to rub her head back and forth on the ground, like she is scratching off the biggest horsefly ever.

"Oh, what a good feeling!" She moans and snorts again. She stands back up and shakes her whole body, in one long satisfying tremor. "Who's the boss now?"

I don't know what would have happened if my mom's friend hadn't been there to witness this event, but for this time anyway, my mom conceded and I was left to patch up my wounds, and to cry to the early evening sun, as there were no other witnesses.

There have been so many times as an adult, that I have treated myself in this same cold way. I had not taken the time to listen to valid reasons, to figure out better ways of doing things. Instead I berated myself to do the same thing over and over again. Failure is not an option. They say the definition of insanity is doing the same thing over and over again and expecting different results. "Don't feel; don't think; don't talk, just do!" my mother's motto, adopted as my own.

Now, on my spiritual journey, I'm able to tell this

beautiful, brave girl, "The horse was too old and too cranky to have been ridden. It should have been put out to pasture years prior. It was nothing you did. You were only following the rules imposed upon you. You were so brave! You handled it the best way possible and I don't know of anyone else who could have stayed on. The horse never got ridden again and died of old age. I'm so sorry there was no one there to rescue you! There should have been. Now, if you sense that something is off, please tell me and I will listen. We will work together to find safer options."

Even though this message gets delivered many years later, perhaps the universe might let it slip through the cracks of time. Perhaps, a special sliver of light fortified her, as she cried out to the sun on that day.

Now, years later, I needed to find out what the spiritual significance of this lesson was. I found Gabby at the Center and sat down for a spell.

Her teaching voice was always soothing, "We spoke very briefly about Spirit-First last time. There is a Universal Principle of Spirit-first, mind follows and body belongs." She began.

She said, "Think of a river. Upstream is the spiritual aspect. The middle stream is the mental or emotional aspect. The downstream is the physical. If you were to purify the river, where would you start? Upstream of course! This is exactly what we have to focus on as humans: Spirit-First."

"We need to focus on the core or the spirit-centered actions that are 'spiritual' in nature, everything else doesn't matter." She stated.

She said, "You really need to understand that we're

NOT speaking of anything religious or even about religion, we are simply using words to easily connect with ideas. We use 'spiritual realm' to talk about the realm of 'spirit' or the concept of 'spirit-first' ---the innermost realm of spirit-----the unseen realm.

She gently intoned, "Your mom's innermost attitude was focused only on herself and how she looked to her friend. She didn't even try to climb on your rock and see where you were coming from. When we take a 'Spirit-First' approach, we are always looking at how can we impact others, how can we help their spirit, and most importantly, how can we help God—-the Core Spirit?"

She saw the look on my face and knew what question was coming, "No, that doesn't mean we need to be door-mats and forget ourselves. We need to always look for the core or the truth, and work from there. We need to find the God-spark in everyone and to honor that in them—to draw out the divinity that is in everyone, including ourselves. The best way to do this is to concentrate only on the good points of everyone. If we draw attention to only someone's good points, they will succeed and the good in them will grow and prosper. If we draw attention to the negative, then this is what will grow and expand. Energy directed must move. Either it will harden down on itself, or it will open up and spiral upward and outward. This works in harmony with the Principle of Echo—what we send out, comes back multiplied.

Finally she said, "Also, remember, as you grow spiritually, so do your guardian spirits. Imagine being on a mountain and they are always climbing a little higher than you. If you have a very low spiritual level, then your guardian spirits look out over the valley and can only see a couple days ahead. If you have a very high spiritual level, then they can see years ahead, far into the valley and they are able to help you make wise decisions. This is why some people who commit crimes look silly because they didn't see that they actually had no chance at all. Also, likewise, someone who is highly spiritually evolved can have great intuition that is astounding to the rest of us. We can all be someone who has great intuition. This intuition comes from our Ancestors whom are also our guardian spirits. Every time you offer altruistic service and put Spirit-First, you and your ancestors are elevating spiritually. With this, brings more freedom, spiritual knowledge, and power—God's Love, Wisdom, and Will."

As Gabby walked me to the door, she said, "Remember, these are 'living teachings,' so find ways to put them into actual daily practice and you will start to have those 'a ha' moments of deep spiritual clarity."

Gabby always gave me something to think about. I hugged her fiercely with great gratitude, as this had become our parting ritual.

Let's connect back with the small child…

Chapter 5

When we moved to Whitecourt, my parents built their home from scratch. They imported pre-packaged logs and we all helped putting them together, quite like a jigsaw puzzle. Each of the round logs had letters and numbers and would only fit in one spot.

When completed, it was a breathtaking beautiful open-beam, log house filled with antiques. My parents bought and sold antiques. I spent many hours traveling to auctions with my parents, all across the country.

Everything in the house, it seemed, had a price tag on it. We never got bored with the surroundings as one piece was sold, another took its place. One month, my bed was a beautiful carved rosewood piece and the next month it was solid brass. My parents were shrewd business people.

I used to enjoy spending time alone in the small cabin, down from the main house, refinishing antique furniture. They would buy a piece for $50. I would strip the multiple layers of paint. I would rub a beautiful stain into the wood and add a clear smooth varnish that did a beautiful job emphasizing the solid oak or walnut wood underneath. They then would sell the piece for $800 or more.

I loved feeling the wood and was able to sense energy flowing from each piece. I'm forever grateful for this experience, because it taught me how to touch something and send actual gratitude vibrations into it. I think it's kind of like blessing something. When I do this, I sense it becoming less dense and having a brighter and lighter feel, all the way through. I sense this in people as well.

This way of sensing energy, actually saved my life on the streets, many times. I could tell in an instant if someone had a dark, dense aura. I would immediately turn away—as long as I wasn't in a haze of drugs, that is.

My parents were raised as Christian, even though they didn't actively practice. We celebrated Christmas in the traditional way. The other holidays were passed over like they didn't exist.

This one year, in particular, when I was about ten years old, I had just come into the main house and had let my mom know I had completed refinishing the new bedroom set. I was allowed to be alone in the cabin, as long as I produced according to her expectations.

I was so glad I had finished on her timeline.

I looked over at her sitting in her favorite, leather, easy chair. Next to her was the immaculate Christmas tree. It was a real spruce tree that had been cut by my brother a few days prior. It had beautiful matching ornaments of dark green, and deep red bows hidden under a bushel of tinsel. I wasn't a fan of the decorations, but it wasn't my tree and I wasn't dumb enough to complain.

She was clutching the phone and her mouth was set in a hard line that I knew all too well. She didn't respond to my comment about the furniture.

"Warning! Warning! This isn't going to be good." Bells were ringing in my head.

My mom spoke, "I just got off the phone with the neighbor. She said that her kids talked to their neighbors, and found out that the bus driver had handed out boxes of chocolate to all the kids on the bus, for Christmas."

Oh dear, I knew where this was going.

"She said they found out the bus driver gave you two extra boxes of chocolate, to give to them. Where are they?"

I don't know how I thought I could get away with it. Actually, I think at the time, I didn't care. I was so hurt and angry that I made an impulsive decision and then regretted it later.

Our neighbors were a family of three kids and their parents. Their religion dictated they couldn't celebrate any holidays. Therefore, they never went to school on the last day before Christmas, because that day was always the school party.

Their mom held a similar view as ours and actually came over one day, when my parents were gone and spoke to my brother and me. She thought our parents weren't strict enough and we needed to smarten up. My brother walked away in the middle of her spiel, but I was too scared to. To this day, I have no idea why she felt the need to berate us.

She had two daughters and a son. The oldest daughter, Melanie, had a mental disability and was homeschooled. Her son, Michael, was the middle one and he was a year younger than me. He and his younger sister, Misty, were the ones whom I had taken the chocolates for.

Michael happened to be extremely short for his age and was a fire cracker. He would try to start fights with anyone near him. He disliked me and would constantly tease and harass me on the school bus. He was fast and cunning.

One time, he came over to our place.

My mom heard the doorbell and went to answer.

"Hi, Mrs Edwards. How are you today?" Michael stood at the door, smiling like an angel.

"Oh what can we do for you, Michael?" Her voice sounded like honey, as she smiled.

"I just want to see Judy outside for a bit, if that's okay?" He asked.

She turned away from him and looked at me. I had told her in the past what he would do to me and how much he tormented me. She knew. Even at this moment, they both seem to be conspiring together. As he looked at me, his evil grin was exactly like that of a hawk about to pounce on its prey. Yum! Yum! He even rubbed his hands together.

He quickly adjusted his facial expression when my mom turned back to him.

As I'm shaking my head, she replied to him, "Sure, but don't be too long. She has work to do."

They both acted like the other didn't know what was going on. They might as well of agreed, without all this subterfuge. Between the two of them I was doomed anyway.

I'm filled with dread. I put my shoes on and stumble

out the door. He takes me around to the back of the house. Without a hint of what's to come, he balls his fists and wallops me in the stomach, a one-two punch. I drop to my knees, trying to make sense of what just happened. The pain morphs into a ball of hot lead and I'm about to throw-up. I can't though, because that movement will make it worse. I take short little puffs, trying not to cause any vibrations. I can taste blood in the back of my mouth. I must have bitten my tongue.

"Don't ever laugh at me in front of anyone, again!" He kicks me hard in the thigh as I fall to the ground. "And don't think your mom is going to come rescue you! She doesn't give a shit about you!"

The pain in my stomach still overrides the pain in my thigh. I start to cry. The tears flow like a dam unleashed. The shaking makes me start to puke, and my stomach convulses as the dry heaves heat up the hot lead, once again. I feel sick, as a river of tears reach the ground.

"Oh shut up! You cry baby! It serves you right! Nobody likes you anyway!" He starts to walk away, and looks back over his shoulder laughing at me.

"Now who gets the last laugh?" he taunts, just before he turns the corner of the house, and disappears.

I had endured his bullying and his beatings. The moment the bus driver entrusted me with the chocolates for safe keeping, I knew I wasn't going to deliver them.

I enjoyed every one of those chocolates. But now, I had to pay the piper.

My mom was livid!

They say that people lie for different reasons. One of them is self-preservation. That was me. I lied because I knew I was going to get beat anyway, so if there was a tiny bit of hope that it might be believed and I could avoid a beating, I would take it.

"I lost them. I can't find them," I quietly said.

"You are an absolute liar! You stole them and then ate them all!" She raged at me. "I should call the police and have you take a lie detector test, and then they can throw your ass in Juvenile hall!"

"Oh my God! I've done it now!" I scramble with a newfound terror. My mom had always reminded us kids that we would one day find ourselves in the Juvenile Detention Center, and the kids there would knife and rape us, and we would never survive.

I knew I had to come forward and tell the truth and accept just a beating. This new threat was too much!

"I'm sorry. I ate them." I mumbled.

"Go cut a switch, and bring it back!" She directed.

I stumbled down the back trail. I couldn't stop the tears. I had to be careful not to trip with the hatchet. I wasn't prepared for that type of death. I walked out onto a cut-line and looked for a willow tree with the right green branch that would whistle in just the correct way. Imagine chopping your own switch that will be used to cut through your flesh and blood; knowing that the pain from it is like an entire nest of angry hornets, funneled into one spot and then moved to spot after spot.

I spotted a mushroom and picked it up. "If I eat it, will I die?" I thought as I held it to my mouth. I couldn't do it and, disgusted, threw it away.

The beating was severe, and I couldn't sleep on my backside for days. My mom also decided that wasn't the end of it. She threw away all my presents. There would be nothing under the Christmas tree, for me, this year.

It didn't seem like that much of a loss, because she always picked practical stuff and never the toys we really wanted. It still hurt, though, on Christmas morning. It seemed bizarre, and out of the ordinary, that this year of all years, my brother got the exact toy he wanted. He grinned at me from ear to ear. At least the bulls-eye was off him for a moment.

Well, my mom was good at inflicting maximum damage.

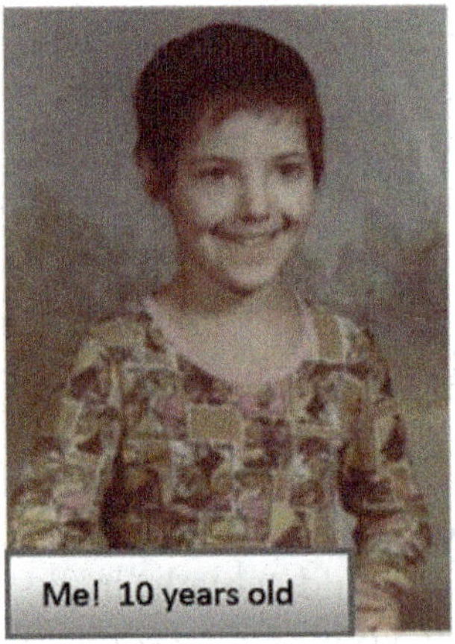

To this ten year old girl who endured beating after beating, I can only deeply apologize and hold her tightly and fiercely against my chest, "I will never let you get beat again. If you feel any intense pain coming on, I will wipe your brow and calm your soul and hold you with love, until it passes. Please know that I will not let anyone touch you again or they will be charged to the fullest extent of the law. I will protect you and help you heal. You are so precious and beautiful!"

It has taken me many years to trust people enough to be truthful. I can easily revert to lying and believing it with my whole being. I had lots of practice. However, these days I am very careful and always ask myself, what is my intent?

As an adult, in order to understand the spiritual aspect, I needed to ask Gabby, "Is it a great sin to lie? What if it can prevent a beating or pain for someone?"

Her response was, as always, very articulate, "You already know about reincarnation and karma. We don't need to go over that again. Just remember they do play a role in this answer. Also, again, what we know of the unseen realm is paper thin and what we don't know is higher than the Empire State Building. So we have not been given the authority by God to judge another human being. There is too much about any given circumstance that we are NOT aware of."

She continued, "Nothing is black and white in the unseen realm. There are degrees to sins and to karma. It depends on what our innermost attitude is, at the time. If we are just in it for ourselves and we have manipulated the outcome, than this adds more negative karma to our cup, then if it was done by accident."

She concluded by saying, "Of course, when acting in Spirit-First, it is important to always tell the truth. This is first and foremost. However, there are times when you are thinking about the welfare of others, for example you tell a 'white-lie' to keep someone from knowing what their present is. In this case, you are only accumulating a tiny amount of negative karma. As long as we, ourselves, are not benefiting from the lie, it is allowed. The universe always makes exceptions, but that's what they are…exceptions. If we become too rigid about rules and laws, this can also end up in a negative situation. Also, likewise, we must be very careful not to get into the habit of lying and using it for our own purpose. The Principle of Balance also comes into play here. This goes the same for stealing. What is our intent and why are we doing it. Is it because we are starving or someone we know is? Have we exhausted all other options, first?"

"Wow! You are a wealth of knowledge! Thank you!" I said good-bye to Gabby; gave her a big hug and headed home.

I had stolen out of malice and anger towards them. I had lied out of great fear. I had a lot of soul searching to do. I knew I couldn't be too hard on myself. As a child, I did the very best; but as an adult, I had to draw some boundaries and make sure that my future actions were altruistic in nature.

For now, more memories were surfacing, of a lost youth…

Section 2

The Lost Youth

Chapter 1

The first time I ran away, I was twelve years old. My brother offered to help me, and he was true to his word. It was a daunting task. We lived in a remote area, miles from civilization. Looking back now, I shake my head. It's hard to believe I made it.

Before we head down that path, allow me to share some background information.

Two years after we moved to Whitecourt, (4 years before I first ran away), we went to meet the neighbors. They were known to have goats for sale, and my parents were very interested in buying some.

We drove a few miles south. We pulled into a driveway, but I didn't see a house. All I could see was a two story, red and white, platform with stairs going up. It had a massive cable extending out, which disappeared across the mile expanse of the Athabasca River. The tall trees hugged the platform closely, almost obscuring its view. If your eyes went a little fuzzy, you'd miss it. You had to look through the trees to see the platform.

We heard a repetitive clanging, and watched the cable swing up and down at the top of the platform. It looked like a clothesline made for a goliath. A tiny carriage came into view. Inside was a short elderly lady, with what looked like an ogre's wrench held over her head. She was using it to pull herself and the carriage up to the base of the platform. She would fasten the wrench on the cable, pull herself and the carriage along a foot or two, then slide the wrench forward and pull again. She came into view with short, jerky movements. The carriage hit the back of the platform, and she wrapped a giant hook to secure it in place. She climbed down and met us on the ground.

She was the matriarch, and she had come to bring us across the river to her home. It was the only way there, in the summer. I had no choice but to climb into this creaky carriage. It had a seat on either side, with a bar in the middle to put your feet on. In between the bar you could see straight down, for half a mile, to the river below. Once we started, gravity shot us, like a bullet, across the river. As soon as we started going up the other side, the carriage slowed to a stop, and that's where the wrench was needed to pull us up the rest of the way; otherwise, we would start sliding backwards. It never seemed to stop swinging from side to side, either. Especially, if a gust of wind hit it. We didn't need to pay money to go on a hair-raising ride!

I had a blast! They had nine children in the family. The two sets of twin girls were around my age. We played and romped like kids were meant to. They had boxes and boxes of fruit, which they generously shared. My brother turned his nose up and refused to eat. He told me to stay away from it. I ignored him.

I paid the price later. My parents had nothing good to say about them and I got a beating for eating the fruit, which came from, "the garbage bins at the back of the stores!" How stupid could I be?

My mom became judge and jury, "We don't eat garbage! How can the government allow them to have so many kids while on welfare? What a filthy shack they live in! I will never buy goats from them. That place should be condemned!" My dad listened and agreed.

My parents were cut from the same cloth.

I think it was pretty ingenious of their Dad to find such good fruit for free. It was still in good shape and they had washed it. I was always confused with my parent's logic.

Over the next four years, I developed a close friendship with the older twin, Betty. She was my age and she was an identical twin. The only way I could tell them apart was she had a freckle on her left cheek and her twin, Letty, didn't. Also, she was the calm and organized one.

I was never allowed to have any sleepovers or go to her place. She went to the regular school so I couldn't even connect with her there. The only time we had together was the 45 minute bus ride in the morning and at night. It became the most precious allotment of time.

On this particular day, after school, the beating was severe, again. I was washing dishes and my mother snuck up behind me and yanked my hair almost out of my head. She dragged me over to the cupboard, where she had taken out a pot for supper.

She tried to shove my head into the pot, "Are you so lazy and blind that you can't see the food left in it?" She raged at me and pointed to a small piece of burnt food on the inside of the pot.

She didn't have to build up her anger. She could go from zero to ten in a millisecond. Cool as a cucumber, then off her rocker—in the blink of an eye. I'd hate to be inside her brain!

"You lazy son of a bitch!" She cuffed me across the head and shoulders again and again. She kicked me in the butt and I went flying across the floor. "Get off your lazy ass and do the dishes right, this time!"

I moved around like a zombie for the rest of the night. If I showed any emotion at all, it would have set her off. It was best to lock it down. The adrenaline would bring out a large supply of emotions later, for what I had planned.

I was leaving this night, before I became a beaten-down doormat, unable to move.

The night is so still and quiet. I think they're asleep. I'm under the covers with my clothes on. Every time I wiggle my toes the cat pounces on them. She's attacking my feet, but I have my boots on, so I'm gonna ignore her. She's having too much fun!

I look up at the ceiling. I wonder if I can pull this off? I hope they don't catch me! Please God, let me make it!

I have to stay awake. I burrow under the covers and start reading my 'Hardy Boys' book with a flashlight. I wish one of these brothers would rescue me! For a short while, I'm lost in a world of detectives and heroes.

I've been waiting for this night for a long time. A little travel bag is tucked under my bed. My brother helped me fill it. It has a flashlight, some food, water, and a change of clothes. I followed the directions of the 'Hardy boys.' They always know best. They are good at sneaking in and out of places. So is 'Nancy Drew.' But, they're cuter.

I almost scream as my door creaks open. I peek out from under the covers. Whew! It's just my brother. He has unlocked my door for me. He knows how to unlock our bedroom doors, but our parents haven't figured this out yet.

We don't hug, he's not into that. 'That's for sissies,' he always says. He helps me sneak out the window. So far so good! He hands me a little hand watch. "It's 2 AM now. If you hustle, you can make it to Betty's place by morning. I put extra batteries in the bag for you." He takes a last look at me and closes the window. I see him move into the darkness of his room.

I head down the long driveway. It's cold and a little windy; but, I'm prepared. I stop and put on my toque and gloves. I see my breath billowing out, like smoke from a dragon's nostrils. I puff my cheeks out and blow for good luck. It would be so cool to ride a dragon!

It's too easy for me to get lost in a make-believe world.

I force my mind into the present. I need it if I'm going to survive this night. I look up. I can't find the moon. The stars are bright, though.

I hope I don't freeze to death! What if nobody finds me? "Isn't that the point?" I chastise myself, trying to boost my courage. I can't stop now.

Two things happen at once. I look down and see my brother's pure white dog, Boo, wagging her tail and looking up at me. Then, I look up at the house and everything is blurry! I can't see properly! I squint. Am I that scared?

I realize that my brother forgot to lock up his dog AND that I had forgotten my glasses. Oh my God! I can't do this over again. But, I have to. I take the walk of shame back up the driveway and knock on my brother's window. I can't stop trembling.

All-consuming fear threatens to knock me out. It's a relentless boxer. Can fear kill someone? I shake my head as the jabs come in fast and furious. If my parents wake up, they will kill me! That's for sure. I can't make any more mistakes! Get it together! This is it! There's no going back! I manage to take a deep breath and slow down the onslaught.

Puff the magic dragon, I can do it!

My brother realized what happened, so he's ready for me. He hands me my glasses. Better! I can see now! He snaps his fingers and Boo jumps in through the ground floor window. No need for another good-bye.

Okay. I need to do this one more time.

I race down the driveway and hit the gravel running. I swing the flashlight side to side, like a metal detector—only this one's checking for possible assaults or ambush.

Now that I'm away from the house and its outdoor lamps, I run into a wall of black. The flashlight penetrates only a foot or two. The sounds of the night threaten to unhinge me, as the blackness opens its arms and pulls me into the dark void.

My heart misses a beat as a large branch cracks and splinters, very close. I jump sideways and almost scramble backwards! What was that? 'You don't want to know! Just run!'

I repeatedly swing the flashlight behind me, looking for 2 lights that signal a car heading in my direction. Please, don't let there be any! Please, let them still be sleeping!

I've gone about 3 miles and I hear a sound that rips into my chest and squeezes my heart—cold as ice! **The darkness literally screams at me, like a tortured soul being delivered to hell!** *The flashlight flies out of my hand and scatters to the gravel. Oh my God, I've just* *tripped over it. I think I twisted my ankle. I fumble for the light, before I trip again.*

What was that? I frantically swing the flashlight around in circles. It sounded human and very close! There it is again! ***A high pitched scream!*** *Oh my God! I'm in the twilight zone! I stumble again.*

As my mind is about to fall over the edge of insanity, something nibbles at the far reaches of it. Oh yes! Occasionally, we have cougars in the area, and their screams sound eerily human.

Oh no! Run!

Adrenaline seizes me and I take off running, like death is nipping at my heels! I can't stop running. I ignore the throbbing in my ankle. My legs ache. I have a stitch in my side. I can't breathe! How long before I get to the highway?

I take a look behind me again for the hundredth time. Lights scare me far worse than an animal. I'm so overwhelmed that I think I hear a vehicle. I slip into the woods and crouch for a few moments. There is a light layer of snow on the ground and the cold seeps through my jacket and pants. I can't stop shivering. I need to move to stay warm.

The stars are bright tonight! I can see the big dipper! There's the little one! I finally reach the highway. I don't have far to go to Betty's place.

I'm exhausted! All I want to do is stop. Everything hurts! I have been limping for a while. My ankle is demanding attention.

I look at my little watch, with its Mickey Mouse dial, and see it's six in the morning. The sun is starting to come up. I have run for four hours. Wow! Fear and adrenaline are a perfect recipe to get an 'A' in gym. Maybe my teacher should look into it. I chuckle insanely. The sound startles me back to reality. I shake my head.

I limp on, for about ten more minutes. I reach my friend's driveway. Oh my God, I'm safe. They will help me. Thank you!

I remember reaching her place around sunrise. It was a beautiful, crisp October day. The sun was bouncing through the tall trees. The river was shimmering and blinking with diamonds. I think I was coming close to hyperthermia from the cold and from pure exhaustion.

I realized that nobody knew I was coming. I started yelling at the top of my lungs, across the river. I yelled "Help!" over and over again, until I was hoarse. I was just about to give up, when I saw the cable jump and jerk. I knew someone was on it. After 10 minutes, Betty's oldest sister, Laura stepped out of the carriage.

I begged her to take me over to the other side. I knew my parents couldn't get there, when the river was flowing. That would be the ONLY safe place.

She was about seventeen, at the time, and her parents weren't home. She didn't know what to do, so she didn't move. I could see she wanted to do something, but was stuck. Cell phones didn't exist in those days.

I could hear a vehicle arriving. I hoped it was her parents, but my gut told me otherwise.

Panic rolled over me in waves. I looked over at my parents driving their white pickup. Everything inside of me ripped open. I had done all of this for nothing. Rather, I had done all of this for more torture!

They got out and signaled for me to get in the vehicle. They looked like ogres that were about to have me for lunch. They spoke to Laura for a moment, and then got back in the vehicle.

Their silence weighted me down like a wet blanket, and fear and exhaustion prevented me from moving. I was done.

They stopped on the way home, and my dad got out and walked around to the back passenger side. He grabbed my arm and hauled me out. I forgot he was an excellent tracker. He pointed to my tracks going into the bush a short distance, "Are those yours?" There was no point in lying. He grabbed a stick and started to beat me. My mom urged him to stop. They couldn't have witnesses.

As soon as we got home, he dragged me by my hair to the bedroom. He had saved the stick for further discipline. He ripped off my shirt, my pants and underwear and threw me over the bed! I was bent over, completely naked! I was almost 13 years old and just entering puberty! Physically, I was a young woman forced to submit to a 35 year old man. Something cracked in my head and all feeling suddenly stopped! I completely disassociated. I continued to scream, but didn't feel connected to my body. My mom finally entered the bedroom and begged him to stop. Not to help me, but because she was sure they had called Child Welfare.

I believe that the brutality of the beating was due to his ego being stepped on. 'How dare I run away to those neighbors!' They were beneath my parents. By doing this, I had slapped him in the face.

Laura's parents called Child Welfare. The next day a worker showed up. Low and behold, it was a friend of my mom's. My mom had taken in foster kids and they had become friends. I sat at the table, having been directed not to say anything. The two of them conversed and my mom explained that I was being teased at school and was depressed, but they were trying to help me through it. The lady bought it. She didn't even take me into the bedroom and look at all the bruises that were so fresh and large.

I remember her driving away, and drowning in absolute hopelessness. My parents were all powerful. End of story.

I thought I was dumb and stupid and they were gods. It wasn't until years later that my brother revealed that they had been reading my diary. Finally, I was able to take a look at it from a different angle and begin to heal.

I had a beautiful colored diary that came with a strap and a lock on it. I wrote about everything and about all my fears. It was my release.

Over a two year period, my mom screwed with my head. She was cunning and smart and she knew how to cut to the core. I believed she had extra powers. I was blown away by how she could read my mind!

If I wrote in my diary that I was terrified to look into their eyes, she would taunt me and make me look into hers, as she blasted pure hate like a sword. If I wrote that I didn't like to watch animals being killed, she would make sure I had front stage when the butchering started. It went on and on.

I couldn't fathom that she could pick the lock, so instead I just thought she was all powerful—that she could actually see what I was thinking! She was very sneaky. She didn't use the diary immediately after I wrote in it. She would wait for these assaults, sometimes a week or more.

She also drilled the message into my brain that I was completely and utterly stupid, and dumber than a doornail—that I would never amount to anything. This, I began to believe with my whole being, as everything I wrote in my diary, she affirmed and reaffirmed, day in and day out. The destruction of my soul was pre-meditated and cunning. It was an all-out assault.

I was a broken, terrified, crushed, ugly, stupid, fat, lazy, 'no good for nothing' bitch of a girl.

Yet, there were moments as a small child when I looked up at the universe, at the stars in the sky, and I knew there was something far greater out there! I could feel this warm sense of awe seep through my entire being! This energy wrapped me in its glow and it was far more powerful than the force trying to break me. It gifted me with a little more strength, a little more courage, and the Will to never give up. It mended enough of the broken seams to help me survive, until I could grow up and learn more about the mysteries of this amazing Universe.

You go girl!!

Chapter 2

Days, at home, were filled with work, work, and more work. The only break was if we were being productive outside the house. Our parents did not believe in children playing. That was a monumental waste of time, when they could put us to work.

My brother could trap animals, as long as he brought back the hides for sale. I could go berry picking, as long as I brought back a full pail. I loved summers for this reason. I could get a break from the 'fight or flight' response that was always set like an alarm. I could relax for a few hours and just be.

The beginning of summer brought the strawberries; then, the raspberries made their appearance; and by the end of summer, the high bush cranberries were ripe.

I brought the two dogs with me so I didn't have to worry about bears. The only problem I had with nature was the wasps. More times than I could count, I stepped on a nest. They loved to hang out where the raspberries and high bush cranberries grew. Their nests were always low to the ground.

I always heard the buzzing first. It sounds exactly like an angry swarm of wasps! There is no other sound like it in the world. I would look down and see them swarming up my legs. The first few times, I threw my pail at them and start running! I had to change that behavior quickly, because I would get beat for returning home with no pail! Oh my God! I got good at hanging on to the pail and high-tailing it away from the source. I wasn't going to let those little buggers sting me twice!

My mom made fabulous jam and jelly from all the berries! It was amazing! But, she was a horrible, terrible cook! She would often cook wild meat, such as moose or bear and it would be tough like leather, and taste gritty and gamey. Most of the time, she cooked the liver and forced us to eat that.

So many times, I remember gagging and still having to put it in my mouth and chew. We were threatened with a beating if we threw it up. It was so horrible that even when we tried to secretly feed it to the dog, under the table, she would turn her nose up at it!

The other food that makes me gag to this day, is 'All Bran.' It's a cereal that contains all the husks, or the fibre, from the wheat. I had problems with constipation, growing up, so Mom decided that I needed to eat a bowl of this every day. It was disgusting!

I thought I was a smart little puppy when I figured out how to fool my parents. I would stir a little of this crap into a bowl with a drop of milk. I would put just enough of it in the bowl to dirty it, and then leave it with the spoon in the sink. This kept my mom off my back for exactly two wonderful weeks!

Then she bought groceries. I had forgotten to throw enough of it into the garbage, to gradually empty the box. How dumb could I be? Oh my!

I paid the price for that. Not only did I get a beating, but she decided to bake it into biscuits that were brown 'hockey-pucks.' They were dried out and rock-hard. Bon appetite!!

During the winter, we were forced to cut, chop, and haul wood for the furnace. This would be great and refreshing exercise, except when its -40 degrees Celsius and you are under the orders of a man who loves to come up behind you, and either cuff you or savagely kick you in the butt for being too slow. Then, this becomes a hard-labor prison sentence.

Sometimes, I think the universe does have a sense of humor. One winter, it was minus 42 degrees Celsius, so we brought the goats into the house to keep warm. They were about to have kids, and we couldn't take the chance the little ones would freeze to death in the barn.

My mom had been up all night watching over them, but my dad had gone to bed. I woke up, after I heard all the commotion. One of the goats snuck into my parent's bedroom. Goats tend to chew on anything and everything. This one was nibbling at my parent's wood dresser, and in the process had backed up to the edge of their bed.

It had already just birthed a kid, but with goats they usually come in pairs. It started 'bleating,' which woke my dad up. The bloody entrails were coming out the back end, as the goat was pushing. My dad's head was so close to the edge of the bed, that the view and the smell must have been spectacular!

Oh dear! I heard about it, when he started yelling at the top of his lungs. But, I would have given anything to have seen it! I guess he scared the goat so bad, everything came flying out. Unfortunately, my dad got out of the way in time. Too bad!

Experiencing death is normal on a farm. The short lifespan of animals pushes life and death into close proximity—as does predator and prey.

Two experiences I remember very well:

My dad grabbed his shotgun and ordered me to

follow him. I watched my dad separate a yearling calf from the herd, and place a pail of oats on the ground in front of him. I watched the calf hesitate out of fear, then shake it off and come running to the pail.

In my mind, I was thinking, "No, no! Don't come, don't come!" Not that it would have helped.

It dug into the oats, having abandoned all fear. Cows and goats won't stop eating oats, even when they are full. They keep eating until their stomachs actually explode.

This one didn't get that far.

At that moment, my dad shot it through the head. It died instantly.

It struck a chord in me, that something we believe is so wonderful and delicious (like the oats), could actually turn out to be our demise.

Shortly after this, the other incident happened. We had fifty, young fluffy, yellow chicks that we had just moved into the large barn. They had graduated from the warming lights.

One morning, I entered the barn to feed them and complete my chores. It was quiet, which was unusual. I looked around. I saw little piles of fluff everywhere! I took a close look at one, and saw the tell-tale sign of two red holes, where the weasel had sucked all the blood out and left the carcass.

In the midst of death and sadness, I heard one lonely peep. It peeped again and again, sounding very distressed. I followed the sound. I found it. It had frantically jumped inside an old teapot, and the lid had flipped over, sealing its good fortune.

It seemed a strange leap for my brain to make as a child, but, I saw it as a metaphor for life. There may be times when jumping into a deep dark hole could actually save our lives. We never know the outcome of any situation, and therefore we can't judge people by where they are in life—good or bad.

Someone with great material wealth could become so obsessed and indulgent that death comes knocking sooner than expected. Or, that person could fall down a deep dark hole, lose everything, and be forced to reflect and change, thereby actually gaining back the most precious wealth in existence—their soul. The universe loves irony.

I realized that what humans think of as good, may not necessarily be; and what humans think of as bad, might be the beginning of something truly great!

This is the door to a spiritual way of thinking—a thinking that demands a greater and broader perspective. WE are not the center of our universe.

To this young girl, on the verge of becoming a teenager, I wish to impart this: "You always had an uncanny ability to see the hidden layers of life. However, you locked your intuition away, because they had you convinced that you were stupid. I think you were wise beyond your years, and this scared them. When a bully is scared they often lash out more. Please know that you are NOT stupid. On the contrary, you are brilliant! You see things in a way that stretches the normal boundaries of perception. You have a gift that can't be broken or taken away. I know that you will use it wisely and for the good of humanity."

I headed to Gabby's place. I had some strange questions. I lived right behind her, so I would come to the Center every time I could. I loved offering service there and listening to her guidance. I knew she wouldn't think they were strange questions.

She was in her office with a stack of paperwork. She loved a break and a chance to teach.

I shared my memories and asked her, "What happens when we die?"

Well, I could see this was a good question, by the way Gabby smiled. She pointed to the only other chair in the office. "Have a seat."

She used the air to draw a triangle with her pen, "If you draw a pyramid, the divine realm is the top, with many levels. Then the astral world is underneath, also with many levels. Finally, the base is the physical world."

"The laws are different with animals and humans. Humans reincarnate after spending 200–300 years in the astral world—meaning they keep coming back to earth for more training until they have elevated enough to enter the divine realm. Animals do not. Animal spirits stay in the Astral World and offer a different kind of service."

The only exception is, if a human transmigrates for one lifetime as an animal. Meaning, the human soul comes to earth as an animal. Perhaps they spent the previous life as an abusive boss, raging at their employees. They probably need to go through intense 'humility' training, so they are made to come back to earth as a dog—a dog that must obey its master at all costs. Once this temporary training is done and they die, then they go back to a human form, to continue their training in the astral realm. This doesn't mean that all dogs are human."

I blinked as if she was nuts, "What?" Gabby

clarified, "Haven't you ever seen an animal, like a dog for instance, act like a human being. They have a unique character that is completely different from the rest of their own species?"

Actually, I had. It kind of made sense. I had seen a dog howl, along with us, as we chanted a certain prayer, and I always thought the dog was more in tune then the rest of us!

"It's like the human soul is wearing an animal costume. They can only do what that costume allows them to; but they still think like a human, and have desires that are humanlike." Gabby said.

She placed her pen down on the desk, and began to tidy the scattered papers, "When humans die, they have up to 49 days to go anywhere on earth they want, just by thinking about it. This gives them the chance to say good-bye to loved ones, and let go of any attachments. Then, they move on to the Astral World for a different kind of training. However, some souls escape the astral world and become earthbound spirits, where they haunt different places and people."

I nodded, even though I was still trying to digest this, "But what about killing animals?"

She responded, "We, as humans, do NOT have the authority to kill another human being, ever. But, as humans, we have been given authority over the animal and plant kingdoms, in the sense that we are here to look after them, and protect them. If we need to use their essence for food, then we do it with the utmost respect and in a humane fashion. The best way to honor the life of animals and plants is to expend the energy we receive from them, towards divine service—to help others and to save the planet. This transmutes their energy in the unseen realm and stops their resentment towards humans from building into a huge, dark, mass. This dark energy materializes when we callously kill and abuse animals with no regard for their welfare. Of course, when we have to euthanize our pets, we do it in the most humane way possible, as well. However, we don't have the authority to do this to humans, no matter what the circumstances are."

Gabby got side-tracked as she answered the phone. I half listened to her, as I reflected on what she shared. This helped me understand and realize that I wasn't condemned to hell for euthanizing my cats. I was devastated when I was put in this position, and wasn't sure I would ever recover.

"Judy, I need to get going. We'll have to continue this discussion another time." As Gabby rose and escorted me to the door, I continued to ponder.

I'm not one to believe everything I hear, until I experience it myself. Little did I know that later on in life, I would have several amazing experiences around death and these 49 days she mentioned.

Of course, I'm getting ahead of myself; first, let's go back and continue with my lost youth…

Chapter 3

Every day we rode the yellow school bus for forty-five minutes. It carried us into the town of Whitecourt. The public Elementary school was downtown, and both high schools were located up on the hill. One was the Catholic school which actually had k-to-12 and the public 'Hilltop High' which started at Grade 7, located a few blocks away.

My brother and I had gone to the public elementary school, until my mom got the brilliant idea that the Catholic school would be stricter, even though both of our parents were not Catholic nor practiced any type of religion. They needed to create more upheaval—like they weren't strict enough. I loved the elementary school. The kids were fun to play with, and the teachers were sweet and kind. The Catholic school was a nightmare! The teachers were tough and distant. The kids were mean and cliquish.

I had been attending Grade 7 at the Catholic school for a few months. Every day, I had to say good-bye to my friends on the bus, as they got off at the public school, and I continued on to the next stop. Again, I was isolated and the constant thought of being bullied, cloaked me like an itchy wool blanket, I could never shake off. I had no friends here. The boys ignored me. The teachers ignored me. The only attention I got was the incessant teasing from the girls, like being in front of a hornets nest, and not being able to even swat them away.

There were four girls who were the worst offenders, and they never missed a chance to make my life miserable. These four girls were from middle class Catholic families. They all had long hair. They all wore brightly colored handkerchiefs to hold their hair back. They all dressed alike—skin-tight jeans, the type that you had to use a hanger to pull the zipper up with, and slutty, low-cut, T-Shirts. All birds of a feather. They believed that together they were stronger. Together they were greater. Together they were a gang—a silly gang of twelve year old girls.

Their radar always seemed to know where I was. They were looking for a victim, a punching bag, an easy target. For me, they didn't even have to turn their radar on. The years of terror and abuse had branded me a red, neon, bull's-eye, blinking in staccato, as I moved. A homing pigeon could have found me. I was the full package. Come pick on me, whenever you want. My mind lived in a dark cave. A heavy wet cover of fear and powerlessness wrapped my soul.

I was the lost one and no adult seemed to care or even notice. Except my parents, who guarded the cave of my existence with iron bars and iron fists. They didn't even need to be physically there to imprison me. They had adopted advanced remote technology.

Theirs was a sneaky assault. "We are all mighty and all powerful. You will bend to our will, now and forever. If not—you know what will happen! Don't even try to run!" The permanent tape of their voices rolling over and over in my head, never runs silent. Welcome to my prison.I always stood out. But on this day, my hair was recently cropped short and more uneven than usual. I had cried the night before, as the scissors did their routine damage. I had just started to get bangs and was able to pull the hair behind my ear. I knew the haircut was looming, but had hoped it would be forgotten. But I had ticked my mom off, and the repercussions were always great and personal. She knew what was important to me.

You couldn't even call my hair a boy's style. I had no style. Mine would never be in style. My mother made sure of that. It wasn't enough to be in prison at home, she had to enforce it, by proxy, at school too.

"Let's check your pants. Are you sure you're a girl?" One of the girls whispered, always able to avoid the teacher's ears. Their giggling sent shivers down my spine. I wanted to instantly disappear.

Now! Right now! Luckily, the bell rang and recess saved me. The same group of girls, fed off each other as their combined energy took on a power of its own. On this day, they seemed to take extra notice of me. Part of the school hallway had a short incline, with a handrail separating it into two directions. I saw them before they spotted me. They were headed to the washroom. They never went anywhere alone.

I purposely moved over to the other side and squeezed my little frame together, hoping to make myself smaller, hoping they wouldn't see; hoping I could be invisible even for just a few more seconds. As always, I walked with my head down. A tiny dot of existence always centered toward the earth—a moving spotlight of pain and torment.

"Hey, ugly two shoes! What dumpster did you find those clothes in?" The oldest of the four ducked under the rail and stopped short to block my path.

She sneered at me and pushed me hard against the wall. Her breathe was tinged with cigarette smoke and wet ash. "We will find you after school, so don't go anywhere. We have a present for you!"

The hall echoed with their laughter, as she released me and they moved to class as one unit. I trembled and fought not to cry. It was a losing battle. I knew I needed to run. I knew I needed to run fast and hard at the end of this day. My life depended on it.

Time sped up. It's such a tricky partner—always by your side but never consistent. *I make it a block and a half down the back alley. I can't breathe. I bend over to try to catch my breath. My eyes search frantically for a hiding place. I only have a moment.*

I hear the familiar ebb and flow of their voices, not too far behind me. I can hear them laughing and speaking of boys and natural, teenage, girl things. I catch little snippets of biting, cold words of torture and torment which they plan to inflict on me.

This spurs me on. I feel an icy chill crawl up my back. I catch a sense of pure darkness from one of them.

I have to find cover, now! By sheer force of will, I move into the darkness.

"What did I ever do to deserve this?" My thoughts echo. I shudder and fight for a breath. I quickly pull myself up short, as the large, metal garbage can I'm hiding in, starts to sway to my frantic movements. I steady it with my arms out.

I have to be still. Perfectly still! Don't breathe!

"We'll break every one of her fingers!"

"Yeah, and smash her face and cut her ears off!" They're frenzy and excitement is building. They have a plan. They just need to execute it. They are close, and they are getting prepared for battle.

"I saw her leave by the south door! We should be on her right away!" That's the voice of the youngest girl, whom I encountered earlier on in the day, by the Principal's office. By herself, she had held her head down, and mumbled what sounded like an apology to me. She had quickly moved past me, so I'm not sure, but it seemed like she didn't want to tease me, when we were alone. What's changed now?

I hear their voices moving away from me down the alley. Only now, I smell the rotten stink of garbage. Perhaps that's me? This thought clings to me as I climb out. I feel like something discarded—something no one wants and I'm rotting away.

In their world, they couldn't fathom anyone hiding in a garbage can. They had no idea what fear was. This was a game to them, a nasty one. Their world was small and narrow.

My world had cracked open at the seams.

I dodged a bullet that day. A few years later, when I returned to Whitecourt, I had heard that two of these same girls were convicted of a similar crime, where they had taken scissors and cut off the ear of a girl and broke many of her fingers. They beat her up in such a savage manner. They were locked up at the Juvenile Detention Center. The other 2 were involved, but had not been charged.

As an adult reflecting on this scene, I realize that I had, also, become this little girl's tormentor and abuser. I had treated her with absolute meanness and total distain. I had no use for her, and would beat her up every chance. I was adept at ripping her to shreds with the slightest provocation.

"Shut up! You don't know anything! You're stupid and lazy!" These words uttered in my head, effectively, knocked her down over and over again.

This little girl lived for many more years, than was necessary, in a silent tomb. It is only in the most recent years, of my spiritual journey, that I have begun to gently coax her out of the deep, dark hole and say hi to her. It is only recently that I have begun to acknowledge her with hugs and a soft touch. It is only recently that I have apologized to her and she, with her ever buoyant spirit has accepted this, and is beginning her journey into the light. She even comes out to play, now and again. She has a gentle, beautiful, nurturing spirit! I feel so blessed to know her.

I couldn't sleep, so I grabbed my jacket and headed over to Gabby's. I knew she would be up, doing papers for College. Because English was her second language, she would often ask me to look at them for grammatical support. I loved helping her in any way I could. She has never said 'no' to me, anytime I have asked her for assistance.

She welcomed me in, and put on a pot of tea. "What's bugging you tonight, Judy?"

I relayed my memories, and asked her about the spiritual significance of bullying.

I entered her little kitchen and sat at the nook table, in the chair, by the window. The only thing on her table was an aloe vera plant resting on a doily. Everything had its place. I loved coming here.

Gabby, sat down with 2 cups and some sugar. She had just plugged in the teakettle. "Well, we need to start at the beginning of time. The divine plan is actually progressing. As you've seen with the pyramid, there is only one God. He created the universe and all the realms. He created the divine realm, and then created gods and deities under him to have different missions in the universe. Much like we have the Prime Minister and all the ministers.

"Then, He created the Spiritual World where many saints, sages, angels, and holy souls reside. Then, the astral world was created, where all our souls travel, when we pass on. Finally, He created the physical realm, by first creating spiritual patterns for everything and then using the Principle of Hardening, materialized everything into the physical dimension."

If you were to look down through the center of the pyramid, you would see (draw a circle with a dot in the middle). This is the core of God running straight through all and everything."

"Are you still with me?" I smiled. Sometimes she talks in a roundabout way, to get to the point. I should be used to it by now. I took my jacket off and dug in for the long haul.

Gabby continued, "The divine plan is actually progressing. During the ancient divine era, or in other words the time of the 'Garden of Eden,' humans lived closely with the deities and gods. In fact humans were half human and half God. They lived for 500 to 600 years. They were taught everything they needed to know. They were happy and prosperous."

"This, however, caused a problem with motivating humans to develop the material resources on earth. So, God created within us 'desire' the area just under our belly button, where our desires both negative/positive come from. Some of these negative desires include: the desire to compete; the desire to want beautiful woman; the desire for lots of wealth and prestige; the desire for more land; and the desire to be at the highest echelons of society. At that time in divine history, these negative desires were needed and allowed, so that the material civilization could advance at record speed."

"Then, God sent down saints, sages, prophets, Jesus, Buddha, etc. to try to slow down the onslaught to the earth. People had lost sight of the spiritual principles completely, and had become too materialistic."

"During the ancient divine era, the 'fire' deities were controlling the earth and they were strict. They included both male and female. It was like looking at your house in the middle of a sunny day. You can't hide any dirt or secrets. It was because they were so pure and spiritually straightforward. So in order to advance material civilization, they were moved into the background, and the 'water' deities were allowed to take temporary control over the earth. They also included both male and female. They were very lenient: 'No problem, we will look the other way on your affair, as long as you are fighting for more land and building more factories. No problem, if you have to steal a little, as long as you are learning new technologies to take over your competitor. No problem! Just advance the material world.'"

The kettle started whistling, so Gabby got up to unplug it , "During the time of the water lineage, any families who had 'righteous desires' or who were trying to practice spiritual principles, were prosecuted and stepped on. Many were killed, as we can see in our world history. They were taken advantage of, because they were considered 'weak.'

She carried two full cups of Earl Grey tea to the table and gently placed one in front of me, "This is how it has been for the last few thousand years. The problem now, is that humanity has taken it too far. We may be close to destroying the earth. So now, there has been a change. The 'fire' deities are steadily and step by step coming back into the forefront. Secrets that have been kept secret will start to come out.

The spiritual essence of fire is increasing day by day. We are in the age of the 'baptism by fire' instead of the age of 'baptism by water.' Even Christian religions make reference to this new age. The Principle of Dawning plays a role here, as the spiritual pressure of the light is increasing day by day, so people will be spiritually waking-up, all over the world."

She took a long, slow sip of her tea and closed her eyes for a second. I stopped myself from speaking, just as she opened her eyes and continued, "Now, we will start to see a reversal in fortune. Those who are looking for only material indulgence will come to a complete deadlock, until they change. The pressure of the light will become so intense, many may go insane before they change."

"Now, the people who are standing up for what's right and following a spiritual way of life, will receive **great** blessings from the 'fire' deities. It you think of the power from the Sun, nothing is impossible to achieve."

"People have spent many lifetimes stepping on the 'weak' and bullying them. This comes from our divine history. We all have lived during the time of the great renaissance, so we all have accumulated this kind of karma. You were able to erase your 'bulling' karma and it has now been engraved on your soul to honor all life, at all times. You have transitioned to a practitioner of the Universal Principles. Congratulations!"

Gabby placed our cups in the sink. I knew she would clean them the moment I walked out the door. I smiled and felt absolute gratitude for being allowed to know someone of her calibre.

I don't know who first said it, but I've heard that "An ordinary man thinks he is extraordinary, and an extraordinary man thinks he is ordinary."

Gabby is truly humble and gentle and so spiritually in tune with the universe. She believes she is fallible, and though she may be, in my world she is extraordinary!

Let's check in again with my lost youth…

Chapter 4

The second time I ran away, I was thirteen years old. I had, already, endured a lifetime of pain and suffering.

It started out very similar to the first time. I put together a pack with essential items, and I left in the middle of the night. Only this time it was June and very warm out. I didn't need my brother's help. I locked the dogs in the barn and dug in for a long hike.

I made it down to the highway in three hours. I didn't hear any cougars, but I had also become hardened, and able to withstand more. They should be worried about me!

Oh my! Teenagers, often, have no comprehension of the scope of the world, nor of their fragile existence.

This time, I thought I was so prepared. I had made a friend on the school bus. Her name was Cindy and she was friendly and kind. She was naive to my world. I didn't share it with her. I liked her innocence. She had recently moved to Edmonton. She gave me her address, and said if I ever go to the City, look her up.

I planned to do just that.

As soon as I made it to the highway, I stuck my thumb out. Within minutes I got a ride. In those days, hitchhiking was as common as breathing. Everyone did it. It would be extremely rude to pass someone by, and NOT pick them up.

A middle aged man in a blue utility truck pulled over. He was another version of my dad—hard working, blue collar, built from grit.

I blurted out my name without thinking. Oh my God!

I had to get this together. Of all the luck in the world, he knew my dad.

He looked over at me as he shifted into higher gear, “You know, I worked with your dad in Edson on a fire call.” He chuckled and shook his head, “Man, I remember when the fire came up over the north ridge and caught a sidewinder (a cross wind). It changed directions so fast, we didn’t have time to pull out. All we could do was crawl under the Cat and pull the fire blankets over us. Holy Christ, the heat was enough to bake us into instant cement!”

He said, “Your dad stayed cool as a cucumber. I have a lot of respect for him.”

My dad flew water bombers, for years, for the forestry and then he traded the plane for one of those big Caterpillars and he would clear a ‘fire swathe.’ He cleared all the trees and debris from around a large fire to keep it from jumping. He rented out his ‘Cat’ and his time, for hundreds of dollars an hour, to the Forestry. He received danger pay for dangerous work.

Of all my luck in the world, I had to run into someone he knew. I had to think quickly on my feet and I was getting good at it. Over the coming years I had honed it to a fine art.

I responded, “Yeah, sometimes he’s gone for weeks at a time. My little Volkswagen broke down on the Windfall road and I need to get to Town to get the proper parts. Thank you so much for picking me up!” I had a hunch this guy hadn’t seen my dad for a few years and didn’t know our family situation well. I was right.

He did look sideways at me a few times, so I’m not sure if he bought what I was selling, but he drove me into town, and dropped me off at the gas station. That's all I needed from him.

I made it to the Greyhound bus station, with just minutes to spare. I remember climbing the stairs and heading to the back of the bus. My spider senses were tingling, so I went on high alert. The fear was climbing up my spine and I could feel that my parents were close by, somewhere.

"Please, please, let me get out of here!" I was starting to panic as I monitored all the windows.

Once the bus started moving, I expected it to come to an abrupt halt. In my mind, I saw my mom climb aboard and stare me down with her evil eyes. I couldn't see straight. I was hyper-ventilating and needed to calm my breathing down. Good thing the bus was almost empty.

I took a deep cleansing breathe, once we were well outside the Town limits. I made it! Now the real adventure begins.

Three hours later, I climbed off in the city of Edmonton. I had never been to the city before. It was overwhelming! It was like those Amish teens, on that reality show, seeing the big city for the first time—wide open mouths and big eyes, trying to take it all in. We were lost in another dimension that was moving along at a rapid-fire pace.

It was late afternoon by the time I found her home. I had a lot of difficulty with the streets and understanding how addresses worked. In Edmonton, streets run North and South. Avenues run East and West. To me, that was like Greek. I couldn't comprehend it, and had to ask for help every step of the way. Many strangers were kind enough to assist me.

I rang her doorbell. I smiled as she opened the door and instantly recognized me. She gave me a big hug, and let me in, "It's good to see you Judy! Wow! What are you doing here?"

I walked in and sat down at the kitchen chair. I put my bag down and noticed her eyes follow its movement. I could see she was curious, but too friendly to ask out right. "Do you want some juice?" She got out two glasses and poured some orange.

I started, "Remember when you said I could come see you any time? Well I need a place to stay, just for a short while." I didn't think it would be easy to convince her; but I didn't expect to see panic set into her eyes so quickly. What was going on with her? I wondered.

She quickly looked around, "My mom has been stressed out lately, and she won't let me have any visitors. You need to find another place."

"I don't have anywhere else to go." I blurted. This was not going as I had imagined.

"Let's go to the park near here." She said. I grabbed my bag as she herded me out of the house, as fast as she could.

We sat on the swing and talked about the bus rides we shared. We laughed about the one winter when the bus couldn't make it up the hill, because the road had become a thick sheet of ice. We all played in the snow, till a new bus came. We missed half a day of school, having fun and sliding down the hill on the ice. The bus driver had no chance of controlling us, but to his credit he never gave up trying.

"My mom is getting a divorce." She blurted. "I guess that's why we moved to the City to give them some time apart, to see if they could fix it that way. It didn't work." Cindy started to cry. I, quickly, gave her a hug.

"My older sister is coming tonight and sleeping downstairs. She's going back to College tomorrow and then, maybe, I can sneak you downstairs after she leaves." She was trying her best.

"What about tonight?" I stammered. I was on the verge of crying myself.

Cindy pointed to the hockey arena, which was now filled with grass. There was an overhang above the penalty box. "Let's make a bed for you there. I can bring you a sleeping bag and some food, a little later, when my Mom and sister go to bed."

This was the first night that I spent homeless. I didn't get any sleep. I cried most of the night. I wasn't used to the sounds of the City and all the lights at night. How can anyone sleep with so many lights on?

The next day, Cindy skipped school and brought me back to her home, after her mom and sister left. I had a wonderful day playing and laughing and just being a typical teenager. We ransacked her mom's makeup and did ourselves up. We laughed so hard our stomachs hurt.

Around six pm, when her mom got home from work, she put me in the basement bedroom and I had to be extra quiet so her mom wouldn't come down. I slept the whole night through, like a baby. She didn't. She was the one scared all night, thinking we were going to get caught. I slept from pure exhaustion.

The next morning, my picture was all over the news. They didn't have the 'Amber Alert' in those days. They just had my picture and a warrant out for my arrest. Back then, runaways were dumped into the same category as criminals.

Cindy was terrified! I could see it in her aura. She was putting her walls up and shutting me out. She was too scared to talk to me alone, so she waited until her boyfriend showed up. She needed his moral support to send me away. He brought the address to the Youth Hostel, and they walked me to the bus stop.

If I was her, I probably would have done the same. I held no ill will towards her. I could see her future and mine were worlds apart. I didn't want to inflict any deeper scar on hers. She was too innocent and too fragile. If she even peeked into my world, it would be enough to break her. I said goodbye and thanked her.

I found my way on the Transit bus to 'Downtown Edmonton.' That was the easy part. I got on the only bus that had it written across the top. Now, knowing Edmonton very well, I knew I had ended up only blocks away from the Youth Hostel. At the time, though, I was lost. I remember looking out of the phone booth and seeing strange characters walking by.

It looked like a Comic book spread. There were Goth teenagers, hookers, pimps, leather-bound bikers, with more tattoos then skin, etc.; all strolling up the sidewalk like they had nowhere to go. In the middle of this spread, was a damsel in distress who seemed to have an invisible cloak. Everyone cut a wide swathe around me. They didn't want to get involved. Perhaps they thought it was a set-up or an ambush.

I phoned the Youth Hostel and the lady sounded harried and stressed. Probably overworked and underpaid. She tried hard to give me directions, but I couldn't understand.

I was falling over the edge, and my mind couldn't compute anymore—sensory overload. I hung up and stumbled down the sidewalk. Dusk was coming and I was lost in a strange dark world. I wished I was in my bed reading my favorite novel. I wished I was back with my parents. At least I knew what to expect with them, and how to survive it. Here, I was in a foreign land with no bearings.

I stepped onto a Transit bus, to ask the driver for help. (Now, years later it seems a strange coincidence that my husband was an Edmonton Transit bus driver, and then a Transit dispatcher for years, right up till he died) The bus driver could see that I was spooked and ready to bolt.

He was so nice and caring. I saw him take some money out of his wallet and put it in his upper shirt pocket. I knew he was going to give it to me at the next stop. I sat down and started to cry. I could handle pain, but kindness undid me. That I couldn't handle. I gave up. I could see him looking through the large mirror at me and speaking into his CB radio, but I didn't care. I knew there was a warrant out for my arrest. I was done. I didn't want to stay in this City any longer.

The police boarded the bus at the Transit Center. One cop climbed aboard the front steps and another climbed through the middle door. I stood up. There was no point in resisting. I could see the bus driver had gotten involved because he cared. He had no choice. I didn't blame him. The cop escorted me off the bus and put me in the back of the cruiser.

All he said to me was, "If you run, I will shoot you!"

That was the exact moment that I lost it. I couldn't

hold back, anymore. I cried my heart out. They were long, gut wrenching sobs. I couldn't catch my breath and then I couldn't breathe through the snot. I was desperately trying to get oxygen in and trying to clear my nose at same time. I was a mess! I couldn't fathom how running away from abuse warranted being shot and killed! I couldn't get it to compute in my brain at all! I hadn't hurt anyone! Ever! I wasn't even a bully! Yet I came close to being shot?

Not registering! Scrambled! Done!

The cop looked back at me several times in the mirror. He didn't speak a word until we got inside the station. I noticed that he handled me with a gentle hand, when he escorted me out of the cruiser. Something had caused his manner to change.

He brought me into his private office. (They still had those back in the day) I think if he was permitted to hug me, he would have.

In a firm voice, he said, "Look at me." I wouldn't. He sighed, "Please, look at me." His tone became kinder, gentler. I looked up.

He handed me another Kleenex. "I'm so sorry! I thought you were different. I thought you were a hardened teen, like the ones we deal with all the time. I can see that you're not. I'm sorry for what I said. I would never have drawn my weapon, even if you ran. I would have just chased you down and caught you. I just wanted to scare you." He smiled sadly, "Which, I see worked. Too well!"

I learned about transference later in life, where a professional helps you and you feel so safe with them, that you think you have fallen in love with them. He was about six foot, two inches tall. He had short blond hair. He was a little bald up front, but he had the kindest blue eyes I had ever seen. I could get lost in them.

I loved him! Maybe that's why today, when I see any man in uniform, I get turned on. Oh, he was so cute!

I told him my story. He listened to every word. He told me that he had kids, and that his heart breaks for what kids like us have to go through. He said that I wouldn't have survived on the street. I was too honest and too kind. I would have gotten eaten up—whatever that meant.

He had no choice but to call my parents. They would have to come get me and keep me for the night, BUT child welfare would be at my place tomorrow, and would do an investigation. He tried to calm me down and reassure me that they wouldn't touch me tonight. He would make sure of it, he said.

My parents showed up three hours later. They had to drive into the City. I could see they weren't happy. I saw the officer speak to my dad, and move up really close to him. I don't know what was said, but I got the impression that my dad didn't like him at all.

My parents never said a word to me on the long drive home. They never said a word to me the rest of the night. The next day Welfare came. This time it was two ladies, whom my mom didn't know. They decided to take me and put me in a foster home for two weeks, until the case could be brought in front of a judge.

I had the best two weeks of my life! There were four other kids in the home, and we only had a few rules and a few chores. The foster mother had a large trampoline in the back yard, and we spent hours and hours bouncing, laughing, and gossiping, as teenagers do.

The judge knew my parents, and decided that they were upstanding citizens, and that I needed to be returned home for another try.

What other try? Years of abuse, wasn't enough?

In those days corporal punishment was the norm and there was no proof that they were beating us with a stick or a switch. It was legal to use a leather strap, as long as it had the right dimensions. The strap was even used in the schools for discipline. So really, my parents weren't breaking the law.

Well let's look at the lines around sexual abuse:

Hmm, a man pulling down the pants and underwear of a teenage girl and beating her bare bottom with a stick, doesn't fit anywhere in sexual abuse? Because, this sure as hell, abuses and confuses the sexual neuro-pathways to the girl's brain. It disrupts the pain/pleasure receptors until one overrides the other.

A painful incident such as this one, repeated over and over, causes the body to release pleasurable endorphins, especially around the age when the hormones are 'raging' in a teenager. When these same neuro-pathways are lit up again, they create a 'horny' signal. The body then responds with a dump of endorphins. In the extreme, this leads to S&M's and 'Fifty Shades of Grey.'

The other mix up in the pain/pleasure receptors for abused teenagers is 'power.' When someone has ultimate power over me and I'm the helpless victim, I start to get horny. I HATED that for years, but couldn't get my body to stop betraying me! For so many years, I believed I was flawed and disgusting. It wasn't until I started researching the physiological effects on abused kids, did it begin to make sense, and I could start to heal.

The first experience, of this, was when my mom sent me to the doctor, at thirteen, to see if I was a virgin. This doctor was creepy, and loved his job too much. I remember lying down, with my legs in the cold stirrups while he stuck his hand up my vagina. I could feel his icky fingers moving around far too long. My body started responding, and I hated myself for the betrayal! I thought I was exactly what my parents said, a dirty slut!

Wow! The path of destruction cuts wide and deep.

To this beautiful young teenager: "First of all, you were so brave in Edmonton! I notice that you sense a lot of things, but don't trust your intuition. Please trust it. You are gifted with this ability to sense people's auras. Don't waste this talent. Also, your young body is changing and flowering into a beautiful woman. I wish you had a mom who could sit down with you and explain this once in a lifetime celebration of entering womanhood. She could explain the physiological changes and what to watch out for and what to avoid.

She could make sure that you were safe and that you would undress for no man and no stranger, even if they were a doctor! Not only should a nurse have been present; but you weren't sick, so that procedure should never have been performed in the first place! It's not too late to re-wire your brain. Now that you're aware of it, let's work together to create some new and beautiful experiences. I love you so much!

The lost youth is waiting…

Chapter 5

"This time, when I get a chance, I will get as far away from this hellhole as possible!" I silently raged at the world, as I squeezed my books and walked into the school.

My parents toned it down for a few weeks, after I returned from the Foster Home. Then a shift happened, and it was like they were making up for lost time! It got worse than before. It felt like payback! I'm sure my dad didn't like anyone in authority telling him what to do, like with the cop. He was used to getting his way, like with the Judge. How dare I disgrace him!

Now, they were locking me up all the time in my bedroom. I was allowed to do chores and go to school, but that was it. It was like living in a concentration camp. If I looked the wrong way, I would get slapped. The hatred in my Dad's eyes, whenever he looked at me, was like getting scorched with a branding iron. It burned my soul! They even discussed keeping me at home, from school, so they could have more control. I was mortified! I wouldn't survive that torture!

Again, I had become a trapped animal—clawing at the cage to find a way out. Any crack would do! I was terrified! I wasn't going to get beat again! Something snapped in me and there was no other choice available.

"Just don't touch me again!" I shook off the painful memories, and sat down at my desk. I had to watch for a crack, to slip through. If it came, I would be ready. I was beyond my limits. I could bear no more!

The crack appeared, that day at school. It was second

period of the day, and she walked in behind the teacher. She sat down directly behind me. The teacher introduced her as Lisa. Today she would be labeled as 'Goth'. She had black lips and black fingernails. Actually, everything about her was black, even her 'stay away from me' dark persona. Except her skin.

She had on white powdered make-up over top of already translucent, white skin. I thought she made a good imitation of a Vampire. My four female tormenters at the back of class giggled, and continued dive bombing rolled up 'spit-wads' at my head. I wondered how long, before she would join them.

I was shocked when I heard her speak, "What the fuck?" I turned around in my seat and saw her bend over and pick up one of the spit-wads. She walked to the back of the class and handed it to the owner. "I think this is yours." She leaned over and whispered in the girl's ear, "Leave her the fuck alone, if you know what's good for you!"

I had never seen them so still or so silent. Their mouths hung open in a perpetual 'Oh!'

Complete shock! I loved it! Nobody had dared speak to them that way. There was no chance, they would be friends with her. I was ecstatic!

The gang, who had tormented me for years, had nothing on this girl! Lisa knew how to be a rebel. She wasn't scared of anyone. These girls were small potatoes to her. She had moved to Whitecourt from the big city. The big city of Edmonton was like the mother-ship of teens in rebellion. I had been to Edmonton, I knew how foreign and crazy it was. At fourteen, most of us were still naïve to the world outside this small town. Even, if we pretended otherwise.

I was drawn to her. She was drawn to me. She took me under her wing. We started skipping school together and hanging out with some older Vietnamese men, whom she knew. Looking back, I think she was hooked on drugs, and I was the gift she served up to these guys, to guarantee her supply.

Lisa partied and loved drugs! One day, we skipped school and she convinced me to go to this apartment downtown.

"Come on! I don't want to walk around Whitecourt anymore! If we're gonna skip school, then let's make it count!" She pleaded with me, twiddling with her braids. "Your parents won't find out and if they do, who cares! They beat you anyway."

"Fine! But, only this one time!" I had said 'no' so many times in the past, I felt like she was getting bored with me. I agreed to go. I couldn't bear the thought of losing her as a friend. I didn't have any others.

We walked into this crappy hole of an apartment. There were two guys sitting at an old Formica table playing cards, and another was watching a small black and white TV. The curtains were thick and drawn, and it was dark and dingy. There was dust everywhere, and junk scattered all over the floor. Dirty dishes were stacked high in the sink. You could see small particles of dust floating in the air.

I could visualize my Mom's disgusted look, as her nose got bent out of shape, looking at this dive. She would have NEVER crossed this threshold! I smiled at the thought, as I entered.

I noticed we were the only girls, and as soon as we

walked in, all eyes shifted to us.

Lisa, immediately, grabbed a joint from the nearest guy. She took a deep, long puff and blew it into his mouth, while climbing on his lap, "Look what I've brought you guys!" She looked up and pointed to me, like I was a gift. I watched as the drug morphed her face into an instant mask of pleasure, and the tension drained from her body. She hung her head over his arm and closed her eyes. Just as I thought she was asleep, she said "She's all yours. Just don't hurt her!"

The smell of weed permeated the place. I noticed right away that everyone was happy! I hadn't been around drugs before, but it didn't seem like a bad thing to me. No one was yelling and there was no sense of impending danger. They were all extremely friendly. Little did I know, I was walking into the lion's den. I was so very naïve.

I was extremely shy at first, but the weed had a way of making small and insignificant things seem larger than life, and extremely funny. I quickly slid down the rabbit hole. I had never laughed so hard in my life. I found a whole new world, far removed from the pain and torment waiting for me at home and at school. Sure, it was a false sense of peace and happiness, but I didn't care. For the first time, I wasn't in the 'fight or flight' mode. For the first time, I wasn't sitting in a pool of dread, being eaten alive. 'I will take an unlimited supply, please. Keep it coming!'

It wasn't long before the owner of the place, Tam, started cozying up to me. I knew what he wanted, and it was on the 3rd visit that he made his move. I knew it was time to deliver or I wouldn't be allowed back.

"Come with me." I follow him into the bedroom. He sits on the edge of the bed and starts to unbutton his shirt. I almost walk out. He grabs my arm and pulls me down next to him. There is a moment of fear. The only time I have undressed in front of anyone is right before a beating! I clear my mind. This is not going to happen that way. I look around. The room is semi-dark. The curtains are drawn. I'm glad.

I feel a strange change in my body—a warm feeling down below and extra sensitivity when I wiggle. I steal a glance at him. He has darker skin. He is Vietnamese. His stomach is flabby. He seems older than Lisa said. Maybe I should ask how old he is? No, it doesn't matter. He grabs my hand and places it over his penis. What am I supposed to do? He holds his hand over mine and starts to rub in circular motions. Ahh, okay I can do that.

He lets go and backs onto the bed. I quickly undress and jump under the sheets. I don't want him to see my body. He laughs, as he rolls the condom on. He climbs in next to me. Oh my God! He's squeezing my breasts with his hands and it's hurting! I try to pull away. Any sexual feelings I had are completely gone. I don't want to do this anymore! I tell him I've changed my mind. He laughs, again. This isn't going well. He's already climbing on me! Isn't he supposed to go slower? He finds the entryway and pushes into me. I feel something break. I turn my head away as he builds to a frenzy, and quickly ejaculates, lost in his own world of pleasure. It's done. He climbs off me.

Isn't there supposed to be some chemistry between us? Isn't my heart supposed to go pitter patter? I don't even think he's cute. Well, at least it didn't hurt. Thank

God we didn't kiss. I'll save that for someone else.

He walks out, towards the bathroom. I'm left with silence and a ton of regrets. I push them away. A survivor won't make it with regrets.

We walked back into the living room together. He was smiling and whistling. I was his new girlfriend. He bought me gifts and drugs to keep me happy, and bought himself plenty of condoms to keep him happy. I realized, at that moment, that I was no longer powerless. It was a strange feeling. If I gave him sex, which didn't hurt, he became happy and generous. Since he was the head of his gang, I had an unlimited supply of weed. Even Lisa bowed to me. Wow—a wonderful new world had opened up!

The rest of his gang was jealous of him. This became a paradox for me over the next fifteen years. I always saw myself as ugly, yet wherever I went, men would whistle and stare. I had a bright energy and a look that drove them crazy. This always confused me. At the time, I didn't know what they were seeing. All I saw was ugliness, exactly what my parents had drilled into me.

Now looking back at the pictures, I can say that I was gorgeous! I have beautiful brown eyes, dark brown hair, and at that time, I had a very tiny physique. I had a narrow waist and large hips. I had very beautiful, long, legs. I also had an innocence about me, and a gentle spirit that combined with the learned ability to be provocative, drove men insane, no matter where I went.

Within a couple of weeks, my parents found out we were skipping school. They told the school that I was the bad influence on Lisa. My mom felt that we needed to be separated. They discussed the possibility of homeschooling me for the next semester. I was beyond terrified. I would not let this happen! Once stuck at home, it would be almost impossible to escape! They had already started locking my brother and I in our rooms at night!

I was followed closely, over the next couple days. The principal's daughter, who was my age, stayed on me like white on rice. I couldn't shake her. Finally I managed to sneak out during the school assembly. She lost sight of me for a moment and I booked it.

I found the nearest convenience store, as they always had phone booths on the corner. It was 10 cents a call and Tam was always home. I quickly explained that I needed to get out of town. I lied and told him that I had an old lover looking for me, and I needed to get away.

The jealousy angle worked. Tam had no idea how young I was and he didn't even realize that he had been the one to take my virginity! It was easy to play him. I needed him. He was my ticket out of town.

"I'm heading to Red Deer. Come with me. I'll take care of you." He said all the right words.

I was excited! Red Deer was about 350 kilometers south of Whitecourt and my parents didn't know anyone there. They would never find me!

"Please, come pick me up now!" I hung up.

The time in Red Deer was a blur of smoking dope and drinking. I don't remember what else we did for those two weeks. The haze suddenly cleared when Tam decided he was going to go back to Whitecourt. He assumed that I was going with him. He said he would protect me, and he wasn't taking no for an answer.

"Not in a million years buddy! I'm never going

back!" I thought. I'll do whatever it takes.

He just happened to have a friend heading to Calgary, which was about 150 km *further* south of Red Deer. I immediately dumped Tam and latched on to his friend. Neither of them had any idea what hit them. Tam headed back to Whitecourt very confused and hurt. I had no sympathy for him. He had used me, as well, for one-way gratification in the sex department. He must have had an idea of how young I was, yet his needs were all that mattered.

I don't even remember his friend's name. Within two days of being in Calgary, one of his friends asked me if I wanted to make a lot of money. He said I could come and see the business, and if I didn't like it, no problem, I could leave. He gave enough hints that I knew what I was getting into. I needed money to survive. I was game.

The next day, I walked into this upscale condo/hotel complex, and never left. They rented furnished apartments by the month.

I remember walking in and the first thing I saw were four other girls lounging around the living room coffee table. They were all dressed in sleazy, sheer robes and Teddys. A lot of boob was visible. Two of them were smoking. As I was escorted down the hallway, I could hear what sounded like lively sex going on in both bedrooms. This was a happening place.

When I first looked at the girls, I remembered thinking, "Wow, they look gorgeous! They're all done up like actresses!" It was only days later, I realized that thick make-up and expensive outfits can cover wrinkles and flaws, but it's a false mirage. The bared truth is harsh, and not all it's cracked up to be. On closer inspection, sadness and despair were the dominate coverings.

I was escorted in by a Frenchman named Andre, in his late 50's. He had strawberry blond hair and was covered in freckles. He was built sturdy and large—close to 6 feet. He had a thick mustache and his French accent was just as thick. He had a gorgeous blond, bombshell, hanging over his arm. Sarah, looked to be in her 30's and she was the house mother. She, also, had a thick French accent.

Andre spoke, "We don't force anyone to be here. We take only the best. You come with a good reference. If you choose to stay, you will follow everything we tell you. You will be well looked after, and you will make us a lot of money." They both were inspecting me from head to toe. I felt like a horse at an auction. What a strange feeling!

I guess they liked what they saw, except for the clothes. Andre said, "We will send Sarah's sister, Tina, out with you to get some clothes. They will accent your feminine curves. He started to run his finger over my shoulder and down my arm. The look in his eyes unnerved me. I didn't like his touch either. But, it was the look in Sarah's eyes that really scared me. She didn't like me on sight.

Andre had the final say, and Sarah listened to him with abject loyalty. I needed money to survive and I didn't have a SSN nor a driver's license to get a legal job. This was my only option. It seemed safe enough. I didn't have to go outside. I didn't have to solicit the men. They were brought in to the location, and they picked from the circle of women/girls in the living room. Many of these girls were close to my age.

I smoothly transitioned into the world of prostitution. I made them a boatload of money. I had repeat business. I was the only girl who never sat, alone, long. I was the most popular. I learned how to pleasure the johns, most intently. I learned how to draw out an orgasm and bring them to a quick climax. I was an honest businesswoman. I believed in giving a generous trade for their dollar. I became one of the best in that industry.

I grew up fast. Buying new and beautiful clothes grew old. Besides, I always had to buy whatever Tina thought was cute. I was never allowed to go anywhere by myself. I never saw the money. Based on conversations, I knew that Andre was making $600 to $800 a day on me. I had become trapped again. I wanted out, but had no place to go. This was still better than being at home. There was no pain inflicted; but we weren't allowed to party and especially no drugs were allowed, because that interfered in business. I often thought about being my own boss and I began to have many days when I was too sick to work. I knew, I had to balance this very carefully or they would throw me out.

I had seen Andre's temper many times. However, it had never been directed at me. I was his top girl and he didn't want anything to get in the way. He directed his anger towards his girlfriend. Their fights were loud and intense!

"I want to go back to Montreal!" Sarah came around the kitchen corner and started in on him, as he walked through the door. All the girls were either out or busy. The living room was strangely quiet. I was in the bathroom and had just started to open the door. I quickly closed it to a sliver. I wanted to hear.

"We've had this discussion, before. Drop it if you know what's good for you!" He growled.

She swung her blond, dyed locks over her shoulders. She stood with her hands on her hips, blocking his way into the kitchen. "Move your ass, or I will bruise it badly!" his voice dropped even more menacing.

She moved out of the way, but refused to back down. "I miss being alone with you!" Her lower lip stuck out, like a child about to throw a temper tantrum.

"Look, I'm not giving this up! It's too good. We can settle down later." He moved to the coffee pot and poured a cup.

He brought it to his lips and said, "If we ever move to Montreal, you can bet your beautiful ass, we're bringing the girls. They are my business. We would be stupid to dump them! If any one of them stops making money, we WILL dump them, but not before."

This was the moment the light turned on, for me. I realized that he didn't care about me. I was only a tool in his business. I wasn't even getting any money to save. I needed to get out, but I didn't have a plan.

Providence intervened a week later.

A rumor had started that the police were on our tail; they had found our location, and they had put surveillance on us. Plans were set in motion to move us all to Montreal. Andre paid to have his brother fly in from Montreal, so he could help drive us across the country.

I didn't want to go to Montreal! I didn't even want to be in the same vicinity as his brother. He was creepy and covered in dark energy. I didn't like him. I don't even want to remember his name. For the sake of this story, let's call him Evil-weasel. During a private moment, he had tried to strangle me and get off on it. We had been interrupted by Andre, who had lost it on his brother! I could NOT be alone with him again. Andre acted like he had the same goal as well—but he was protecting his asset.

They knew I didn't want to go. The pretext of being able to leave had disappeared long ago. They were not going to let me leave. I was their biggest source of income. Andre had Sarah's sister tail me every moment, even to go to the washroom!

I wasn't meant to escape until later. Looking back, I can see that the unseen realm had arranged it beautifully. My guardian spirits had arranged it. Thank you!

Andre drove the white van, with his girlfriend, Sarah; her sister, Tina; and two other girls. They had let the rest of the girls go. They weren't worth the trip out east.

I rode in his 1979, black Z28, Chevrolet Camaro, with Evil-weasel driving. It was a sleek two door sports car. It was Andre's pride and joy. He must have owed his brother something big, because it was very unusual for him to concede anything, much less this baby.

Of course, I could care less about the car. All I wanted to do was escape.

We had been driving for hours, when everyone decided to pull over to eat. The brothers always spoke in French and always seemed to be arguing. I sensed a lot of their arguments were over me, and I didn't like how possessive Evil-weasel was acting towards me. He scared me more than my parents did. There was something truly dark about him. I think his brother knew this.

We headed back onto the main highway, just before Saskatoon, a large city located in the province of Saskatchewan. Evil-weasel had just put the 'petal to the metal' and we were flying like a black bird veering over the horizon. This province has miles and miles of straight, flat, roads as far as the eye can see. It doesn't take much to drive at unbelievable speeds.

Within two minutes, we heard the police siren behind us. The black bird had just been grounded. The cop drove along side and waved us to the curb. He pulled off the road directly in front of us. Evil-weasel punched the steering wheel with his fists.

"Shut up and let me do all the talking!" he ordered.

I knew there was a Canada wide warrant for my arrest. I also knew I would do ANYTHING to get away from this evil monster and take my chances later.

The officer bent at the waist, to fit his head into the low window of the Camaro. He moved sideways to the car, with one hand on his gun, "Good day!"

He tipped his hat. He was a young officer, not jaded yet. Still friendly, "Do you guys know how fast you were going?"

Neither of us said anything. I saw Evil-weasel's hand move towards the hidden gun between our seats. I literally offered a prayer, "Please God, don't let him do it!"

I don't know if the prayer helped, but I felt an immediate shift in the air, and for some reason his hand stopped. He quickly moved it back to his lap.

After this moment of silence, the officer asked, "Can

I get your registration and insurance, please." His smile was gone.

He wrote down what he saw on Evil-weasel's form. He then looked at me, "Can I see your ID, please, ma'am,"

Here was my chance. I could have easily lied, but I needed the officer's help. I gave him my real name. I crossed my fingers as I watched him walk to his cruiser. I prayed for a completely different outcome, than Evil-weasel did.

The officer reached inside his driver window and picked up the CB radio. He didn't have the luxury of computers yet. It only took a moment of talking.

It worked. The officer walked back to the driver side of the Camaro. "Sir, I'm going to need you to step out of the vehicle and put your hands on the hood." Evil-weasel looked in the direction of the gun, but something changed his mind, and he got out of the vehicle. Whew!!

We were separated, as another police cruiser came and picked me up. It was driven by a female cop. She was very pleasant and considerate. They took me to the police station in Saskatoon.

I never saw that bunch again. I heard that Evil-weasel got charged with statutory rape and possession of a concealed weapon. He did a lengthy stint in prison. Andre and his girlfriend probably made it to Montreal.

Our roads finally diverged, and I was on a new adventure.

The police station was antiquated by today's standards. It was small and had only a handful of rooms. The front desk was an old wooden one. It had an officer sitting at it, manning a black phone with lots of buttons and lights going off. There were no plastic partitions or any cameras for security.

It was around 8:00 pm. They must have taken Evil-weasel to a different station. I could hear mumbled conversations in the back rooms, but the front was deserted. They escorted me to one of these back rooms. It had a desk heaped with junk. There were multiple files scattered across it. They left me there for a good hour or more.

I always thought it was odd that they didn't put me in an actual jail cell. I think they were trying to be nice to me, considering I was only fourteen. I wasn't used to being treated like a child, or even treated with respect. That made me nervous.

I could only watch the clock for so long, before my eyes started to wander over the desk. What was in those files? I looked around them to the far side. I strained my neck to get a good look. I couldn't believe what I saw! Was that blond hashish?

It looked like little chunks of blond hashish, nestled on some tinfoil. Before I could think it through, I quickly jumped up and broke off two small pieces. I shoved them down my bra and sat back down.

Now I was really scared, "What if they come in and strip search me? Oh crap! What had I done!"

Before I could put it back, the same officer walked in, "We've located a foster home for you to stay in tonight, and by tomorrow we'll fly you back to Whitecourt. He looked happy to have this resolved.

I walked in a stupor, outside, with the foster parents right behind me. I don't remember what they said, probably the usual, 'don't be afraid' 'we're here to keep you safe' diatribe. Whatever the foster classes had taught them to say.

I managed to smoke the hashish outside, on their property, once the sun had gone down. Now I was probably pretty stoned, so what I did next needs to be excused. Also, to my benefit, it motivated me the next day when I really needed it to.

I confided in the other foster kid about my escape plans.

I was going to run that night, as far and as fast as I could get. Looking back now, I realize that I NEVER would have been able to find the highway. They didn't have computers or cell-phones back then. No Google maps or GPS navigation. No stores would have been open in the middle of the night. I would have been completely lost in a large city, inside a large province that I had never been to, before. What was I thinking? But, who needs a plan when you are in a drug-induced euphoric high. Anything is possible in that state.

Within a half hour of spilling the beans, the RCMP knocked on the door. "We've been told that Judy is thinking of running, so she needs to come with us."

Oh my God! Well at least I didn't have any drugs left. I walked out and was placed in the back of the cruiser. This time they weren't friendly at all.

They took me to the Juvenile Detention Jail. It was my first time in jail.

I can't get out of these handcuffs! They are so cold and tight. Impossible! The RCMP constable hands me over to a lady guard. She isn't smiling. She is gruff and cold. She gives my bag of clothes to another guard. She takes me into a small room with only a chair in the middle. She takes a key and removes the cuffs. I wiggle my wrists to encourage circulation.

"Take your clothes off! All of them! Underwear too!" she orders. The drugs are wearing off. I feel jumpy and scared. I try to follow her orders. I start to fall, but she catches me gruffly. Her fingers are cold and hard, like the handcuffs. I wince.

She orders, "Watch what you're doing, if you know what's good for you!" I think she has done this many times. I'm cold. The floor is an ice cube. The lights hurt my eyes.

"Now grab the chair with both arms and bend over!" I look at the chair and my mind goes blank. I see myself following her orders, as if from a great distance. I watch as she sticks her gloved finger into my bottom. I don't even remember her putting the glove on. I see that I'm crying, but I don't feel it. I don't feel anything anymore. Something cracks in my head. I bounce back into my body with a jolt. Now, the raw emotions are almost too overwhelming! They are sizzling. Pain, embarrassment, terror, they all vie for attention. I can't stop my body from shaking! This has happened before! My brain has done this in the past! I wish I could control it.

"I would like to leave again. Now, please!" I whisper in my head.

Nothing happens. Of course not!

"Alright, put these pajama's on!" She throws me a blue regulation top and bottom. No underwear? She watches me dress. She has completely turned off her empathy receptors. I don't exist as a person—just a job that needs doing, so she can go home to her family.

She walks me into the dorm. I sit on the edge of the

bed and look around. The other girls look like they're sleeping. Mom told me that if we were put here, we would be knifed and beaten, within the first 24 hours. I don't think I'm going to make it the first hour! Panic threatens to send me over the edge. I can't get my breath! I'm going to pass out!

The guard leaves me in utter pieces, and I hear the lock slide into place. Such a scary, lonely sound!

I move to the window next to my bed and lean into it. I can't see out! All I see is sadness and desolation in the millions of scratches covering the plexi-glass. A window that can't be opened. A window etched with the broken dreams of the youth. I sit back down on the edge of the bed. I must be diligent! I can't sleep! That's when the attack will come! I sit at the head of the bed, and pull my knees up. It's going to be a very long night! If I get out of here, I'm NEVER coming back to a place like this.

I boarded the plane with a police escort. It was an interesting arrangement, because they couldn't get a flight directly to Edmonton, where the social worker was waiting for me. They had to send me on a flight to Calgary first, with a two hour lay-over. I was handcuffed again, and received multiple stares from passengers. What kind of a criminal is she? Is she a murderer?

The cop said they had found a social worker in Calgary, who would stay with me for the 2 hours, until I boarded the plane for Edmonton.

This social worker was nasty. She was cold and withdrawn. She could care less about me. She told me that my parents wanted me arrested and put into the Yellowhead Youth Detention Center in Edmonton, and that was probably where I was going. Loud bells went off in my head!! This was not going to happen again! I couldn't spend two years there, let alone another night!

She escorted me onto the plane, and explained to the stewardess that my social worker would be waiting for me in Edmonton. The stewardess asked me if I wanted to sit at the front of the plane, or the back. She was extremely friendly and would comply with whatever my answer was.

Now here is the defining moment, where I believe I got help from my guardian spirits: In those days, we could still smoke at the back of the plane. I knew if I sat at the back, I could easily bum a smoke off of someone, anyone. That would be easy. I desperately needed a smoke! Especially, if I was going to be locked up! If I sat in the front of the plane, then the plan went out the window. No smoking allowed at the front!

I went to open my mouth and confidently say 'the back, please!'

What came out of my mouth, was instead, "I'll sit at the front." What the hell!

I tried to correct myself to her, but started stuttering. I sat down in the front seat and she patted my back. I was dumbfounded! What was going on with me? Was this some kind of shock?

The next chain of events happened very quickly. As the stewardess headed past the washrooms, she moved aside for another stewardess to pass her by. I watched them closely and saw that they only spoke for two seconds and didn't have time to talk about me. She mentioned to her peer that she needed to talk to the Captain, and would be back in two minutes.

Had I sat at the back of the plane, I would have

missed this golden opportunity!

I didn't think at all, just acted. I jumped up and quickly got the new stewardess's attention. I showed just enough panic and concern to illicit her help. I had left a piece of luggage downstairs in the restaurant and I needed to get it, immediately!

I knew the social worker was outside the entrance, watching the planes take off at the window. I couldn't be seen going back that way. I asked the stewardess if there was a shortcut, maybe some stairs that would get me down to the restaurant quicker, and I could be back in a jiffy. I couldn't leave this luggage, as it contained all my money.

She, most kindly, directed me down a stairwell, and said they could only hold the plane for ten minutes. No problem, that's all I needed, I assured her.

A year later, I did talk to my social worker. They were dumbfounded on how I escaped. When the plane landed in Edmonton, she said they watched everyone walk off, except me. I had vanished! It didn't take them long to figure it out. She stated that I would have been in lock-up for only a couple of nights, until they found a foster home for me. She didn't understand that one night in lock-up felt like eternity. If I ended back there, I would have done whatever it took to be forced into isolation, just so I could sleep safely. I can't imagine surviving.

I found my way back to the apartment. I had dealings with the landlord a couple of times, so she knew who I was. I didn't think the police were staking it out. I think paranoia can cause people to act in very irrational ways. She agreed to give me a key. She was a cranky old lady and a very cunning one. She knew a good deal when she saw it. She knew what I was up to, but she couldn't resist the extra $100 a week that would line her pockets well.

I had become my own boss! I had a steady clientele. They just kept coming and knocking at all hours. I was making money, hand over fist. The landlord eventually let me move into a one bedroom furnished loft, and I re-directed the good clients there.

All good things must come to an end. Eventually, I had such a massive party, that the damage to the loft was extensive. Furniture was broken and large holes in the walls showed the electrical wires. The landlord finally kicked me out. She was getting too much pressure from the other tenants. They didn't like the men entering the apartment night and day, nor the loud music at all hours.

At this point, I ended up homeless and truly 'on the streets.'

To this young teenage girl, I wish to express:

"Your mom should have sat you down, and gently and lovingly explained the changes occurring in your body. She should have wrapped her arms around you, and guided you into the world of feminine power and responsibilities. She should have explained to you that your 'virginity' is something to be valued and treasured. That you, yourself, are worth so much more!"

"It is the most precious gift that you can give a man. He must first show his worthiness by committing his life and soul to protect you. He must cherish you; be kind to you; honor you and never abandon you. This is what marriage is. It is the spiritual bond and signed contract, before God, that two people agree to protect each other, over an entire lifetime. Also, this marriage ceremony exists simultaneously in the divine, astral, and physical realms. It is an actual contract before God, in the divine realm—the deities are present and observing. In the astral realm, both Ancestors celebrate the marriage and agree to work together to support this new family. In the physical realm, a great celebration occurs."

"If a man can't wait for this, or chooses that he doesn't want it, does he really deserve you?"

"I want to roll back time and give you this precious bonding experience, but I can't. All I can do, is tell you how very brave you are! You are so special! You are a survivor! I will be with you, from now on. I will help you through these moments of confusion and fear. If a man tries to seduce and abuse you, again, I will help you stand strong and firm—to repel him with power and grace! I will be there to support you, and help you heal from the grievous wounds that were inflicted. I love you so very much!"

These memories evoked powerful feelings! I really needed some spiritual guidance from Gabby.

I made it to her place, just before she was locking up for the day. She smiled and let me in. I would often come at this time, as I was in College during the day.

"Let's make some tea." She went into her tiny kitchen and plugged the kettle in. "What's the direction of your thoughts, today?" She asked as she placed the cups and utensils on the table.

"I have been thinking about sex and how youth tend to give it up so easy. Can you help me understand the spiritual aspect of this?" I asked her. I also shared my memories with her.

She sighed. This was her element, “God arranged balance in the universe. Since humans are his highest art form, he also placed them in a state of intricate balance. Teenagers enter a phase of their lives where we say, ‘their hormones are raging.’ In actual fact, God arranged this, so that they could step away from their parents and create grand new designs. This doesn’t mean they should treat their parents with disrespect. Only, that they must move beyond the norm, and create. Sometimes, this requires a small amount of rebellion.”

“Remember, we must never judge negative as bad, and positive as good. They both have a mission in the universe.” She poured the tea and sat back down.

“As humans, we have a ‘negative’ ball of energy stored in our pituitary gland and a ‘positive’ ball of energy stored in our pineal gland, the area where our main soul resides. (She points to her forehead) Because energy can never be still, the negative ball of energy travels down our spine into our ‘area of desire.’ (She places two fingers below her belly-button) Here, where our desires come from.”

“Teenagers receive huge waves of this ‘negative’ energy into this ‘area of desire.’ (She points just below her belly-button again) This causes them to have intense desires. It is the responsibility of the parent to direct these desires for good. They need to guide their teenager to change society and the world for the better. When this happens, the ‘negative’ energy is converted to ‘positive’ energy and travels back up to the main soul which increases the youth’s spiritual power. Then, they have the ability to move mountains!”

I pondered this as I sipped the tea.

She continued, "As adults, this process still happens but 'the hormones settle down' and it isn't so intense. However, if our desires become obsessive and we give into sex all the time, then we become unbalanced. Sex is actually a gift given by God to couples, so that they can first procreate, and then it's given as a gift to get through the difficult 'soul scrubbing' times together. When we have an orgasm, it is a release. But it also depletes a small amount our spiritual power. So, if we engage in sex, we must do it with reverence, and a high innermost attitude. This will balance the energy."

"If we find ourselves having too many negative or addictive desires, then we need to balance our energies by stopping the illicit act, and immediately offering an altruistic 'act of service' that will benefit others and our community. This act of service immediately moves the excessive energy from our 'sub soul' back up to our 'main soul' and increases our spiritual power as a human being." She drank the last of her tea and sat the cup down.

Wow, where did the time go. I loved listening to her!

She moved on, "Also, if two people have sex and they are not married, this causes fighting amongst the Ancestors in the astral world. The laws and principles in the Astral World are very strict; not like down here. There are lines drawn between families, and contracts are living documents there. It would be like us walking into someone's house without permission and partaking of their food. It is considered 'breaking and entering' here. It is the same spiritual law, when a man enters a woman without a proper contract."

"We aren't able to see the immediate effect of the

accumulation of spiritual impurities. However, we see the 'relationship cleansings,' which come in the painful form of: male/female fights, miscarriages/abortions, any diseases within the reproductive organs, etc. The universe will cleanse any energy that is out of balance. This is the great universal Principle of Cleansing. As soon as someone thinks it's 'unfair,' they have forgotten about reincarnation. We have spent many lifetimes accumulating negative and positive deeds."

"Free Will comes into play when we choose either the passive, painful cleansing or the active, altruistic acts of service. Both eliminate the negative energy; but one is joyful and fun. The other is painful, just like trying to scrub a huge stain off our arm—ouch! It hurts, but it needs to be done."

"When we clean our body and our house a little every day, we don't need to do a major cleaning. This is the same for our spiritual impurities. If we go through small cleansings with gratitude, and we offer altruistic 'acts of service' every day, then we don't need to go through a major catastrophic cleansing. Yet, even if this happens, have you noticed that it often changes that person's life? They may have been so materially absorbed in their jobs, or accumulating wealth, that they forgot what was important, until they nearly lost their life. We see a sudden reversal in how they live their lives, and we call it a miracle! It is, but actually, it was because they erased a huge amount of negative impurities, all at once."

"Humanity is lost in a quagmire of negative actions. We have wrapped generation after generation of spiritual impurities around ourselves. We have lost sight of what cleansing is, and how important it is to restore balance.

This is why we need extraordinary gratitude to move through it. It is difficult to see the light at the end of the tunnel, especially while we are in the middle of utter darkness. This is why the Universal Principles will become our road map, through the dark times ahead."

Gabby could go on and on. In fact, she seemed to absorb great amounts of energy as she talked. I, on the other hand, needed to absorb this and ponder it for a while.

I hugged her with my whole being, and walked home.

That night, I dreamt of a young hooker, working the streets of Calgary…

Section 3

The Young Hooker

Chapter 1

Hooker, prostitute, whore—what term is politically correct today? It's the oldest profession in the world, yet the most controversial career in existence.

I shall use the term 'hooker.' I like how it sounds. As hookers, we cruise the streets, projecting our most salient resources, like models on a runway. As the vehicle slows, we cast our hook and voila, we reel the sucker in. We make huge sums of money! We party all night long! We love this life, and we feel so blessed…

Wait a second, rewind…

Shake out the marbles! That only happens in movies. 'Pretty Woman' gave it a great spin!

In real life, this profession is a sneaky, black witch. She rips your heart out and steals your soul for breakfast. For lunch, she feasts on your youthful attributes, and by supper has cast the spell to chew you up and spit you out, with no regrets. As daylight fades, so does your light and innocence, and she is ready to snuff out the torch. Death is her final spell.

She is dangerous, dirty, and demented. She carries no remorse.

If you are a teenager reading this, I hope I am extremely clear that this is NOT a profession, or a journey, you choose—ever!!! If this is the only option you think you have, please know that the Universe always gives us choices—a crossroad—a time to make a tough decision to move through the pain and make a 'Spirit-first' choice. Only your soul will know what that 'spiritually-correct' choice is. Sometimes, at first glance, it may seem like the hardest and toughest one. Later, we look back and see divine providence at work, only then we know for sure if it was the right choice.

There are a few places in the world, where this profession is legal. Perhaps, their souls and their lives are better protected by the government. I can't speak for them.

Around the time I got involved, the prostitution law was being challenged in the Canadian Supreme Court, so there were a couple of years where they couldn't arrest us. Instead, the police picked us up and tried to scare us into quitting. One cop said, "We need to take your picture, so when we pull your body out of the river, we will be able to identify it."

We didn't have any groups or agencies trying to help us, like the ones that exist now. It was us against the police and the inept foster-care system. Today the bundle of support, for teens on the street, is wrapped in many layers and many options. It will continue to evolve, as long as there are lost kids needing help.

As I heal, I must honor the past. I share my memories of a fragile time, when I was a young hooker…

Once I got evicted from the hotel/condo complex in Calgary, I was literally homeless at fourteen.

Even though I had worked as a hooker in a 'brothel,' I was completely naïve to life on the streets. My time in this profession was like living in a penthouse suite, then abruptly thrown into the gutter.

I had a few friends who brought me to a place, in downtown Calgary, called the Basement. It was run by a retired nurse, Linda, using her own money to try to give us teenagers a safe place to rest during the day. It had a weird name, because it actually existed on the second floor of an old building. It had the word 'Basement' on the side wall and an arrow slanted up the stairs. Only teenagers were allowed upstairs and only during the day. She couldn't get proper funding to have it open all night, and the fire coding wouldn't allow it to happen, anyway.

We were able to have a shower, eat some sugary snacks, and play cards and games until it closed at the end of each day. Every night, we were on our own to find a place to sleep.

Some of the kids at the Basement introduced me to Mama G. She had a low-rental, two bedroom apartment in a cheap section of the city. All her furniture was mix and match. Probably, most of it donated, having survived the 30's and 40's. Around the same era that saw her into the world. She cared about teens, but that went only so far. She expected to be reimbursed one way or another. She was world weary and weather worn. When she saw a good deal, she capitalized on it. Many teens needed a place to stay. Most wouldn't stay long, as their transient life-style forbade it.

She let kids stay with her, as long as they helped out with chores, groceries, etc. She took a liking to me and allowed me to move in. Her eighteen year old daughter and her daughter's boyfriend lived with her. I was always nice to the boyfriend, but I made sure I never crossed the line. There was something creepy and dark about both of them. Right away, Mama G's daughter became extremely jealous and angry of me. She wanted me out!

One night, I was finally told to leave. Mama G felt bad. I think she knew how vindictive her daughter could be, so she gave me some supplies with a small pup tent.

She gave me directions to the nearest park, and advised me to find a secluded place to set it up. She also gave me some food and water; enough for a couple days.

It's getting dark already! The ground seems level enough to put up a tent. I hear the City sounds in the distance.

A car horn blasts, a few teens laugh while playing soccer, a dog barks—they are a soothing balm to my nerves. Life is still playing out, all around me. The night has not staked its claim, yet.

I finish staking the tent in place. I arrange all my items in the tent. I grab the roll of toilet paper and find a remote spot to take care of business.

As I return, I see the shadows grow large and dark. Night is coming. I feel my body filtering between dimensions. Not on earth anymore. Twilight uses the lengthening shadows to play havoc with my imagination. Monsters are unleashed to creep out and touch, only to instantly retract as my eyes attempt to locate them. I shiver.

I crawl into the tent. The thin fabric feels like a thick wall of security. Insane! However, I'll take it. I need sleep. I'm exhausted.

I jolt awake! My head is fuzzy. Where am I? I don't know what time it is. Something woke me up. Its pitch black and I hear twigs snapping and branches moving. I remember where I am. I strain to hear, and I make out two people moving in my direction. Goosebumps instantly sweep my arms. I know these voices. They are good friends with Mama G's daughter. I only remember Mike's name. The other is his sidekick, who follows him everywhere.

Were they told to come get me? Can I go back? My senses are telling me 'no,' they're up to no good. I didn't like their energy then, I don't like it now. I think her daughter commanded them forth, like a black queen to her pawns.

"Hello, Judy are you there? We know you're there! Come out, come out, wherever you are!" Whack! Whack! It must be a stick they're using to hit the tent—over and over. I hear his sidekick chuckle.

I take a deep breath and finally unhook the flap. There is no point pretending. "What do you want?" Mike sees the fear in my eyes. It emboldens him. I see shifty eyes, up to no good. They are pinpoint small, so I know he's flying high.

"I heard you're a hooker. We want some!" His sidekick snorts the words and grabs his crotch. Mike smirks and directs his friend into the tent first.

What happened next is unbearable. I can only describe it from a safe distance:

Mike knew I would fight, and he wanted to see what I would do. That's why he let his friend go first. I fought and scratched, and beat his chest with my fists, but he was too strong and too powerful. He was thin, but extremely wiry. He had dirty hair that hung to his shoulders in dreads--more due to laziness, then an actual style. I had such a tiny frame, it was easy for him to overpower me. I screamed until I was hoarse. He slapped my face several times. I remember his breath and his hair stunk like rotten potatoes—probably due to whatever drug he had ingested, and the black-rot that was left of his teeth. When it was over, all my clothes were ripped and bloody. The tent was destroyed.

Well, you know my history. When you think something is as bad as it's going to get—for me, it gets a whole lot worse.

I'm finally alone in the tent with my shattered psyche. Mike crawls in the tent. Really? I'm dumbfounded. I can't fathom what he's going to do. Sex doesn't seem to be his thing. Perhaps, tonight my life will end. I have come to the edge, and I might be thrown over this time.

Something shifted in my brain. I decided it wasn't worth the fight. I just had to endure it, like a trick that I'm not getting paid for. That's it. I drifted. I disassociated.

Mike expected resistance. In fact, he tried everything to get me to fight. The body was there, but the mind was absent.

'Go ahead and finish, so I can come back.' This thought floated, as I drifted.

He gave me a tongue lashing. While he was raping me and his face was inches from my ear, his voice hissed like a viper, as it vehemently whispered how disgustingly wet and dirty I was.

Like he didn't know he had just directed his friend to the same place, moments before! Really!

He taunted me and told me that I needed to shower, and not be such a dirty whore. That I should be more prepared and ready for him in the future.

He went on and on. As he emptied everything into me, he sensed an opening. He was a predator, pushing through the fog to yank me back. He didn't want me drifting. Unlike his sidekick, he raped for power and control. His energy smothered me, like a sandstorm invading every orifice. I felt the intense danger, like a hot iron ready to scorch everything in its path. I realized, I needed to give him his drug, or he would never leave me alive. Fear was his drug.

I gave. I lived.

Survival is required. I can't heal now. That has to come years later. Today, I have to put one foot in front of the other…

I found new friends at the 'Basement.' They were around my age and together we started working the streets of Calgary. I started to trust my instincts. These new friends had a bright aura and we connected. We became as close as you can get to family. They taught me the ropes. We watched out for each other. Collette was the oldest female, at sixteen. She was short and wiry and tough. She had a nose ring, which in those days was rare for women. She spoke with a gravelly voice and if you didn't look too closely, she could pass for a boy.

Her brother was Simon and he was gay. It was my first experience around that and I loved him!! He was your typical flamboyant, saucy, gay teen with beautiful blond locks and a boyish face. He knew how to pick any lock and he was an expert at math. Numbers were his elixir. We had picked up two stragglers along the way, Wendy and Linda. Sisters, fifteen and sixteen, they would wander in and out of our lives, sometimes disappearing for days on end. They were quiet and a little strange. They often used a weird language when talking to each other. They wouldn't divulge what country they were from, perhaps from Scandinavia or Yugoslavia. I think they liked the break of being with us. We wouldn't hurt or steal from them. They were safe with us.

We got into a routine. During the day we rested at the Basement. Once evening arrived, we worked downtown Calgary, 1st avenue. The first one to grab a 'trick,' would take them to the closest 'Motel 7,' within a 10 minute drive, and not too far from the bus stop. This is the motel we would use for the night. After that, we just needed a couple more 'tricks' for $30 each, and then we were set to party for the remainder of the night.

I have met many types of people on the street. You might think that we were all dishonest and untrustworthy. You would be wrong. There is a code of honor, even on the streets.

There were many girls who would 'jack up' the trick—instead of giving them sex, they would stick a knife to their throat, and steal all their money. What would the 'John' do? Call the cops?

They were the soulless ones… The lost ones…The ones that were strung out on heroin…The ones that would do anything for their next high…

They were the ones that WE crossed the street to stay away from. We knew not to tangle with them.

Our group had a code. We kept our word. I had regular customers, who would meet me at the same street corner, the same time every day. They trusted me and I trusted them. It was a business transaction. Everybody left satisfied.

I saw all types. There were the usual, young, horny guys looking for a quick fix. There were the elderly gents, who were probably too scared to ask anyone else out. I was escorted up to the most lavish penthouse suites, but only for short moments. I could only catch a glimpse of their affluent lives, and wonder why they needed a hooker.

The ones that caught my heart, were those like Larry. He was the Fire Chief of the downtown Fire Station. He was one of my regulars. He was average in all his features—nondescript. You couldn't pick him out of a crowd. He was bald, with a slight paunch to his belly. He had been in the fire business for many years.

He always brought a condom, and yes he had a wife and teenagers. We met at least once a week, on a Friday. The sex was spectacular. He wanted to please me. Mostly, he wanted to have a smoke and talk. He talked of an aching loneliness. He didn't want to leave his wife, because of the kids. He had tried counseling with her, etc. She wouldn't let him touch her. His language of love was touch. His soul was withering and dying.

I don't know if he was feeding me a line of bull. But, I do know that I felt the ache of his loneliness, like a tooth that requires pulling. I felt his kind heart and his utter confusion on how to heal the brokenness of his family. These things I felt intensely, whenever I was with him. I had become a great listener. Sometimes, that's what they craved more than sex.

The next few months flew by.

Then, the unthinkable happened. Collette got abducted. We lost her for four days. Simon went insane. It all fell apart. The police came to the 'Basement.' They weren't allowed inside, so Simon was escorted out. He had to go to the hospital. With their permission, I came a day later.

I witnessed a completely broken shell. Collette had

been locked up in a boarded-up, vacant house and beaten to within an inch of her life. He would strangle her, and then bring her back, multiple times. The worst was the, horrific, cigarette burns all over her chest and arms. When the nurse removed the bandages to clean, I had to look away. Her soul was shattered.

She told the police that she escaped while he was gone. He would leave her for many hours at a time. Perhaps, he had another life he had to show up for. They never caught him.

I never saw her again. She moved back to Vancouver, where her older sister could take care of her. I heard that Simon got arrested, but gossip is never reliable.

I asked the nurse, Linda, at the 'Basement' to find something for me to do. I didn't want to work the streets again…

To this beautiful, brave teen, "You have experienced more in your young life, than most see in ten lifetimes. At one point, I couldn't see a way in to help you. You constructed such a solid, load-bearing, wall, that, at first, I couldn't find any cracks. I almost gave up. I'm so sorry! Now, with the divine light, I found a way in. I see the beautiful 'God-spark' in you. I see how you hid it so deeply and thoroughly. You had to make sure that it wouldn't get crushed or stolen. I see that you protected it with your life, for so long! Well done!"

"Now, it's time to heal. Now, it's time to let me in. Now, it's time to open the passageway into your home, into your soul. Now, the longer you keep it shored up, the opposite starts to happen. All that negative energy, from the past, causes damage and corrosion—if it's not released."

"Now, I'm asking the opposite of you. To release it, I'm asking you to be vulnerable, to open your heart and soul. You might need to be a little brave, because you are used to hiding and protecting. It will require you to open the doors and welcome the world in. I will be here with you, to protect you. I will make sure all appropriate boundaries and consequences are set up between us and the world. I will not abandon you!"

Chapter 2

Just because we're in shock and we don't want to continue, doesn't mean it all stops. We, still, need a roof over our heads. We, still, need materials to survive. I, still, had to go to work.

About a week after Collette left for Vancouver, I was heading out of the Basement, around closing time. I pushed the glass doors open and exited onto the sidewalk. I adjusted my eyes to the harsh glare of the sun, so it took me a few seconds to register what was right in front of me. I think, I noticed Pup first. My brain went into slow motion, like the movies. I saw a little, brown Chihuahua with one floppy ear, sniffing the parking meter, about to mark it. I raised my eyes higher, and there she was. My mom had her leather bag in one hand, and she was pinching the bridge of her nose with the other, as if the smells were placed there just to accost her. The dog didn't have a leash, but she was well trained. She kept close to mom. Mom was trying to side-step around some disgusting mess, only she could see.

My heart banged in my chest. The wild beats made me dizzy. I was instantly cemented to the sidewalk. I was terrified. I wanted to bolt, but couldn't move. It was the twilight zone, magnified. I would have sold my soul, to change the picture in front of me.

However, believe it or not, this moment saved my life.

Linda was worried about me, so she called my parents, not knowing the history of abuse.

Of course, they came immediately to pick me up.

My mom appraised me, up and down, then looked away as if to dismiss me. Her eyes switched to laser beam and focused on the street, "So this is where you've been hiding."

"It figures, you'd pick the worst area of the City!" She pointed to the four door, white, pickup truck where my Dad's arm was resting, partway out the window with a smoke. "Let's go! We have a long drive home!"

I walked with lead shoes, and climbed into the back seat, like a prisoner heading for a life sentence. What just happened to my world?

A week later, we went to visit my grandparents in Tofield. They were old. At least as a teen, I thought they were. They were in their 70's, and very old fashioned. The two-story, farm, house was built in 1910 and hadn't seen very many upgrades. It needed a new paint job. It had these strange vines covering it, like they had been growing for a century or more. Inside, the wood stairs creaked and moaned. Everything, from the wallpaper to the couch, had large flowers and large square patterns. The colors were at odds with each other—nothing matched. It was hard on the eyes. The basement was dark and creepy, and had an actual dirt floor. I avoided going down there!

I was told to go to bed early, that night, around 7 pm. That was usual, when they wanted to have an adult-only conversation. I felt a bit of pain throughout the day, but ignored it. I got up moments later, and sat on the edge of the bed. The pain suddenly ripped through my right, lower side. It was like a knife being thrust in me, over and over again. I was dizzy and scared. I was scared enough, that I had to go find Mom. She thought it was just constipation, "Go sit your ass on the toilet, and stop complaining!"

Every time I tried to push, the pain seared my insides, and I almost blacked out. It was my grandma who realized something was terribly wrong. She forced my Mom to take me to the hospital. Bless her heart, for her role in saving my life.

I had a ruptured ectopic. It's where the fertilized egg grows in the fallopian tube, instead of in the uterus. After 3 months, it ruptures the tube and you have internal bleeding. You can bleed to death in an hour or two. I was in critical shape, by the time they wheeled me into the surgical bay. I was moments from death. I had lost a lot of blood.

If I was still on the street, I know, without a doubt, as soon as I experienced the pain, I would have gotten stoned and drunk, and passed out. I NEVER would have gone near a hospital! I didn't have the proper identification.

Death would have claimed me that night.

Many elements had to come together, in a harmonious fashion, for me to still be alive. Imagine if my grandma wasn't there. Imagine if my parents never got that call from Linda. Imagine if Linda never made the call. Imagine if I never asked Linda for help. Imagine if that horrible event never happened to Collette. How did this all happen? What took place in the unseen realm to choreograph this? It all came together in perfect sync. I will never see this as a random act, or a coincidence.

Once we returned home, I started getting morning sickness. My mom figured out what was happening. I would have had fraternal twins. It's where two separate eggs are fertilized. One made it to the uterus and the other ruptured in my tube.

I was four months pregnant, by the time they figured it out—a month after the first surgery. My parents sent me to several doctors, who refused to do the abortion. Finally, they found one who agreed to perform it. I didn't have a say.

It was the last time I saw my parents for years. Two weeks after that surgery, I ran away for the final time…

This is a memory that I will never forget. I had to connect with Gabby to find answers to my questions.

I found her in the garden. I loved watching her work. She had on them crazy, garden, gloves with orange and green gnomes. While she was bent over, it seemed like the gnomes were magically dancing, and tending to their foliage. Her floppy hat completed the strange scene, as if she was the giant caretaker to this miniature fantasy world. She was about to exit a tree-sized weed from their lives, when I showed up.

Gabby greeted me and sat down on the bench with a sigh. She turned her big, floppy, purple and yellow hat into a fan, in hopes of a breeze. Mud warm air was all that resulted, but every bit helped. It was mid July, and one of the hottest days of the year, topping out at 35 degrees Celsius. We managed a little better in the shade of the large oak tree. Though, I was a little jumpy, seeing too many wasps massing around me.

Gabby had no fear of them, nor they of her. She seemed to fit right in with nature, as though she was part fairy, and part flower.

I entrusted to her my full memories, as I knew she

would never abuse that privilege. She listened and smiled.

I loved to hear her speak. She started, "The unseen realm has structure and laws. It is dynamic and fluid, much like our realm. To be clearer, the souls, angels, deities, and gods all have personalities and missions. It is a living realm." She watched as I was deciding whether to jump up or to ignore the wasp. I chose to lean away from it—ready to bolt if needed.

She continued, "All three realms, the spiritual, the astral, and the physical are all linked, but not in a straight line. They overlap each other, and blend together. If we look at you, you have a guardian spirit who stays beside you, and sends you intuition and guidance. That guardian spirit can go to a group of guardian spirits when he/she needs extra support. Those guardian spirits are linked to a deity, who is linked to a god, all the way up to the one great God, the Creator of the Universe. There are also deities and gods who have other missions, such as looking after different countries and territories, etc. The types of missions and responsibilities are endless, much like human missions, here, on earth."

I settled back against the bench, and lifted my face to the sun. My vitamin D had been low that winter. I needed every opportunity to absorb the rays.

I listened, "Also, we all have 'attaching spirits' who are angry at us, and want revenge for things we've done to them in previous lives. They plot ways to cause problems in our lives, much like when you were at the tent. They helped the boys find you. However, they are ultimately controlled by the gods, who allow only certain activities, due to the Principle of Balance and the law of

Free Will: What we give out, comes back. It always goes back to the balance of Yin and Yang—positive and negative." She took a breath, folded her gloves and crossed her legs on the bench.

"You know," she said. "Your guardian spirits connected with my guardian spirits earlier on, to make sure we had this time now. I wanted to go shopping, but felt a weird urge to work in the garden. I don't normally do that in the heat of the day. I would have been gone, if I hadn't followed my intuition." She gazed up at a small cumulus cloud, in a sea of blue.

"Wow." I said. I was so absorbed in her story, and then the cloud, I couldn't think of anything else to say.

She continued, "Also, we are all connected to the gods of Character. Meaning, that each of us comes from a distinct 'soul' group. Each of these gods has a unique and strong character type, like leadership, or supporting leadership, or finance etc. One day, our society will allow each person to work in the area that displays their unique talents. It is these unique talents that evolve from their essential character. This is why not everyone can be a multi-millionaire, like Donald Trump. It's not their destiny, or part of their character. People like him, have trained for many lifetimes in just finance. His character and his mission are directed towards building industry and cities in a certain fashion. You come from a different character, or deity. Your mission might be to teach, like mine. Only you know, for sure."

She added, "In the Astral world, it took many guardian spirits connecting through you, your parents, Linda, your grandma, the doctors, etc. to ensure that you survived. They, also, have different characters and support each other in different ways."

I finally had a question. "Why can't we remember our previous lives? If the attaching spirits are after us, wouldn't it be better to know why they are angry?"

"Good question." She said. "Our soul remembers the essential trainings from previous lives. This is seen in our talents, and in our values. However, if we were to remember our previous lives, we would not be able to focus on this one. We would go crazy, if we knew the extent of our actions. It is a delicate balance of knowledge and free will. We need to be able to make clear decisions in this life, without being haunted by previous ones. The attaching spirits are allowed to give us 'training' and 'cleansing' in the areas that we need. The intensity and severity is always predetermined by God, based on our own negative actions, and how willing we are to change and grow.

"The average soul is around 15,000 years old. If we look at that timeline, we have lived many lifetimes, and accumulated a great deal of karma—good and bad. However, if we look only at this lifetime, everything seems so unfair. To grow spiritually, requires a broader viewpoint—a greater understanding of the universe and how we fit in it."

She stopped for a moment and we drifted in silence, listening to the sounds of nature, on a hot muggy day, enjoying each other's company.

Then she spoke again, "We need to stop looking for instant gratification and start finding ways to move through difficult situations, with grace and an inner strength. We must teach our youth to actually 'pay' to go through difficult situations, just to build strong character.

That's how important it is. Instead, many of them have been babied, and coddled, and rescued. We have to be careful that we are not building a generation of soft, pliant, youth who are unable to shoulder the responsibilities of the world. Again, we moved from being too hard and too abrupt on them, to being too soft and too gentle with them. It is always a delicate balance."

"*Great Love* is a perfect balance of gentleness and strictness—this is God's love. It is a great art to achieve." She had moved into her teacher mode. I could see the deep concern for children, permanently etched in her soul. She would always be their advocate. I loved her for so many reasons, including this one.

She looked into my eyes, "This doesn't mean we want anyone to go through what you went through. It was horrific! This is why it is so important to teach how to accumulate 'meritorious' deeds—good karma. If we look at this in a spiritual way, you are stopping the 'cycle' of abuse. By following this path, you will not die and choose to become an attaching spirit yourself, who continues looking for revenge. You have already made a positive impact on all realms, and the future of many, by this choice alone. Because we're all connected through each realm—we are all one. When one changes, it impacts the entire world. The ripple effect can change the tide of all humanity. This is already happening around the world, as more and more souls are awakening."

It truly was, one of those hot days where conversation is broken by a communal drift into silence, not wanting to expend too much energy at once.

Does this help? Hearing these teachings?" She finally asked.

I took a deep, cleansing breath and pondered all that she had revealed. "Yes, it does."

It was wonderful to get some answers, but I knew that realistically it would take years of experiences and learning, before this would fully sink in. I needed to have many opportunities to change the neuro-pathways in my brain—new patterns of behaving and doing, equals new neuro-pathways.

"Thank you Gabby!! I love you so much!" I hugged her fiercely. She was my anchor in this crazy world.

Chapter 3

It was the last time I ever lived at home. I left within two weeks of the abortion. This time, I moved to Edmonton. I was 16 years old in body, and so much older in spirit.

The years between 16 and 18 are a blur. I know that at some point, I spent time in three different foster homes. It was like I gave off a signal with my body—come use it and abuse it whenever you want. I always seemed to have a foster brother, or a doctor, who would take their fill of me, without my consent. The important point here, is that I didn't stay anywhere for too long because, by then, I had the mentality: "If I'm going to be forced to do it, I might as well get paid for it."

I started working the streets of Edmonton at 16. Actually, right in front of the main police station, across from the York Hotel, around 95 Street and 105 Avenue—it was labeled 'the drag.' The police station was the only new building in an ocean of dilapidated ones. It was an old section of the city and at that time, it was not well maintained. Garbage, used condoms and needles, etc., were common place to walk through, like the street was the actual waste basket. Most average citizens never ventured into this area, especially not at night.

I rarely left this area. It was my home. I lived a couple of blocks away, on 93 Street. There was a cheap yellow building that rented out rooms only.

Of course, I got involved in drugs. It was the only balm to cover the grievous wounds. Wounds that kept re-opening every time I went to work.

I started out with pot and hashish. I didn't like

drinking, unless I combined it with these. The drinking made me tired, but when combined with pot, I could party all night. I soon moved to cocaine. I didn't really like this either, but it was available.

It was the T's & R's that almost did me in. A friend took me to a party house, and this was the party favor. They had a nurse willing to shoot it into me, if I wanted to try. Why not? She found a vein quickly, and the liquid gold entered my bloodstream.

I will never forget these three hours. I was floating for the first time in my life. I was having an orgasmic experience, one after another; more accurately on top of one another. Each breath was an orgasm of pleasure. Each thought and each touch elicited the same orgasmic response, throughout my entire body. If my toes moved, I felt it intimately. If I spoke, I felt the orgasmic pleasure of the sound. I couldn't get enough!

T's & R's are called the 'cheap form of Heroin.' It was Talwin–a painkiller, and Ritalin–an upper for kids.$20 for the 2 pills. Cut in half—two doses, about 6-8 hours of non-stop, pain-free, drug induced, orgasmic high.

Did I say orgasmic enough? There is no other word to accurately describe it. Liquid pleasure gently caressed every pore of my body, for three solid hours. I don't think that describes it better.

I chased that initial high for 6 months. Though the ones after were good, I never experienced the same feeling, again. Knowing the spiritual laws now, I'm sure the attaching spirits used that first time to hook me, all the way in. They knew my body constitution, thoroughly.

To make a long, sad, story short, I saw a lady on the street one day, Cindy, who had been on these drugs for five years. Her soul had been eaten away. She was an empty shell. Usually, I would stay far away from her. But, on that day, she snuck up behind me and confronted me.

She yelled, "You have on my eye-shadow! I want it back!" In the blink of an eye, she slapped me across the face.

I was bewildered, at first. We've never talked, much less shared items. I could see that she was mentally unstable. I walked away, rubbing my face and shaking my head.

A difficult, painful moment? Yes!

But, the best thing for my soul! This slap in the face woke me up!! Loud and clear!! I didn't want to end up like her. I had to get off these drugs, no matter what it took!! I had already seen changes in my personality. I would do whatever it took to get the next high—I would compromise my own values, because, by now, the drug owned me, outright. I was dying already.

I tried to get off, but they had a strong hold on me. One more event happened, before I was able to be free of them:

I just need to find a vein. Oh my God! I shake my arm. I'm usually good at hitting it. Ah, finally! That was just enough to bring me back to normal. I don't even get high, anymore. At least it took the sickness away. Okay, now I have to go to work. Hmm, my roommate left a line of cocaine on the table. Normally, I don't partake until I'm done working for the night. Screw it!

Wow! Okay, a little much! I gotta go! I need

money!

I go to my usual spot, just off 95 Street. I grab a smoke from my purse. Hopefully, I get something right away.

Hey, a two door black Honda. Hmm, two guys looking for a nice night. Over here! I wave. I sashay across the back alley to where they've stopped.

"What you lookin for?" I sway a little, then try to hide it with a provocative swing of the boobs.

The driver comments, "Two for $60?"

"No problemo"

The cute passenger gets out and pulls the seat forward, so I slip into the back.

"My, you two are cute!" They are both in their 30's, with dark skin, dark hair. I try to start a conversation, but they don't seem interested. They don't smile and they don't speak to me.

I think about what I'm going to do with the money. My mind wanders, as it normally does on Cocaine. I lay my head back on the seat.

I notice we've been driving for a while, now. "Hey, where are we going?"

They don't respond to me. I'm not really paying attention to them. My mind is wandering, as I gaze out the window.

A tick slips into my brain and starts to nibble. Something is a little off. I blink and try to focus in. They are arguing in a strange language.

"Hey, I need to know where we're going?"

The driver looks in the rear-view mirror at me. "We will be there right away. Keep quiet!"

"What a rude guy, I should charge you double!" I

think to myself. I chuckle.

It's extremely dark. We pull up next to the river. "What the heck?" I roll down my window. There are no buildings, no lights, only the rushing sound of the river, and darkness.

They start arguing, violently now. I don't know what language it is. The passenger pulls out a knife and keeps waving it towards me. Well, I know it's me he's talking about.

The passenger guy wants me out of the vehicle. He is gesturing wildly, as he stands outside. "No problemo!" I think to myself, "I want out too!" I start to comply.

I want to get as far away from them, as possible!

He pulls the seat forward and reaches for me.

"DO NOT GET OUT OF THE VEHICLE!" What the fuck? Where did that come from? I shake my head.

I decide to kick him. He can't get me out, but he keeps trying. They are still arguing this whole time. Finally the guy climbs partway into the backseat and pulls a knife to my neck. I feel a trickle of blood.

"Get out! Let's go! Now!" He's yelling right in my face!

The driver is yelling at him!

"DO NOT GET OUT OF THE VEHICLE!" Someone is yelling at me!

What a cluster fuck!

I struggle some more, but I think it'll be over in seconds.

I'm dumbfounded. He moves away with the knife and gets back out. He climbs into the front seat. They continue yelling at each other. Finally, the driver gets in the back with me, and decides to have his way with me.

Okay, no problemo! That I can handle.

Now, can I go? I really want out, and away from these guys! They are freaking me out!

"DO NOT GET OUT OF THE VEHICLE!"

ALRIGHT!!! HOLY FUCK!!!!

The driver tries to pull me, but I have long legs and I brace them against the seat, so they don't bend. He finally gives up. They drive me back to the same back alley and let me out. I feel like I've been dumped from the twilight zone back into civilization.

This was the first time that a voice in my head was that loud, that clear, and that persistent. I heard it three separate times. If it was up to me, I would have gotten out of that vehicle, three separate times.

Two weeks later, I picked up the Edmonton Journal, newspaper, and these same two guys were on the front page. They had been arrested for killing six prostitutes in the Edmonton area.

I pieced it together. They were arguing over whether they should kill me in the vehicle. They realized, they needed to get me out of the vehicle, or else there would be too much blood and DNA evidence left behind. By staying in the vehicle, my life was spared.

My guardian spirit knew that!

I can only imagine the scene from their realm. Here my guardian spirit is trying to save my life, and I'm higher than a kite, swearing up a storm, and not really listening. What an infinite amount of patience and love, they expended to me. Oh my! I'm not sure I would have had the same.

I knew the rules of the street. Never, under any circumstances get in a car with two people. Never, under any circumstances get in the back seat of a two-door car. The last one, though wasn't needed here, is never kiss on the lips.

I had broken the most important two rules. I was beyond lucky to be alive! I had to get off this drug…

That memory was a tough one. I had just one quick question for Gabby. This time, I called her on the phone.

"Hi Gabby! What happens to us spiritually, when we take drugs or do alcohol?" I asked her.

She replied, "Depends on the drug, however, most drugs and alcohol drop our inhibitions, and open us up to the other realms. Meaning, they cause a switch in our brain, which gives us more of a psychic link to the other realms. So, depending on the situation, either the attaching spirits can completely manifest and take over the body, or our guardian spirits can come through stronger. Remember, how the aboriginals used it for 'spirit journeys' to the other side, so they could learn something positive?"

"Uh huh," I said.

She continued, "Most people, now days, don't know how to control it, so the majority of the time it is an attaching spirit that comes through. You've told me about Lisa who used to get drunk and her voice and mannerisms would completely change. She went from being nice to being a mean drunk. That would be a good example of an attaching spirit manifesting through her."

"Okay, makes sense. Thanks, Gabby! Love you!" I hung up.

I reflected on this information. I had indeed seen strange things happen with people under the influence, including myself.

I will have many more experiences with my guardian spirits, but for now, back to my time as a young hooker…

Chapter 4

I couldn't get off this drug on my own. I tried AADAC. Nothing worked. It had a powerful hold on me.

When I look back, now, I see that the streets also had a powerful hold on me. Where was the only place I could obtain this drug? On the 'drag.' I had to get away from that area of the City.

Providence intervened long enough to wean me off.

I got extremely sick. It acted like pneumonia. Even the medical staff thought it was pneumonia. It actually was the 'chalk' buildup in my lungs from the effects of this drug.

They admitted me to the University Hospital. While I was there, I was having horrific nightmares. They asked me if they could send someone to speak to me.

It was a psychiatrist. I shall call him Doctor U. He listened. I spoke. He invited me down to his territory. I went for a tour and stayed.

During those days, the psych ward had its crazies, but mostly it held a lot of people who were just depressed. They seemed like normal everyday people. There were a lot of empty beds, so the hospital admitted many people who wouldn't even come close to qualifying today. Today, they probably would be waiting months and months, just to see a counselor.

On the tour, I liked what I saw. A free bed, free TV, a beautiful games room with a large pool-table in the center, and wonderful, interesting company. The nurses were a bonus too, because I knew how to stir up trouble and keep from being bored.

Also, don't forget the drugs. I was coming off the street drugs, but this place had their own cornucopia of drugs. That helped with the withdrawals.

Mostly, it was the energy of Doctor U that made me stay. It was confirmed by the nurse, who thought they were alone in the back medication room, "Well, Doctor U's got another young, cute, one admitted today!"

I could tell he wanted something, and it wasn't just my history.

I stayed three months. I would say I became 'institutionalized.' I remember, I couldn't think for myself on that first day out. The structure was rigid, and there were multiple rules to ordinary, daily tasks, such as eating, bedtime, etc. I quickly overcame it, but never forgot the initial feeling of helplessness.

Doctor U would use 'sodium amatol' treatments. Another term they use for this is, 'truth serum.' I wouldn't remember what I said under the influence, but I vaguely remember some inappropriate activity happening.

There were times when I would cut my arm. Not deep cuts, just enough to draw blood and have the nurses spin into a frenzy. They would instantly jab a needle in my butt and I would be out for 24 hours. I didn't realize it at the time, but I was bored and needed attention. These events cut up the monotony of psych life.

I was extremely bored and wanted out after three months, so I confronted the shrink. I hugged him after the sex, while he had on his white jacket, and purposely left a brilliant red kiss on the upper left collar. I lied and told him I had a hidden camera. Doctor U was not pleased by my change in behavior, and promptly kicked me out. He knew the well had run dry.

I left willingly. I had gotten off the drugs and had spent the cold winter months in a warm, free sanitarium. What more could a young hooker want…

Chapter 5

I went back to being a young hooker…

However, I never went near those drugs again. My soul learned I was very lucky to have gotten a new lease on life! Because, that's what it was. I was no longer chained to this beast that couldn't be satisfied. The gnawing hunger was sated. The itch just under the skin had disappeared. I was free.

I was seventeen, by now. I still wasn't a legal adult. Therefore, I didn't have a lot of options when it came to working.

I worked the street for several months, before I ran into Tom. He was a Vietnam War Veteran and he had flown a medical helicopter that was shot down. He survived as a paraplegic. He had partial feeling in his male parts and his right leg, but for the most part, his legs were useless.

He originally came from Trinidad. He had a dark black hue to his skin. He was going bald with only a few tufts of black and white, wiry, hair circling the sides of his head.

He saw me, for the first time, on the street corner, wearing a red dress. I went with him, thinking I would only see him the one time. He fell in love with me. He intrigued me. He had a brilliant mind. He could open any lock placed in front of him, and he had an interesting history. I'm not sure if I believed his stories about the CIA, but they were colorful.

He asked me to move in with him. I agreed. He lived far away from downtown. He didn't mind me working, as long as his friends could watch me from a safe distance, to protect me. They were from the 'Montreal Mafia.' They were well connected. They were temporarily in town for a few months, and Tom was the head of this ring. There were seven, including Tom.

He wanted to introduce me to them, but they refused. They felt that if I could identify them, the police wouldn't leave me alone. I would catch a glance of them occasionally, as they followed me at work.

My relationship with Tom was very bizarre. There was always this weird energy that manifested around us. It had its own entity, even though, I know that sounds absolutely crazy!

This all started out with me putting on a provocative dance-show for him, in my red dress. I always danced to the same song, 'Lady in Red,' by Phil Collins. I would sway to the music, and I could feel the rhythm of this energy hit him, all the way across the room. It was the strangest sensation. His body would jolt a split second after my hips would swing forward in the rhythm. I realized I was sending him shock waves of energy!

It revitalized him, but exhausted me. This went on for the whole time I was with him.

As time went by, I noticed he became more possessive of me. Right after these dance rituals, his aura would grow in darkness and strength, and mine would fade weaker and weaker. It was like he could enter my mind and dig around, but I needed to be weak, first.

I would have moments of shear panic and one time, even ran out of the house, into the street, wielding a hammer, yelling, "Get out! Leave me alone!"

I'd never been prone to psychotic episodes like this. I

remember looking up and down the street, thinking in a second of clarity, if anyone saw me, they would indeed think I was insane.

Something in that house was growing stronger, day by day…stealing my essence in the process.

My friends came over, one time, and Tom lost it on them. All they wanted to do was go down into the basement and find a wrench to help me fix the sink. He went insane! He was now holding the hammer and threatening to kill them, if they didn't leave immediately!

Tom trusted me enough, that he finally confided his secret. The reason his Mafia friends were here in Edmonton, was that they'd all robbed an American bank, out east, on the Canadian border. Each of them was carrying a portion of the money, and they were moving it around every few months, waiting for the seven year Statute of Limitations to run out. They only had five months to go.

Tom had become extremely paranoid. He had, temporarily, placed the money in the basement, and needed to move it soon. He thought the police were hot on his tail. I never saw the police.

I didn't believe him at the time. I thought this was all a game, so I pretended to believe, and we didn't discuss it for two more months.

The following is very difficult to explain. It was my first paranormal event:

I think we need a bigger bed, the springs are creaking. Oh well, he's under me so I don't feel them. The sex takes on a life of its own, and I lose track of time.

The room darkens. The air thickens. Is there a storm in the middle of the afternoon? I glance out the side window. The sun is shining through. What the fuck?

I focus on the sex. I thrust harder and harder. Tom's eyes are closed and he's moving in rhythm. Suddenly IT enters. I can feel the shift. Now I'm fighting for my life. The IT has thrust itself right between us.

"You are mine!" It rages at me!

"No, never!" I thrust harder to show my power.

"Stop fighting, and be mine!" It tantalizes me, hoping to weaken me.

"Never!" I continue to thrust over and over.

I feel a war waging over my soul. I can NOT lose!!

Suddenly, I think to offer a prayer, "God, please help me!"

Instantly, the connection breaks. The feeling of being airborne is overwhelming, as we hit the bed hard.

Tom bounces and instantly comes to, "What the fuck just happened?" He shoves me aside, sits up and quickly moves to the edge of the bed.

"Did you drug me?" He accuses me.

That was the first paranormal experience. Here's what happened in a nutshell: As the war raged over my soul, we were levitating off the bed. When I won, with God's help, the entity let go and we fell back down.

I didn't know it then, but I had been giving IT a little of my soul every time I danced, and in so many other small ways. Over the months, I felt the energy draining, but I didn't understand what was going on. My ego was too big. I thought it was cool that I had the power to send energy across a room.

I could feel the entity, through Tom, pulling my essence from me and becoming stronger and more possessive. It wasn't going to let me go easily. I was having fun with this new 'power.' I was a baby, playing with fire. About to be burned.

I finally asked Tom to prove to me that this money was real. He drove me to downtown Edmonton, to a major Hotel. He instructed me to walk in and ask for a package for so and so. I complied. I brought this old record album box that was wrapped securely in Saran Wrap—multiple layers. He then drove me to the bus station and gave me a key for a locker. I retrieved another similar package.

I still thought this was a game. I laughed at him, and taunted him, until he opened the package, bringing reality into sharp focus. He used his knife to slice through the saran, like butter. He nodded for me to peek inside.

There were stacks and stacks of American $100 bills—in both packages.

I estimated three million dollars, if not more. Oh my God! This was real and not a game! I needed out. I stopped smiling and contemplated leaving ASAP. He sensed my shift and told me that if I ever left, he would find me and perform a murder, suicide. The hairs on the back of my neck stood up. This was no idle threat.

A couple days later, the next paranormal event occurred:

"I don't want sex. I just want to lay here next to you." I convince Tom.

"Okay, sure." He finally agrees.

I'm on my back, looking up at the ceiling. Suddenly the air thickens and the room darkens, again. I feel the shift. It's like I'm suddenly suffocating under a heavy, wet blanket. I can't move. I look over at Tom and see that he has disappeared. IT has entered. IT has replaced him.

"You need to stop fighting" IT says. Tom's hand moves to hold mine. I yank away.

"Go away!" I speak in my mind, as that's the stage for this conversation.

"You're already mine, so stop fighting and come..." IT is very deceptive.

Every time IT speaks, Tom's body and hands move, as if IT has taken over completely.

I remember the key. This time, I pray, "Please God, take this away and I promise I will get off the street forever! Please, please, please!"

Suddenly, a silent vacuum switched on. IT and all the dark energy was, instantaneously, sucked out of the room—with a whoosh! My spirit could breathe! There were no windows, but it felt as if the room suddenly breathed sunlight.

Tom came to and thought I had drugged him, again. I swear to God, we were not using any drugs during these experiences.

Within a few short days, I left him and moved in with a friend of mine. He had no idea where I was staying and I wanted it that way.

I was now 18 and could look for a legal job. My life was about to change in the most profound and beautiful way…

As I reflect back on these memories, I don't need to talk to Gabby. I have enough information to understand what happened.

I think that in order for me to understand how powerful and positive the divine light is, I had to experience the exact opposite—how blackness, the sheer absence of light, ignites primal fear and sucks us down into its dark depths, and WE as mortals are powerless to stop it. I had to see and witness for myself, the blinding power of the dark side.

If I had never experienced this, I would NOT believe it—at least not so easily. It lands far outside the boundaries of our normal senses. However, once we live it, we can't so easily dismiss it. Actually, it is impossible.

I realized, as powerful as this entity was, it couldn't hold a candle to the light. God knocked it on its ass, quickly and effectively.

I did see Tom one last time, months later. I had already been receiving sessions of light, and felt so spiritually strong. I ran into him on the street, as I was waiting for a bus.

I remember starting to feel that familiar 'opening up' sensation, but this time I felt it as a prodding, an invasion, like the entity was trying to worm in. I quickly stopped the desire to send my energy his way, effectively closing the door. Now, I knew it wasn't something good.

Again, to describe this is very difficult. I could feel ITs thoughts and Tom's thoughts, but through a very weak connection. For a split second, I sensed him wanting to aim the gun he brought, then changing his mind and removing his hand from the bag. Then, suddenly, the connection was severed and I sensed nothing from that point on. I was completely released from bondage. I could feel his eyes on me, as I walked away. The very last thought was that Tom, himself, had cut the connection through the sheer force of his love for me. He had let me go.

I was free to move on.
An old life discarded, and a new one borne…

Section 4

Birth

Chapter 1

They say we live many lifetimes in one. I agree. Two lives are about to be born and reborn, together—my son's birth, and my rebirth into an exciting, awe-inspiring, new way of being!

I moved in with Sally. She worked part-time at Zellers, while going to College to get her Accounting degree. She was a year older, at 20. She loved plants and had an amazing 'green thumb.' She was always bringing home wilted plants from Zellers, and nursing them back to life. She didn't look anything like me. I was tiny with dark hair and she was tall, heavy-set, with blond curly hair. We met several years prior, lost contact, and then found each other again at a nightclub.

Together, we rented a small basement, two-bedroom suite, on the south side of the City, far away from the 'drag.' A place called Strathern Heights. She quickly filled it with her 'lost & found' plants.

I was bound by my contract with God to find a legal job, so after two months of looking for work, I was hired by Kirby Vacuums.

Now, the only agreement I made with God was never to work the streets again. I didn't agree to anything else—I didn't have the spiritual fortitude, at that point.

The guys who hired me at Kirby were young and they loved to party. They knew I had connections to pot and hashish, which I gladly obliged them. Of course, it helps to use my feminine wiles to get hired. What else did I have? I didn't have the proper work experience. I didn't have an education.

It was here, where I first met Doug, my future husband. They would drive us out for the day in Vans, in groups of 6-8. Doug wasn't in my Van, so I only saw him in the mornings. He would find some excuse to talk to me, or just smile at me from across the room. I remember he always wore this white suit, with a pink shirt. He definitely stood out.

It was door-to-door selling. It was a tough business. This vacuum was close to $2000. We had to really work, to sell it to the housewives. We used round, white papers to show all the dirt the vacuum sucked up. It was a monstrous looking thing, and heavy! It looked built to show off its brute force. I wouldn't have bought it. In the entire three months at this company, I sold only three, and two of the customers backed out within the grace period. Go figure!

One day, Doug approached me, to talk in private. He begged, "A good friend of mine is getting married on Saturday. I need a date to attend. Would you go with me? It's only for the day. You'd be doing me a huge favor! I know we're just friends. I don't expect anything more."

His face was beet red and damp. He wore his nervousness like an excited boy, going in for his first kiss, knowing it may be rejected. I had no desire to go with him. I had no desire to EVER go out with him, let alone kiss him. I was about to say that to him, and something stopped me. Like all the other times, providence intervened; I said instead, "Okay, it'll give me a good excuse not to come to work Saturday!"

I need to give some background information here. There was a time on the street (I was around 16) when I wanted to find a legal job but couldn't, so I answered an Ad in the paper for someone looking for a nanny. It was a guy looking for help with his two children.

Doug happened to look exactly like this guy.

This creep had red hair, and a red beard. He was very broad shouldered and the only fat on him, extended from his belly like a large, round ball.

When I first laid eyes on this guy and his two small children of 4 and 5, he had his pickup truck fully loaded with mining supplies. He was heading up into the interior of northern British Columbia to do some gold mining. He wanted a nanny to support the children. I wanted away from Calgary so badly, that I jumped in without a second thought.

Let's keep this part really short, this time: He brutally raped me, the second night in the hotel, and then decided to try and sneak out with the children, before I woke up. I never went to sleep that night. I stuck to his kids like glue, and forced him to pay for a Greyhound bus ticket. I spent two days on the bus, back to Calgary, with no food or water. I had to beg customers on the bus, for sustenance.

So, here I am, years later, standing in front of an absolute replica of this creep. In my mind, I'm thinking, "Not on God's green earth, will I ever go out with you. Ever! Ever! Ever!"

Then I say yes! What was I thinking? It obviously wasn't me. I should know by now.

We attended the wedding. Sally warned me that morning, if he shows up with a gift, his intentions are more than he agreed to.

He showed up with a 'Zipper' necklace. Oh my

goodness! Really!

In the car, I attempted to be clear. “You know, I can’t accept this gift. I just want to be friends.”

He lost it with me! “I’m sick of just having girls as friends. Why can’t we ever be more than friends?” Oh dear! I sunk deeper into the seat and decided not to respond. I planned to NEVER see him again, after this day, so it didn’t matter. He apologized, but I wasn’t listening.

Both the day and evening ended without any other mishap. The wedding went off without a hitch. It was your typical Christian wedding. He walked me to my door, and we said goodbye—for good! At least that’s my conclusion.

He showed up at my apartment the next night! I had spent most of the night with my boss, from Kirby, doing the ‘humpity bumpity.’ When I walked in, at four in the morning, Sally met me at the door. “Guess who’s been here all night, with a bouquet of flowers?”

What the hell?

He was determined not to let me go. He even spent the next six nights just listening to me talk, without pushing sex. I asked him years later, how he managed to do that so well. He replied “Cause I knew that was the only way to hook you. Sex wouldn’t do it. You would just dump me right after. But, believe me, all I had was sex on the brain. I couldn’t believe how patient I had to be to get it!” He was right.

We moved in together and sex was all he had on his mind. We did the deed 3-4 times a day. We would have done it more, if he could help it.

Even though I had gotten off the street, I still had the

mentality of a hooker, and intense rage and anger towards men that could scorch the hair off their chest at ten paces. I was an absolute mess.

We had rip-roaring fights. Then we'd have make-up sex, like monkeys, and go through the same cycle again. It was crazy!

My neighbour, Melodie, came over one day. She had a toddler and was looking for a babysitter. She saw that I was sick and, instead, asked me if I wanted to receive a session of light. What?

She seemed perfectly sane. In fact, she had a beautiful aura which matched her angelic singing voice. I would hear her through the walls, since she lived next door. It didn't matter what I was doing, I would stop and listen—she was that good!

She worked for the forestry, at the time. She had an amazing life story, herself. She went to boarding school in Switzerland and she was one of those souls who had a solid, stable energy that can only come from growing up with the great love of her parents.

Remember, I mentioned the balance of strict and gentle love equals Great Love? That's what she had growing up, with a tangle of brothers and sisters to keep it interesting.

She wanted to give me light. I'm always up for something new. I get bored easy. I ventured over to her place. She collected unusual artifacts from around the world, and a lot of sandstone sculptures. Her place felt like walking into a desert oasis. It had such a beautiful, calm energy!

She started by raising her hand and kept it a foot away from me. She, first, directed it to my 'main soul' area—the center of the forehead. She described this as the area where my soul resides. She also stated that when I receive light there, my ancestors and any spiritually related souls would also receive, at the same time.

Hmmm. Okay, I didn't care about that, at least then.

She gave to the back of my neck and, then, asked me to lie down. She gave to my back, and then she indicated that she was going to give to the back of my uterus.

This is where I felt something. I was lying on my stomach, and I looked up and over to see where her hands were. I saw both of them and they were NOT touching me, though one was a foot away directing the energy through my back. I felt pressure, as if her hand was pushing on the back of my 'upper butt/lower back' region. Wow! I didn't expect that.

Melodie spoke up, "I think you might be pregnant. The light feels so strong, radiating through this point."

"No! You're wrong!" I very confidently explained, "There is no way I can get pregnant. I've only got one tube, and too much scar tissue."

"What a flake!" I thought.

I've learned that when we are too confident, that is right when the universe delivers its punch. The last laugh is usually on us.

I went to the doctor, the next day, just because I thought I had the flu. I was pregnant! I was in complete shock! Doug wanted to marry me. He was ecstatic! I wanted to throw up!

I received light two more times, before I noticed a small change in my thoughts. I found the intense rage, I had, seemed to settle down a few notches. I had a long way to go, but I started to feel how powerful this energy was. I was intrigued by it.

Melodie said that, "big problems will become small problems, and small problems will naturally disappear. The light purifies in this way."

One day, she gave me the key to her place and asked if I could take care of her plants, as she was heading to Calgary for three weeks. I was devastated! Who would give me light? She gave me the address to the Centre, on the south side of the City, and the hours they were open.

Okay, here's where I tell you that I had become a recluse. I no longer worked the streets, but I also started having panic attacks, whenever I left the house. So I wouldn't go anywhere, unless I was forced to. It was becoming quite serious.

I was craving this energy, so I braved the bus system and showed up at the Centre. This was where I first met Gabrielle, or Gabby, as we call her.

When I first met her, she didn't impress me. Actually, she irritated me. She kept telling stories about spiritual stuff and all I wanted to do was receive this energy, and get the hell out of there. Oh boy, she drove me nuts!!

'Stop talking to me about gratitude! It took everything I had to get here, and I don't feel very grateful at the moment!' These were the thoughts rolling around in my head. Outwardly, I just smiled and nodded.

Every time I went to that place, I felt disturbed! Why did I keep going then? Well, Gabby talked about that too! She said something about some spirit attachment, and that we have to be stronger than they are.

Well, I'm not one to back away from anything tough.

I would show them, and Gabby!

I started coming 3-4 times a week, and gradually my world started to truly open up. The change was gradual, but there was definitely a change. I knew this was the path for me. I even started to like Gabby! Go figure!

Doug refused to receive light after the first time. He had so much rage towards women, it didn't surprise me.

When he was ten years old, he, his mom, his six year old sister, another lady and her two kids were all camping at Michelon Lake. They decided to go to town for groceries. Doug fell asleep in the back seat behind the lady driver. His mom was in the front passenger seat, with his little sister in the front middle seat. The other boy and girl, the same ages as Doug and his sister, were in the back seat with Doug.

A fully loaded gravel truck went through a stop sign, and tipped over onto their car. The driver was drunk. Everyone was killed instantly, except Doug and the lady driver. They both sustained major injuries, and both were in a coma for several weeks. Doug woke up from his coma, to find his little sister and mom had gone to heaven.

Within a year, his dad remarried a lady with four daughters. She became extremely abusive to Doug, and allowed the girls to act the same way.

We were an interesting pair. I had been severely hurt by men, and he had been severely hurt by women. We just didn't understand the irony at the time, nor would it have made a difference. We were extremely dysfunctional together. I knew this much.

I finally kicked Doug out, and went about looking for another place to live. He kept saying how much he loved me, but within a week of leaving, he had another girlfriend. I couldn't wrap my brain around that.

Chapter 2

I found a beautiful one bedroom apartment, and began to 'nest' as they say. I needed to get the space ready for the baby. I even got a cat with red fur. A crazy, spooky, little thing that would race at lightening-speed, take a flying leap up the wall and then slide down, digging her nails in. She always did it at night too, like the boogy-man clawing through my dreams. Oh my goodness! Used to scare the crap out of me! The little brat!

I went for a regular check-up with the dentist. I was told this was important to do while pregnant. They put one of those led blankets on me to protect my belly, and took x-rays. The doctor walked in and delivered the news. I had a huge hole in my jaw, a bone cyst. The doctor showed me the x-ray. What the hell?

During one of my short stays at a foster home, I managed to get my wisdom teeth pulled. I was seventeen. The idiot doctor did it while I was awake, with local freezing. I still remember him yanking and pulling my jaw around, just to get pieces of bone out. They were impacted and he couldn't get them out in one piece. Four hours later, my face and neck swelled out three times the size. I looked like an alien. I had to go back to the dentist to show him, but all he gave me were painkillers. By the next day, the foster family took me to the hospital. They instantly admitted me with IV antibiotics and morphine for six days. It was touch and go. The infection had run rampant.

I refused to go back for a check-up. Now, this dentist was telling me that for the last three years, a bone cyst has been growing on the right side of my jaw, eating away all the bone. Even though I felt no pain, if I just knocked it the right way, my jaw would break into a million little pieces. I needed surgery the next day… but, I was four months pregnant!!!

I ended up having two surgeries. The first one, they scraped the hole out, to try to get it to fill in with new bone. Then, they realized three days later, they needed to put a drain in. I was admitted to the hospital for two weeks. Not only did I have two surgeries, but I was getting IV antibiotics and strong painkillers, all while I was four months pregnant.

Gabby, bless her heart, came every single day to give me a full session of light. Prior, I would feel sluggish, achy, and in severe pain. Afterwards, I always felt clearheaded and refreshed. I really felt a difference, like a spiritual make-over. This was one of many amazing experiences I continued to receive with the light.

I healed and settled into a routine at home.

Pregnancy was a blast! I loved it! I had the 'glow' that everyone talks about. By the time I was seven months, I was a regular at the Centre. I was making plans to go to Seattle for the three day course, so I could receive this Holy Pendant called an 'Omitama.' It would allow me to radiate light. This way I could give back, instead of coming to the Centre and only receiving.

The Centre was actually part of Gabby's house. It had an Altar in the living room that had a picture in the middle of it. Gabby explained that at the center of the picture was a 'chon' that allowed the divine light to enter, much like the window lets in the sun's rays. Some psychic people can see golden energy swirling from it, but most of us can't see anything.

However, I have to admit, I felt something strange, whenever I was in front of it. It felt like a portal, an opening between realms. I sensed there was unlimited space between me and that 'chon.' Strange! But beautiful!

On this particular day, I was receiving a session of light from Melodie. Once I got into the position, where I was lying down on my back, she knelt on my right side and started radiating light towards my belly. Instantly, my son, Brydon, rolled over, in my belly, and started pushing up against the spot she was giving to. We both saw my belly flatten on the opposite side. We got excited!

She immediately rose, put her finger to her mouth, "Shush" and quietly went around to my left side and repeated the same thing. She made sure NOT to touch my belly, at all. Immediately, Brydon rolled to the left side and my opposite side went flat. We were absolutely amazed! It was like he was pushing towards Melodie, to absorb as much light as he could. I could feel the pressure in that spot, each time.

If someone repeated this story to me, I wouldn't believe it. Not in a million years. I was that much of a pessimist.

I finally received my Holy Pendant. I remember moving my hand over everything to radiate this light, and I marvelled at the heat and pressure coming from my hand. I could feel this energy leaving my hand, and it was the exact opposite of what I felt on the street. I knew I had hit the jackpot. Now, I just needed to accumulate experiences, and see if this was real.

I gave birth to Brydon at the Grey Nuns hospital, on the south side of the City. This hospital had the only new 'birthing' rooms, out of all them in Edmonton.

Brydon didn't want to leave me,(He's still living with me, 26 years later) I was two weeks overdue. I had missed the 'Lamaze' classes, where they teach you how to breathe, during labour. I figured, in my infinite wisdom, that it can't be too hard to breathe! Can it?

I started having labour pains on a Wednesday. I couldn't sleep because each episode ripped through me. Melodie agreed to be my coach and take me to the hospital, once they were two minutes apart. I hadn't slept for the last two days.

When I got to the hospital and they watched the next contraction, they asked me why I wasn't breathing properly? What the hell? Of course, I'm breathing properly! I felt indignant! What was wrong with my breathing?

The nurse, patiently, showed me how to breathe, by taking long deep breaths and matching the build-up of the contraction with faster, more intense breaths. Well, what a difference! It took the pain away completely! Well, oh my goodness! Why didn't anyone tell me it would work so well?

I was in for a long spell. It was Thursday afternoon, and the doctor felt that I was exhausted and not ready to move through the difficult stage.

Difficult stage? Wasn't I already in the difficult stage?

He wanted to give me a shot and have me sleep for several hours. The shot caused extreme fuzziness, which made me paranoid and mentally weak. I decided right then, that I didn't want to be pregnant, and that I could NOT go through with this labour. I was serious! Get me out of here! I was ready to run! I was good at that! As I tried to scheme, I knew I couldn't figure a way out through the haze.

Melodie had gone home to get some rest, so I couldn't receive any light or encouragement. I had to do this on my own. I needed my faculties back, this drug was causing my brain to be sluggish and weak. I was in panic mode. I, finally, decided to do the labour breathing to ease off the panic. Forget the pain! It worked! Whew!

I did NOT get any sleep, and was so grateful after four hours when I started thinking clearly. When the doctor returned, I pretended to be well rested. I wasn't going through that again!

Melodie showed up while they were hooking me up to the 'Pitocin' IV drip, Friday morning. Intense contractions immediately started—one after another. Here we go! I was just starting to understand difficult…

She gave me a session of light and I felt like I had slept a full night. I was getting into a good rhythm of breathing to move through the pain and contraction with relative ease. The new birthing rooms were amazing! They used to move the mother into a surgical bay, right around the time she was ready to push. This was very distracting and upsetting for the pregnant mom. Then, they changed it so that we could stay in this beautiful, homey, room and complete the entire birthing process in one place. This room had a couch, rocking chair, TV, phone, etc. They made it look as close as one can, to a typical bedroom.

They had these surgical carts they would wheel into the room, once the lady was ready to deliver. My room was next to the carts, so over a span of 48 hours, I would see the nurse come for them, and deliver them to the other ladies, one after the other. The first day I was there, I heard a woman screaming, as if something was ripping her to shreds!

I asked the nurse, who was about to deliver the cart to that woman's room, "Will I scream like that too?" "Oh, yes!" She replied. "Oh my god! Really, I'm going to be screaming like that?" I couldn't fathom it. What the hell had I gotten into? I don't want difficult!

Around 4 pm, something shifted with the contractions. They had to give me a shot for pain. In those days, it wasn't routine to get a spinal shot to numb everything, and the staff never offered it. The painkiller was so ineffective, it didn't seem to work at all.

Once we got to the 'difficult' stage, Melodie, bless her, was too gentle. She was trying to get me to follow her breathing, but it wasn't working. Her gentle voice, which had been a balm for the last several hours, was now irritating me, because the intense pain was overriding her sweet gentleness.

A wonderful nurse clued in and took over the reins. She had a powerful, authoritative, voice and 'commanded' me to follow her. She was almost shouting. Her power and strength overrode the pain, like a professional rider, taking control of a bucking bronco. The special breathing wasn't working anymore, and I was slipping over the edge, into a world of sheer panic and chaos. Panic is pain's ultimate weapon. The nurse reined in the panic, and expertly guided me through the chaos.

Someone looking in, may judge it as bad that the nurse was yelling at me, but that was exactly what I needed to make it through. I needed gentle care in the beginning, and then as the energy intensified, I needed it matched.

Often partners sustain the gentleness from beginning to end, or sustain the intensity from beginning to end. Not many can adapt to the changing requirements. Or, many get mad when they can't be all, and storm out of the room, feeling inadequate. They think they've let their partner down.

However, when I pull back and look at this from a spiritual point of view, I remember when Gabby told me about the Character Gods. Let's say this is true. Let's say the Creator of the Universe divided, or birthed himself into different characters. Let's say that each of us has a 'part' of God's essence, and therefore we are under one of those deities. Well, I received the most beautiful and gentle support from Melodie's character; and then when needed, God sent me the nurse, and I received the powerful strength of her character, to complete the journey. Together, they brought more of God into the room. When more people come together, more 'parts' of God are present, and when you have families, communities, countries and the world working together, the Creator is able to fully manifest on our beautiful planet!

Melodie understood this teaching. This is why she never once felt inadequate. She, humbly, and with great gratitude stepped back. Once her part was complete, she, graciously, allowed the nurse to utilize her strengths and complete the mission. They worked together, and a harmonious power was generated.

At 9 pm, I started pushing. I pushed for an hour and broke every blood vessel in my face and neck. They speak about the 'ring of fire,' which is right when the baby's head is crowning. That is the most intense pain that exists. Plus, the doctor decided to use forceps.

I had just noticed that he showed up in hip waders and I had a brief panicked question about what and how much was going to come out? What the heck? He was a strange doctor, but a good one. The thought quickly left, as I started to scream and scream and scream! "Get it out!" I repeated over and over, in between screams.

At 10 pm on Friday, July 15, 1988, my son was born!

"It's a boy!" I kept repeating to Melodie. We were both laughing and crying! We couldn't stop! Melodie gave him light for the first time, while they were stitching me up. I will always remember how peaceful he looked. I don't remember him crying at all.

To this day, Melodie and my son have an unbreakable bond! They don't live in the same City, nor do they see each other often, but time disappears when they do.

Welcome to this world, my beautiful, gentle boy!

Chapter 3

Brydon is an amazing gentle man and a wonderful gentleman. He has grown up to be a very responsible, spiritual, individual.

I decided to give him a session of light every day, during his first year. I was a single parent and I definitely had the time. He never cried. Seriously, he never cried. He would start to whine a little, and I would assist him with either a feeding, or changing, or a hug, and he would immediately settle down.

I will say that I was an amazing mother! I was determined to give him a hug, a cuddle, a kiss, and a smile, every single day, and more often whenever I could.

The only black mark on my mother sheet, was one night around 3:00 AM, when Brydon was a year old, he was playing in his crib and refused to go back to sleep. I was grouchy and addicted to sleep. I had grown up with Epilepsy and sleep helped control it, so I always got 10-12 hours. Imagine as a mother, having to adapt to very little. Without thinking, I swatted his butt in anger! Oh my God! The virgin look of shock and pain on his face did me in! I swore NEVER to do it again!

Well that's easy to say, but hard to do. It's easy when they are babies and especially when they are never fussy. As he got older, I realized I had no clue how to be an effective parent.

Here's when I got introduced to some parenting books, that were written by Barbara Coloroso. They blew me away! She teaches how to get children to think for themselves; to be strong enough to move through natural consequences. She teaches parents the difference between the brick wall parent (overbearing), the jellyfish parent (spoil the kid with no guidelines or rules) and the backbone parent (one who utilises both strict and gentle love-flexible). Her teachings became my backbone for parenting. I read her books several times, and even attended her workshops when she came to Edmonton.

When Brydon was two, I moved directly behind the back alley to Gabby's place. Gabby helped me stay on track, and was always there to give me spiritual guidance.

Brydon and me.

We lived in the basement of this old house. A Lebanese lady, Janine, lived upstairs by herself. She was in her 50's and she rarely left the house. She would always wear these pink, one piece, 'mu-mu's. Right from when I moved in, she would come down and play with Brydon, and act completely normal for a few moments or even a day, then, mysteriously, she would start yelling at me and blaming me for spying on her, and trying to break into her place. She had paranoid delusions and they would come without notice. One moment she was friendly, and in the blink of an eye she would completely change.

I asked Gabby for guidance. She directed me to radiate light through the ceiling to her, with sincere apology to her Ancestors. Gabby said that I had done something wrong to her or her Ancestors in a previous life, and they were hanging on to a grudge.

Well, forget that! I was too busy. I was in College taking Secretarial courses. Why can't she just leave me alone? She's crazy! That's why she's doing this! Ask anybody else! It doesn't have anything to do with me! I wouldn't go as far as saying Gabby was crazy, but sometimes, really?

Janine kept this behavior up. To the point, that one night at 2 AM she started banging on the floor with a stick, yelling at me. I woke up, in a rage. I had exams the next day! I took a few cleansing breathes, and thought about what Gabby had, patiently, been trying to teach me.

Okay. I started radiating light through the ceiling, and thought about the possibility that I might have done something to her Ancestors in a previous life. I felt a shift, and the apology started coming out very sincere. I quietly, and with great sincerity, offered an intense apology to her ancestors. I told them I was truly sorry, and to please accept this. I prayed for Janine's happiness as well.

Immediately, the banging stopped and my phone rang. I kid you not, I knew who it was. I picked up the phone, "Hello?"

A moment of silence, then, "Judy, is that you? I'm so sorry! I don't know what gets into me. My family won't even come around anymore."

In shock, I responded, “It’s okay, no worries. You know you’re always welcome down here, no matter what! Good night!”

I stayed there for another six months and she NEVER acted that way again. Yet, she had been doing this for over a year, prior. She hugged me when we moved out.

I know that she, herself, didn’t know what actually happened in the unseen realm, to get her to stop. I do know that her Ancestors forgave me and my training was complete. Gabby said that if it doesn’t instantly improve like that, it just means the negative karma runs very deep, and may require a whole lot more effort and altruism to balance it out.

I understood. If I destroyed their family and children, well a simple apology wouldn’t cut it. For her Ancestors, this sincere apology was enough.

Chapter 4

Brydon was three years old, when I decided to get my Secondary Omitama. Gabby opened my eyes to this possibility. They were holding that three day course in Mexico City. At first, I couldn't even fathom I would be able to go. Where in the world would I get the money? Gabby gave me spiritual homework to do and I accomplished it. My world was opening up. I was caring about others. She had said to not focus on the 'lack of money,' but rather to 'be of service' to others.

To this day, anyone who knows this story, shakes their head. I was able to borrow money from someone who is extremely tight with money. Many who know him, can't believe that this arrangement occurred. Of course, since he was an Economics Professor, he laid out a plan for me to pay him back with interest. I agreed. I now had the money to go to Mexico City! I also understood that his mission, in this lifetime, is all about money and he was excellent at managing it!

The day I handed in my application for Secondary, my world did a flip. Gabby says that whenever we go through major cleansing, right after, we receive a major blessing. I knew that Secondary was the major blessing—it would cause a huge, spiritual, shift in my soul. So, I knew a 'cleansing' was coming. It came and it was big!

For a few days prior, I noticed Brydon had an ear infection. I had been giving him light to his ear points, and it seemed like it was getting better. He wasn't crying anymore. All of a sudden, that night the right side of his head started swelling out.

I immediately took him to the hospital. They advised me that they needed to admit him. I asked them to wait until I could make a phone call before they put the IV line in his arm. They agreed. We didn't have cell-phones in those days, so I went to the bank of payphones to let Gabby know, so she could offer prayers.

I could hear him screaming, as I went back down the hall to his room. I sprinted as fast as I could, yelling at them to stop! I had NEVER heard him scream like that, and it ripped my heart out!

A different nurse had strapped him down to the gurney, and was poking him with the IV needle. Oh, I wanted to slap her! But, I calmed down and tried to be there for Brydon. The interesting thing about this, was three days later when they had to change the site, he sat on my lap and only winced a little when they stuck the needle in. He knew he was safe with me there, protecting him.

Remember, when I told you I was addicted to sleep? Well here was my training to overcome that. I would help anyone during the day, but don't ask me for help at night—ever! Well, because I saw what happened when I left the room, I moved into his hospital room. I refused to leave him, and I refuse to sleep for any length of time.

We had a wonderful arrangement, because my training could have been a whole lot worse. Because they didn't know what was going on with him, they moved us into a private room. Well, normally, that's unheard of. We should've had to share space with four other families.

Gabby helped me by teaching me to take this time of

‘no sleep’ and try to stretch myself, and offer ‘gratitude’ with my innermost attitude, no matter what was going on around me.

This is the practice that I trained myself with. Every time the nurse or doctor came into the room, I would sit up and smile and tell them how grateful I was for their services, etc. I opened myself up to Brydon and tried to not focus on how tired I was—at all. I would give him light and be there for him in the middle of the night, with gratitude in my voice.

It was difficult! Any stretching, or growth, is supposed to be difficult. Just like when we go work-out in a gym. We start out with ten pound weights. If we never increase the amount, we never see any result. Whenever we increase it, it is a struggle for the first while, until our body gets used to the new increment. Then, we do the whole thing over again, until in six months we are lifting 75-100 pounds.

Gabby taught me, this is exactly like spiritual growth. People often think this is stagnant, meaning a person is looked at as either spiritual or not. In reality, if we put the universal principles into actual daily practice, we can achieve great spiritual growth in a short amount of time!

My training, at this time, was to deepen my gratitude and to put it into actual practice, especially when I was tired. The universe always brings us the appropriate training. We don’t need to worry.

I felt the shift. There came a point, when it was no longer an effort to be positive. After four days there, I was smiling day and night. I had made friends with many families, and I received multiple compliments from the team of doctors and nurses. They had no clue how difficult this training started out as.

I took Brydon home, and I felt so much stronger and ready to elevate my Holy Pendant! Even today, I no longer have such intense attachment to sleep. It was a great life lesson! Thank you!

I went to Mexico City and was in awe of the people! They were so humble and so beautiful! They welcomed me into the Centre, like I was family! It was a magical four days! Thank you, to all those bright souls who dedicate their lives to helping others, in a place where hardship and survival is an everyday struggle.

A wonderful event occurred within a week of returning home from Secondary.

My parents called, out of the blue, and advised that I should come to Whitecourt and pick up this inheritance that they had been holding. Both my brother and I had heard rumours, years prior, that one of our Great Uncles had left us some money and land. Because we never heard anything when we turned 21, we gave up thinking we would get it.

My parents didn't want to give it to us, ever. However, they were being pushed by the lawyers and told that it had to be done legally.

Both my brother and I, each, received $30,000 and a parcel of land! We were supposed to have received it when we turned 18. (We thought maybe 21)

There were different times on the street where I saw visions of the future. One time I told Tom, out of the blue, that I would be doing something with my hands that would help people, and I would live through a cataclysmic event…now only the first part of that came true, and hopefully the second won't.

However, I also had a vision of receiving a large sum of money, three different times; each time the amount would get a whole lot bigger. It would be contingent on me using it to help others and our beautiful earth. If I succeeded, I wouldn't have to worry, the next increment would come.

I immediately offered 10% to God. I have heard of the spiritual power of numbers and that the number 10 represents 'God.' They say if we offer that amount to any charity or spiritual organization, essentially to do God's work, then the Universe will protect the other 90% for us, so we never have to worry. I believe this.

I was able to pay everyone back, and still had money to go to College and get my degree in Administration.

Looking back, if I'd received the money at 18, I would have partied until I died of an overdose. I would NEVER have done anything wise or smart with it.

Providence at work, again? Well, by now I know it's our guardian spirits working hard in the Astral World to protect us.

Chapter 5

There was one tough decision that I had to make with Brydon—whether or not to immunize him. Now, I know this is a very hotly debated topic!

I didn't make this decision lightly. I put forth a lot of research and questions, before I made it.

Physically, they say that if everyone is immunized, this stops the major diseases from running rampant. Spiritually, they say, first of all, it is our choice, and either choice is okay. Secondly, they say that all diseases are forms of 'cleansing' and if we don't need to go through it (ie, we don't have this type of karma) we could have direct contact with the contagion, and still NOT get ill.

I, also, have read quite a bit of material on children getting Autism from immunization shots.

I don't know if any of the physical stuff is true. However, my gut said not to do it, for spiritual reasons. Gabby said that once I made the decision I had to not worry, or else it was better to just immunize, if not doing it caused such great duress.

Brydon was spending his days at a daycare, while I was working. They had approximately 20 children. I picked him up one day, when he was around three years old, and they told me he had direct contact with a child that had a confirmed case of Whooping Cough. The child had its first immunization, but for some reason had still contracted the disease. I was told to either immunize Brydon or take him home and put him on antibiotics for the duration of two weeks. They were pretty sure that

Brydon would contract the disease, because both kids had eaten from the same spoon, and the child had coughed and sneezed directly on Brydon.

I took Brydon out for two weeks, but I did not put him on antibiotics or immunize him. Many of the children got sick, and six more confirmed cases came out of that daycare. Brydon never got sick!

I, finally, was able to let my worries go and knew that, for me, I had made the right decision—not to immunize. This doesn't mean I judge anyone else for whatever decision they need to make for their family. I honor the right to choose, and trust that we will all make the right choices for our families, even if they aren't the same ones.

Around this time, I was allowed to go give light to someone who had recently passed away. This was my first experience. Six months prior, I was working as a Residential Aide. I had looked after a lady, Karen, in her home, who had brain cancer. I told her sister about light and mentioned that we offer this when someone passes. They didn't want anything to do with it while she was alive, so I gave them that final option, right before I changed jobs. I never expected to hear from them.

Her sister called me, out of the blue, and asked if we could go. Karen had passed away that morning.

Lisa could also give light, so I asked her to go with me.

We arrive at the Grey Nuns hospital. Gabby told me what to do, but I'm so nervous! Oh my god! If my mom could see me now, she would know for sure I've lost it. I've gone crazy! What am I going to do with a dead body? I've never even seen one before!

Thank god, Lisa's with me! "I think we need to ask for the pastor of the hospital." I tell Lisa, as we walk through the entrance to the front desk. She nods. "Okay."

The pastor is a woman! Wow! We step into the elevator. She's taking us down to the basement, to the morgue! My heart is beating wildly, as I watch the numbers change! I could still change my mind. The doors slide open.

I can smell death! I'm in shock! I breathe through my mouth. I will never forget that smell. The pastor leaves us in a tiny room, for a few minutes. There's nothing in this room. It's cold! She wheels the gurney in, and gently lowers the sheet and tucks it around Karen's face.

Karen looks glassy, like a doll. She also has dark blue spots around her mouth. She looks like she may have died in pain. I think I'm going to pass out! Breathe!

I start to give her 'main soul.' I put my hand about a foot above her forehead, and aim the energy through. My hand is shaking, but nobody notices. Lisa starts giving light towards Karen's feet, through her body.

After two minutes, the pastor asks to see my Prayer Book. She starts to read it to herself and we continue to give light.

I take a few cleansing breathes, and forget about my fear. Something has shifted in the room.

I feel heaviness and sadness throughout the room, like the room itself is very sad and about to cry. It's similar to when I was with Tom, but this doesn't feel evil—only very sad.

I tell Lisa this and she acknowledges. The pastor

remains silent.

We've been giving light for 20 minutes now. I feel a shift in the room, again. This time, I feel the weight completely gone. I feel joy and happiness, like Karen is trying to give me a hug! How can that be? I look at Lisa and she's smiling.

I look at Karen's face and I see a change. Impossible! That can't be. It looks softer and more relaxed. I mention this to Lisa and she agrees. I think she is just agreeing with me to support me. I'll take it for now.

The pastor finally speaks as she hands me the Prayer Book. She said, "Well I don't know what you are radiating, but I feel as if she is suddenly happy and I noticed a small change on her face. Tell me more about this!"

I've had the privilege of giving light to over 30 bodies in the last 26 years. Every single time, there is a massive shift in the room, from sadness to joy and every single person, whether they know anything about the light or not, feels it.

My friend Rose, from Newfoundland, had become a member and she moved back there for a year. She was allowed to give a half hour of light to her mother-in-law, when she passed away. Her husband didn't say anything until two weeks later, when he was drunk. Then he told her, he felt and saw his mom smile, and he thought he was losing his mind. Rose told me that she noticed it too, but as a social worker, she wasn't sure if I put that thought in her head. She was blown away by her husband's confession.

Later on in the book, I will share my experiences of

giving light to my husband on the day he passed. It was the most profound experience! They say that it is even more amazing when they have Omitama themselves, because in the Astral World, they are radiating divine light back towards us!

Spiritually, Gabby said that when we die, we go to a certain level of training in the Astral World. The light helps us make realizations very quickly and, thus, we are able to go to a much higher level, immediately, after receiving light. This is why we feel their immense joy and gratitude every single time.

Doug is about to enter my life again…

Section 5

Marriage

Chapter 1

They say marriage is the union of two opposites. Where two people of opposite character, join together to create something truly spectacular!

Usually, great offspring! Other times, just a great life together!

Why is it, that our spouse can 'push our buttons' in a heartbeat? Why does it feel like a soul scrubbing? *Because, they are the closest to our heart and soul!* The unseen realm set it up this way, to create a harmonious union—where we're no longer TWO, but ONE. In order to 'blend' well, the edges need to be smoothed with a grinding or whetstone—life. Boy, did life ever throw us some major 'polishing' experiences! As a jewel is shined to a priceless value, so were we.

Doug and I had the great offspring first. Then we scrubbed each other's soul. Oh my! Did we ever scrub and scrub, to the point where we had to take a few breaks in between. It was a painful, deeply scouring, awe-inspiring, profoundly sweet journey!

During most of our marriage, it was agonizing. It was a tunnel filled with darkness. I was completely trapped, like a caged animal. Yet, I couldn't give up and I had to navigate through; I had to find a way. Now, having made it through, I wouldn't change it. We took breaks, but we never quit. We needed to be 'scrubbed,' or 'tempered,' to forge souls who could be of great service in this world.

'It is only in climbing the mountain, through blood, sweat, and tears, that we are able to fully savour the view!' I still hear Gabby in my ear, though she now, physically, lives 300 kilometres away in Calgary.

Our souls needed to be scrubbed. As painful as that is, and most of us would quit or run from it, the spiritual blessings at the end of this journey, have been priceless.

Knowing what I know now, I would do it again, in a heartbeat. It doesn't mean I would like it any better, or complain any less. Gabby taught me that the deeper the 'cleansing' or soul scrubbing, the deeper and older the negative karma. It means we are cleaning out some very old, stinky garbage.

Doug and I filled the entire dump with our garbage!

Welcome, to our tumultuous journey together.

This is the most painful part of my life to share. When a person departs from this world, we are inclined, out of respect, to place them high on a pedestal and 'never speak ill of the dead.' My first instinct is to glaze over it and move on. However, this pain was as much a part of my final healing, as the childhood abuse and my life on the street. Just know, at the end of this journey,

Doug and I found a beautiful and awe-inspiring love for each other!

I shall attempt to reconstruct some of the important events throughout our marriage:

Doug was terrified to be by himself. During the first three years we were apart, he scurried through girlfriends, like a mouse through a house.

When Brydon was three, and shortly after I returned from Secondary in Mexico City, Doug called, out of the blue. He was having difficulty with his current girlfriend.

Really? You call your ex-girlfriend for support with your current one?

It was strange, because the day before his call, Brydon and I were in an elevator, and he looked up at the stranger standing next to me and, with so much innocence, asked, "Are you my Daddy?" Oh, break my heart, good buddy!

When Doug called, I extended great altruistic love. I gave guidance on how to really listen to his girlfriend, and on how to get to the Center in Toronto. Toronto had been his new home for two years. I let him know how receiving light would resolve the underlying issues. He said he would go, but I held no expectations.

When Brydon was first born, I received partial financial support from the government. They went after Doug for child support. Doug decided to fight the DNA testing. He didn't want to pay for anything.

His lawyer got the DNA test results and advised Doug to drop the fight. Immediately! The test results showed that not only was Brydon his son, but they might as well have been twins. His lawyer advised that he had never seen results so high!

Doug also had two children from a previous marriage, whom he rarely saw. The oldest boy, Sam, has red hair and looks just like him. Sam was his absolute favourite, whenever they were together. Tina is his daughter, and she is a spit-fire. She can look you directly in the eye and tell a bold-face lie, even when you have the evidence to prove otherwise. She does care deeply about others. She's just been through so much abuse in her short little life, long before she came to stay with us. Sam is six years older than Brydon, and Tina is five years older.

Doug had no interest in connecting with me or Brydon for the first three years. He wanted to party and have fun in Toronto. So when he called, I was shocked. Over the next six months, he called a few more times, and informed me that he had actually gone to receive light at the Center in Toronto, and loved it. Well, go figure!

My friend Rose and her daughter moved back to Edmonton, from Newfoundland, and we moved in together. She got a job as a social worker and as two ladies who love to talk, we had a beautiful year of peace, tremendous fun, and lots of laughter.

We had been living together for about a year, when Doug called and stated, "By the way, I went to the Primary Course and received my Omitama." Say what? Give my head a shake. Holy smokes!

I had sworn to God that I would only marry someone who could give light.

We started talking on the phone on a regular basis. Doug had a deep baritone voice that washed over me like a smooth fine wine. I could listen to him non-stop. He also played the guitar and sang. Though he was good, he would've been great, if he'd had more confidence. In singing, he always held back.

Doug decided to move back to Edmonton and marry me. He proposed over the phone and I said yes. I thought married life would be a fairy tale with a beautiful ending. I ignored all the signs.

I was clueless to what Rose, her daughter Trish, and Doug were up to, prior to him moving back. He was going to arrive just before my 25th birthday, March 4th. A week before my birthday, I went down to Trish's bedroom, as usual, to get the towels from her laundry and she snapped at me. I just thought she was being a moody teenager, I never once thought she was hiding party supplies. I never even clued in when Rose would talk to Doug on the phone, while I was on another level. I just thought they were getting to know each other.

I had no inkling, no clue, no warning, no intuition. My ancestors did an amazing, wonderful job making sure I was totally surprised!

Doug had been with us for only a few days and he was taking me to West Edmonton Mall for my birthday. We were going to see a movie and have dinner. I dressed in my best and strutted down the stairs. He never once commented on how good I looked. That frustrated me. We went for supper and all the way through, he was so distracted. That frustrated me. Even in the vehicle, he wouldn't follow a conversation, he was so distracted. I was beyond frustration! I wanted to thump him! By this time, I gave up. I suggested we buy a bottle of wine and head home to play cards with Rose and her husband. He came alive, like a burst of wind stirring a marionette! Well finally! Something was pulling his strings and it wasn't me.

On the way home, he drove down the alley and crawled past our house. Then, he couldn't find parking, so he repeated it. I didn't think it was that strange. I already had him pinned as acting bizarre. I just wanted to get home and not have to spend another moment with him!

Finally, he parked and escorted me up the stairs. I opened the door, and voila! About 30 balloons floated down from the ceiling, while a chorus of people yelled, "Happy Birthday!" I was stunned! The house was filled with at least 25 people! Oh my gosh! They even had a birthday cake that looked exactly like a typewriter! My mouth hung open as I walked in!

It took a massive effort to pull this party together. Doug was frantic, trying to figure out how to get me out of watching the movie. He couldn't believe his good fortune when I asked not to go. Then, when he was driving home, since we didn't have cell-phones, he had to drive by the house and see if the outdoor light was on. His first drive through showed they weren't ready. Next time around, the light was finally on. He was frazzled by the time we walked in.

I completely forgave him! I had the most amazing, 25th surprise birthday party! I had a blast! I felt so special and loved for that one night! I had never experienced this unique feeling before.

Doug was a big man. He had thick, curly red hair that faded to a strawberry blond over the years, including his 'fu man chu' beard. He wore bifocals, which he never really adapted to. He would, often, look over the glasses at you, like a professor determining if you pass or fail. He would fall asleep sitting up, hunched over his belly, like a boy refusing to let go of his beach ball. A silent giggle would start out of nowhere, and all you saw was his belly bouncing up and down, like the ball was about to take off. Then we'd hear the most contagious, deep throat laugh. He'd of woken up and listened in on a conversation, and something had struck him funny. He had a dry sense of humour.

My humour was a little different. Prior to our marriage, Doug and I slept in different bedrooms. One night I got up, around 3 am, and headed to the bathroom. I had on a long, flowing, white nightgown. As I, silently, retraced my steps down the hallway, I ran into Doug, literally. He screamed and trembled, like quivering jelly, and collapsed against the wall.

I used every ounce of muscle to hold him up, but I couldn't stop laughing, as he was positive he'd seen a ghost! Doug's main act was 'tough and manly,' so this memory still sends me into a fit of giggles. For a moment in time, he was a helpless boy!

When Doug moved in, he had his own idea on how to be a parent. He was abrupt and forceful and he didn't seem to realize that Brydon had a very gentle spirit. Doug's idea was to 'toughen him up.'

We fought, constantly, over how to raise Brydon. Brydon never had anyone yell at him. Rose and I never needed to. We were firm with him, when needed, but rarely. He had such a gentle spirit, that he never talked back and he always listened. Doug thought we were raising him 'to be a sissy girl.' Trust me, though I don't care what people wear, I always dressed Brydon in 'boy' clothes. I knew he was a boy, and I always honoured that in him. But, I knew, he had a very gentle soul.

On the medical front, I always wondered if my surgeries affected how much testosterone Brydon received. It is between three and four months, when the sex organs develop. I don't care if Brydon turns out 'gay.' I would love and support him equally. Due to his gentle nature, I always watched for the signs, so I could support him through it. I can say for sure, though, that he is straight. As a mother, I have caught him, on more than one occasion, on websites with very provocative women. He's still a virgin at 26 years old, and is adamant that he will remain, until he is married. He holds himself to a very high standard. When he turned 18, I bought every kind of alcohol available and lined it up for him. He refused all of it. He walks his own path.

Doug continued to bully Brydon. Rose was worried and thought we weren't ready for marriage. She thought it was a mistake and that it would only get worse. I ignored her, I thought everything would be okay. I thought if I did the 'spiritually correct' thing, and marry my son's father, it would turn out fine. I felt compelled. I can't say for sure if it was love, at that time. I think if I'd have chosen to marry for love, the future, as we know it, would never exist.

Chapter 2

We held our wedding on September 26, 1992. It was a small one, because we didn't have a lot of money. I borrowed a white top and skirt from Rose. I had hoped, one day, to renew our vows in a beautiful wedding dress. What girl doesn't dream of walking down the aisle looking amazing! Doug's sister took care of the flower arrangements, purple and white, which matched the cake that another friend donated. Brydon was the ring bearer.

The wedding took place at the United Church, since that was Doug's church. Our home became the reception venue. My parents attended. They were ecstatic that I would now be a 'respectable wife!' I don't know how my dad accomplished it, but he walked me down the aisle, while my arm was linked in his, having not said a word to me the entire day! Not a word, even when we were standing outside the door ready to walk. He spoke to Brydon and completely ignored me. He was forced to perform the role by my mom. It was awkward and embarrassing, for me, to walk down the aisle with him, knowing the extent of our relationship, or rather the absence of one.

Our friends paid for a night at the most expensive hotel in Edmonton, the MacDonald Hotel. I thought it was wasted. Doug had gotten drunk and ended up passing out as soon as we got to the hotel, and it was only 11:00 pm. I was frustrated with him throughout the evening, when he drank more and more, because his behavior became more sexually overt and sloppy.

We moved into our own place in November.

It got worse. Way worse. Doug and I fought like crazy! It was always over Brydon. I didn't handle it well. Doug would trip Brydon and then tease him, to toughen him up and make him more of a man. Doug was very competitive and definitely a man's man. He wanted his son to be the same. They were opposites. They would never be the same. Doug couldn't see this.

Doug started spending long days away from home. Yet he made very little money. Whenever he came home, he would start yelling and cursing over small things. He thought I was too gentle with Brydon. He would get jealous if I went out with friends. He would find some reason to complain and yell.

We stopped having sex. This drove him nuts. His irritation and anger would build to a crescendo, until we'd have sex again. Then he would literally whistle for a day or two. To him, all problems were solved with sex. That was his language of love—touch.

Mine was words of comfort—emotional. He would sit on the same couch as me, and ignore me crying my eyes out. Completely ignore me. So I ignored his sexual needs. This would go on for extended periods, until he would force us to have sex again, and the cycle would repeat.

One day I was watching TV and a commercial came on. For a second the TV went black and I saw Doug's image reflected in the TV. He was in the hallway, silently stalking me. When I finally got the confidence to confront him, after seeing this several times, he stated that he was making sure I wasn't 'masturbating,' because I wasn't sharing it with him. His usual sexual trick was to make a move while I was sleeping, when my defenses were down; but that hadn't worked for a few months, because he was working nights driving the Transit bus. He craved sex like I craved drugs. Intensely!

There were some very dark moments, in our past, around sex. I don't wish to explore them here. Suffice it to say, it is clear, that we both acted out in dysfunctional ways around the opposite sex.

On the emotional level, he was dysfunctional as well. He would shut down completely. One day, we were all in the vehicle and he accidentally ran over a squirrel. We heard it. Brydon and I gave it a burial and sobbed! Doug sat at the wheel, like a stone. He never uttered a word, nor shed a tear. Not even when we got home. He was so irritated with us, because we were emotional and upset.

I would talk to him about the spiritual teachings for hours. He would agree to come to the Centre or agree to try to practice them. I noticed all he got good at, was repeating what, he thought, I wanted to hear. Later, when he was working with Edmonton Transit, the ladies would all line up for guidance and he would repeat to them exactly what I taught him. They loved coming to him! When he first shared this with me, he thought it was so funny. I didn't.

It was only in these recent years, when I learned more about Aspergers, which Doug had, that I finally understood. They are excellent at 'rote' memory. Meaning, they can memorize facts and spout them off, but they have an extremely hard time with anything, 'abstract.' Doug would listen intently to me talking about abstract spiritual concepts, and he would sincerely agree with me, but a moment later, he would do the exact opposite! Yet, he could go to work and recite word for word, to the ladies, all that I had imparted. They thought he was so wise and I thought he was so dumb! Perhaps, we all needed to find the middle ground.

I, also, didn't understand what a 'spiritual watering hole' was. Gabby explained that it's where the 'water' never dries up. A person can come to you, time and again, maybe even for the same spiritual guidance, over and over, until they eventually get it. This is what I represented for Doug. Though I had to repeat, several times in one day, even, he knew he could come to me for spiritual guidance. Though this would frustrate me to no end, at the time, I'm so grateful, now, for being allowed to be of service in this small way.

I finally got pregnant again and thought for sure this would help our marriage. I felt that if he actually had a child to raise from the beginning, he might be different.

Instead, I had another ectopic. I went in for surgery. They gave me Demerol after the surgery. Demerol affected me exactly like T's & R's. What a drug!

I came home to try to recover and Doug was emotionally absent. He had become verbally abusive. He knew how to raise his voice and rip into me with horrific words. He never hit, but we would push each other and I would throw food at him when we fought. He would come at me with eyes bulging, fists clenched, exactly like a raging bull, and I wouldn't back down. Where most sane people would, I pushed back more. I hated the 'build up.' I wanted it over with, as quickly as possible, because only then, would it feel safe.

I got diagnosed with severe 'endometriosis.' This is where the lining in the uterus floats through the fallopian tube and enters your abdomen, instead of flushing out, once a month. It would bleed on my ovary, or on my bowels, etc., and they would have to go in, with surgery, and burn it off. It was extremely painful. The common drug to use at that time, was Demerol.

The last time, they admitted me, and told me I needed to have a 'hysterectomy, within the next few months.' This is where they remove the uterus, and I wouldn't be able to have any more children. I remember telling the doctor I wanted the surgery right then, as soon as possible. I didn't want to go home, I just wanted to 'float' away with the drugs.

I could've waited for the surgery. Only I know what my innermost attitude was, and it took many years to forgive myself. I'm not sure I have, fully.

There was a time, when Doug convinced me to sell my land for $15,000 and to give it all to him to start a new business. He hired guys to sell coupons door to door, and he thought he could make a profit. I didn't see him for three months, while Brydon and I almost starved. We couldn't get help from Social Services, because we had received this money. Later I found receipts for party after party. He had rented an office above a bar and had gone through all the money, partying with the guys. He was angry when I finally went through the receipts. By this point, I just felt so sad and lost.

Looking back now, I see that leaving him never entered my mind. It wasn't an option. The choice didn't exist. I thought the proverbial 'flyswatter' would come down from the sky, and I wouldn't survive.

I had trapped myself, with my own judgments and spiritual misconceptions.

Gabby used to say that people get stuck in either

delusion, anger, or greed, and sometimes all three—for long periods of time. Mine was pure delusion—and for a long period of time.

To add to our dysfunctional family, Doug's 13 year old daughter, Trish, moved in with us, when Brydon was eight. I had no idea how to deal with a teenager, and especially one who was an expert at stealing and lying. Within the first week of living with us, she got caught stealing cigarettes at Safeway. The court gave her probation.

It got so severe, that one day Doug threw his daughter across the room in a fit of anger. I shared this with my friend, Rose, and she said if I didn't call Child welfare and get help, she would.

I made the dreaded call. A lady came in and took four days to assess us, as a family. I was terrified! Doug had me convinced that I was a horrible parent and that everything was my fault, because I wouldn't listen to him. He tried, his best, to convince the Child Welfare lady, as well. The lady sat me down, privately, and advised me that I was an amazing mom; but, that I needed to take Brydon and get as far away from Doug, as possible. Immediately! She stated that he had too many issues, and his rage was out of control! She called in Doug's aunt and uncle to take care of Trish. She felt I needed to focus on me and my son's healing, only. She suggested that I go to WIN House—a shelter for abused women and children.

I was shocked! I knew I didn't have a choice. I left. As I walked out the door, Doug raged at me and then started crying (finally). It was painful! However, that night when we were admitted and Brydon and I were alone in the bedroom, I felt a spark of freedom! The oppressive weight shifted, like shedding a hundred-pound pack. I could breathe! I had escaped prison! I had lost all my self-esteem and hadn't realized it, till that moment. I had lost everything, except my son. I was surprised at the rush of feelings, like a dam with a major hole sprung! A blended river of sorrow and joy sped down my cheeks, as a new reality began to emerge.

After the maximum 30 days at WIN house, I was fortunate to be allowed to move into WINGS. It's a long term shelter for abused women and children. We could stay there between six months and a year. We had our own private, one-bedroom, apartment, and I was required to attend group therapy in the basement, five days a week, while Brydon played at their daycare.

I never realized how much I didn't know, until I learned how to communicate effectively. In therapy, I was astounded to learn that there were rules and guidelines around communication! It was like learning a whole new language. I loved it! I absorbed as much as possible. I felt like I had entered kindergarten. In reality, I did. My parents never communicated effectively, so how could they teach me.

Doug went to therapy as well. He knew I would never get back with him, otherwise. He entered 'Changing Ways.' It's a group for abusive men. Some are even mandated by the Court to take it. Doug used a lot of 'spiritual talk' in the group. He was mimicking what he'd heard from me. For the first two months, he pretended to 'get it.' He was the one everyone listened to. Finally, the coordinator and the men confronted him. Once he was laid out bare, he finally started tackling the real work and making real changes. He cried in front of the group that day, and he felt a major shift from that point on.

Prior to this, I could tell he was faking it. He would call and beg to get back together, but as soon as I would confront him on his previous behaviour, he would fly into a rage. It was after the group confronted him, that I noticed real change. He finally took responsibility for his actions, and would listen and sincerely apologize.

The day they confronted him, was the same day Gabby guided me to do a very special 'apology' offering at the Centre for my ancestors and my family, for previous life negative karma. Every single time, I would do something spiritual, a wonderful result would happen, immediately after. I share with others that if this is coincidence, than I like the odds that it happens every single time.

I poured my heart and soul into this prayer, and that night Doug called me with the news of his breakthrough. This is the life of spiritual blessings. I was so grateful!

During all this, I never gave up on going to the Centre, nor on giving and receiving sessions of light. During our time apart, Doug started going more often, as well.

Gabby taught us both that when two people marry the karma is equal. We have the same positive karma and the same negative karma, or else our Ancestors would never allow us to marry. Even though, at times, I thought he was far worse than me, he was actually equal to me, spiritually. We both had different 'bad habits,' but they all added up equally in intensity. We scrubbed each other in different ways, but the cup of karma was exactly equal.

I loved learning the broader view, or the spiritual view of things! I thought about drug addiction and how that shuts me down emotionally from the world. This puts me at one end of the stick. Doug would go into constant rages, which is, hypersensitivity to the world. It is the exact opposite end of the same stick. The unseen realm put two opposites together to find the middle ground and to 'harmonize.'

There were so many miracles and amazing experiences around all of this 'soul scrubbing.' One of them was Doug, himself. They say that less than 2% of abusive men ever change. He heard this from the group coordinator. Doug changed. We both attribute this to his spiritual growth with the light. The Principle of Dawning dictates that it is a step-by-step process. This was the case with Doug. This is, also, a testament to his beautiful soul!

Doug learned better ways to cope and once he did, he put them into actual practice. We got back together and life became bearable.

In between our trainings, the unseen realm gave me many beautiful, spiritual experiences like the following:

In 1990, I received a little, three inch, car shrine from the spiritual organization. It rests on the inner dash of my vehicle, held in place with a magnet. It has an invisible 'spiritual cord' connecting the car to the 'divine realm.' This gives members extra protection while they are driving. It allows the 'spiritual bumper' around the vehicle to thicken over time. I have seen many miracles with it, as has my husband, who doesn't usually show excitement. He came home one day and shared that a woman almost hit him, with her vehicle, then she circled around quickly, while he was at a red light, to tell him that she felt a 'slip in time' and that there is 'no way they should have missed each other!' She was beside herself with astonishment! As was he! All I could do was laugh, because by this point I had had many of my own experiences.

The most amazing, was on a trip to Seattle. I wanted to review the three day, spiritual, course with my friends, Donna and Bruce. They were members and could, also, give light. We took turns driving straight through. We didn't want to stop and sleep. It was a long 16-17 hour drive. We were using Donna's car, a little 2-door white, Honda Civic.

She had a car shrine as well. Donna had just finished her driving stint and had crawled into the back seat to sleep. She had one of those black masks on, to effectively block out all light. She confided with me later that she was about to fall asleep, when she felt her car getting 'raped.' That was the only way she could, accurately, describe it.

Before we left, Donna and I offered an intense prayer that we could put 'Gratitude' into actual practice. We really needed help, because we knew that Bruce could get 'disturbed' and had a reputation for getting angry and trying to cause fights. He loved arguing and 'pushing our buttons.' When he asked to come with us, we didn't want to turn him down, because we felt that any opportunity to receive intense light should never be refused. Also, like all humans, he had a deep, sensitive side that we loved.

Bruce started driving, with me resting in the

passenger seat. I noticed he was grumpy about something, but he wasn't ready to share. I was about to close my eyes to sleep, when I had a strong inspiration to raise my hand and radiate light. I was exhausted! But, I couldn't ignore my gut, and just as I raised my hand, I looked over at the speedometer and noticed he was stepping on the gas and it was reaching over 140 kilometres! I looked up and saw a sharp right-hand turn, with a sheer drop-off on the left side. We were cruising through the Rocky Mountains and this was a dangerous section of road. To top it off, there were semi-trucks slamming past us in the blink of an eye. They seemed to be traveling at suicidal speed. The bell was ringing in my gut. It was deafening! I knew something was about to happen!

He wasn't going to make the turn. It was like he didn't even see it. He just punched the gas more. We barrelled through the turn and went airborne as he over-yanked the wheel. I quickly offered a prayer and asked for help. I was still radiating light, as well, from the palm of my hand.

I glanced out his window and saw a semi-truck! I heard its breaks and honking, like a monster roaring up to engulf us! As we were about to hit it, I felt a 'cushion' of light surround us. We were circling in the air, end for end. It was like we slipped into another dimension for those precious few seconds. I don't know how we missed the Semi or the cliff. We landed yards down the road, in a ditch—the only ditch for miles.

When Donna and I crawled out, on shaky legs, we immediately kissed the ground with intense waves of gratitude! We were alive and we weren't earthbound by the side of the road, with Bruce, for 300 – 400 years. Intense gratitude gushed from every pore, like new life springing forth! We bathed in it! We exalted in it!

We attended the course, being absolutely present in the moment, and feeling waves of intense gratitude pour through our spiritual bodies! We gained a profound understanding of putting 'true' gratitude into actual practice! We even had a stranger at the course comment that we looked as if we were 'shimmering,' with this profound bright aura!

When I returned from this amazing trip, Doug convinced me that we should visit my parents. My husband liked them. He felt a strong connection with them. I was full of light and love, so I agreed to go.

Chapter 3

From the passenger seat, I watched as my husband navigated the narrow gravel road leading up to my parent's long driveway. Our son, Brydon, sat in the back, staring out at the fall scenery, ensconced with the northern trinity of birch, popular, and spruce. The trees waved us in, as the day yawned cold and blistery.

Sitting in the passenger seat, I watched it slide by like a film. I reflected on the horrific memories that were also projecting by slide after slide. My memories of this area were not good. Not good at all.

As we drew nearer to the great log house, my heart rate accelerated and my breathing became laboured. I felt pinpricks of fear traveling up my spine and a heavy rock in my stomach. The memories were clawing at the edge of my vision. I blinked as if to clear my eyes. I wasn't about to let them in.

"I will be okay. We can leave if we need to. I can handle it." I tried to convince myself, as I took a great cleansing breath.

The tires of our brand new 1998, black Dodge Caravan crushed the leaves, like a monster munching its way through a snack, excited for the main course ahead.

My parents were in their early 60's at the time of this visit. They had literally carved a spot into this untamed land, about 20 years prior. They showed no signs of slowing down.

They loved my husband, Doug, and he thrived on being around them. My mom and he would tease each other, and he would spend time with my Dad outside on the farm. I was a ghost around them—my speaking was not required, wanted, nor valued.

I don't think my husband really believed the horrific abuse I went through until this day, when he caught a glimpse of my hell.

It was shortly after we parked. Mom met us at the end of the driveway and mentioned to Doug to head to the barn, as my dad was there doing chores. It seemed like he had planned it that way, so he wouldn't have to greet me. I was used to this.

My husband told me, later, that they were in the middle of a conversation when my dad immediately grabbed a huge stick and began to beat this stray dog that had shown up out of nowhere. The dog howled in extreme pain, and still my dad continued to beat it. He held its collar with one hand and brought the stick down on its backside, over and over. It howled in greater agony. My dad finally released his grip and chased it, as it sped away, frantically trying to put distance between itself and this new predator.

My dad explained, to Doug, that it was the neighbour's dog and that he was teaching it a lesson. He firmly believed that this dog would never run away again, despite the fact that the neighbours lived miles and miles away.

When they walked into the house, I could see Doug visibly shaken. We made eye contact and we converged in the bathroom.

"What happened?" I closed the door and leaned against the countertop.

He was in shock, and for a moment said nothing. A tear rolled down his face. "I believe you! Your dad is psychotic!"

"He didn't break a sweat! He didn't show any remorse! He didn't show any feeling at all! He just beat and beat and beat that poor dog! Then he continued talking, as if nothing happened! I can't get that sound out of my head!" Doug held his head in his hands, trembling.

"I'm so glad you got out!" He, swiftly, pulled me into a great bear hug.

I hugged him and rubbed his back gently. I realized, at that moment, that my husband hadn't fully believed me until this day. I wasn't sure how I felt about that. Many families of survivors of abuse, sometimes wonder if that person is making it up or wonder if they are exaggerating. Perhaps, they are having false memories. Even the survivor, themselves, may question their own sanity. I've been there and I've pondered it. I, myself, would've had a hard time with my story, if my brother hadn't been there to witness a large portion of it and to survive his own brand of hell with our parents.

My husband never liked confrontation with anyone else, besides me, so we pulled ourselves together; checked the mirror to put everything back in order, and he followed me out to my parent's dining room for a classic meat and potato dinner.

At the supper table, it was like the incident never took place. The topic up for discussion was local sports. The night droned on in a traditional way, as the men took their place in front of the TV and the women washed dishes. My parents were consummate actors and denial was their specialty.

Chapter 4

Life can become stagnant and move in a slow, downward spiral without us even registering the event, until one day we are hit with such force and magnitude, that the veil is immediately lifted. What we do at that point becomes the fork in the road—the ripple that changes our destiny, either for good or bad.

This is what happened to us as parents.

It was shortly after the visit with my parents that Brydon started having great difficulty in school. The previous year, his principal got moved to a new school and several parents were upset, including us. We were about to lose a great soul who cared deeply for his students and displayed a great balance of gentleness and strictness.

The new principal didn't have any previous experience. She was hired from her old position as a vice principal. She was clueless on how to deal with bullying in her school. Many parents started removing their kids from this, once, popular school.

Brydon was a minority. There were only six 'white' kids in the whole school, including him. The rest of the children were either Asian or Aboriginal.

His dad would tease him at home, and the kids would tease him at school. He started teasing himself and having suicidal thoughts. I stepped in as soon as he confided in me. He didn't know what to do anymore, and he was only ten years old. My heart was breaking!

I went, several times, to talk to the counsellor and the principal. They kept saying it was Brydon's fault. He over-reacted. He had to learn not to cause a scene when the children knocked him down, or snuck their own medication into his milk, etc. The staff had so many excuses. They, simply, didn't know how to get on top of bullying. They would bring the kids in for questioning, and these little ones would deny any involvement. Well of course they would! That's not how to deal with bullying!

I finally lost my patience with the principal. Her only solution was to get Brydon to not 'over-react.' One day, I responded, "Really, so you wouldn't cause a scene or 'over-react,' if one of your teachers came in and decided to punch you? I think you'd definitely react! The police would be called in!" I walked out! I was so frustrated with the system.

Brydon wasn't allowed to hang out with the teachers at break and lunch anymore, because then 'he would never learn to defend himself.' It went on and on, both the excuses and the bullying. I had called the school board and had made multiple trips to the school. I couldn't find a way through. Though that guidance might work for other children, depending on their personality, it wasn't working for Brydon. He had a gentle spirit and needed proper support.

As soon as they realized he'd made a 'suicidal' comment, the school suggested he get diagnosed from a psychiatrist. He saw one of the best in Edmonton. The psychiatrist diagnosed Brydon with Asperger's Syndrome—a high functioning form of Autism.

The psychiatrist brought all of us together into a room with Brydon's principal, teacher, and counsellor. (Except Brydon, of course) He asked the school how they were dealing with bullying. They made excuses and blamed Brydon, again.

After several minutes of listening, and right in front of them, he turned to me and asked, "They don't have a clue on how to deal with bullying in their school. Can you remove Brydon immediately, and start homeschooling him?"

I was dumbfounded! I thought they'd all gang up on me, including the psychiatrist. I didn't expect to have someone on my side. I answered, "Absolutely!"

I home-schooled Brydon for eighteen months. He stayed home for part of Grade 5 and all of Grade 6. I taught him a balance of spiritual values, principles, core subjects, and physical activity. I was lucky, because in Edmonton we have Argyll Home Schooling, where Brydon worked online and an actual teacher corrected his material and sent him new stuff to work on. He had to follow a curriculum and he had timelines to completion.

He loved it! He relaxed and his self-confidence grew. He was ready for Grade 7. Brydon went to Spruce Avenue and adjusted well. Around this time, he also joined Air Cadets. He entered their music program and excelled! During the next six summers, he got paid to go to camp and learn music for six whole weeks! He loved the structure, discipline, and the experience as a young leader. As a parent, I learned how important it is for young teenagers to be in a structured program, where they must give back to society and in doing so, learn fine leadership qualities.

During his last three years of school, he made it into Victoria School of Performing Arts and graduated there. He excelled in music and the baritone/alto saxophones.

He learned to follow his own groove and find unique friends that fit in with him.

Gabby and I have talked many times about our schools, and how we need to incorporate values at a young age. The kids are ready for them! They want them! They need them! Brydon is now guiding me, in much the same way Gabby used to. He blows me away with what comes out of his mouth. He is so stable and amazing! He is now the head of the Youth Group at our Centre and helps guide and shape the youth on becoming pure, radiant, virtuous, courageous, and open to helping others and their communities.

Recently, when they were practicing in a nearby park, many strangers came up and expressed how radiant and full of energy the Youth looked! They felt there was something beautiful and unique about these youth. The Youth had just finished picking up garbage all through the park, and were practicing some amazing marching skills.

Some parents have a hard time with kids marching. Gabby and I guide them, where possible, that marching is a way for the youth to bring together a powerful energy and to use it for a good purpose. For them, it's to promote the divine light. Marching is a powerful tool to unite the branches of a tree to its trunk. It generates a great spiritual power. The real question parents need to ask is: Who is the master of this particular tree? A great master leads great souls.

Once Brydon had settled into high school and was doing extremely well, I had an opportunity to put into actual practice some universal teachings, I had learned from Gabby.

I began working for a Call Center company. We assisted American customers with wireless phones. I started out on the ground floor and quickly moved up. Within two months, I was on the 'resolution' team. We were the ones who managed calls from angry customers. I became adept at calming them down and resolving the issue. Our team started having some problems, at the same time there were changes in management. Everybody was scared to come forward and speak up for fear of their job. The issues were not getting resolved and had actually escalated. I did NOT want to be the spokesperson. It was the last thing I wanted to do. This is why I knew it was going to be me. I had to move past the fear of speaking, to help my fellow peers.

I decided to come forward. It was around the same time they were having interviews for the Assistant Team Lead positions. I aced the test and did extremely well in the interview. I was sure I would get the job. They were looking for eight positions, and I knew that I scored well above most of the others.

After having sent multiple emails about the valid issues on our team and hearing nothing back in response, they finally called me into the office. They sat me down and instead of really listening to me about the issues at hand, they started grilling me, "Do you like your job here? Do you like stirring up trouble? Do you want to stay with us?"

What the heck? It was like stepping into the twilight zone! You know when you walk into a room and you are missing some vital information that everyone else has—I was missing something big here.

I ignored it and let them know that the issues were

valid and needed addressing. They already had the emails. They took notes, but I could see that nothing would be taken seriously.

Well, I had done my part and spoken up for the team. To me this was Spirit-First. I had done everything I could humanly do to help others, now I had to leave the rest up to God. If I lost my job, then that was divine arrangement too.

Well, even though I didn't know it at the time—this was the beginning of a huge miracle!

I didn't get the assistant job and I was devastated beyond!! All my friends got the position and were allowed to be off the phones taking care of their own teams while the Team Leads were away, etc. I was the only one left behind with a new group of 'resolution' specialists. This was a very difficult year, because I didn't think I would ever get the position. Another round of assistants was hired a few months later, and still I was overlooked. Finally, my friend asked the Supervisor in charge and he told her I was black-listed because they thought I was a racist.

What? I had friends from all over the world and loved them like family. Where was this coming from?

My friend, who had made it all the way up to Team Lead, dug into it a little further and found out that when I spoke up against management, they assumed that it was only because this Supervisor was an African Canadian. My friend immediately set them straight and told them that these issues were valid and that I was the ONLY brave person to come forward. They had to believe her because she was one of my peers, at that time, on the Resolution Team and she had been too scared to come forward as well. She felt terrible, once she found out the true reason. I believe she was able to find redemption by setting them straight.

This African-Canadian Supervisor brought me into his office and deeply apologized to me. He immediately gave me the Assistant position and then even went further and told me that he would prepare me for the interview for the Team Lead position. When we went over the interview, I was astounded at how it works on a point system and how many buzz words are needed to be said, to get the points. He told me exactly what to say.

Wow! I had no idea and would have NEVER been able to get the position on my own. There is no way I would have said what was needed and would have NEVER been considered. What a gift!

I went in front of two Supervisors and gave the best interview of my life! They were nodding and smiling and writing. Everyone was shocked that I got the highest points out of over 30 applicants.

I got one of the coveted positions!

So putting Spirit-First, seemed like it was the worst decision I ever did in the moment, but later turned out to be the greatest blessing! Wow!

The next principle I put into actual practice was The Principle of Echo-what we send out, comes back multiplied. I wanted to emphasize someone's good points and ignore their bad ones, then see the impact. I was curious to see how well it would work.

Within a couple of months of having my own team, I sent in a proposal to have a specialized 'Commitment' team offline doing research into accounts that needed a lot of time to fix. This team could also help with other offline work. They would only be making out-bound calls and not on the phones accepting any inbound. The Company loved the proposal! I worked closely with all fifteen employees. They became the best and happiest employees in the entire company! I even won a "Powered by the People" coveted award, that was open to all Supervisors both in Canada and the U.S. This was due to the success of my team members and their willingness to follow and unite as one unit. I could not accomplish this alone.

I taught my team not to be lazy, in the sense that we, especially as North Americans tend to be complacent and shy away from anything that hurts or is 'inconvenient.' As a society, we have trended towards wanting 'instant gratification' at any expense. Often, we think that blood, sweat, and tears are bad and should be avoided at all costs. We have become like little saplings, young trees that are easily knocked over at the slightest gust of wind.

I taught them that it is good to 'irritate,' like an oyster producing a priceless pearl from a simple grain of sand. The more we 'irritate' and move OUT of our comfort zone, the faster we build our character. We become strong, solid trees with deep roots. We increase our value as human beings and as employees.

I challenged my team once a week, at our Team Meetings, to read their experience stories of 'how did you move out of your comfort zone?' and 'what did you learn from it?' The change and growth in my team was phenomenal! They squirmed at first and tried to get out of writing them, but after a few months, I was amazed at how excited they were to share their growth and experiences!

My team became so successful that we doubled in size and required another Team Lead to assist me. I had a new boss, by this time, and he was a womanizer and didn't care about anything else. A couple of years later, six female employees handed in sexual harassment letters to HR against him. But in the meantime, he was my boss and I had to respect the title, if not the man.

He refused to look at the resumes and knew, even before the closing date on submissions, who he was going to pick. I had built a very close knit team. We would go through a wall for each other and sometimes we had done just that. I knew I would have to tell them who he picked and they weren't going to like it. This person was going to be their new boss, next to me.

He officially introduced Jean to the team. You could hear a pin drop. I quickly turned to face my team, and clapped my hands and whispered for them to do the same. They finally followed in a stunned fashion and congratulated her. They knew her and her reputation. She was mean and she had no idea how to run a team. She had openly admitted to having recently used 'crack cocaine' and she was nasty to whoever she was speaking with. The only thing going for her, at that point, was her physical beauty. I could see why my boss had a crush on her.

I quickly brought my team into a private room and told them that we had no choice. I stated that I would work with her and they had to give her a chance! At first, they weren't budging, but gradually they started to come around. They trusted me, not her. I had my work cut out for me.

I knew, without a doubt, that if I had written her off

right then, they would have too. I carried that much weight and respect with my team. It was a pivotal moment.

I directed Jean, "For the next 2 weeks, while you are waiting to come on board, I want you to go around every morning and say 'hi' to each member of the team. Do not reprimand them for anything! Ask them some questions about themselves and just listen!"

"Why do I need to do that?" she snapped.

"Because, you need to earn their trust!"

"Fine, whatever…okay!" She walked away.

I shook my head "Oh boy! This is going to be tough!" I thought.

She had a difficult time doing this, but she accomplished it. I was so proud of her! By the end of 2 weeks, they were actually teasing her and she was not reacting. I told her this was a good thing and she could tease them back.

What I realized, is that she wanted to learn 'people skills' from me, and she was a quick study. I taught her how to approach people and how to market their best attributes. I taught her how to give respect and that it needs to be earned and not just demanded.

I found out she was a whiz with computer programs and was able to produce some amazing ones that helped our team be more productive. This was what I needed to learn from her. I absorbed as much as I could and she was eager to teach me.

Through this amazing experience, I have learned that all difficult relationships are actually symbiotic opportunities for inner growth and powerful connections. Since God tore off a piece of His spiritual essence to create us, then it makes sense that the more we gather and unite our energies, the more God is present. This then produces a great power, like a master electrical puzzle being linked together. This is why it's so important not to give up and walk away. Blood, sweat, and tears are the universe's fire tools that help our souls become tempered, like a sword being repeatedly heated and cooled. We gain inner strength and are able to withstand anything that comes our way—we create a master sword that is priceless. Our souls emerge with an inner strength that is both graceful and powerful—but only if we approach it with true gratitude and fortitude!

I purposely focused on only the positive in her and it brought out the positive in all of us! The energy opened up and expanded beyond what I thought possible! I was practicing the Universal Principle of Echo—what is sent out, comes back multiplied. I loved it! What a powerful tool!

It took a team of misfits to see and accept the eccentricities of another misfit and accept her into the fold. They just needed a little push in a positive direction! Isn't this what the human experience is all about? None of us are perfect, we are all misfits in one way or another.

In the end, when everyone moved on, she went from being the most feared and the meanest supervisor to one of the best loved and most missed. She moved into the Tax Department with the City and combines her love of numbers with her newfound expertise as a Supervisor. I wish her all the best! I'm so grateful to her.

Within this spiritual path, I have learned that when we set out to help others, we are stepping into foreign territory. We need to move out of our comfort zone and into that person's zone. If we are able to do this effectively, then the lines blur on who is helping whom. This is the truly altruistic form of service, because every single human being can teach each other something. If we allow ourselves to become vulnerable, and to be open to the experience, then our ego disappears. We need to know that the initial feeling of irritation will pass, as long as we push through and don't run from it.

We have to be careful NOT to put ourselves above that person and think we are better than they are. If we think that we are only here to help or fix THEM, then we have immediately separated ourselves from them and from the universe. Not only does this thought separate us, but it prevents us from receiving a divine arrangement from the unseen realm. We, both, lose the chance to receive a precious spiritual nugget. I am learning that separation and division affect all the realms.

This is where 'humility' is put into actual practice; where we completely ignore any and all *negative* qualities of that person, 'I bow to your divinity and I speak only to the God-spark that exists within you. I'm open to any and all outcomes. Let's move forward together.'

I have learned that even though I may have the knowledge and the intense desire to practice these teachings, it is NOT easy. This is not an easy path. It is because it is so hard, that we are being stretched spiritually. It's like working out in the gym. If we go and lift ten pound weights forever, we will never see a change. We won't sweat or hurt at all; but, likewise we won't change at all. Sometimes, people lift ten pound weights forever, and then complain that nothing is getting better in their lives; that they don't see any miracles or amazing divine arrangements. It's only when we embrace the difficulty, and search for a Spirit-First way through, without giving up, that we spiritually become stronger. It is in the journey, that we grow.

We have to willingly take on more difficult, spiritual, challenges to grow our spirit. Then the divine arrangements that unfold in our lives are awe-inspiring!

Whether we ask or not, the universe will always give us many opportunities to put into actual daily practice the three great virtues of gratitude, humility, and acceptance. It's just more fun and intriguing when you know what to do with them.

Chapter 5

Doug and I went through a second intense period of scrubbing. Communication between us improved, but we still had a long way to go. We drifted apart. He got hired with Edmonton Transit and drove bus at all hours of the day and night. We rarely saw each other, and when we did, it was like we were roommates. He still didn't know how to support me emotionally, and I still didn't know how to support him physically—interesting, that our upbringings molded us in these opposite ways.

Gabby has guided me, many times, that the unseen realm brings together things and people of 'opposite nature,' to practice 'uniting together in loving harmony.' This is what true balance in the universe is all about. It's not easy. It's not supposed to be easy. The more difficult it is, the more sweet the victory. Extreme heat and cold temper a great and priceless sword. Blood, sweat, and tears temper the human to be a great and worthy soul.

That all seemed like 'hogwash' to me, while I was in the middle of it. But, okay, it helped me to not give up and quit. The unseen realm knew that was all I needed.

Doug and I went further into our corners and became more extreme in our behaviours. We were both so hurt that neither of us would budge, at least not then.

We had great egos! Therefore, it only stands to reason that for us to unite as ONE, we would've generated a lot of power.

Again, Gabby's voice comes to the forefront, "Our worst enemies are our greatest allies. The 'attaching spirits' of the unseen realm, try to cause discourse so that a union never happens, because they know a great power will be generated if we harmonize! Of course, they don't want that! This is why it's so important to never give up finding a way to 'harmonize' with the people we are feuding with. If we hang in there and don't give up, our 'guardian spirits' will show us a way through, and we will see a divine miracle."

Gratitude, humility and acceptance are the three great virtues that the unseen realm, constantly, gives us training and opportunities to practice. Since our egos were so great, the unseen realm had to give Doug and me, a lot of humility training to break them down.

Remember I talked about pain earlier on, and how I had to build a relationship with it? I had no idea at this time, what was going on with me. I just knew that I was in tremendous pain and had to go to emergency on several occasions. I remember my inordinate fear and panic around the pain. It made the pain worse. I can't deny there was a physical problem, but I had an unusual intense response to it. I, always, thought I was dying and that the medical system was inadequate and couldn't locate the problem. There was this built in trigger that would go off, at the first sign of pain. It was shockingly effective in shutting down my 'common sense' detector and raising the alarm bells. Pain—Panic! Pain—Panic! Pain—Panic!

I'm a drug addict. I will be for the rest of my life. I can cope with it now. I work on it daily. I know, now, that I was seeking an external 'womb of love' whenever life became too painful. If anyone had told me this at the time, I would have thought they were crazy. Even the doctors eventually found my last ovary twisted and adhered to my bowel. They agreed that I would have been in a lot of pain.

However, between you and me, my innermost attitude at the time was to run away and succumb to the sweet tide of painkillers. That was easier then dealing with someone who refused to emotionally support me.

I, finally, decided to get some help with my drug addiction. I worked for the City of Edmonton and they had a new program. I came forward and asked for support. Because this was a fairly new program, they were pretty naïve to the difference between drug addiction and pain management. Prior to going through this program, I didn't know the difference, either.

My doctor had put me on Oxycontin and every time the pain increased, he increased the amount. Pretty soon, I noticed I had holed up in the bedroom. I had reverted back to the way I was years ago. I felt my soul dying, again. I knew I had to get off these potent killers. I was on such a high dose, that I had no idea what sort of 'real' pain I had.

They instructed me to come off everything! I had to be completely clean before entering the program, which meant I had to go to AADAC for five days first. I decided to come off at home instead, but was forced to do the five days, anyway.

I walked into AADAC without my divine pendant. I had to keep it safe at home. I was terrified to go, because we had to sleep in a ward with many people in rough shape. I didn't need to worry, because once I went off everything, I couldn't sleep for three weeks, because of the intense pain in my neck and back.

I had offered a prayer, at home, for Humility training, with great hopes that I would succeed.

I walked in and a nurse assessed me. They felt that I was actually in good shape, even though I hadn't slept for four days. They allowed me into the back and I entered the activities. The first night, my blood pressure skyrocketed and they decided to move me back to the front. Well, this is where they kept all the active drunks until they've dried out, having just come in off the street. They gave me a double dose of Valium and put me on a stretcher, in the middle of the room. I couldn't believe it, but I slept soundly for two hours.

I woke up listening to a commotion, and opened my eyes to a seven foot tall First Nation's man, with an extreme case of scarring on his face, becoming agitated and sparing with the nurse, like a bear on a hound. He was coming down off multiple drugs and not coping well. He was throwing out, crumpled, $100 bills from his pockets and he wanted to leave.

I closed my eyes very quickly and prayed to be anywhere else, but here.

I remembered my humility prayer, and opened my eyes again. I sat up on the edge of the stretcher. He noticed me, immediately. I looked directly into his eyes. I took a deep breath and said, "It's okay! I know how difficult this is!"

He got up and that's when I realized just how big he was. I had a moment of fear, but I pushed it away and, instead, sent loving vibrations towards him. As he lurched towards me, I held out my arms and gave him the most intense hug, "You can get through this. This horrible feeling is only temporary. It will get so much better!" I quietly spoke into his ear.

As I hugged him, I felt his tremors instantly stop and a river of calm move through him. I felt this powerful surge of energy move through me, to him. He sat down and shook his head. The nurse used that moment to check my blood pressure. It was normal. I knew it would be, because my training, at the front, was completed. She sent me to the back.

I saw him, the next day, talking to other people at a table. He was telling them he had witnessed an 'angel' who had hugged him, and that was why he was still there. He didn't recognize me. I didn't think he would, once he came down off the drugs.

After five days at AADAC, I was sent to a program for women in Calgary. I started working out and walking twice a day, while I was there. I still couldn't sleep. I would fall asleep in the group therapy sessions, sitting up. I noticed that the other women would talk about partying and seeing multiple doctors for prescriptions, etc. Though that didn't fit for me, I listened to the rest of it with interest.

After not sleeping for two weeks, they sent me to their doctor. The women advised me that I would hate him. He was 80 years old and had been working with these types of women for over 35 years, they advised me. You can't fool him, they said. I actually liked him. He looked over my MRI and CT scans and checked my neck and back. He advised me that I was in the wrong program. He said I needed to be in a 'pain management' program. He wrote a note for me and within a week, I left the program early.

I entered a pain management program in Edmonton.

I learned that I needed to manage some very serious pain, but I needed different drugs and I didn't need such high doses. They had researched narcotics and they found that the Bu-trans patch (buprenorephine) kept the brain chemicals steady and still worked on the pain. I didn't get that euphoric high and then the major crash. I started with these patches and was able to get the proper rest and sleep. I still use them today, and I'm so grateful to have gotten off some heavy duty drugs. I went into therapy, and was ready to engage with the world, again.

Shortly after coming home, I was reading my emails and one got returned. The system had been trying to send it multiple times, but one letter in the email address had been typed wrong.

This, one, wrong letter was used by the unseen realm to draw my attention to something of massive importance:

As I'm reading the email, the floor starts falling out from under my feet. I lose my bearing! My nose burns as I try to hold back the tears. I can't hold them back. If I start, the dam will break!

This can't be. I'm sliding down the rabbit hole, again!

I stare off into space for a moment.

I look back at the letter and read it over and over. It's from my husband and it's not addressed to me!

"Dear Jane! I miss you! I have fallen in love with you! I can't wait until we're together, again. Brydon will graduate soon, and then I will feel more comfortable leaving Judy on her own. Please let me know when I can see you. Love, Doug."

The letter is so much longer, but these are the words I

focus on.

I never saw the signs! Dear God, what is happening? He is my anchor!

It pierces my heart, as I'm tossed about in the ocean currents.

Now, the tears are flowing... for all that is truly lost.

I called Doug and confronted him. What could he say? Here is the interesting thing. He never even kissed her. He met her and went out with her several times to talk. When she found out he was married, she stopped it. She didn't want to be with him, while we were together. Yet, he thought he was in love with her. I wrote her a letter thanking her for her discretion.

Any love I had left, for Doug, died. I wasn't even angry with him anymore. I wanted a divorce. What existed in the past was:

DEAD... DONE... FINISHED... FLATLINED... OVER...

Donna, actually, guided me NOT to make any decisions until we got back from Montreal. It turned out that the spiritual leader would be traveling there and we could 'shake hands' with him. On the unseen realm, the deities use that moment to strengthen our 'spiritual cords' and we would experience a huge spiritual shift. In other words, many miracles would happen, after.

I held no belief that this would work, but decided it didn't matter. Everything could wait a week. Doug and I flew down to Montreal. It was a historical time for all of Canada. Well over 200 people participated. When the gentleman entered, I felt a wave of light spread across the room. It was like I was floating in another realm!

Upon arriving home, we had a serious conversation.

This is so hard to explain, but I felt a massive shift in my thinking and being. I, all of a sudden, got it. I got my part in it. I got that we had moved to opposite extremes because of our egos. I got that our languages of love were not being met. I got that I had become the 'ice queen' to him and his soul was withering and dying, just like mine. I was able to truly stand on his rock and view his world.

Wow! This is why, Gabby says, we as humans have NOT been given the authority to judge, good or bad, because our scope of view is so narrow and limited. Even, when we step back and gain a broader view, we still miss so much! All we can ever say, for sure, is that 'a positive result will come out the other end of it.' How long that may take, is not up to us. Our only responsibility is TO NEVER GIVE UP!! TO FIND A WAY THROUGH!

I humbly and deeply apologized to Doug. I, also, established a good balance of great love. This part was important. I let him know he was deceitful, and he had a huge mountain to climb to regain my trust. I let him know, I would help him; but, I expected full cooperation and emotional support in return. He sincerely apologized and fully agreed. Though I had heard that before, this felt different…

The unseen realm knew we had a great mountain to climb, and we needed to accomplish it together.

Cancer was knocking on our door.

Section 6

Death

Chapter 1

Doug's reaction to pain was the exact opposite of mine. He ignored it and hoped it would go away. It didn't. He'd been having pain on his right side for a few months.

His routine blood-test showed his prostate (PSA) levels were extremely high. He endured more testing, and they found a tumor pushing through his bladder, which was preventing his right kidney from functioning. It had started in his prostate. The day he went for a routine test, the doctor advised us that he had to be admitted right away, 'because of the Cancer.' We went into immediate shock, like getting hit with a sledgehammer! Is that how you tell someone they have cancer? He thought we already knew. Well, that was nice of him to assume.

Doug was, immediately, admitted to the Misercordia Hospital, so they could put in a tube, to help drain the urine from his kidney. They also performed a biopsy of his prostate. One in ten thousand, go into septic shock from this procedure. (13 little biopsies are taken at one time, and they enter through the bowel wall) Doug happened to be the one. He spiked a 42 degree fever and they had to move him to ICU. For the first 24 hours, we weren't sure if he was going to make it. Then, the IV antibiotics knocked out the infection, and he recovered quickly. He was sent home three days after this episode.

He was advised to take a hormone that would stop his prostate from producing testosterone. Effectively, they call it 'medical castration.'

He went on the hormone and within two months, he

was emotional and 'tear infested,' as he'd describe it. He completely changed. He wrote a short experience story about how he, finally, was able to climb on his wife's rock, and that the view from there was extraordinary! In the past, he stated, he had so much rage and testosterone that he couldn't see anything, beyond anger and sex. He entered a new world of emoting and feeling. He liked how he could see my side, but hated how he no longer felt 'like a man.' He was stuck between two worlds.

He decided he wanted to live his last few months as a man, so he stopped his hormone treatments. However, he never forgot his experience, as a 'gal.'

He surprised me. He started going to the Center on his own, without me! He had never done this before. He started offering tremendous amounts of 'divine service.' He started putting others first. He boasted of his love for me to anyone who would listen!

He still had his fierce competition streak. I always taught Brydon to cheer for whoever won the game, especially if it wasn't him. Brydon didn't like any games that had a loser. He was into win-win only. His dad, however, loved competition and winning. One day, the director of our Centre, Rocky, challenged him to her famous, home-made hot-sauce. She is on a life mission to engineer sauce that is exceptionally hot!

Doug took the challenge, of course, and swallowed a teaspoon full, with great gusto! Within seconds, his face turned beet red! He started sweating, profusely! Everyone asked if he was alright, and he refused to complain, although he couldn't speak, he just nodded his head. Actually, I was proud of him, he refused to admit it was too hot.

The next day, he confided in me that it hurt so bad, he thought he was going to pass out, then to make matters worse, he said it 'burned like a bloody bugger coming out the other end!'

He was the first to laugh and the last to cry. He was a man who lived with intense loss, and intense pain. He was a man that I fell madly and deeply in love with, finally.

Many will ask, "Why didn't the light save him?" Well, it did! Most definitely! Without a doubt! He even agreed, through a medium, which I'll explain, in detail, later.

His innermost attitude completely changed, and his soul elevated because of it. I know that our 'lives' continue on in the Astral World. That is our true home. This is like a vacation home. We spend 200-300 years there and only 60-80 years here.

I wish to share with you the most beautiful stories around his journey to the astral world. I believe all the amazing arrangements occurred because he changed and spiritually awakened. Some of us are needed more in the astral world to be of service, and some are needed, here, on earth.

Within a year of getting diagnosed, the Cancer spread to his bones. He was on high levels of painkillers. He was admitted to one of the major hospitals in Edmonton, because his permanent 'urine' bag was getting clogged with blood clots and he had an ongoing infection. They kept him there for 2 weeks, in a tiny, 2 person room. It was so small, you could barely fit a chair next to his bed. He room was also right beside the nurses' station and extremely noisy. Also, his neighbor was noisy.

It wasn't a place to get any type of rest. Plus, the nurses were always busy, and many were rather abrupt. I could tell they were burnt out, but I still wished for their best efforts with my husband.

I didn't want to take him home. I didn't have the physical strength to support him. He was 300 pounds and had fallen several times. I asked them about palliative care and they said he didn't qualify, because it had to be within the last 3 months of his life. Well, who decides that? As it turned out, he was in the last 2 weeks of his life.

I was so angry with them! They discharged him without proper support! They even dumped him by the outer door, to wait for me, to come pick him up. I was furious! They don't normally do this in Alberta. Usually the support is amazing, throughout all the hospitals. I was dumbfounded!

It was a huge divine arrangement, when they discharged him and forgot about him. Go figure! The unseen realm was supporting Doug, and taking very good care of him. They had an amazing plan in place, I just hadn't figured it out, yet.

Again, Gabby's voice was ringing in my ears, "Often, what we think of as bad, from our human point of view, turns out to be the source of something good. This is why it's so important to offer gratitude for everything!"

Yes, Gabby, thank you very much!

Doug was determined to go to the Secondary Course in Vancouver, which was taking place two weeks after he was discharged from the hospital. I figured out, later, that he was acting a lot tougher and stronger than he really was, just so he could go. I had given him guidelines that the only way he could travel, was if he showed he was strong enough to see it through. He wanted this more than anything he ever wanted. He was determined to go.

A week before the trip, we were sitting at a Japanese restaurant and he started crying, out of the blue. Big fat tears started gathering speed down his cheeks.

Before he said anything, I spoke, "Oh my gosh! I actually feel your mom and sister here! I sense your sister has grown up in the Astral world. I feel her energy as an adult! This is bizarre!"

Suddenly and mysteriously, I had felt their presence. His sister passed away at six years old, yet I felt her energy come through as an adult. If she was still alive, she would have been 46 years old.

He peered over his glasses, which were now soaked in tears, "I miss them so much! I feel them here!" I reached over and lovingly removed his glasses, as his belly was shaking, betraying his intense sorrow!

I cleaned his glasses with my shirt, knowing I would have to do the same with mine, as my tears had joined in. I got up and hugged him, deeply.

Later, when I saw a medium, she backed up our story. Though, I didn't need her to, it was very refreshing.

Just before a person passes on, it feels like the veil thins between the physical and astral realms. Often, before people pass, they will have paranormal events happen, and temporarily see loved ones waiting for them on the other side. During these times, there is so much preparation happening in the Astral World, it is like the door is cracked open and small amounts of energy escape from one realm to the next. This was why both of us could, out of nowhere, feel his family come through, for that precious moment.

This journey, for Doug, was an extremely painful one, but I saw his soul come alive for the first time, ever. He was letting go of old hurts. His inner strength blew me away. He had bone cancer and every movement hurt, yet he was focused on walking up and down two flights of stairs, everyday, at the Centre, to go and give sessions of light to others. In the past, he would go only with me, and only to receive. His sorrow and apology were bone deep, when offering prayers.

A month prior to our trip, I felt a strong urge to invite his best friend, Cris, to fly into Vancouver and be there to watch Doug receive his very special, divine pendant. Cris didn't want to bother us and he didn't have the money. The urge was so strong, I wouldn't take no for an answer. I had extra air-miles, so I used those to purchase him a two day ticket. Done deal, he was coming. He was excited!

The day arrived for our trip. Doug, I, a friend of ours, Serena, and Brydon drove to Vancouver in our Dodge caravan. Doug stayed in the front passenger seat and we made frequent stops so he could have a smoke. Yes, even in the end he craved them. We figured at this point, he might as well, thoroughly, enjoy them.

He followed our conversations through the mountains and seemed mentally stable, throughout the trip. He loved the Rocky Mountains! The first night in Vancouver, he stayed with my son and another member in a room, next to us girls. The following morning, I had three guys help me move him into the van. He seemed to be a lot weaker than the day before. He spent the first day of the course in a wheelchair they provided for us.

The next morning, he was not mentally present. I walked into the room and he was smiling into space and not moving. I had to coax him and dress him. Serena and I, managed to pull him onto the floor of the van. All the men had left the hotel earlier, for a short walk to the Centre. We contacted them via cell-phone and they managed to get him into the wheelchair outside the Centre. That morning, all the candidates were to receive the 'main soul' point for 10 minutes. I gave Doug light and noticed that he refused to follow directions. He had a permanent 'vacant' smile.

I started to panic, and Donna, who was reviewing the course, walked over and put her hand on my shoulder. Instantly, I calmed down. After I finished giving him light, the staff informed me that it was imperative we take him to the hospital.

I was in denial. I advised them that perhaps it was just the infection again and all he needed was some more antibiotics. I agreed to take him, but informed staff that we would be back for the next day.

The ambulance brought us both to the hospital. The last thing Doug said to me was, "I feel strange!" He lapsed into a coma.

Chapter 2

The doctor on duty was a beautiful lady, and she watched me holding Doug's hand for a moment and then spoke, "You know, I have a good friend who is the doctor in Palliative Care upstairs. Normally, it takes a few months to get moved to this ward, but I know they have a room just opened up. Perhaps, we can get your husband in there. It's a slim chance, but I will try." At that moment, I had no idea how large that offer was, but I was grateful.

We got accepted. This is unheard of. Within three hours of being in Emergency, in a different province, Doug got wheeled into the most beautiful, private, room I had ever seen. The whole unit was extraordinary! Her friend, Dr. Williams, greeted us right away. Doug's new room was 5 times the size of the rooms in the Edmonton hospital! (In Edmonton, there were no private rooms that we knew of)

This one even had a built-in bed for family, right under a beautiful, bay window looking out over the mountains. It had hardwood floors and a solid wood hutch with a flat-screen TV. Even the hospital bed had an expensive air mattress. It was better than a 5 Star hotel. What was even more exquisite, than all of the beautiful surroundings, were the nurses and doctor. The doctor was always available at the front desk. But, it was the nurses that moved me to tears. They were extraordinary in their gentleness and care!

This was a Saturday afternoon. The doctor sat me down in a beautiful, private sitting room. She could tell I was in denial. She was gentle, and persistent at the same time. Doug was not leaving here and may not even make it through the weekend, she advised me. Probably, he wouldn't even wake up again. She showed me his MRI scan of his brain, he had recently. It showed that the brain had shrunk considerably from the Cancer. She was shocked that they had discharged him in Edmonton!

On Sunday, his best friend Cris arrived and stayed at the hospital with Doug. We both realized the great divine arrangement that had occurred to have Cris there, because neither of us had any money to have flown him in later. He wouldn't have made it. Cris watched over Doug with great love, attending to all his needs. He called me that morning, while I was at the hotel, and handed the phone over to Doug. Doug had woken up from his coma! He just thought he'd been sleeping. He wanted a smoke! I laughed and let him know that probably wasn't going to happen.

Cris shared with me what had occurred. He was in Doug's washroom cleaning up, when the nurse walked in, smelling the air. The nurse had walked up and down the hallway, smelling a strong odour of 'Nag Champa.' It's an incense that, supposedly, Sai Baba used. He's a famous Indian Guru. The nurse walked into Doug's room and said to Cris, "This is the strongest spot! I smell Nag Champa and it's coming from here! Well hello, Doug! How are you?"

Doug had just woken up from his coma. Cris told me that if someone brings this essence back with them, they are arriving from a great and holy place. Cris, also, smelled it as he stepped out of the washroom.

Interesting, I thought. I had no idea what this incense was. I had never heard of it before.

I walked into the room and almost cried when Doug gazed at me. He was smiling, and he recognized me! He was very quiet and mostly just observed us. Within a couple of hours, he slipped back into a 'light' coma. The nurse explained that though he wasn't waking up with painful stimuli, his body still responded to it.

Later that evening, he woke up again, just in time to say good-bye to many of our friends who were heading back to Edmonton. Plus, due to the conference, we had several staff come and gave Doug light. He was bathing in everyone's love and kindness.

Cris had to head back to Edmonton, and was able to say good-bye to his best buddy. I cried when the two hugged. It would be for the last time.

Monday morning, the nurses advised me that he had slipped back into a deeper coma through the night, and they thought he wouldn't wake up this time. I hadn't had a chance to be alone with him and say my good-byes.

Then, Gabby showed up around 1 pm on Monday. She had rearranged her trip to come and stay with Doug! She started giving him light and singing special prayers. She continued for the next 10 hours, non-stop! She was our angel! I was too emotionally and physically drained to focus on giving him light, so the unseen realm brought Gabby!

Doug woke up one final time. I was able to have precious time alone with him and Brydon. I knew this would be the last time. I said to him, "You know, you are going to the Astral World, but you will be well supported. We will all give you light as you pass and you will have your Omitama there, so you can give light too."

Doug, very gently, like a child, replied, "I wish I'd been a better parent to Brydon!" His tears rained down.

I wiped them away and replied, "It's okay! I think you two were brothers in a previous life and you had to go through training together in this one. You need to let this go and offer gratitude! Brydon totally forgives you!"

Brydon nodded his head up and down, his face full of tears too, "I do, dad."

"Okay!" Doug meekly replied.

I hugged him and kissed him on the forehead. He slipped into his final coma.

Doug's 2 kids showed up late in the afternoon, after having traveled from Kelowna.

I noticed something very interesting. As Doug received light, he began to sweat and his body was discharging a tremendous amount of toxins. We were changing his nightgown, once every 20 minutes as it was wringing wet. Finally after five hours of this, he stopped sweating completely and went bone dry. His breathing also changed. The nurses advised that it would only be a few more hours.

The nurses removed his oxygen and his IV bag.

After a few hours, he was still hanging in there, so Brydon and the kids, stepped out with me to have supper. Gabby stayed with Doug.

Chapter 3

On August 2, 2011, Gabby called us at 9:27 pm and advised us to return as quickly as possible. Doug had taken his final breath. They say this often happens, where the soul will pass while the family is not present, to make it easier on them.

We arrived within minutes. His daughter lost it. She fell to the floor next to the bed and started pulling on his arm and screaming. The rest of us tried to focus on giving him light, during those crucial first few minutes. The staff of our Centre arrived within 10 minutes and brought his Holy Pendant.

I felt the shift in the air, as soon as they placed it around his neck. Even his daughter quieted. It was like HE was giving US light from the Astral World! I was blown away.

Also, the staff of our Centre took me to a private room and advised me that Doug would be of 'great' service in the Astral World. They indicated that he had a great mission and I would see it.

When I was finally alone with him, I got the nurses help to put his clothes on. I noticed immediately how thin his legs were and how easily I could lift them! Just that morning, they had a routine of putting fresh pillows under his legs because the swelling was so intense, and the legs had felt like a hundred pounds each. He was admitted in this condition.

It, then, made sense where all the toxins had come from. I kid you not, his legs had NO swelling and NO edema. They looked beautiful! Even the nurses were shocked and amazed!

British Columbia is one hour behind Alberta. So precisely, 10:27 several people back at home had extraordinary experiences! We had a set of identical twins who were members, and they were extra sensitive. One of them was in bed with her husband and he happened to glance at the clock, when she started mumbling in her sleep about a guy named Doug, and that he would have an amazing journey! Precisely 10:27! She saw her sister's text the next morning, and her husband shared his observation from the night before.

Also, the director of our Centre, turned to her husband and said she felt like Doug had just passed. Precisely 10:27! She then got a text from Brydon indicating this, a few minutes later.

Also, another friend felt his passing and immediately offered a prayer for him. These two shared the same birthday, right down to the same year. She said in that moment she was transported out of her kitchen and was standing next to Doug. She remembers smelling an ancient incense but didn't know what it was. She had NO idea he was even in the hospital or had passed away at that moment. She didn't find out until a couple of days later.

Here's where a lot of cool things started happening one after another. We were broke. We had bad credit. We had saved the last penny to go to Vancouver and we were in such denial, that we hadn't prepared for a funeral.

Here I was devastated and penny-less. Though members attempted to pitch in and we were so grateful, $240 wasn't going to help with cremation. The cheapest was $1400.

Two members, a husband and a wife, who usually keep to themselves, sat down next to me at the hospital, on the Sunday, and asked what help I needed. At first I didn't respond and they repeated it, saying they knew I probably needed money. I explained that I would be getting some money with his insurance, but not for weeks.

They, generously, lent us $4000, without batting an eye. What would we've done? I couldn't get a loan, because of bad credit. I can't even imagine how horrible it would've been. There were no other options. We had no other family, and his kids were broke. My son and I even had to help his kids with gas so they could come.

The unseen realm sent angels to help us. We didn't even ask. This still blows me away, thinking about it! They know who they are. From the bottom of my heart, to the moon and back, thank you so very much!!!!

We had to wait several days for the ashes from the cremation. So we moved out of the hotel and into my birth dad's apartment. I had met him a few years earlier and though we didn't communicate a lot, he offered to give us a place to stay. To make a long story short on this one, I had also located my birth mom, but she had passed away, long before I could meet her.

While we were waiting, Brydon and I went to Grouse Mountain, and in honor of his dad, we went zip-lining. Wow! I loved it! There was a point where the fog had rolled in and all I could see was the line ahead of me and it felt like I had entered the Astral Realm with Doug. I felt his presence so strong!

We brought his ashes home to Edmonton, nine days

later.

I've been taught that the spirit remains on earth for up to 49 days, to say good-bye and let go of any attachments they have. Then a guide takes them to the Astral realm to begin a different type of training. If they refuse to go to the Astral realm, then they become 'earth-bound' or 'attaching' spirits. This usually happens when they know their training will be unbearable in the Astral world—they try to escape it.

During the 49 days, whenever Doug's spirit was present, I felt a sudden shift in the atmosphere and I would feel his unique 'character.' Suddenly, I would be bathed in liquid warmth, from head to toe. The constant pain in my hip and back would magically disappear.

It was a unique sensation, and it would only last while he was in the room. As soon as he disappeared, my pain would return with a vengeance and I would feel devastatingly alone! Because the change was so drastic, I felt it, like a knife wound! It was sharp! It took my breath away.

If anyone tried to tell me this, I would say they were imagining it, because they wanted it so bad.

Too many of my senses were being activated during these 'episodes.' I didn't expect it. Also, I never pined over him. There were times when I was extremely busy, and not thinking of him, and he would surprise the hell out of me, when he popped up! Also, others would call me and respond with a multitude of their own experiences.

I remember the very first time, I felt Doug's presence so strongly.

Brydon and I, were still in Vancouver, waiting for

Doug's ashes. We were at my dad's place and he was at work for the day. My dad was a typical bachelor, and his house was extremely dark and dirty. I felt Doug's energy so strong, one day I decided to offer a 'divine service' to materialize my gratitude to my birth dad, on behalf of Doug and me. I cleaned his bathroom, but I also cleaned the 'energy' in it.

I felt Doug giving light at the same time as me, and I wept tears of joy! It was an intense bonding moment. I didn't expect this, and it was extremely weird, but I felt closer to Doug during these 49 days, then ever before.

My study class, below, explains what happened in my dad's washroom. Within a month of returning to Edmonton, I was asked to hold a study class at the Centre. I decided to pull this one together, to honor Doug, and I felt his soul supporting me, all the way through.

This study class holds a very special place in my heart!

Another opportunity to practice Spirit-First:

The Ability to Affect the Spiritual Imprint of an Object or Room

This begins with understanding, again, that we communicate 90% of the time in the unseen realm, and that everything is made up of energy.

Objects accumulate Spiritual impurities from a multitude of things, such as the environment, people, nature, etc. When a place does not get cleaned for a long time, it exudes clutter and dirt and can cause someone to feel depressed, and they don't have a clue why.

Also, that depression, negativity, swearing, shouting, etc. are vibrations that enter the spiritual patterns of whatever is nearest. So the wood, chrome, metal, etc. absorbs these energies and casts a cloudy energy back. Likewise, any positive vibrations also enter and create the opposite effect.

We have the ability to change this imprint and affect someone's destiny, without them even knowing.

First, we need to discuss the subject of 'service.' This can range from giving a present to someone with strings attached, even if we don't openly admit it; to offering something to someone, altruistically (anonymously) so they benefit in a massive way. This continuum is infinite.

If we change it to 'divine' service, (Don't get caught up in the words, it's just another word for the energy of the spiritual realm) we are offering 90% of it in the unseen realm:

As an option (not necessary) we can first offer a prayer to send it out to the universe. (Again remember that prayer is just very concentrated thought, bringing the energy waves into concentrated form.) We can ask the universe (or God) to accept our 'service that we are about to offer' either for ourselves or on behalf of someone that may be going through a hard time, etc.

<u>The most important part</u>: Does everyone hate cleaning their house? Here is the way to change it and make it something very meaningful: Do it as 'divine service' instead and immediately see the difference. Take your cleaning supplies and thank them, very much, for their hard work and ask them to work hard for you. Whatever you are cleaning, offer a "thank you!" to it every second you are cleaning. (To keep from being bored, I try to say 'thank you' in multiple languages.)

You have to be absolutely present in every moment when doing this. You are literally sending wave after wave vibrations of **gratitude** into the object while you are cleaning it!!! Think of all the people who had a hand in making it, from the farmers, to the truckers, to the warehousemen, etc. and thank all of them.

This energy that you are sending into the object literally changes the "spiritual imprint" of it, and eliminates all the impurities that it once contained.

The cool thing is that the next person who comes into contact or into the vicinity of the object or room will experience amazing vibrations. They will suddenly feel happy, lighter, brighter, etc. The room will even change and feel brighter and lighter, even sound emitted in the room will come out crisper and sharper. Etc. A buoyancy effect will happen.

You can also offer this anywhere!! I did it one time for my birth dad and he couldn't get over what I had done and said that he couldn't understand why every time he went into the bathroom, he wanted to sing and hadn't felt that way in years. I only was able to offer this in his washroom!!! He had no idea that I offered it as 'divine service.'

If you offer a prayer at the beginning, then remember to offer a closing one when you are done and ask the universe to accept this as divine service, etc.

This type of spiritual imprinting can be done with anything, anywhere, and at anytime AND it is always free and unlimited!!!!! Also, what you send out comes back a hundred fold!!!

Enjoy going out and offering true 'divine service!!'

Chapter 4

His memorial service was held on September 10, 2011 at the McDougall United Church in Edmonton. I knew he had grown up in Strome and had been baptised in his family's United Church. (His mom's maiden name was McDougall)

There were over 150 people in attendance. His co-workers had set up a memorial page on Facebook. I was astounded at the flurry of activity on the site. All his kids were present. I lost it, emotionally, when a representative of the Edmonton Pipes and Drums walked in playing the bag pipes! What a haunting sound!

One of our friends, who is very open to other realms, told us a story, which, at first, sounded crazy. She said she went into her garage, where there is no wind and she lit up a cigarette for herself and offered one to Doug. She said the end of his cigarette went deeply red, as if he were puffing on it. She then had a brief conversation with him. He told her to tell me that yes, he and Brydon had been brothers in a previous life and that, now, he was allowed to help many people. I was blown away! Brydon and I never shared a word of our last conversation with Doug, to anyone!! Brydon never opens up anyway, let alone talk about something so deeply personal.

Another friend, on the day we were driving home, said she kept seeing him riding this crazy jet plane all over the world, helping people. Well, on the way back, suddenly, Brydon and I couldn't get this crazy song out of our heads, "Riding on a Jet Plane."

The following is the most amazing story. My friend, Rose, had been a member for 20 years. I had guided her many years ago. She wasn't very active and she would, usually, only come to the Centre with me. She decided to quit, completely, and we lost contact with her for 2 years.

Five weeks before Doug passed, her daughter ran into us, and confided that her father had committed suicide in the hospital. We were devastated. Doug wanted to sit outside the hospital and direct divine light towards it, to help her husband. I watched Doug use the walker to painfully walk the half block to a bench, across from the hospital, where we sat down and started radiating light.

Her husband had been taken to the hospital because he had ingested a bottle of sleeping pills. He'd had a history of mental illness. This time, the hospital had closed down their locked ward, where the nurse watches constantly through the glass. The psychiatric nurses would come into his room for a check, only, every 15 minutes. Late at night, he used a cord from his pajamas and hung himself. There was a public inquiry, and hopefully it resulted in some, much needed, changes in their procedures.

I remember the day was Sept 12th, in the afternoon. I felt Doug's spirit come and I asked him to go find her husband. I felt him return twice and indicate that he couldn't find him, than on the third try, I felt a resounding 'yes.' Doug had located him and had given him light. This may seem absolutely crazy, but I got confirmation, later, from Rose.

Rose and I connected for the first time in over two years. We both cried and I gave her a full session of light. She went from being a broken shell, to finding some peace. I could see the shift in her aura. She confided in me that something happened on Sept 12th. She had a golden retriever, Buddy, who would act a certain way, only around Doug. (Doug's sign was the dog and he had a special connection with all dogs) She said on that day, she started thinking of Doug, and suddenly her dog went crazy. She felt Doug's presence so strongly, and she felt a wave of spiritual energy envelope her. She said, from that day on she felt a huge shift in her world.

Her daughter, Trish, attended the memorial and confided that she doesn't believe in spirits at all, yet she felt Doug sit beside her and she 'felt' him whisper in her ear, that her dad would be okay. I was dumbfounded, because she and I never talk about the unseen realm. I always thought she was closed to it. She was 'blown away' with this experience, yet she said she couldn't deny it, even though she wanted to.

My friend's teenage daughter also shared something with me. Ever since she was born, she could see spirits. This gift has been passed down to her through her 'First-Nations' heritage. She shared what she saw at Doug's memorial.

She said, "Imagine a bottle. That's our body, and our spirit is stuck in the bottle. Once we die, our spirit can move freely and isn't contained to this shape. We take on the shape of our innermost attitude, whether it is beautiful and light, or ugly and dark. Your husband looked beautiful and he went to every single person there and whispered something to them. He was a true host. Then, at the very end, as the bag pipes were playing he appeared at the front of the church and, from him, I saw a massive gold explosion of energy that filled the entire church. Then he disappeared."

I was grateful to have received this precious knowledge from the mouth of a fourteen year old. Someone who sees clearly, and is not involved with any organization. Bless you, and thank you!

During the 49 days, I felt so close to Doug and many different people would call me and share their stories of how his spirit had come to help their family members. I was blown away!

I felt closer to him during the 49 days, then ever before. I knew on the 49th day, without even counting the days, that it was the last one. He was headed to the Astral World, and although he would still be able to connect with me, it would be completely different. It's like having someone right there with you, verses talking to them on the phone, from a great distance.

On the 49th day, I said goodbye to him and then I mourned, deeply and thoroughly. I felt the loss of him like an ache that burned through my heart. For the first time, I felt truly alone.

Yet, the strangest thing started happening. Whenever I'm in either intense pain or intense joy, Doug shows up! Otherwise, he's busy with his training in the Astral World. I think his training, now, is to come and support me emotionally, as he hadn't been able to do it in the physical dimension. I, also, feel that he willingly accepts this new form of service.

Here's one example of many. When Doug was alive, I had to put my oldest cat, Kit, down because she had Cancer. She had lived 16 beautiful years, but she was in extreme pain. A friend came with me and we gave Kit light during and after. I cried and cried, and I couldn't stop even when my nose was stuffed. It was painful and emotionally shocking. It took a few days to recover.

A year after Doug died, I had to put Sully, our other cat, down. Sully was 15 years old and we had built a special bond over the many years. I was prepared to have the same horrific day. I brought Rose with me and Brydon waited in the vehicle, because he couldn't be that close to the event. As they injected the needle into Sully, I felt a huge welling up of tears and sorrow in my chest. I was about to wail! You know when you are just starting to cry, and it's going to be a good one? Well, that was me. It was coming up and building in intensity, nothing would stop it.

Suddenly, it was like all my grief got sucked out and the intense pressure in my chest disappeared! I felt instant peace! Yet, Sully, had just passed and my grief had just been building! What in the world happened? I looked over at Rose and she was in shock! She felt it too! She, also, had put pets down and never experienced this. We both felt Doug's presence and we felt the warm flow of divine light. This caused an instant shift in all the realms. The rest of the day, though sad, was peaceful. I missed Sully, but knew he wasn't suffering.

Chapter 5

My parents refused to come to Doug's memorial. In fact, they even stopped sending cheques. They used to send gifts of $100 for Doug and Brydon's birthdays, and for Christmas. Once in a while, they would remember my birthday.

I finally called my mom and she didn't want to talk, even after 3 years of no communication. She asked if I had heard from my brother recently. That's all she wanted to know. There was nothing left to say. There was no anger, hate, love, or joy, just a flat-line. Our training was over.

Recently, I attended a three day spiritual course that we held at our Centre. I had been to many of these, and during this one I was doing service behind the scenes and in the office, so I only heard parts of it.

I walked into the lecture hall, and something the Speaker was saying struck a chord in me. However, it wasn't until later that I realized why. It had to do with reincarnation. Based on many experiences up to this point, I firmly believed in this concept.

One of the new participants had asked a question, "Are we always re-born into our family lineage?"

I remember the Speaker replied, "Usually, yes. Males are born directly into their ancestral lineage. Females are born outside of their spiritual lineage, and marry back into it. Occasionally, a person can be re-born into their 'enemy's' family for special training. They are able to erase tremendous negative karma during their childhood, and often have a great mission as an adult."

I already knew and believed the first part. We had always been taught that even though women marry into their spiritual lineage, the family that they are raised in spiritually agrees to take care of them, protect them, and love them, like one of their own, until the day they are handed back to their original family. This happens when the father gives the bride away at the wedding. Over the years, we have forgotten the spiritual significance of many of these traditions.

It was the first time, however, that I had heard the second part about being born into the 'enemy's' family. It resonated with me on a very deep level.

"Could this be true? Could this fit for me?" I pondered this.

Now, at 47 years old, I have spent the last 26 years on this unique spiritual path, working on healing my spirit and utilizing many principles, including the Principle of Dawning. I have completed tremendous spiritual work on myself. I have, consistently, offered prayers and service in apology and gratitude to my parents, for our past life karma.

Over the years, I have seen a gradual change in their behavior and feelings towards me. They have moved from rage and hatred to more neutral ground.

I have always expected that this change would continue and that we would move to love and acceptance. Now, it hit me that this will never happen and I understood for the first time, why.

If you could look into a lens and see my life only in this lifetime, you would, without a doubt, hate my parents and want them to experience exactly what they put me through. Mostly you would just want them to stop. Now, you are looking into the lens at our previous lives. You see that I have destroyed their family and abused their child. I have left their family in utter devastation. Now, you are cheering for them and hating me.

The cycle of both abuse and revenge needs to stop. Where does one begin and the other end? We have seen where wars are created over lifetimes and lifecycles of abuse and even killings go on and on. Each generation refuses to let go and they carry the torch of hatred and revenge with honor.

Gabby says we create our own heaven and our own hell, both in this lifetime and in the astral world, simply by how we live our life and how we direct our innermost thoughts. I can say without a doubt, that if I had died 26 years ago, before I knew anything about this divine energy or this spiritual path, I would have become an attaching spirit and would have made my parents lives a living hell. I would have attached to them and caused them great suffering and hardship! Without knowing the laws of the unseen realm, I wouldn't have known any other way to exist. This cycle of hell and revenge would have continued for many more lifetimes, probably ruining all of us.

Now, due to my years of experience on this spiritual path, I know, without a doubt, that it is up to me to change and stop this cycle with my parents. I must first understand this karmic journey and then offer humble and deep prayers of apology, and yes, even gratitude for my parents. I don't have to say anything to them. This is a process of healing within my innermost attitude. Thoughts and feelings carry power, and have a life of their own.

My parents took care of me, to the best of their ability, in this lifetime and allowed me to erase a huge karmic debt. "Thank you so very much!" My parents went through extreme pain. This is why they can look into a five year old, child's eyes, with absolute hatred. They were looking into an old soul that had wronged them. "I'm so very sorry for the pain I put you through!"

This all may seem bizarre. However, this journey worked for me. I saw a shift in them over the years as I tried to practice the 3 great virtues of gratitude, acceptance, and humility. Books have been written about these three virtues. They have a profundity and then an even deeper profundity. There is no limit to the depth at which we can practice them.

It was only recently at this 3 day course that I received the final piece of the puzzle:

I had been born into the 'enemy's family' to heal the wounds and to end this war that has been going on for many lifetimes. Now that my mission is complete and karmic balance has been restored, my journey with them is almost over. I forgive them unconditionally and with no conditions. I love them unconditionally and with no conditions. We don't need to ever speak again in this lifetime. It is complete.

Throughout my life, I have witnessed miracles that have moved me to tears, and filled me with joy and awe! I have experienced the crashing waves of intense pain and suffered both mentally and physically, due to my, extremely, dense negative karma! I have journeyed many lifetimes in one!

I share this last part of the story with you, where my

soul embarks on a new journey of awakening…

Section 7

Awakening

Chapter 1

Who am I?

I'm a beautiful woman, borne of intense pain and sorrow. I'm a seeker of mysteries and adventure. I'm a child of God, still filled with wonder and awe. I am a divine soul!

I have come to a place of acceptance and peace. I'm learning to love myself, including the parts of me that are still healing, and still clinging to a darker side. I'm NOT perfect, nor even all good. I honour my 'imperfect perfectness.' This is the miracle of human life. We are sentient beings with Free Will. We are bound to make mistakes, and bound by them to grow.

Today, I'm grateful! My son, Brydon, and I enjoy each day! The house is quiet. We never argue with each other, ever. Though, sometimes I still want to parent him, and sometimes, he still lets me. We are two adults living together as friends, each honouring the other's ability to carve a unique journey in this world.

I feel extra support and love from the Ancestors. We have an Ancestor Altar in our home, so we are able to serve them food, cigarettes, etc. We serve them things that Doug would love. Gabby says, although this is a good start, the best 'service,' to help our Ancestors, is the active one, where we support others in their journey to heal and grow.

I hope my story blends in with the efforts of millions of people around the world, who are also taking an active role in healing and mending our planet. I remember Gabby saying, when we unite as ONE around the globe, the spiritual, astral, and physical realms will unite as ONE, and the (ONE) Creator will become fully present on this earth, within the 21st Holy Century. What an amazing miracle to witness!

Brydon and I began singing lessons. Who knew Brydon had such a natural, deep, baritone voice! He has the innate ability to listen to a song once, and then sing it straight through. I don't have any ability in this department! When I first stood up to the microphone, I started crying, out of intense fear and longing. I wanted to sing, but nothing came out. For years, I was told that I was tone deaf and couldn't sing. For years, I believed this, deep down in my soul. And so it was.

My son, Brydon, and me. He had just received his Secondary Spiritual Pendant

Our singing instructor, Mike, worked with me for a couple of years, to remove some of this intense fear. He scoffed at the excuse of being tone deaf. He said that if I can hear, I can sing, period.

I will never forget, when he said, "Singing is

curvaceous. You can't *think* your way through it; you have to *feel* your way through. In order to *feel*, you have to allow yourself to be vulnerable, to emote." Mike has the patience and skill of the best. I will never have the talent that Brydon does, but now I can, at least, stand up to the microphone and 'pretend' to sing. I enjoy it.

In 2012, I had to go for major surgery. I needed my left hip replaced. I was terrified and had an awful, sinking, feeling, for a month prior. I let the surgeon know all of my fears. I was on a special, new, pain patch. It's a 'partial agonist,' meaning it blocks other painkillers from working. Normally, you are supposed to go off it, completely, more than a week before surgery. The surgeon sent me to see an anaesthesiologist. He listened to my concerns and, then, said that he would pass it on to the hospital, but that I didn't need to go off the patches, they would just give extra pain control after the surgery. The hospital staff didn't realize I was on three of the strongest patches, although I tried to tell them. It's a new medication, and many doctors had never worked with it.

I went in, with absolute dread surging through my body. I knew it wasn't just about the surgery; I was an old hat at surgeries, that didn't bother me. I felt something else way off, but didn't know what it was and therefore couldn't stop it, quite like a runaway train.

I woke up, after surgery, in severe, agonizing pain! The nurse gave me some painkiller through the IV and said it should take the pain away completely. It didn't! They tried more. It didn't work! By this time, they didn't know what to do, so they sent me up to the room. I was screaming! It was like being given aspirin for a leg that's just been hacked off. It felt like I was left on the battlefield to die.

The nurses didn't know what to do, so they got irritated and aggressive. I wanted to pass out from the smallest movement, yet, they would move my legs around in an abrupt manner, then 'tsk, tsk' when I reacted. When they wheeled me to x-ray, they snapped at me, "Be quiet, you're disturbing the other patients!"

"Really? What about me? Don't my needs count?" I remember thinking.

I was thrown into hell, I couldn't talk or even open my eyes; all I could do was moan in wretched, mind-blowing, agony. I remember the doctor asking Rocky if I had emotional or drug-seeking problems. Thank god she was there to let them know she had known me for over 20 years, and this was NOT the case!

There was a point, where I hit the edge. I started producing a fever, so the nurse snatched ALL the blankets away. I couldn't stop shivering, like I'd been thrown in an ice pond. I remember feeling my body didn't have the strength to fight the agonizing pain, AND try to get warm too. It was unbearable. I felt my soul about to cross over. (I think they call this 'shock') Then, I realized that I had to find 'gratitude' somewhere, even if it was the smallest spark imaginable. I had pillows tucked in around me, so I squeezed into them with great gratitude, and drew in all the warmth from them that my body could pull. Through this small act, I was able to step back from the edge. Whew! It was a very close call!

This took place about 26 hours after surgery. The second day, a nurse came in and advised us that she had been off the unit, the previous two days, but that she was trained in pain management and knew about the new patch I was on. She apologized that the other staff weren't trained yet. She spoke to the doctor and within moments, they came back with a much higher dose of painkillers. The agonizing pain became bearable. It was still rough, but doable, with gratitude.

From the moment I found gratitude, and put it into actual practice, my training completely changed.

The ambulance arrived to take me to the rehabilitation hospital. While we were traveling, the attendant asked me what song I wanted to hear and since he had his laptop with him, I could watch the video too. My son had been learning the song, "A Pittance of Time," by Terry Kelly. It's about observing a moment of silence for war heroes. I watched the video and cried my eyes out.

When I got to the rehab hospital, the doctor asked me if I wanted a higher dose of painkillers; he didn't see a problem with it. I told him I was fine, I could manage at this level. All the nurses were so kind and caring, it made me cry again! It was the exact opposite care from when I first had the surgery.

After having gone through this horrific experience, I always wonder if in a previous life, I did kill people on a battlefield. I wonder if my intense fear of pain is due to this karma. Regardless, I came out the other side stronger. I don't fear pain, anymore! In fact, while I was recovering, I made a board game about 'cleansing' and the 'waves' of life. I sent four copies of the board game to different places around the world, and the reports were absolutely positive. People loved playing it! It brought them together, sharing a powerful bond.

I couldn't stop this experience, no matter how hard I tried. This is where I had to put 'Acceptance' into actual practice. My soul needed this to grow, so I hold no grudge or ill will towards the staff at the hospital. However, I did report the incident to the hospital's internal department, so they would have the opportunity to make some positive changes. Some people get confused over this. It's important to report and be strict when necessary; however, it's even more important to let go of any negative feelings or attachment to the outcome.

Acceptance, Gratitude, and Humility—these are the three great virtues. For as long as we are alive, the Universe will send us opportunities to put these into actual practice.

In October, of 2012, I journeyed to Japan and received my Tertiary level divine pendant. While I toured the Holy Sites, I was bathing in dense gold energy. I could feel the pressure, like I was living halfway between the spiritual world and earth. The door to heaven opened and I was allowed to step into this mysterious realm for a few days. Everything was crisp and clear, and time flowed at a smoother pace. I noticed the pain in my neck and back disappeared, only while in Japan. Also, any mental anguish that usually rears its ugly head was extinguished in moments, rather than hours. It was similar to riding a flat escalator, like those at airports—my thoughts and interactions would flow smoothly and peacefully, like I was being carried along by an unseen spiritual force.

When I returned, I felt a major shift in my destiny. I was able to understand spiritual concepts that had alluded me before. I had stronger spiritual discernment when making decisions. I, also, noticed that I could read people's auras on a far deeper and clearer level. I still suffer from physical/emotional pain, but I have a deeper understanding of why I'm going through it.

I have attained many exceptional friends, who would require another book to pay proper homage to. They know who they are. They have supported me through many rough times, and I continue to count on their friendship.

Recently, one these good friends, Lynn, referred me to a medium for fun. I tried very hard to discredit the medium, just to see if she was the real deal. This one blew me away!

She spoke of my journey as being 'brave,' and that I needed to start public speaking, as a way to support those who've been abused. She drew three cards when she was ready to speak directly to Doug:

1st Card – I'm with family and friends.

She said that Doug finally had closure with his mom and sister.

2nd Card – My mind is free.

She said that in this physical world, Doug had a type of 'misfiring' with his brain that caused extreme anger. However, in the astral world, he no longer had this disability. Doug wanted to apologize to me for the pain he inflicted. She saw him as an 'explorer' in the Astral World, looking after the land and animals. He was extremely happy. She said he wanted me to know he wouldn't be at this high level in the Astral World, without my spiritual support. He wanted to thank me.

3rd Card – We are soul mates.

She said that, actually, she doesn't see this card very often. She said that Doug kept apologizing for not taking me to 'higher energy places.' She couldn't get what he was trying to convey, until I clued in and remembered that I, desperately, wanted to take him to Japan and we had it all set up, until he got angry and changed his mind.

She said that he and I were from the same 'soul group.' She said that I will find another 'soul mate' in this lifetime, and Doug will assist in making sure this man understands me, and takes better care of me.

She chuckled and asked if we thought Brydon would never get married. I advised her that he was still a virgin at 26 and never had a girlfriend yet. Yes, I was more than a little worried. She said that Doug was sure he would get married in the next couple of years in a 'blue type blazer.' She was adamant about this color. I told her she was wrong. If Brydon gets married, it would be in his official youth, green, blazer. She refused to budge on this point.

It was only a couple of days later, at the Centre, when Donna reminded us that Brydon was waiting to get his blue blazer from Japan. He had ordered it many months prior, and we had completely forgotten!

The reading was cathartic. I cried and cried! I closed the circle with Doug, and thanked him from the bottom of my heart! I know I will see him again.

My life has been filled with many 'nodes' and times of intense, unbearable pain. There have been many times when I've judged myself harshly, and thought, for sure, I was going 'backwards.'

I still have days where I'm cranky and cantankerous, though not many. There are moments when I drive, I feel like a hissing cat with its claws extended. I want to throttle some of these idiot drivers! Our city seems to have an epidemic of drivers who turn left on red lights. Our light has gone green and they still enter the intersection and tailgate the car ahead to sneak through, sometimes even 3 vehicles will attempt this at once. Here is the most interesting thing: nobody honks at them! They just let them do it! They just sit at their own green light! I can only honk if I'm at the front, and that doesn't happen very often. It's like they won't honk, because they've just done the illegal act themselves, at a previous intersection.

When I do honk, I usually get the middle finger pointed at me. Yet, they are clearly in the wrong! I finally realized that it was the Creator teaching me that all of us, as humans, have gone so far against the principles that even when WE are wrong, we won't take responsibility for it. We blame others, instead. We have become so spoiled, so egotistical, and so self-indulgent! I realized why we need the strictness, if we are going to reverse our innermost attitude in time.

If God, or the universe, was allowing me to witness this, then I had to examine my own life and see where I was trying to get away with something—some sort of bad habit I didn't want to fix. Of course, I could find a few things! I'm sure we all can.

Even knowing this is a lesson, there are times when I want to clobber them upside the head! I know it would be satisfying only in the moment, and then I would own double the negative karma. Why double the karma? Because, spiritually, it is the difference between a young child not knowing and a university student having been well taught. Who would you be tougher on?

Ah well, life goes on! The universe will keep bringing me lessons. I will pass some and fail some. Those that I fail will be my constant companions, until I can close the circle and say good-bye for good.

I HAVE stopped judging myself. This is the biggest lesson I cherish. I have gone from being my own judge, jury, and executioner, to accepting all of me and my actions. I used to rip my soul to shreds at the slightest provocation. There were times, my mind just stopped working. It would freeze in abject terror from the internal onslaught. Yet, on the outside, a regular day was playing out. Nobody else would notice. It's like there were two of me in my brain—the abuser and the victim.

The abuser has been stopped. A line has been drawn. The victim has gained a wonderful balance of gentleness and strictness. In victims the pendulum often swings to the extreme. As a victim, I would either give everything of me away, with no boundaries; or, I would beat myself up with the proverbial stick. Now, each day I balance both, sometimes I need to be gentle with myself and others, and other times I need to be strict.

I'm learning that balance is the key in all things and with all people.

I realize, I can't put myself above God and think I know better than the entire divine realm! It just doesn't work that way. I haven't been granted the authority to judge, because what I see is paper-thin and what, actually, exists is higher than the Empire State Building. This, I fully believe.

Now, I can laugh at myself and allow myself to survive mistakes without being condemned to a lasting hell. It's very freeing.

Having gone through many lifetimes in one, I have discovered the following universal truths have been etched, forever, in my psyche:

All who exist in the Universe are bound by the same laws and principles. Even plants and trees go through a similar growth. They have fast growth, and then they slow right down, when they are creating a node or a knot. We think they are NOT growing at all during this period, but this is not true. The more nodes and knots the tree has, the stronger it can withstand 'mother nature.' It must grow them to survive. It is very obedient to the principles of the universe. Trees bend as needed, and grow strong to withstand the harsh winters.

We, as humans, are part of the universe and have our own cycles to go through, for as long as we are alive. The universe will put us into situations over and over again, until we learn what we need to. Once we learn one lesson, we will be granted a temporary reprieve and then another will be placed in front of us. **Spirit growth is limitless.** The more we roll up our sleeves and accept hard work is necessary, the greater the rewards!!!

I try to listen to the truth that resonates from the unseen realm of SPIRIT and dedicate my life to embracing, experiencing, protecting, and passing on this ancient power. The Laws of the Universe have placed the Spirit as the upstream of the mind and body, and therefore it must always come first. As in all things, when the correct balance is restored, magic unfolds within the physical realm and the alchemy of the moment produces sustainable Health, Harmony, and Prosperity.

This, immediately, creates an awareness and

responsibility to 'right-action. It is a paradigm shift of knowing what is right and WANTING to do what is right—being excited to roll up our sleeves and gratefully allow the universe to train our spirit. To look at challenging and tough situations as an opportunity to grow the spirit and awaken even more. When we combine colors and textures in a unique way, they create something bigger then themselves – a priceless tapestry of art. In the same way, the greatest ART that exists is fully empowered human beings using their unique talents to support each other in true harmony! This is the self-actualization of manifesting the gifts of the unseen realm and materializing them into the physical realm, using concrete tools to practice on a daily basis.

Now, I experience this higher realm of 'spirit-first' every day. It is truly alive and vibrant! It is a world where movement is choreographed by Divine Will and free-will becomes a dance of unimaginable beauty and joy! Its clarity moves me to tears, even at this moment...as a soul awakening!

THE END.

CPSIA information can be obtained at www.ICGtesting.com
Printed in the USA
LVOW05s2339300715

448305LV00014B/25/P

9 780994 76740